MULTI-THREADED GAME ENGINE DESIGN

JONATHAN S. HARBOUR

Course Technology PTR
A part of Cengage Learning

COURSE TECHNOLOGY
CENGAGE Learning

Australia • Brazil • Japan • Korea • Mexico • Singapore • Spain • United Kingdom • United States

COURSE TECHNOLOGY
CENGAGE Learning

Multi-Threaded Game Engine Design
Jonathan S. Harbour

Publisher and General Manager,
Course Technology PTR: Stacy L. Hiquet

Associate Director of Marketing: Sarah Panella

Manager of Editorial Services: Heather Talbot

Marketing Manager: Jordan Castellani

Senior Acquisitions Editor: Emi Smith

Project Editor: Jenny Davidson

Technical Reviewer: Joshua Smith

Interior Layout Tech: MPS Limited, a Macmillan Company

Cover Designer: Mike Tanamachi

Indexer: Larry Sweazy

Proofreader: Michael Beady

For product information and technology assistance, contact us at
Cengage Learning Customer & Sales Support, 1-800-354-9706

For permission to use material from this text or product,
submit all requests online at **www.cengage.com/permissions**
Further permissions questions can be emailed to
permissionrequest@cengage.com

All trademarks are the property of their respective owners.

All images © Cengage Learning unless otherwise noted.

Library of Congress Control Number: 2010922087

ISBN-13: 978-1-4354-5417-0

ISBN-10: 1-4354-5417-0

Course Technology, a part of Cengage Learning
20 Channel Center Street
Boston, MA 02210
USA

Cengage Learning is a leading provider of customized learning solutions with office locations around the globe, including Singapore, the United Kingdom, Australia, Mexico, Brazil, and Japan. Locate your local office at: **international.cengage.com/region**

Cengage Learning products are represented in Canada by Nelson Education, Ltd.

For your lifelong learning solutions, visit **courseptr.com**

Visit our corporate website at **cengage.com**

Printed in the United States of America
1 2 3 4 5 6 7 12 11 10

To the talented faculty at UAT—and especially those in Game Studies—with whom I shared five arduous but rewarding years: Michael Eilers, Ken Adams, Arnaud Ehgner, Justin Selgrad, Dave Wessman, and Bill Fox.

ACKNOWLEDGMENTS

Thank you to Emi Smith, Jenny Davidson, and Joshua Smith, for your efforts to get this long-overdue book into publishable condition. Thanks to Dave Wessman for many diversionary hours playing *Twilight Struggle* and *Memoir 44*. Thanks to my favorite game studios Bungie, Obsidian Entertainment, Firaxis Games, and BioWare, for their inspiring works of creativity. Thanks to Misriah Armory for their SRS99D 14.5mm and M6G 12.7mm semi-automatic weapons, which are a lot of fun to shoot (only at the range, of course!).

AUTHOR BIO

Jonathan S. Harbour is a freelance writer, teacher, and indie game developer, whose first experience with a computer was with a cassette-based Commodore PET, and first video game system, an Atari 2600. His website at www.jharbour. com includes a forum for book support and game development discussions.

He has been involved in two recent indie games: *Starflight—The Lost Colony* (www.starflightgame.com) and (with Dave Wessman) *Aquaphobia: Mutant Brain Sponge Madness* (www.aquaphobiagame.com). He loves to read science fiction and comic books and to play video games with his four kids, and even after "growing up," he is still an unapologetic Trekkie. When virtual reality technology progresses to the full holodeck experience, he will still spend time playing shoot-em-ups, role-playing games, and turn-based strategy games. There's always a new story waiting to be told.

He has studied many programming languages and SDKs for his courses and books, primarily: C++, C#, Visual Basic, Java, DirectX, Allegro, Python, LUA, DarkBasic, Java Wireless Toolkit, and XNA Game Studio. He is also the author of *Visual C# Game Programming for Teens*; *Beginning Java Game Programming, Third Edition*; *Visual Basic Game Programming for Teens, Third Edition*; *Beginning Game Programming, Third Edition*; and *Advanced 2D Game Development*. He lives in Arizona with his wife, Jennifer, and kids Jeremiah, Kayleigh, Kaitlyn, and Kourtney.

CONTENTS

INTRODUCTION

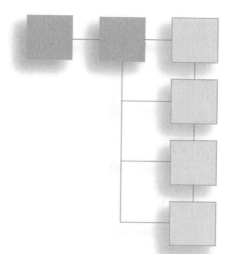

Today's modern processors come with multiple cores, each of which runs independently to run programs and significantly increase the throughput compared to a single-core processor. The clock speed is no longer the most important factor, because a quad-core processor will outperform most dual-core processors even if there is a clock speed discrepancy.

The purpose of this book is not to teach game engine development in depth, but to teach multi-threading in the context of Direct3D rendering. While we do build a decent Direct3D-based game engine with most of the modern conveniences one would expect, the goal is not to try to build a commercial game engine. The engine architecture is simple, with one library project consisting of a class for each component and limited inheritance. I believe that complex designs lead to expensive code (that is, code that consumes more processor cycles than necessary). While a professional engine might have an interface for each module (input, networking, rendering, etc.), with each implemented as a DLL, we only need a single engine project that compiles to a static library.

This book does not attempt to present a cutting-edge game engine that is competitive with commercial offerings or even with open-source engines such as OGRE and Illricht, but only as a platform for demonstrating multi-core threading concepts. We could implement numerous optimizations into the renderer (such as a BSP tree with frustum-based leaf rejection and terrain splitting), but the goal is not to build an exemplary engine, only a usable one for this stated purpose: to explore multi-core game programming. In the interest of exploring multi-threaded optimizations, over and above algorithms, we really do want to approach the subject from the brute force point of view in order to see how multiple processors and threads help to improve performance. Therefore, I will not attempt to offer creative algorithms to optimize the engine.

There are many components of the engine that are not discussed in the pages of this book. Engine building is covered, but not line by line, function by function, class by class. In the interest of time and space considerations, some pieces have been purposely left out even though the code does exist and these features are part of the completed engine.

Visit www.jharbour.com/forum for details on the entire engine, which is located on a subversion code repository as an open source project. Here are some components not covered in the book:

- **Scripting**. This extremely important subject was left out due to space considerations. A fully featured script system is available for the Octane engine.

- **Audio.** A fully featured audio system based on the award-winning FMOD library is also present in the Octane engine, waiting to be plugged in to your projects.

- **Command console.** A drop-down console is a helpful feature in a scripted engine such as this one, but not extremely important to the discussion of multi-core programming. This feature too is available.

- **GUI system**. A GUI is an important part of an engine, especially when game editors are planned. A rudimentary GUI system is available for the engine, and we are experimenting with third-party options such as CEGUI and GWEN as well.

SDKs and Libraries

This book primarily uses DirectX 9 for rendering, and all source code is in C++. If you want to focus entirely on 10 or 11 for rendering, you will face the challenge of replacing the utility code from D3DX9 (such as .X file loading) that is no longer available. The PC game industry is still in a transition period today with regard to DirectX 9, 10, and 11. Unless you are writing Geometry Shader code, there is no other compelling reason to limit your game's audience to PCs equipped with DirectX 11-capable video cards. So, we might expect to see a mix of library versions in a project, with DirectInput 8, Direct3D 9, DirectCompute 11, and so on (and yes, this works fine).

The "Indie" market is most certainly a consumer for the type of engine developed in these pages, with good performance and features, without complexity or high cost. Suffice it to say, we will not try to compete, but only to show what multi-core programming brings to a "sample engine" in terms of performance. Neither is the goal of this book to provide extensive theory on symmetric multi-processing (SMP) technology for use in a computer science classroom, since there are already many excellent resources devoted solely to the topic. In the first five chapters, we do explore threading libraries in detail. I have striven to give this book a unique place on your game development bookshelf by covering the most significant thread libraries in an applied approach that any intermediate C++ programmer should be able to immediately use without difficulty. We will use the OpenMP and Boost.Thread libraries, while examining and tinkering with Windows Threads.

Advice

The C++ Boost library (an extension of the STL) is *required* to build the source code in this book. Since the C++0x standard is not ratified yet, it is not part of the STL and must be installed. Please see Chapter 1 for details on how to install Boost and configure Visual C++ to use it.

CPUs and GPUs

This book will explore the current applied techniques available to do multi-threaded programming, with a multi-threaded game engine developed as an example of the technology. A strong early emphasis on software engineering will fully describe the design of a multi-threaded architecture with the goal of improving game performance. The game engine is based on Direct3D and C++, and is constructed step by step with threading built in—and based on the engine developed in *Advanced 2D Game Development* (published in 2008), but significantly upgraded with shader-based rendering. Many examples will demonstrate the concepts in each chapter, while a simulation is developed in the last chapter to show the overall benefits of multi-core programming—a trend that will only continue to evolve, as evidenced by NVIDIA's custom processing "supercomputer" expansion card, the TESLA.

Massive multi-processing has traditionally been limited to expensive, custom-built supercomputers, like IBM's Deep Blue (which defeated chess master Garry Kasparov), and IBM's BlueGene series, which are used to simulate nuclear explosions, global weather patterns, and earthquakes. This level of performance will soon be in the hands of consumers, because PCs are already equipped with multi-core processors, and the trend today is to increase the cores rather than just to increase clock speed. Intel's newest architecture is the Core i7 (http://www.intel.com/products/processor/corei7), which features 8 hardware threads. Intel and AMD are both working on massively multi-core processors with at least 80 cores, which are expected to be available to consumers within five years (see story: http://news.cnet.com/Intel-shows-off-80-core-processor/2100-1006_3-6158181.html). This is a cutting-edge trend that will continue, and game developers need to learn about the tools already available to add multi-threading support to their game engines.

To show that massively multi-core processing is available even today, it is now possible for a hobbyist to build a personal supercomputer for under $3,000 using a typical "gamer" motherboard (equipped with two or more PCI-Express video card slots) and one or more NVIDIA TESLA processing cards. The TESLA is based on an NVIDIA multi-core GPU that can be programmed using NVIDIA's CORE compiler and device driver. A four-card setup on a quad-SLI mother-board is capable of teraflop performance, and some studios have replaced render farm clusters with single TESLA PCs. At under $2,000 for each TESLA card, a quad-TESLA machine can be built for only about $8,000. This demonstrates that affordable massive multi-processing is now available, and we are at the forefront of this technology today. Over the next two years, consumers will be able to buy this caliber of processor at retail for the same price as current chips, and the performance will continue to increase according to Moore's Law, which shows no inkling of slowing down.

Hardware discussions aside, this book is about game programming. This is a very important subject that is prevalent in most game engines today, but has received very little attention because it is such a challenging subject: multi-threading, symmetric multi-processing (SMP), parallel processing. Several presentations at GDC 2008 touched on this topic, directly or indirectly, but there is still very little information about threaded game engines in print or on the web. We feel that this is the most important topic in game engine development for the upcoming decade, because massively multi-threaded processors will soon be the norm, and we will look back on the days of dual and quad chips as a novelty, the way we look back today at archaic single-core processors. This topic is absolutely hot right now, and will continue to be in the news and in industry presentations for the next decade.

COMPILER SUPPORT

The code in this book follows the C++ standard and makes extensive use of the Standard Template Library and the Boost library. The projects were developed with Visual C++ 2008. Your best bet is to use the Professional (or Enterprise) edition. If you are using the Express edition of Visual C++ 2008, then there is one key disadvantage: OpenMP is not supported in the Express edition. I will suggest a *legal* workaround using Microsoft's own download packages, but be aware of this limitation.

The threaded game engine will be modular, comprised of C++ classes, and will be simple in design (so we can focus more attention on threads, less on Direct3D). The reader will be able to create a new project, write a few lines of code, and try out a simple thread example without knowing anything about our engine. This I am adamant about, because so many game dev books feature an incomprehensible engine that is all but impossible to use in a simple context (where a quick demo is desired). For instance, I will be able to create a new project, connect to the engine API, and load up several objects and render them, and print out details of the engine's performance. This will be possible due to the engine's loosely coupled components. The engine developed in this book is simple and to the point. I have made huge improvements to the engine over the past two years, so this is not a fly-by-night book engine. We will be able to expand upon it without starting from scratch and enjoy the benefit of the work already put into it, thus reducing mistakes and coding problems.

Academic Adoption

If you are considering this book for a course, I can tell you that I *have* used this material successfully in both an advanced rendering course and a game engine course. There are no course materials (exercises, test bank, etc.) officially available at this time, and the chapters herein include no quizzes or exercises. However, I believe this book could be used for a rendering or hardware course on threaded multi-core programming, or as a supplemental resource for such a course. If you are pioneering such a course, please do contact me so we can discuss your needs, and I will be happy to share what materials I do have on hand.

DirectX SDK Support

Microsoft's official DirectX SDK can be downloaded from http://msdn.micro-soft.com/directx/sdk. The current version at the time of this writing is dated June 2010. However, we are not using Direct3D 10 or 11—this book does not venture beyond Direct3D 9.

Advice
_____

Direct3D is the only DirectX component that has been updated to version 11. None of the other components (DirectSound, DirectInput, and so on) has changed much (if at all) since around 2004. All this means is that DirectInput does what it needs to do just fine and needs no new updates, just as DirectSound supports high-definition audio systems and 3D positional sound without needing to be updated further. However, Direct3D is updated regularly to keep up with the latest graphics hardware.

_____

This may sound strange, but I often recommend using an older version of DirectX, even when using the latest version of Visual C++. Although the June 2010 and future releases *may work* with source code in print, there is no guarantee of this since Microsoft is not dedicated to preserving backward-compatibility (as an historical fact). For instance, the October 2006 release is a good one that I use often, and the code compiles and runs just as well as it does with the latest version (when code is based on DirectX 9). Just remember this advice when it comes to game development—the latest and greatest tools are not always *preferable* for every game project.

Advice

We do not study the basics of DirectX in this advanced book. If you have never written a line of DirectX code in your life, then you will need a crash course first. I recommend *Beginning Game Programming, Third Edition* (Course Technology, 2009), which will teach you all of the basics at a very slow pace. The first four chapters cover Windows programming before even getting into DirectX, and only ambient lighting is covered to keep the examples simple for beginners. We go *quite* a bit further beyond the basics in this book! If you are already familiar with my work, then I might recommend *Advanced 2D Game Development* as a follow-up. Those two lead up to the material covered in this book, in a sort of trilogy. Those familiar with the Beginning book will feel at home here.

HARDWARE REQUIREMENTS

The example programs presented in this book were tested on several Windows systems to ensure compatibility on a wide range of hardware configurations. Although a single-core CPU will run all of the code presented in this book, there will be negligible performance gains from threaded code. Even a fast dual-core CPU will have a hard time keeping up with an average quad-core CPU as far as threading goes. Obviously, a dual-core 3.2GHz Intel i5 will outpace a 2.66GHz Core2Quad when running a game, but not a threaded prime number algorithm. I'll leave system performance comparisons to the hot rod gamer magazines and only suggest using a quad- or hexa-core processor over a high-end dual if possible. (Yes, even an Atom CPU in a netbook will run our code!)

Minimum System Requirements

- Dual-core 2GHz processor
- 2GB system memory
- Windows XP SP3 or later

The following operating systems should run the code in this book.

- Windows XP SP3
- Windows Vista 32-bit and 64-bit
- Windows 7 32-bit and 64-bit

Test Systems

The following systems were used to test the examples in this book:

CPU	System RAM	GPU	Video RAM
Intel Q6600	4GB	NVIDIA 8800 GT	512MB GDDR3
Intel E6850	2GB	NVIDIA 8600 GT	512MB GDDR3
Intel P4 3.2GHz	2GB	NVIDIA 8500 GT	512MB GDDR3
AMD Turion X2	4GB	ATI Radeon HD 3200	2GB DDR2 (shared)

CONVENTIONS USED IN THIS BOOK

This book was written for intermediate-level programmers, so many of the beginning-level callouts are omitted in the interest of simplicity. We want to focus more on detailed explanations of concepts and source code with as little distraction as possible.

Advice

This is an Advice callout, which will highlight any important piece of information or supplemental issue related to the main thread of a chapter.

Source code is presented in fixed-width font for easy readability.

```
/**
This is a sample of what source code will look like in the text of this book.
**/
#include <iostream>
#include <string>
int main(int argc, char argv[])
{
    std::string helloWorldVariable = "Hello World";
    std::cout << helloWorldVariable << std::endl;
    return 0;
}
```

The coding convention followed in this book may be described as "camel case," as the example above illustrates with the helloWorldVariable. All properties and methods within a class follow the camel case format, except where only a single word is needed (such as Update()), in which the first character will be capitalized. Class "methods" are often referred to as functions, for this word offers more clarity and I have never been fond of the term method, the root word of methodology—please consider the words "method" and "function" as synonymous in this book.

In game development, and software engineering in particular, not every function processes data in a methodological manner or produces a clearly object-oriented result. All source code in this book is C++, with no holdovers from the C language (such as printf). The reader is encouraged to brush up on the standard library, which is used extensively within these pages (I recommend Reese's C++ *Standard Library Practical Tips*, published by Charles River).

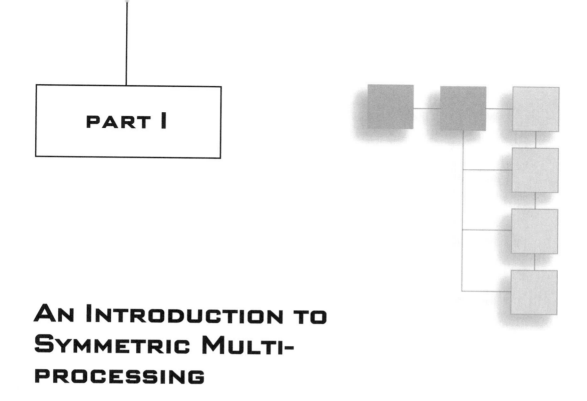

PART I

AN INTRODUCTION TO SYMMETRIC MULTI-PROCESSING

To get started, we will begin with an introduction to parallel programming by exploring symmetric multi-processing technologies that are readily available today as open source software, APIs, or included with Visual C++. These libraries are fairly easy to use, but as with most software, taking that first step can be a bit intimidating. The chapters in Part I will give you an overview of these libraries, with ample examples, to bring you up to speed on multi-threaded programming.

- Chapter 1: Overview of Symmetric Multi-processing Technologies
- Chapter 2: Working with Boost Threads
- Chapter 3: Working with OpenMP
- Chapter 4: Working with Posix Threads
- Chapter 5: Working with Windows Threads

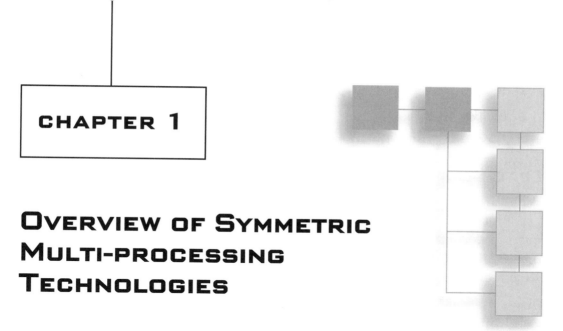

CHAPTER 1

OVERVIEW OF SYMMETRIC MULTI-PROCESSING TECHNOLOGIES

In this chapter, we begin our study of the overall subject of symmetric multi-processing, or SMP. This technology includes multi-threading, which we will use to improve game engine performance—which is the primary goal of this book. SMP has deep roots going back two decades or more, and it has only been in recent years that multi-purpose libraries have become available to take advantage of industry-standard SMP hardware, such as multi-core processors, multi-processor motherboards, and networked clusters of machines (also called "farms"). Until libraries such as OpenMP and boost::thread came along, SMP was largely a proprietary affair limited to rendering studios (such as Pixar Animation Studios, which created *Toy Story*, *Wall-E*, and *UP*; Pixar pioneered the development of shaders for graphics rendering technology needed to render their films[1]) and users of custom-built supercomputers (see www.top500.org). The approach we take, beginning with this chapter, is a *low-impact* approach with regard to the threading code, by working with usable libraries and steering clear of threading implementations.

This chapter covers the following topics:

- Digging in to symmetric multi-processing
- Serial processing with a single thread
- Parallel processing with multiple threads
- OpenMP

- Boost threads
- Windows threads

DIGGING IN TO SMP

What are perhaps the three most important issues to consider in a game's performance as far as the consumer or player is concerned? Think about the question for a minute and consider, from your own experience, what makes or breaks a game? Let's lay down some assumptions in order to narrow down the issue a bit.

First of all, let's assume the rendering performance of your engine is already excellent. This is due primarily to largely over-powered GPU hardware in relation to the actual gameplay—which is terrific for a game programmer, but not so great for the video card industry which keeps trying to come up with new and compelling reasons for enthusiasts to buy new silicon. If your game engine's rendering is subpar, then threading will not make significant improvements; you need to consider the design of your rendering pipeline. We will certainly address threading issues within the rendering pipeline, but since there is only one frame buffer we cannot—for instance—draw each game entity in a separate thread. However, *updating* entities in the game loop is another matter!

Secondly, let's assume the gameplay is already established and initial play testing confirms that the game is fun to play, compelling, and meets the design goals. So, in addition to rendering, we're also not overly concerned about gameplay and can count on consumers to buy our game on that point. Where we will focus our attention with regard to threads is *responsiveness* to player input and on *load times*. The example programs in the next few chapters should give you all the information you need to add a threaded resource to your engine, for example. We will not spend much time exploring inter-process communication, thread lock scenarios, or message-passing schemes within a threaded frame-work. Instead, we will study threading technologies with the intent to improve known gameplay patterns. That is, the issues likely to annoy players or otherwise cause them to stop playing. We ultimately want to attract players to our games, *keep* them playing, and get them to *come back* for more! Load times and user input are of paramount importance.

Thirdly, let's assume the visual style and graphical quality of our game is attractive and compelling, meeting on par or exceeding consumer expectations for the genre, so we can count on sales due to the graphics. Like the previous two points, if graphics are not up to snuff, then the framerate is highly irrelevant.

Now, there are certainly many other aspects of a game that influence a consumer's decision to buy or not, such as the genre, the subject matter (such as a movie adaptation), market share, and studio fame. But, all things being equal, these are the three important issues with regard to sales: Performance, Gameplay, and Graphics.

Avoid Threading for the Sake of Threading

What, then, should we focus our attention on with regard to multi-threading a game engine? What is the first thing you see when a game starts up—regardless of whether it's a console game or PC game? Usually, you will see some introductory videos from the publisher and studio, and then the title screen. What about the *load time* when a level is being prepared? Before the player can jump in to the game, there is always a waiting period while the level *loads*. I submit that this issue is the most notorious killer of even a potentially great game! Without citing any games as case examples, suffice it to say that many a game has been returned to the shelf, never to be played again (or worse, traded in for another)—entirely due to excessive load times.

What does the game industry have to say about load times? Some industry pundits call it a four-letter word, in an obvious but appropriate reference to player frustration.[2] Comparing the Sony PSP with the industry-leading Nintendo DS, the average load times are 103 seconds and 25 seconds, respectively. What is the most likely cause for this huge difference? I do not intend to address the technical differences in any detail, but suffice it to say, the PSP reads data from an optical disc while the DS reads data from a memory chip. Reminding myself that Performance, Gameplay, and Graphics are all equal for the purpose of this discussion, I submit that the load times alone dramatically affect player opinion, with a direct effect on sales.

The next significant area of concern regarding performance, and our ability to increase its efficiency, is arguably game scene and entity management. Threading the update() function in any engine is likely to be where most programmers focus their attention, because rendering *cannot* be threaded—the frame buffer must be monothreaded because the entire buffer memory is used by the video card to light pixels on the display screen.

Design First, Optimize Later

If you have a goal to develop a polythreaded renderer, it *can* be done, but special care must be made to ensure writes to the frame buffer occur *only* during a retrace period when the screen is not reading video memory. In my opinion, that situation will be almost impossible to work out with multiple threads that need to synchronize their work. For instance, what if we were to use a thread to write pixels on the *left* side of the screen, and a second thread to write pixels to the *right* side? That really might work with a raster display, but absolutely will not work within an *accelerated 3D system* based on shaders or fragment programs. And let's suppose it is possible to synchronize two threads within a renderer: will that dramatically improve performance compared to a GPU with 400, 500, or more cores? *I think not!*

The goal of this book is to explore several approaches to CPU-based threading while developing a mid-range game engine, with about equal coverage of both subjects. We will not be building anything like a binary space partition (BSP) optimization system for a first-person shooter (FPS) game engine in this book, but we *will* explore threaded scene and entity management with examples from which you can learn and use for your own engine.

- An entry-level game engine will basically wrap an SDK such as DirectX, providing rudumentary mesh and sprite loading and rendering and a basic while loop with all of the initialization, rendering, and gameplay code together in one project.

- An advanced engine will abstract the renderer so that it can be implemented with any rendering SDK (usually Direct3D or OpenGL), provide scene and entity management, user input, networking (perhaps), GUI features, and often an editor, to name a few things.

With these differences in mind, the mid-range game engine developed in this book falls in somewhere between the two, but leans much closer toward the advanced. Our engine will support features such as managed entities, random textured terrain, and hierarchical mesh animation, but not an abstracted renderer—we're focusing on Direct3D. I will not attempt to build a highly threaded engine from the start, since I'm aware that each reader will have his or her own ideas for an engine, and most readers will simply want to learn the technology in order to implement threading into existing code bases.

Peeking Under the Hood

Let's take a look at the latest multi-core hardware at the time of this writing. The competitive race between semiconductor rivals Intel and AMD continues unabated. Although Intel seems to have the current lead in terms of performance, the two companies tend to leapfrog each other every year or two. Similarly, two companies continue to vie for your hard-earned money in the GPU department, with NVIDIA and ATI duking it out for the highest rendering benchmarks. In this race, the two rivals seem to be leapfrogging each other as well, with NVIDIA having released its next-generation silicon and likely soon to be followed again by ATI.

Flagship Processor Comparison: Intel and AMD

The leader of the CPU performance charts is currently the Intel Core i7 980X, a 6-core screamer at 3.33 GHz, shown in Figure 1.1. Close on its heels, however, is the AMD Phenom II X6, also a 6-core CPU, shown in Figure 1.2.

Image courtesy of Intel, Inc.

Image courtesy of AMD, Inc.

Figure 1.1
Intel Core i7 980X at 3.33 GHz (6 cores).

Figure 1.2
AMD Phenom II X6 1090T at 3.2 GHz (6 cores).

Hexa-core Intel 980X versus AMD 1090T

Although both chips have six cores, they are quite different in architecture. The Intel chip uses a 32nm process technology that squeezes six cores into the same silicon space previously occupied by four cores, while using the same voltage (a *very* crucial issue!). Figure 1.3 shows the internal structure of the Intel chip. The AMD chip uses a 45nm process technology that makes its die size 44% larger than Intel's flagship. Figure 1.4 shows the internal structure of the AMD chip. The second significant difference—which sets Intel over the top (for now)—is the memory bandwidth. The 980X uses triple-channel DDR3 memory, while the 1090T uses dual-channel DDR2.

Hexa-core Architectures

The structure of each microprocessor is somewhat discernible in these photos, but the components will be difficult to make out on a low-resolution printed page, so Figures 1.5 and 1.6 show the two chips with diagram overlays (called a block diagram) to highlight the architecture of each chip. When AMD upgrades its architecture to 32nm, that will make room on the die for DDR3, which will bring its performance up to the level of the Intel 980X.

The One-thousand-dollar Question

I want to point out that, at the time of this writing, the Intel 980X ($999) is over three times ($3\times$) the price of the AMD 1090T ($285). Of course these prices are variable and somewhat meaningless a year hence, but they *are* important right now—and the same holds true of any generation of technology.

Figure 1.3
Photo of the transistors in the Intel 980X.

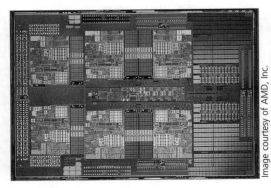

Figure 1.4
Photo of the transistors in the AMD 1090T.

Figure 1.5
Block diagram of the Intel 980X.

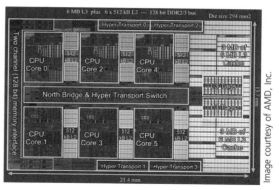

Figure 1.6
Block diagram of the AMD 1090T.

Futurist Ray Kurzweil, whose works include *The Age of Spiritual Machines*, uses a value of $1,000 when evaluating and writing about computer performance. What Kurzweil argues is that vast supercomputers costing tens of millions of dollars cannot be compared with the average home PC, so he breaks down performance into $1,000 pieces for comparative use: in other words, how much computing power does $1,000 produce?

Table 1.1 shows a comparison between our two leading microprocessors, with figures adjusted for cost according to Kurzweil's standard. The goal is not to suggest one processor over another at the consumer level, but only to compare apples to apples at the same price point for these two *flagship processors*. Since the Intel chip is 3.5 times more expensive than the AMD chip, we use that as an adjustment figure to arrive at some intriguing numbers.

What's the outcome? For $1,000, AMD's processors will produce over twice the computational power of Intel's processors.

Graphics Processing Units (GPUs)

We are not focusing too much attention on GPU computing in this book since that is a huge and complex subject on its own (visit www.jharbour.com/forum for details about an upcoming book covering CUDA, OpenCL, and Direct-Compute in early 2011).

Table 1.1 Intel/AMD Processor Comparison: Kurzweil's $1,000 Standard

Cost	Processor	Quantity	Cores	Transistors	Benchmark*
$1,000	Intel 980X	1	6	1.17 B	54,508
$1,000	AMD 1090T	3.5	6 (21)	904M (3.164 B)	31,612 (110,642)

*Lavalys Everest 5.5 CPU Benchmark reported by benchmarkreviews.com[3].

OVERVIEW OF MULTI-THREADING TECHNOLOGY

You do not need a special library to begin exploring multi-processing on your own. Odds are, in fact, that you have been writing multi-processing code for a long time already, but without a formal term for it. *Asymmetric* multi-processing (AMP) is the process of running multiple tasks sequentially, or in a time-slicing manner where each process gets some processor time before being put on hold for the next process. This is how older operating systems (such as Windows 95) functioned. *Symmetric* multi-processing (SMP) is the technology we're striving to tap into to improve the performance of our game code. Let's look at these technologies in more detail.

Serial Processing (Single Thread)

In a non-threaded program, which we can describe as a *serial processing* program because only one process at a time can run, there will still be a while loop with various function calls—because a program that runs once and does not repeat is not only rare, but never used in a game; however, a run-once *thread* is fairly common, as you will see in the next chapter. A single-threaded loop is the most common way to write code today in any language. We can call a *serial* program an *asynchronous* program, which derives the term *asynchronous multi-processing*, or AMP. Here's an example:

```
#include <iostream>
int value = 2;
void process1()
{
    value *= 5;
}
void process2()
{
```

```
        value /= 2;
}
void process3()
{
        std::cout << value << std::endl;
}

int main(int argc, char* argv[])
{
        while (value < 100)
        {
                process1();
                process2();
                process3();
        }

        system("pause");
        return 0;
}
```

Here is the output produced by this program:

```
5
12
30
75
187
```

In this example, a global variable is modified by three different processes (process1, process2, and process3). The order of these processes is known ahead of time, so the programmer can predict how the value will be changed by the three processes.

Parallel Processing (Multiple Threads)

In a threaded program, which we can describe as a *parallel processing* program because many processes will run simultaneously (in parallel), there is still a while loop with various function calls. A multi-threaded loop is becoming more common today as programmers learn about the benefits of a threaded process. We can call a *parallel* program a *synchronous* program. Here's a non-functional example of a program with parallel processes (in order for this to actually run as intended, we would need to add a threading library, so consider this just pseudo-code for now):

```cpp
#include <iostream>
int value = 2;
void process1()
{
    while (value < 100)
    {
     value *= 5;
    }
}
void process2()
{
    while (value < 100)
    {
     value /= 2;
    }
}
int main(int argc, char* argv[])
{
    process1();
    process2();
    while (value < 100)
    {
        std::cout << value << std::endl;
    }

    system("pause");
    return 0;
}
```

Note how the first two processes are launched before the main while loop, and they each have their own loop as well, and how the previous process3 is now running directly inside the main loop. This illustrates how a typical parallel threaded program can be written (although the logic here is nonsensical, as I mentioned earlier, so treat this as pseudo-code). If process1 and process2 were threaded functions, then they would run in parallel with the main loop, and the state of the global variable would be totally unpredictable!

In other words, you cannot share a global variable with more than one thread if the program must rely on the state of that value falling within known limits, because threads will be competing for the variable's state. If a single global variable *must be used*, then we need a way to safely share it among the threads in a way that produces predictable results.

An Example Using Windows Threads

Let's look at a real-world example that calculates distance with a parallel approach. First, distance is calculated serially with a function called `serial_distance`; then a parallel approach is used with a second function called `parallel_distance`, which calls on a helper function, `square`. This `square` function should be launched in a thread so that the two calculations (for delta X and delta Y) are done in parallel:

```
#include <iostream>
#include <cmath>

double serial_distance( double x1,double y1,double x2,double y2 )
{
    double deltaX = (x2-x1);
    double deltaY = (y2-y1);
    return sqrt(deltaX*deltaX + deltaY*deltaY);
}

double square(double base, double exp)
{
    double var = pow(base,exp);
    return var;
}

double parallel_distance( double x1,double y1,double x2,double y2 )
{
    double deltaX = (x2-x1);
    double deltaY = (y2-y1);
    double Xsquared = square(deltaX,2);
    double Ysquared = square(deltaY,2);
    return sqrt( Xsquared + Ysquared );
}
```

```
int main(int argc, char* argv[])
{
    double dist;
    double x1=100,y1=100,x2=200,y2=200;

    std::cout << "Serial version of distance" << std::endl;
    dist = serial_distance( x1, y1, x2, y2 );
    std::cout << dist << std::endl;

    std::cout << "Parallel version of distance" << std::endl;
    dist = parallel_distance( x1, y1, x2, y2 );
    std::cout << dist << std::endl;

    system("pause");
    return 0;

}
```

The square root function, sqrt(), is one of the *slowest* processor instructions because it does not produce an exact result; instead, the processor creates a table of results and chooses the closest approximation of the root. Obviously, if the base number is evenly divisible then the result is easy to calculate, but the square root of a *floating-point number* is problematic. As a result, it's *marvelous* for performance benchmarking! Since calculating distance between two points involves adding the square of two numbers before the square root, and since distance is used often in game code, it's especially relevant as a test function.

It's important to note that *parallel* processing does not have to run with parallel threads running in independent loops to take advantage of multiple processor cores. Instead, consider that two fairly simple calculations are performed in parallel, and the results of both calculations are used in a third calculation that must wait for the first two to complete before proceeding. Here's the output; granted it's not very useful yet without timing data, nor would we notice any improvement with just a single function call—you must call a function thousands of times in a timed loop to get real performance results.

```
Serial version of distance
141.421
Parallel version of distance
141.421
```

Advice

Always use a temporary variable when performing calculations rather than embedding the calculation in the "return" statement. This not only improves the pipelining optimization within the processor (a debatable point depending on your processor model), but it also vastly improves your debugging ability while stepping through a program.

Let's look at a new program that actually creates a thread to demonstrate concurrent or parallel execution, using the Windows threads approach (the multi-threading library in the Windows SDK). This program is called First Threaded Demo and it has two threads—the main program thread and the worker thread that runs in a function called thread_function, both of which have a while loop. Inside the loop a variable is incremented one billion times— which is a cinch for any modern processor and should complete in only a few seconds. Don't be surprised if std::cout is interrupted with both vying for output at the same time! I've used a low-frequency timer function called GetTickCount(), which has millisecond granularity; it's enough to get a ballpark figure and does not require an extra library to compile (just windows.h).

```cpp
#include <iostream>
#include <windows.h>

const long MIL = 1000000;
const long MAX = 1000 * MIL;
long main_counter = 0;
long thread_counter = 0;

DWORD WINAPI thread_function(LPVOID lpParm)
{
    DWORD start = GetTickCount();
    while (thread_counter < MAX)
    {
        thread_counter++;
    }
    DWORD finish = GetTickCount() - start;
    std::cout << "Thread time = " << finish << std::endl;
    return 0;
}

int main(int argc, char* argv[])
```

```
{
    HANDLE handle;
    DWORD id;

    //launch the thread function
    handle = CreateThread( NULL, 0, thread_function, NULL, 0, &id );

    //run main counter
    DWORD start = GetTickCount();
    while (main_counter < MAX)
    {
        main_counter++;
    }
    DWORD finish = GetTickCount() - start;
    std::cout << "Main time = " << finish << std::endl;

    //wait for thread
    WaitForSingleObject(handle, INFINITE);
    CloseHandle(handle);

    system("pause");
    return 0;

}
```

Here is an example of the output from this program (it will be different on every PC):

```
Main time = 3604
Thread time = 3604
```

SMP LIBRARIES

We're going to use several libraries to write test programs while exploring the topic of SMP in order to find not just a library to satisfy the goals of this book, but to provide you with information about what's available for your own uses, since there is never a generic solution that meets every need equally.

OpenMP

OpenMP is an open-source multi-processing API specification. Its home page is at www.openmp.org. OpenMP is not an SDK; you will not find a downloadable *library* for OpenMP at its website. Instead, OpenMP is a specification that vendors can adopt when implementing an OpenMP library on their platform. What this means is that OpenMP is either supported on a certain platform (Windows, Linux, etc.) or it is not—and there's no way to *add it* if it is not available on a given platform. On the Windows platform, Visual C++ 2008 and 2010 support OpenMP 2.0 (see http://msdn.microsoft.com/en-us/library/tt15eb9t.aspx for details); OpenMP is a high-level threading library that functions through a compiler's pre-processor #pragma hooks to work seamlessly with little impact on the source code. It automatically manages its own thread pool and launches threads as needed, and OpenMP is commonly used to optimize for loops.

Visual C++ has built-in support for OpenMP 2.0 via a project configuration flag. Look in Project Properties, Configuration Properties, C/C++, Language, "OpenMP Support," as shown in Figure 1.7. Below is a short test program that

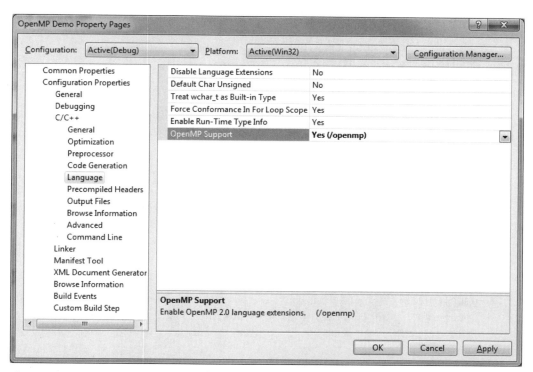

Figure 1.7
Enabling OpenMP support in Visual C++.

demonstrates OpenMP with a timing comparison versus a serial process. The
goal here is not to launch a parallel process but to note the improvement when
crunching numbers in a dense loop.

```cpp
#include <iostream>
#include <cmath>
#include <windows.h>
#include <omp.h>

int main(int argc, char* argv[])
{
    const long MIL = 1000000;
    const long MAX = 100 * MIL;

    //run serial test
    long counter = 0;
    DWORD start = GetTickCount();
    for (counter=0; counter<MAX; counter++)
    {
        double deltaX = counter/2.0;
        double deltaY = counter*2.0;
        double root = sqrt( pow(deltaX,2) + pow(deltaY,2) );
    }
    DWORD finish = GetTickCount() - start;
    std::cout << "Serial time = " << finish << std::endl;

    //run parallel test with OpenMP
    counter = 0;
    start = GetTickCount();

    #pragma omp parallel for
    for (counter=0; counter<MAX; counter++)
    {
        double deltaX = counter/2.0;
        double deltaY = counter*2.0;
        double root = sqrt( pow(deltaX,2) + pow(deltaY,2) );
    }

    finish = GetTickCount() - start;
    std::cout << "OpenMP time = " << finish << std::endl;
```

```
    system("pause");
    return 0;

}
```

The output from this test program reveals a significant improvement in the performance of the OpenMP-enabled loop, which crunched the numbers about 300% faster.

```
Serial time = 17472
OpenMP time = 5491
```

Boost Threads

Boost is a portable C++ extension library that, like the C++ Standard Library, will become part of the C++ standard in the next version of the standard (called C++ 0x). What this means is that you can safely invest time to study the admittedly huge Boost library without getting tangled up in an uncertain open-source project. Boost is a modern library of advanced features that gives the C++ language a huge *boost* in functionality, covering a diversity of subjects, such as threads, socket networking, accumulators, foreach functionality (to simplify iteration), a generic image library, quaternions, statistical distributions, Python scripting, timers, typeof functionality (to determine object type), regular expression parsing, and much more. The entire Boost library, compiled and with all documentation, weighs in at over a gigabyte. Fortunately, the compiler will only link the specific libraries that you use in your code.

Installing Boost

Before you can use Boost, you'll need to install the library and configure Visual C++ with the .\include and .\library folders inside the Boost folder. Download the latest version of Boost from www.boost.org. (The current version at the time of this writing is 1.41.0.) Open the Boost archive file and extract it to the root of your hard drive in a folder such as C:\boost_1_41_0 (depending on the version).

Next, bring up a Command Prompt and change to the Boost folder (such as C:\boost_1_41_0) using the CD command. For instance, type

```
CD \boost_1_41_0
```

From this folder, type

```
bootstrap
```

After the `bootstrap` script runs, which builds some of the tools needed to create the Boost libraries, then type

`.\bjam`

These two commands are all that's required to build the Boost library, and due to environment variables, the process is completely automated. Let's review the steps again just for reference:

1. Download the Boost zip file from www.boost.org.

2. Extract the Boost library to a folder on the root of your hard drive, such as `C:\boost_1_41_0`.

3. Open a Command Prompt, and change to that directory using the CD command.

4. Run `boostrap`.

5. Run `.\bjam`.

Now that the Boost library has been built, you need to configure Visual C++ so that it knows where to find the Boost files. Open Visual C++ and open the Tools, Options dialog, then Projects and Solutions, VC++ Directories. Choose "Include files" from the drop-down list, and add `C:\boost_1_41_0` to the list (note: this folder will depend on the version you're using), as shown in Figure 1.8. Next, choose "Library files" and add `C:\boost_1_41_0\stage\lib` to the list, as shown in Figure 1.9.

Advice

Boost is *required* for nearly all of the projects in the book, so it's important that you take this first step to build the Boost library on your system. Optionally, there are pre-built versions for Windows available (see the Boost website for details—www.boost.org). If you are somewhat inexperienced with Visual C++ and cannot get Boost to work on your system, please visit www.jharbour.com/ forum for assistance.

Testing the boost::thread Library

With all of the technical issues out of the way, you should be able to compile a Boost-enabled C++ project now. The boost::thread library is wonderfully non-convoluted (i.e., *simple*) compared to Windows threads and Posix threads! First

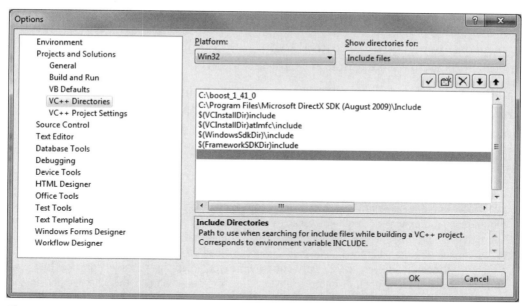

Figure 1.8
Adding the Boost include folder to the list of includes in Visual C++.

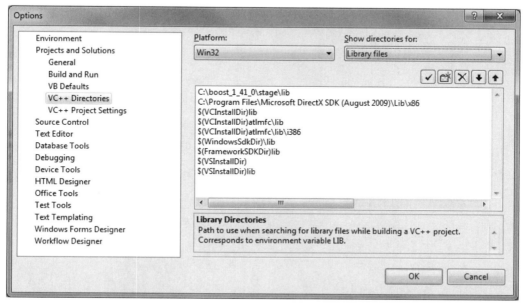

Figure 1.9
Adding the Boost library folder to the list of libraries in Visual C++.

of all, you don't need to use a specific function definition for a thread function when using boost::thread. Instead, you can simply turn a normal-looking function into a threaded function (with any desired return value).

In addition, now that we have Boost available, we can use boost::timer, which is a much more robust and useful means of profiling our code than the old Windows API GetTickCount() function, which was used previously.

Advice

We will not be using the low-level thread libraries Windows threads or Posix threads extensively. I've made this decision primarily due to the complexity involved in protecting shared data and running into mutex locking problems (which I acknowledge is an arguable point), and due to the fact that every programmer has his or her own engine goals that will differ from my own. Far better to let a well-designed library handle such issues instead of getting bogged down in such a quagmire of code ourselves. If you do want to write your own thread code from the low-level libraries, you will learn enough information from the examples later in this chapter and in the chapters to come to help meet your goals.

Here is an example program that demonstrates the boost::thread library:

```cpp
#include <boost/thread/mutex.hpp>
#include <boost/thread/thread.hpp>
#include <boost/timer.hpp>
#include <iostream>

boost::mutex mutex;
boost::timer timer;

const long MIL = 1000000;
long MAX = 2 * MIL;
int counter = 0;
long iter = 0;

int compute()
{
    boost::mutex::scoped_lock lock(mutex);
    int max = MAX;
    for (int n=0; n<max; n++)
```

```
        {
            double deltaX = n/2.0;
            double deltaY = n*2.0;
            double root = sqrt( pow(deltaX,2) + pow(deltaY,2) );
            iter++;
        }
        int c = ++counter;
        std::cout << "# " << c << ": iter = " << iter << std::endl;
        return 0;
    }


int main()
{
        //run parallel test with boost::thread
        std::cout << "boost::thread test" << std::endl;
        timer.restart();
        boost::thread_group thrds;
        for (int n=0; n<10; n++)
            thrds.create_thread( &compute );
        thrds.join_all();
        double finish = timer.elapsed();
        std::cout << "time = " << finish << std::endl;

        //run serial test
        std::cout << std::endl << "serial test" << std::endl;
        timer.restart();
        iter = 0;
        compute();
        finish = timer.elapsed();
        std::cout << "time = " << finish << std::endl;

        return 0;
}
```

Here is the output from the program. As you can see, these worker threads do not overlap, and thus, do not interrupt each other, so the specific boost::thread example used here is not a great choice for a specifically multi-threaded approach to crunching numbers (or polygons, as the case may be), but it is simple and elegant for launching worker threads.

Advice

> For a console application, the window may close before you are able to see its output. Try running the program without debugging (Ctrl+F5), which will keep the window open until you press a key. Another option is to use `system("pause")` at the end of the program to pause before exiting.

```
boost::thread test
# 1: iter = 2000000
# 2: iter = 4000000
# 3: iter = 6000000
# 4: iter = 8000000
# 5: iter = 10000000
# 6: iter = 12000000
# 7: iter = 14000000
# 8: iter = 16000000
# 9: iter = 18000000
# 10: iter = 20000000
time = 3.799

serial test
# 11: iter = 2000000
time = 0.37
```

Windows Threads

We saw an example of threading with the native Windows thread functions such as `CreateThread` earlier in the chapter. This is a low-level thread library used by Windows itself, and as a result, can be very difficult to use. It's not especially hard to *create* a thread the Windows way, but it is a challenge to *manage* threads, once created, unless you are careful not to allow any two threads to share data. Since that restriction usually renders "worker threads" as almost useless—without the ability to synchronize data with the main program thread—the use of a mutex is usually required. (A *mutex* is a trigger mechanism that locks a variable or other data construct while a thread is using it.)

Second Windows Thread Demo

Let's take a look at an example to illustrate these difficulties first hand.

```
#include <iostream>
#include <windows.h>
```

```
const unsigned long MAX = 1000000;
unsigned long counter = 0;
const int THREADS = 10;
HANDLE handles[THREADS];
DWORD ids[THREADS];

DWORD WINAPI thread_counter(LPVOID lpParm)
{
    for (int n=0; n<MAX; n++)
        counter++;

    return 0;
}

int main(int argc, char* argv[])
{
    //launch the threads
    for (int n=0; n<THREADS; n++)
        handles[n] = CreateThread( NULL, 0, thread_counter, NULL, 0, &ids[n] );

    //wait for threads to finish
    WaitForMultipleObjects(THREADS, handles, TRUE, INFINITE);
    for (int n=0; n<THREADS; n++)
        CloseHandle(handles[n]);

    //print results
    std::cout << "Counter = " << counter << std::endl;

    return 0;
}
```

The result will be slightly different on every PC, but on mine the result was:

```
Counter = 4005582
```

Since the thread function was supposed to increment the counter variable 1 million times, and we launched 10 threads, one would expect the result to be 10,000,000, not a value of around 4 million. So what's wrong with this code? The problem is, the threads are fighting over the counter variable and in the fraction of a second that this code is running, wars are waged over who owns the variable at any given nanosecond. Some compilers might even cause this code to crash due to thread conflicts.

Third Windows Thread Demo

Without getting too deep into the details of how this will work this early on, let's examine a modification that makes use of a mutex lock that will protect the counter variable from thread entanglements.

```cpp
#include <iostream>
#include <windows.h>
const int MAX = 1000000;
unsigned long counter = 0;
const unsigned long THREADS = 10;
HANDLE handles[THREADS];
DWORD ids[THREADS];
HANDLE mutex;

DWORD WINAPI thread_counter(LPVOID lpParm)
{
    std::cout << "Thread " << GetCurrentThreadId() << " start." << std::endl;
    for (int n=0; n<MAX; n++)
    {
        //acquire mutex lock
        WaitForSingleObject( mutex, INFINITE );

        //update shared data
        counter++;

        //release mutex
        ReleaseMutex( mutex );
    }
    std::cout << "Thread " << GetCurrentThreadId() << " done." << std::endl;
    return 0;
}

int main(int argc, char* argv[])
{
    //create mutex
    mutex = CreateMutex( NULL, FALSE, NULL );

    //launch the threads
    for (int n=0; n<THREADS; n++)
        handles[n] = CreateThread( NULL, 0, thread_counter, NULL, 0, &ids[n] );
```

```
        //wait for threads to finish
        WaitForMultipleObjects(THREADS, handles, TRUE, INFINITE);

        //cleanup
        for (int n=0; n<THREADS; n++)
            CloseHandle(handles[n]);
        CloseHandle( mutex );

        //print results
        std::cout << "Counter = " << counter << std::endl;

        return 0;
}
```

This new version of the program, which uses a mutex to protect the counter variable, does produce the desired output of exactly 1,000,000 for the counter, but it takes far too long to run (due to the lock), eliminating the whole benefit of threading—which is to increase performance through the use of multiple processor cores.

Fourth Windows Thread Demo

Here's a new and final version of the function that eliminates the mutex locking problem while still protecting the shared data, through the use of a helper variable.

```
DWORD WINAPI thread_counter(LPVOID lpParm)
{
    std::cout << "Thread " << GetCurrentThreadId() << " start." << std::endl;
    unsigned long local_counter = 0;
    for (int n=0; n<MAX; n++) {
        local_counter++;
    }
    //update shared variable
    WaitForSingleObject( mutex, INFINITE );
    counter += local_counter;
    ReleaseMutex( mutex );

    std::cout << "Thread " << GetCurrentThreadId() << " done." << std::endl;
    return 0;
}
```

This new version accomplishes the same task, and runs so quickly that the counter reaches its target immediately—a sign that all 10 threads are running without conflict.

```
Thread Thread 2724 start.
Thread 5772 start.
4488 start.
Thread 2724 done.
Thread 1988 start.
Thread 1376 start.
Thread 4488 done.
Thread 1988 done.
Thread 6040 start.
Thread 2772 start.
Thread 6084 start.
Thread 5772 done.
Thread 1376 done.
Thread 6116 start.
Thread 5428 start.
Thread 2772 done.
Thread 6040 done.
Thread 6084 done.
Thread 5428 done.
Thread 6116 done.
Counter = 10000000
```

Is it cheating to use a local variable as the accumulator and then just "tack it on" to the shared variable at the end in one quick step? Not at all! Passing data around is the single-most effective way to avoid thread locking problems in parallel code. The *whole point* of this series of examples has not been to see how fast the processor cores can increment a variable—that's a ludicrous test of processor power! The point was to demonstrate how threads can increase performance without running into conflicts. Just replace the `local_counter++` line with real-world calculations, and—well, you get the idea.

Final Comments on Windows Threading

Just out of curiosity, try increasing the MAX constant to something larger—much larger—and watch what happens. As far as that goes, try experimenting with the THREADS constant as well. Another change you might try is using MAX as the target value to reach with all threads contributing, rather than using MAX for each thread (in which case the ultimate target is MAX * THREADS). Try using this for the for loop conditional:

```
unsigned long max = MAX / THREADS;
for (int n=0; n < max; n++)  {
    local_counter++;
}
```

Now set MAX to any desired maximum and note how fast the threads reach that level, and experiment with different numbers of threads. The goal is to become familiar with the capabilities afforded your code with the addition of threads!

SUMMARY

In this chapter we have covered a lot of ground in preparation for the chapters to come in an attempt to provide a general overview of the entire book. The threading examples were terse but did convey how to use each of the thread libraries in simple terms. The next few chapters will dig into those thread libraries in more detail to show you how to solve bigger problems with threads. Later, in Part II, we will be building a single-threaded Direct3D-based game engine that you can study and use for your own game projects, including multi-threaded games.

REFERENCES

1. "Pixar"; Wikipedia; Jan. 5, 2010. http://en.wikipedia.org/wiki/Pixar.

2. "Under the Hood: PSP Load Times"; Jan. 5, 2010. GameSpot; http://www.gamespot.com/features/6159832/index.html.

3. "AMD Phenom-II X6-1090T Black Edition Processor Review"; June 5, 2010. http://benchmarkreviews.com/index.php?option=com_content&task=view&id=508&Itemid=63&limit=1&limitstart=8.

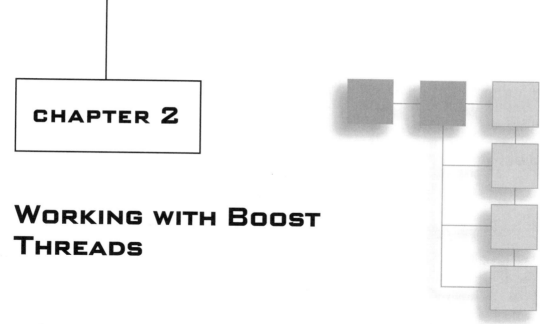

CHAPTER 2

WORKING WITH BOOST THREADS

In this chapter, we will study the boost::thread library in order to add multi-threading capability to our code. The boost::thread component is part of the overall C++ Boost library (introduced in the previous chapter) that provides a standard interface for using multiple threads. Until Boost is fully adopted into the C++ standard, it will need to be installed on your development PC prior to use. Boost is a modern C++ extension library with features that greatly increase the capability of the C++ language. Refer to the previous chapter under the section titled "Boost Threads" for instructions on installing Boost and configuring Visual C++ in order to use it.

This chapter covers the following topics:

- Calculating prime numbers
- Prime divisors optimization
- Odd candidates optimization
- Threaded primality test

PUNISHING A SINGLE CORE

The previous chapter gave an overview—a bit of a snapshot—of the thread libraries we will be examining in the coming chapters. The boost::thread library is a good choice since it is platform independent, and therefore likely to be compatible with more compilers, as well as more reliable than proprietary libraries (such as Windows threads—see Chapter 5, "Working with Windows Threads" for more details).

Advice

We'll assume here that you have already installed the Boost library, built it, and added the .\include and .\library folders to your Visual C++ configuration. For instructions on how to install Boost (required), please refer back to Chapter 1.

Let's begin an experiment. This approach will be used repeatedly as we explore the multi-threading libraries in upcoming chapters. There are many ways to "punish" a single-core processor, or one of the cores of a multi-core processor, which is the more likely scenario today. For this experiment to be statistically useful, we need to make sure the same parameters are used in each situation.

Advice

The game engine developed in this book will function first with a non-threaded update loop so that a base line of performance can be determined. Then, each of the thread libraries and multi-core techniques, using both the CPU and GPU, will be tested to see how we can improve performance by tapping into multiple cores.

Calculating Prime Numbers

A prime number is an indivisible whole number. More specifically, a prime can be divided only by 1 or by itself.[1] For the purpose of testing the performance of code, we do not need to concern ourselves with the most efficient method of calculating primes (and there are many ways to do it!). What we need, really, is just a good algorithm that does something useful for the purpose of *benchmarking* our multi-core code. The actual implementation is not as interesting as the execution time on different types of hardware with the various thread and multi-core libraries we'll be examining in this and later chapters. At the time of this writing in early 2010, the largest prime number ever found has 13 million decimal digits.[2]

To calculate a prime number, you must determine whether a candidate number is divisible by any other number (besides 1 or itself). The program will test divisors from 2 up to the target number's square root. If none of the divisors evenly divide, then the candidate is indeed a prime number. This means it is indivisible. Here now is the source code for the brute force approach:

```
long findPrimes(biglong rangeFirst, biglong rangeLast)
{
    long count = 0;
    biglong candidate = rangeFirst;
    while(candidate <= rangeLast)
    {
        biglong testDivisor = 2;
        bool prime = true;

        //test divisors up through the root of rangeLast
        while(testDivisor * testDivisor <= candidate)
        {
            //test with modulus
            if(candidate % testDivisor == 0)
            {
                prime = false;
                break;
            }
            //next divisor
            testDivisor++;
        }
        //is this candidate prime?
        if (prime)
        {
            count++;
            primes.push_back(candidate);
        }
        //next candidate
        candidate++;
    }
    return count;
}
```

Prime Number Test 1

The Prime Number Test 1 project uses the findPrimes() function above to calculate primes up through the first one million candidates. We can't say that we're calculating "the first one million primes" because that is not the case; we're *testing* the first one million whole number candidates to see if they're prime, and only a small number of them will be.

Add to the function above this declaration code at the top of the code listing. Whenever a prime is found, it is added to the primes list for storage until later.

```
#include <string.h>
#include <iostream>
#include <list>
#include <boost/format.hpp>
#include <boost/timer.hpp>
#include <boost/foreach.hpp>

//declare a 64-bit long integer type
typedef unsigned long long biglong;
biglong highestPrime = 1000000;

boost::timer timer1;
std::list<biglong> primes;
```

And add the `main()` function shown here to finish the program. The primes list is printed out, but limited to only the first 100 and last 100 primes in the list as a quick reference and verification that the prime calculation is functioning correctly. To quickly iterate the list, the `BOOST_FOREACH` #define macro is used (via the boost/foreach.hpp definition).

```
int main(int argc, char *argv[])
{
    biglong first = 0;
    biglong last = highestPrime;
    std::cout << boost::str( boost::format(
        "Calculating primes in range [%i,%i]\n") % first % last);

    timer1.restart();
    long primeCount = findPrimes(0, last);
    double finish = timer1.elapsed();

    std::cout << boost::str(
        boost::format("Found %i primes\n") % primeCount);
    std::cout << boost::str(
        boost::format("Run time = %.8f\n\n") % finish);
```

```
std::cout << "First 100 primes:\n";
int count=0;
BOOST_FOREACH(biglong prime, primes)
{
    count++;
    if (count < 100)
        std::cout << prime << ",";
    else if (count == primeCount-100)
        std::cout << "\n\nLast 100 primes:\n";
    else if (count > primeCount-100)
        std::cout << prime << ",";
}
std::cout << "\n";

system("pause");
return 0;
}
```

Figure 2.1 shows the output of the program, with a result of 78,500 primes in the range of 0 to 1,000,000, calculated in just under one second (0.998).

This time frame is too small for an effective demonstration, so let's bump up the upper range to 10,000,000.

```
biglong highestPrime = 10000000; // 10 million
```

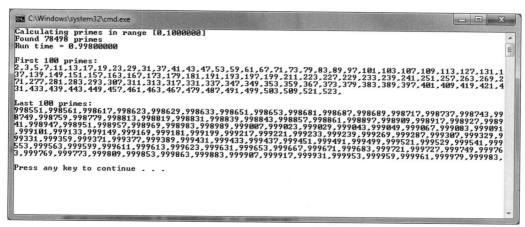

Figure 2.1
The first prime number test project uses the brute force approach.

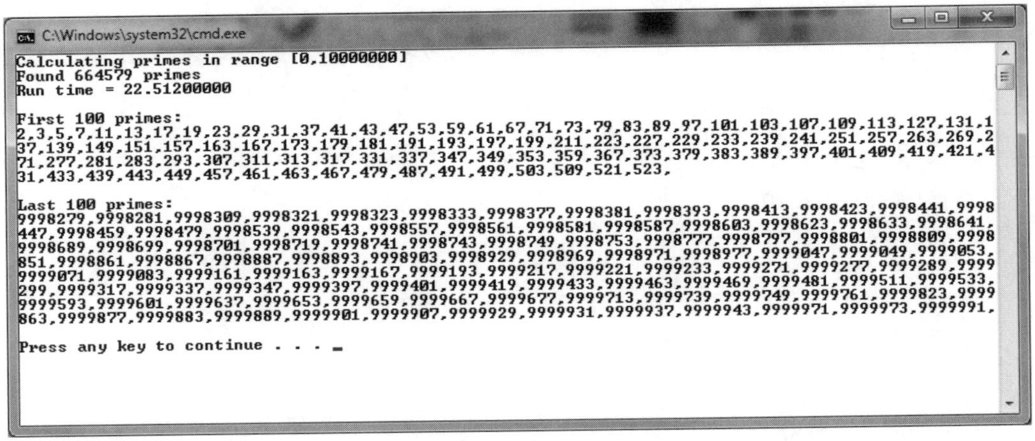

Figure 2.2
The primality test project again with 10 million candidates.

Figure 2.2 shows the output of the primality test with 10 million candidate tests. These numbers will vary widely from one system to another. These results were computed with an Intel Core2Quad Q6600 quad-core processor running at 2.6 GHz (slightly overclocked) with 4GB of DDR2 memory. The number of primes found in the new range is approximately ten times greater than the previous result, which is expected when we increase the range ten-fold. (Note, however, that this will *not* be a logarithmic increase as you explore larger and larger ranges into the billions and beyond.)

664,579 prime numbers exist in the range of the first ten million candidates. Our code calculated these primes in 22.512 seconds, for a throughput of 29,521 primes per second.

Figure 2.3 shows Windows Task Manager's results while the primality test program was running. There were quite a few other tasks running, which accounts for the slightly higher percentage; the prime number crunching was running entirely on one processor core, which is approximately 25% of the "CPU usage."

Optimizing the Primality Test: Prime Divisors

There are faster ways to calculate prime numbers. I mentioned before that we aren't as interested in calculating primes as we are in studying performance differences with different numbers of CPU cores and threads, but a few minor

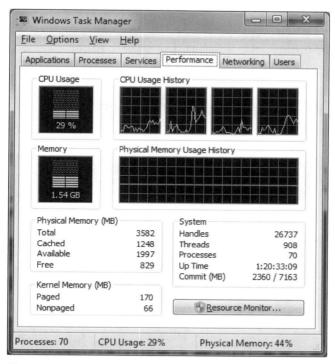

Figure 2.3
Windows Task Manager showing the CPU utilization while the Prime Number Test program is running.

optimizations to the prime number algorithm will at least make the projects in this chapter somewhat more realistic and "real world" in nature. The Lucas-Lehmer test[3] uses fast fourier transforms (FFTs) to calculate Mersenne prime numbers very quickly. But, there are simpler techniques we can use to improve performance in our current code. The best code optimization you can make is to prevent code from running at all. In other words, eliminating test cases from a sequential calculation—such as a primality test—improves performance better than any fancy algorithm.

Again, we are not trying to compete to calculate the largest prime number, or to come up with an innovative new primality test, only to benchmark our loops with various combinations of hardware and multi-threading libraries.

The brute force approach above does work, but it will be somewhat insulting to even the earliest of math majors, so let's at least do the most obvious optimization: eliminating factors that have already been calculated before. A more thorough explanation of primality test optimization can be found in Steve Litt's article entitled "Fun With Prime Numbers."[4] This optimization simply uses the existing list of primes as the divisors rather than going through the *whole range* of divisors (up to the root) every time. We do not need to consider candidates over and over again, just the primes. Here's a new version with an optimized findPrimes() function that uses only primes for the divisors. In the chapter resources, this project is called Prime Number Test 2.

```cpp
#include <string.h>
#include <iostream>
#include <list>
#include <boost/format.hpp>
#include <boost/timer.hpp>
#include <boost/foreach.hpp>

//declare a 64-bit long integer type
typedef unsigned long long biglong;
const long MILLION = 1000000;
biglong highestPrime = 10*MILLION;
boost::timer timer1;
std::list<biglong> primes;

long findPrimes(biglong rangeFirst, biglong rangeLast)
{
    long count = 0;
    biglong candidate = rangeFirst;
    if (candidate < 2) candidate = 2;

    while(candidate <= rangeLast)
    {
        bool prime = true;

        //get divisor from the list of primes
        BOOST_FOREACH(biglong testDivisor, primes)
        {
            //test divisors up through the root of rangeLast
            if (testDivisor * testDivisor <= candidate)
            {
```

```
                    //test primality with modulus
                    if(candidate % testDivisor == 0)
                    {
                        prime = false;
                        break;
                    }
                    if (!prime) break;
                }
                else break;
            }
            //is this candidate prime?
            if (prime)
            {
                count++;
                primes.push_back(candidate);
            }
            //next candidate
            candidate++;
        }
        return count;
}

int main(int argc, char *argv[])
{
    biglong first = 0;
    biglong last = highestPrime;
    std::cout << boost::str(
        boost::format("Calculating primes in range [%i,%i]\n")
        % first % last);

    timer1.restart();
    long primeCount = findPrimes(0, last);
    double finish = timer1.elapsed();

    std::cout << boost::str(
        boost::format("Found %i primes\n") % primeCount);
    std::cout << boost::str(
        boost::format("Run time = %.8f\n\n") % finish);

    std::cout << "First 100 primes:\n";
    int count=0;
```

```
BOOST_FOREACH(biglong prime, primes)
{
    if (count < 100)
        std::cout << prime << ",";
    else if (count == primeCount-100)
        std::cout << "\n\nLast 100 primes:\n";
    else if (count > primeCount-100)
        std::cout << prime << ",";
    count++;
}
std::cout << "\n";
system("pause");
return 0;
}
```

This new version of the primality test replaces the core loop of the findPrimes() function. Previously, variable testDivisor was incremented until the root of a candidate was reached, to test for primality. Now, testDivisor is the increment variable in a BOOST_FOREACH loop which pulls previously stored primes out of the list. This is a significant improvement over testing every divisor from 2 up to the root of a candidate (blindly).

What about the results? As Figure 2.4 shows, the runtime for a 10 million candidate test is down from 22 seconds to 4.7 seconds! This is a new throughput of 141,369 primes per second—nearly five times faster.

Optimizing the Primality Test: Odd Candidates

There is no need to test even candidates because they will never be prime anyway! We can start testing divisors and candidates at 3, rather than 2, and then increment candidates by 2 so that the evens are skipped entirely. We will just have to print out "2" first since it is no longer being tested, but that's no big deal. Here is the improved version. This project is called Prime Number Test 3.

```
#include <string.h>
#include <iostream>
#include <list>
#include <boost/format.hpp>
```

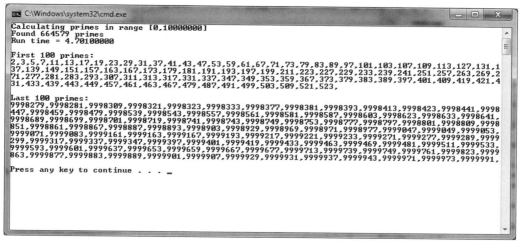

Figure 2.4
Using primes as divisors improves performance nearly five-fold.

```
#include <boost/timer.hpp>
#include <boost/foreach.hpp>

//declare a 64-bit long integer type
typedef unsigned long long biglong;
const long MILLION = 1000000;
biglong highestPrime = 10*MILLION;
boost::timer timer1;
std::list<biglong> primes;

long findPrimes(biglong rangeFirst, biglong rangeLast)
{
    long count = 0;
    biglong candidate = rangeFirst;
    if (candidate < 3) candidate = 3;
    primes.push_back( 2 );
    while(candidate <= rangeLast)
    {
        bool prime = true;

        //get divisor from the list of primes
        BOOST_FOREACH(biglong testDivisor, primes)
        {
```

```
                //test divisors up through the root of rangeLast
                if (testDivisor * testDivisor <= candidate)
                {
                    //test primality with modulus
                    if(candidate % testDivisor == 0)
                    {
                        prime = false;
                        break;
                    }
                    if (!prime) break;
                }
                else break;
            }
            //is this candidate prime?
            if (prime)
            {
                count++;
                primes.push_back(candidate);
            }
            //next ODD candidate
            candidate += 2;
        }
        return count;
}

int main(int argc, char *argv[])
{
    biglong first = 0;
    biglong last = highestPrime;
    std::cout << boost::str(
        boost::format("Calculating primes in range [%i,%i]\n") % first % last);

    timer1.restart();
    long primeCount = findPrimes(0, last);
    double finish = timer1.elapsed();

    std::cout << boost::str( boost::format("Found %i primes\n")
        % primeCount);
    std::cout << boost::str( boost::format("Run time = %.8f\n\n")
        % finish);
```

```
//print last 100 primes
std::cout << "First 100 primes:\n";
int count=0;
BOOST_FOREACH(biglong prime, primes)
{
    if (count < 100)
        std::cout << prime << ",";
    else if (count == primeCount-100)
        std::cout << "\n\nLast 100 primes:\n";
    else if (count > primeCount-100)
        std::cout << prime << ",";
    count++;
}
std::cout << "\n";
system("pause");
return 0;
}
```

This new version of our primality test program, which tests only odd divisors and candidates, does run slightly faster than the previous one, but not as significantly as the previous optimization. As you can see in Figure 2.5, the runtime is 4.484 seconds, down from 4.701, for an improvement of an additional two-tenths of a second. It's not much now, but it would be magnified many-fold

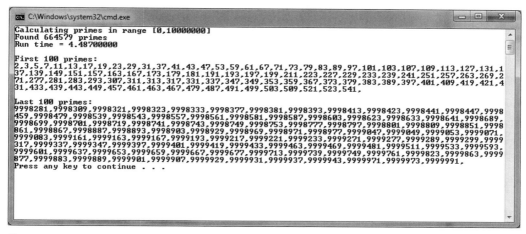

Figure 2.5
New primality test with "odd number" optimization.

Table 2.1 Primality Test Results (1 Core*)

Candidates	Primes	Time (sec)	C/Sec	P/Sec
1,000,000	78,497	0.241	4,166,666	327,070
5,000,000	348,512	1.837	2,721,829	189,718
10,000,000	664,578	4.484	2,230,151	148,211
25,000,000	1,565,926	15.494	1,613,527	101,066
50,000,000	3,001,133	40.244	1,242,421	74,573
100,000,000	5,761,454	102.792	972,838	56,049
1,000,000,000	50,847,533	2,347.162	426,046	21,663

*Intel Q6600 Core 2 Quad CPU, 4GB DDR2 RAM

when you get into billions of candidates. (Note: Results will differ based on processor performance.)

Table 2.1 shows the overall results using the final optimized version of the primality test program. Note the candidates per second (C/Sec) and primes per second (P/Sec) values, which are not at all predictable. This is due to memory consumption. The higher the target prime number, the larger the memory footprint. The 1 billion candidate test consumed over a gigabyte of memory by the time it completed (in 39 minutes). If your system does not have enough memory to handle a huge candidate test, then your system may begin swapping memory out to disk which will destroy any chance of obtaining an accurate timing result.

SPREADING OUT THE WORKLOAD

We can improve these numbers by adding multi-core support to the primality test code with the use of a thread library such as boost::thread. We will compare results with the single-core figures already recorded.

Threaded Primality Test

Using the single-core primality test program as a starting point, I would like to demonstrate a threaded version of the program that takes advantage of the boost::thread library. We won't go overboard yet with a huge group, but just spread the work over two cores instead of one, and then note the difference in performance.

New Boost Headers

We'll need two new header files to work with Boost threads:

```
#include <string.h>
#include <iostream>
#include <list>
#include <boost/format.hpp>
#include <boost/timer.hpp>
#include <boost/foreach.hpp>
#include <boost/thread/mutex.hpp>
#include <boost/thread/thread.hpp>
```

New Boost Variables

In addition to the variable declarations in the previous program, we now need a boost::mutex to protect threads from corrupting shared data (such as the list of primes).

```
//declare a 64-bit long integer type
typedef unsigned long long biglong;
const long MILLION = 1000000;

biglong highestPrime = 10*MILLION;
std::list<biglong> primes;

//this mutex will protect threads from corrupting data
boost::mutex mutex1;

boost::timer timer1;
int thread_counter = 0;
```

Next up in the program listing are two functions that are a derivation of the previous findPrimes() function used to find prime numbers. The new pair of functions accomplish the same task but with thread support. Any variable that will be accessed by a thread must be protected with a mutex lock. If two threads access the same variable at the same time, it could segfault or crash the program. To prevent this possibility, we'll use a boost::mutex::scoped_lock before any code that touches a shared variable. In our case here, the most notable example is the global linked list of prime numbers called *primes*:

```
std::list<biglong> primes;
```

Both the testPrime() and findPrimes() functions must use the primes list: the former to locate divisors, and the latter to add newly identified prime numbers to the list. If one thread finds a prime number, while the other thread is scanning the list of primes, then that first thread must wait for the second thread to finish using the primes list before adding the new number to it.

Are you thinking what I'm thinking? That statement gives me an idea for a future optimization. Rather than requiring threads to wait while the primes list is being used, we could create a new list of primes and then add the new numbers to the *main* list later.

While that idea does have merit, there is one huge flaw: later prime number tests actually rely on there being root numbers already in the list, so we can't test higher candidates as long as the list is not being populated with new primes as they are discovered.

New Prime Number Crunching Functions

Below are the two prime number sniffing functions. You'll note that testPrime() is just a subset of code from the previously larger findPrimes() function, which is now leaner and threaded. This example is not 100% foolproof thread code, though. The testPrime() function, in particular, does not use a mutex lock, so it's very possible that a conflict could occur that would crash the program. We're only using two threads at this point, so conflicts will be rare, but increasing that to 4, 10, 20, or more threads, it could be a problem. We'll deal with that contingency when the time comes, if necessary.

```
bool testPrime( biglong candidate )
{
    bool prime = true;

    //get divisor from the list of primes
    BOOST_FOREACH(biglong testDivisor, primes)
    {
        biglong threadsafe_divisor = testDivisor;
```

```
            //test divisors up through the root of rangeLast
            if (threadsafe_divisor * threadsafe_divisor <= candidate)
            {
                //test primality with modulus
                if(candidate % threadsafe_divisor == 0)
                {
                    prime = false;
                    break;
                }
                if (!prime) break;
            }
            else break;
        }
        return prime;
}


void findPrimes(biglong rangeFirst, biglong rangeLast )
{
    thread_counter++;
    std::cout << "  thread function " << thread_counter << "\n";

    biglong candidate = rangeFirst;
    if (candidate < 3) candidate = 3;

    while(candidate <= rangeLast)
    {
        bool prime = true;
        prime = testPrime( candidate );
        if (prime)
        {
            boost::mutex::scoped_lock lock(mutex1);
            primes.push_back( candidate );
        }

        //next ODD candidate
        candidate += 2;
    }
}
```

New Main Function

Next up is the `main` function with quite a bit of new code over the previous Prime Number Test 3 program.

```cpp
int main(int argc, char *argv[])
{
    biglong first = 0;
    biglong last = highestPrime;
    std::cout << boost::str( boost::format("Calculating primes in range [%i,%i]\n")
        % first % last);

    timer1.restart();
    primes.push_back( 2 );

    std::cout << "creating thread 1\n";
    biglong range1 = highestPrime/2;
    boost::thread thread1( findPrimes, 0, range1 );

    std::cout << "creating thread 2\n";
    biglong range2 = highestPrime;
    boost::thread thread2( findPrimes, range1+1, range2 );

    std::cout << "waiting for threads\n";
    thread1.join();
    thread2.join();

    double finish = timer1.elapsed();

    long primeCount = primes.size();

    std::cout << boost::str( boost::format("\nFound %i primes\n")
        % primeCount );
    std::cout << boost::str( boost::format("Run time = %.8f\n")
        % finish);
    std::cout << boost::str( boost::format("Candidates/sec = %.2f\n")
        % ((double)last / finish));
    std::cout << boost::str( boost::format("Primes/sec = %.2f\n")
        % ((double)primeCount / finish));
```

```
    //print sampling for verification
    std::cout << "\nFirst 100 primes:\n";
    int count=0;
    BOOST_FOREACH(biglong prime, primes)
    {
        count++;
        if (count < 100)
            std::cout << prime << ",";
        else if (count == primeCount-100)
            std::cout << "\n\nLast 100 primes:\n";
        else if (count > primeCount-100)
            std::cout << prime << ",";
    }
    std::cout << "\n";
    system("pause");
    return 0;
}
```

Taking It for a Spin

Figure 2.6 shows the output of the new and improved primality test program
with thread support. The results are very impressive. The previous best time for

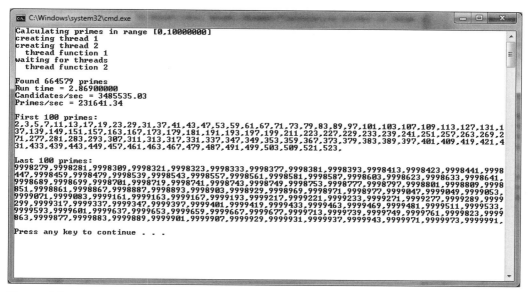

Figure 2.6
New primality test taking advantage of multiple threads.

the 10 million candidate primality test was 4.484 seconds, which is a rate of 2,230,151 candidates per second.

The threaded version of this program crunched through the same 10 million candidates in only 2.869 seconds, a rate of 3,485,535 candidates per second. This is an improvement of 37% with the addition of just one extra worker thread (for a total of two). Assuming the cores are available, a processor should be able to crunch primes even faster with four or more threads.

Getting to Know boost::thread

Let's go over this program in order to understand how the boost::thread library works. First of all, you can create a new thread in several ways with boost::thread, but we'll focus on just two of them right now. The first way to create a thread is with a simple thread function parameter:

```
boost::thread T( threadFunc );
```

where the threadFunc() function is defined like so:

```
void threadFunc()
{
    ...
}
```

As soon as the thread is created, the thread function is called—you do not have to call any additional function to get it started, it just takes off.

The second way to create a thread (among many) is to create a thread definition with optional thread function parameters, as we have seen in the threaded prime number test program.

```
boost::thread T( threadFunc, 100, 234.5 );
```

By adding the parameters you wish to the thread constructor, boost::thread will pass those parameters on to the thread function for you—which is obviously very handy. Here's an example function:

```
void threadFunc( int i, double d )
{
    ...
}
```

In this example, you may use the `int i` and `double d` parameters however you wish in the function. However, if you need to return a value by way of a reference parameter, the value must be passed with the boost reference wrapper, `boost::ref`, to properly make the "pass by reference" variable thread safe (the threaded function cannot return a value directly). Here is an example:

```
int count = 0;
boost::thread T( threadFunc, boost::ref( &count ) );
void threadFunc( int &count )
{
    ...
}
```

SUMMARY

Boost::thread is just the first of four thread libraries we will be examining with the remaining three covered in the next three chapters: OpenMP, Posix threads, and Windows threads. These four are the most common/popular thread libraries in use today in applications as well as games. The prime number calculations explored in this chapter are meant to inspire your imagination! Where will you choose to go in your own multi-threaded coding experiments? Primes can be a lot of fun to explore, and can be very powerful as well—primes are used extensively in cryptography!

REFERENCES

1. "Prime number"; http://en.wikipedia.org/wiki/Prime_number.

2. "Largest known prime number"; http://en.wikipedia.org/wiki/Largest_known_prime_number.

3. "Lucas-Lehmer primality test"; http://en.wikipedia.org/wiki/Lucas%E2%80%93Lehmer_primality_test.

4. Litt, Steve. "Fun With Prime Numbers"; http://www.troubleshooters.com/codecorn/primenumbers/primenumbers.htm.

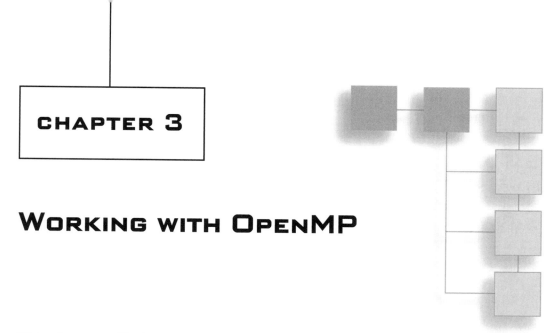

CHAPTER 3

WORKING WITH OPENMP

This chapter will give you an overview of the OpenMP multi-threading library for general-purpose multi-core computing. OpenMP is one of the most widely adopted threading "libraries" in use today, due to its simple requirements and automated code generation (through the use of #pragma statements). We will learn how to use OpenMP in this chapter, culminating in a revisiting of our prime number generator to see how well this new threading capability works. OpenMP will not be used yet in a game engine context, because frankly we have not yet built the engine (see Chapter 6). In Chapter 18, we will use OpenMP to test engine optimizations with OpenMP and other techniques.

This chapter covers the following topics:

- Overview of the OpenMP API
- Advantages of OpenMP
- What is shared memory?
- Threading a loop
- Configuring Visual C++
- Specifying the number of threads
- Sequential ordering

- Controlling thread execution
- Prime numbers revisited

Say Hello To OpenMP

In keeping with the tradition set forth by Kernighan & Ritchie, we will begin this chapter on OpenMP programming with an appropriate "Hello World"–style program.

```
#include <omp.h>
int main(int argc, char* argv[])
{
    #pragma omp parallel num_threads(4)
    printf("Hello World\n");
    return 0;
}
```

Our threaded program produces this output:

```
HelHelo llWoorWlordl
HdeHelllllooWo Wrorld
ld
```

That's not at all what one would expect the code to do! We'll learn why this happens in this chapter.

What Is OpenMP and How Does It Work?

"Let's play a game: Who is your daddy and what does he do?"

—Arnold Schwarzeneggar

OpenMP is a multi-platform shared-memory parallel programming API for CPU-based threading that is portable, scalable, and simple to use.[1] Unlike Windows threads and Boost threads, OpenMP does not give you any functions for working with individual worker threads. Instead, OpenMP uses pre-processor directives to provide a higher level of functionality to the parallel programmer without requiring a large investment of time to handle thread management issues such as mutexes. The OpenMP API standard was initially developed by Silicon Graphics and Kuck & Associates in order to allow programmers the ability to write a single version of their source code that will run on single- and multi-core systems.[2] OpenMP is an application programming interface or API, not an SDK or library. There is no way to download and install or build the OpenMP API, just as it is not possible to install OpenGL on your system—it is built by the video card vendors and distributed with the video drivers. An API is nothing more than a specification or a standard that everyone should follow so that all code based on the API is compatible. Implementation is entirely dependent on vendors. (DirectX, on the other hand, *is* an SDK, and can be downloaded and installed.)

OpenMP is an open standard, which means that an implementation is not provided at the www.openmp.org website (just as you will not find a downloadable SDK at the www.opengl.com website, since OpenGL is also an open standard). An open standard is basically a bunch of header files that describe how a library should function. It is then up to *someone else* to implement the library by actually writing the .cpp files suggested by the headers. In the case of OpenMP, the single `omp.h` header file is needed.

Advice

The Express Edition of Visual Studio does *not* come with OpenMP support! OpenMP was implemented on the Windows platform by Microsoft and distributed with Visual Studio Professional and other purchasable versions. If you want to use OpenMP in your Visual C++ game projects, you will need to purchase a licensed version of Visual Studio. It is possible to copy the OpenMP library into the VC folder of your Visual C++ Express Edition (sourced from the Platform SDK), but that will only allow you to compile the OpenMP code without errors—it will not actually create multiple threads.

Since we're focusing on the Windows platform and Visual C++ in this book, we must use the version of OpenMP supported by Visual C++. Both the 2008 and 2010 versions support the OpenMP 2.0 specification—version 3.0 is not supported.

Advantages of OpenMP

OpenMP offers these key advantages over a custom-programmed lower-level threading library such as Windows threads and Boost threads:[3]

- Good performance and scalability (if done right).
- De facto and mature standard.
- Portability due to wide compiler adoption.
- Requires little extra programming effort.

- Allows incremental parallelization of existing or new programs.
- Ideally suited for multi-core processors.
- Natural memory and threading model mapping.
- Lightweight.
- Mature.

What Is Shared Memory?

When working with variables and objects in a program using a thread library, you must be careful to write code so that your threads do not try to access the same data at the same time, or a crash will occur. The way to protect shared data is with a mutex (mutual context) locking mechanism. When using a mutex, a function or block of code is "locked" until that thread "releases" it, and no other thread may proceed beyond the mutex lock statement until it is unlocked. If coded incorrectly, a mutex lock could result in a situation known as *deadlock*, in which, due to a logic error, the thread locks are never released in the right order so that processing can continue, and the program will appear to freeze up (quite literally since threads cannot continue).

OpenMP handles shared data seamlessly as far as the programmer is concerned. While it is possible to designate data as privately owned by a specific thread, generally, OpenMP code is written in such a way that OpenMP handles the details, while the programmer focuses on solving problems with the support of many threads. A seamless shared-memory system means the mutex locking and unlocking mechanism is automatically handled "behind the scenes," freeing the programmer from writing such code.

How does OpenMP do this so well? Basically, by making a *copy* of data that is being used by a particular thread, and synchronizing each thread's copy of data (such as a string variable) at regular intervals. At any given time, two or more threads may have a different copy of a shared data item that no other thread can access. Each thread is given a time slot wherein it "owns" the shared data, and can make changes to it.[3] While we will make use of similar techniques when writing our own thread code in upcoming chapters, the details behind OpenMP's internal handling of shared data need not be a concern in a normal application (or game engine, as the case may be).

Threading a Loop

A normal loop will iterate through a range from the starting value to the maximum value, usually one item at a time. This for loop is reliable. We can count on a sequential processing of all array elements from item 0 to 999 based on this loop, and know for certain that all 1,000 items will be processed.

```
for (int n = 0; n < 1000; n++)
    c[n] = a[n] + b[n];
```

When writing threaded code to handle the same loop, you might need to break up the loop into several, like we did in the previous chapter to calculate prime numbers with two different threads. Recall that this code:

```
std::cout << "creating thread 1\n";
biglong range1 = highestPrime/2;
boost::thread thread1( findPrimes, 0, range1 );
std::cout << "creating thread 2\n";
biglong range2 = highestPrime;
boost::thread thread2( findPrimes, range1+1, range2 );
std::cout << "waiting for threads\n";
thread1.join();
thread2.join();
```

sends the first half of the prime number candidate range to one worker thread, while the second half was sent to a second worker thread. There are problems with this approach that may or *may not* present themselves. One serious problem is that prime numbers from both ranges, deposited into the list in both thread loops, may fill the prime divisor list with unsorted primes, and this actually breaks the program because it relies on those early primes to test later candidates. One might find 2, 3, 5, 9999991, 7, 11, 13, and so on. While these are all still valid prime numbers, the ordering is broken. While some hooks might be used to sort the numbers as they arrive, we really can't use the same list when using primes themselves as divisors (which, as you'll recall, was a significant optimization). Going with the brute force approach with just the odd number optimization is our best option.

Let us now examine the loop with OpenMP support:

```
#pragma omp parallel for
for (int n = 0; n < 1000; n++)
    c[n] = a[n] + b[n];
```

The OpenMP pragma is a pre-processor "flag," which the compiler will use to thread the loop. This is the simplest form of OpenMP usage, but even this produces surprisingly robust multi-threaded code. We will look at additional OpenMP features in a bit.

Configuring Visual C++

An OpenMP implementation is automatically installed with Visual C++ 2008 and 2010 (Professional edition), so all you will need to do is enable it within project properties. With your Visual C++ project loaded, open the Project menu, and select Properties at the bottom. Then open Configuration Properties, C/C++, and Language. You should see the "OpenMP Support" property at the bottom of the list, as shown in Figure 3.1. Set this property to Yes, which will add the /openmp compile option to turn on OpenMP support. Be sure to always include the omp.h header file as well to avoid compile errors:

```
#include <omp.h>
```

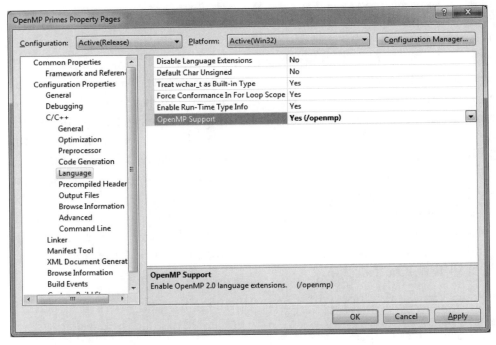

Figure 3.1
Turning on OpenMP Support in the project's properties.

The compiler you choose to use must support OpenMP. There is no OpenMP software development kit (SDK) that can be downloaded and installed. The OpenMP API standard requires a platform vendor to supply an implementation of OpenMP for that platform via the compiler. Microsoft Visual C++ supports OpenMP 2.0.

Advice

For performance testing and optimization work, be sure to enable OpenMP for both the Debug and Release build configurations in Visual C++.

EXPLORING OPENMP

Beyond the basic `#pragma omp parallel for` that we've used, there are many additional options that can be specified in the `#pragma` statement. We will examine the most interesting features, but will by no means exhaust them all in this single chapter.

Advice

For additional books and articles that go into much more depth, see the References section at the end of the chapter.

Specifying the Number of Threads

By default, OpenMP will detect the number of cores in your processor and create the same number of threads. In most cases, you should just let OpenMP choose the thread pool size on its own and not interfere. This should work correctly with technologies such as Intel's HyperThreading, which logically doubles the number of hardware threads in a multi-core processor, essentially handling two or more threads per core in the chip itself. The simple `#pragma` directive we've seen so far is just the beginning. But there may be cases where you do want to specify how many threads to use for a process. Let's take a look at an option to set the number of threads.

```
#pragma omp parallel num_threads(4)
{
}
```

Note the block brackets. This statement instructs the compiler to attempt to create four threads for use in that block of code (not for the rest of the program, just the block). Within the block, you must use additional OpenMP #pragmas to actually use those threads that have been reserved.

Within the #pragma omp parallel block, additional directives can be specified. Since "parallel" was already specified in the parent block, we cannot use "parallel" in code blocks nested within or below the #pragma omp parallel level, but we can use additional #pragma omp options.

Let's try it first with just one thread to start as a baseline for comparison:

```cpp
#include <iostream>
#include <omp.h>
using namespace std;
int main(int argc, char* argv[])
{
    #pragma omp parallel num_threads(1)
    {
        #pragma omp for
        for (int n = 0; n < 10; n++)
        {
            cout << "threaded for loop iteration # " << n << endl;
        }
    }
    system("pause");
    return 0;
}
```

Here is the output, which is nice and orderly:

```
threaded for loop iteration # 0
threaded for loop iteration # 1
threaded for loop iteration # 2
threaded for loop iteration # 3
threaded for loop iteration # 4
threaded for loop iteration # 5
threaded for loop iteration # 6
```

```
threaded for loop iteration # 7
threaded for loop iteration # 8
threaded for loop iteration # 9
```

Now, change the `num_threads` property to 2, like this:

```
#pragma omp parallel num_threads(2)
```

and watch the program run again, now with a threaded for loop using two threads:

```
threaded for loop iteration # threaded for loop iteration # 5
0
threaded for loop iteration # 1
threaded for loop iteration # 2
threaded for loop iteration # 3
threaded for loop iteration # 4
threaded for loop iteration # 6
threaded for loop iteration # 7
threaded for loop iteration # 8
threaded for loop iteration # 9
```

The first line of output with two strings interrupting each other is not an error; that is what the program produces now that two threads are sharing the console. (A similar result was shown at the start of the chapter to help set the reader's expectations!) Let's get a little more bold by switching to four threads:

```
#pragma omp parallel num_threads(4)
```

This produces the following output (which will differ on each PC):

```
threaded for loop iteration # 3
threaded for loop iteration # 0
threaded for loop iteration # 4
threaded for loop iteration # 5
threaded for loop iteration # 1
threaded for loop iteration # threaded for loop iteration # 6
threaded for loop iteration # 8
threaded for loop iteration # 9
threaded for loop iteration # 7
2
```

Notice the ordering of the output, which is even more out of order than before, but there are basically pairs of numbers being output by each thread in some cases (4-5, 8-9). The point is, beyond a certain point, which is quite soon, we lose the ability to predict the order at which items in the loop are processed by the threads. Certainly, this code is running much faster with parallel iteration, but you can't expect ordered output because the for loop cannot be processed sequentially. Or can it?

Sequential Ordering

Fortunately, there *is* a way to guarantee the ordering of sequentially processed items in a for loop. This is done with the "ordered" directive option. However, ordering the processing of the loop requires a different approach in the directives. Now, instead of prefacing a block of code with a directive, it is moved directly above the for loop and a *second* directive is added *inside* the loop block itself. There is, of course, a loss of performance when enforcing the order of processing: depending on the data, using the ordered clause may eliminate all but one thread for a certain block of code.

```cpp
#include <iostream>
#include <omp.h>
using namespace std;
int main(int argc, char* argv[])
{
    #pragma omp parallel for ordered
    for (int n = 0; n < 10; n++)
    {
        #pragma omp ordered
        {
            cout << "threaded for loop iteration # " << n << endl;
        }
    }
    return 0;
}
```

This code produces the following output, which is identical to the output generated when num_threads(1) was used to force the use of only one thread. Now we're taking advantage of many cores and still getting ordered output!

```
threaded for loop iteration # 0
threaded for loop iteration # 1
threaded for loop iteration # 2
threaded for loop iteration # 3
threaded for loop iteration # 4
```

```
threaded for loop iteration # 5
threaded for loop iteration # 6
threaded for loop iteration # 7
threaded for loop iteration # 8
threaded for loop iteration # 9
```

But, this result begs the question: how many threads are being used? The best way to find out is to look up an OpenMP function that will provide the thread count in use. According to the API reference, the OpenMP function omp_get_num_threads() provides this answer. Optionally, we could open up Task Manager and note which processor cores are being used. For the imprecise but gratifying Task Manager test, you will want to set the iteration to a very large number so that it will run for a few seconds—our current 10 iterations returns immediately with no discernible runtime. Here's a new version of the program that displays the thread count:

```
#include <iostream>
#include <omp.h>
using namespace std;
int main(int argc, char* argv[])
{
    int t = omp_get_num_threads();
    cout << "threads at start = " << t << endl;

    #pragma omp parallel for ordered
    for (int n = 0; n < 10; n++)
    {
        t = omp_get_num_threads();
        #pragma omp ordered
        {
            cout << t << " threads, loop iteration # " << n << endl;
        }
    }
    return 0;
}
```

Here is the output:

```
threads at start = 1
4 threads, loop iteration # 0
4 threads, loop iteration # 1
4 threads, loop iteration # 2
```

```
4 threads, loop iteration # 3
4 threads, loop iteration # 4
4 threads, loop iteration # 5
4 threads, loop iteration # 6
4 threads, loop iteration # 7
4 threads, loop iteration # 8
4 threads, loop iteration # 9
```

Advice

See the References at the end of the chapter for a link to the OpenMP C and C++ API, which lists all of the directives and functions available for use.

Bumping the loop count to 10,000 allows you to watch the CPU utilization in Task Manager. In Figure 3.2, you can see that all four cores are in use, which corresponds to the program's output that showed that four threads were in use. Each core is only being partially utilized, though, because printing text is a trivial

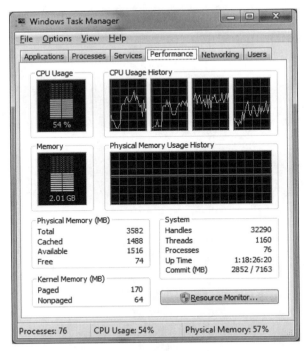

Figure 3.2
Observing the program running with four threads in Task Manager.

thing to do, so the total CPU utilization is hovering at just over 50%. The important thing, though, is that the loop is being processed with multiple threads and the output is ordered—and therefore *predictable*!

Controlling Thread Execution

The ordered clause does help to clean up the normal thread *chaos* that often occurs, making the result of a for loop predictable. In addition to ordered, there are other directive options we can use to help guide OpenMP through difficult parts of our code.

Critical

The `critical` clause restricts a block of code to a single thread at a time. This directive would be used inside a parallel block of code when you want certain data to be protected from unexpected thread mutation, especially when performance in that particular block of code is not paramount.

```
#pragma omp critical
```

Barrier

The `barrier` clause forces all threads to synchronize their data before code execution continues beyond the directive line. When all threads have encountered the barrier, then parallel execution continues.

```
#pragma omp barrier
```

Atomic

The `atomic` clause protects data from thread update conflicts, which can cause a race (or deadlock) condition. This functionality is similar to what we've already seen in *thread mutex* behavior, where a mutex lock prevents any other thread from running the code in the following block until the mutex lock has been released.

```
double counter = 0.0;
#pragma omp parallel
{
    #pragma omp atomic
    counter += 1.0;
}
```

Data Synchronization

The `reduction` clause causes each thread to get a copy of a shared variable, which each thread then uses for processing, and afterward, the copies used by the threads are merged back into the shared variable again. This technique completely avoids any conflicts because the shared variable is named in the `reduction` clause.

```
int main(int argc, char* argv[])
{
    int count = 0;
    omp_set_num_threads(8);
    #pragma omp parallel reduction(+:count)
    {
        count++;
    }
    cout << "count = " << count << endl;
    return 0;
}
```

This code prints out the following (based on the specified thread count):

```
count = 8
```

Try not to be confused by the term "reduction," as this refers not to a variable being reduced in value but rather that it is being modified by multiple threads. It is up to the programmer to be certain the reduction operator ($\pm$, in this case) matches the operation being made to the variable (which was `count++`). The $\pm$ operator simply means that the variable is being *increased*, or is the result of a *summation*, not that it must be incremented by just one. When more than one variable is being increased, all may be included in the $\pm$ `reduction` clause, such as:

```
#pragma omp parallel reduction(+:a,b,c)
```

When a different operator is being used on another variable, then additional `reduction` clauses may be added to the same #pragma line. For example, the following code:

```
int main(int argc, char* argv[])
{
    int count = 0;
    int neg = 0;
    omp_set_num_threads(8);
    #pragma omp parallel reduction(+:count) reduction(-:neg)
```

```
    {
        count++;
        neg--;
    }
    cout << "count = " << count << endl;
    cout << "neg = " << neg << endl;
    return 0;
}
```

produces this output:

```
count = 8
neg = -8
```

PRIME NUMBERS REVISITED

As a comparison, we're going to revisit our prime number code from the previous chapter and tune it for use with OpenMP. For reference, Figure 3.3 shows the output of the original project from the previous chapter—which included no optimizations—not algorithmic or threaded, just simple primality testing. The resulting output of the 10 million–candidate test was 664,579 primes found in 22.5 seconds.

Now we will modify this program to use OpenMP, replacing the BOOST_FOREACH statements with simpler for loops that OpenMP requires.

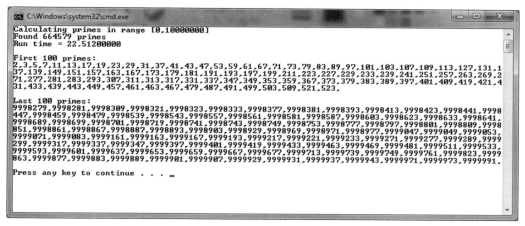

Figure 3.3
The original prime number program with no thread support.

```cpp
#include <string.h>
#include <iostream>
#include <list>
#include <boost/format.hpp>
#include <boost/timer.hpp>
#include <boost/foreach.hpp>
#include <omp.h>

//declare a 64-bit long integer type
typedef unsigned long long biglong;
biglong highestPrime = 10000000;

boost::timer timer1;

std::list<biglong> primes;

int numThreads=0;

long findPrimes(biglong rangeFirst, biglong rangeLast)
{
    long count = 0;
    biglong candidate = rangeFirst;
    if (candidate < 2) candidate = 2;

    //while(candidate <= rangeLast)
    #pragma omp parallel
    {
        #pragma omp for
        for (long n = candidate; n <= rangeLast; n++)
        {
            biglong testDivisor = 2;
            bool prime = true;

            //test divisors up through the root of rangeLast
            while(testDivisor * testDivisor <= n)
            {
                //test with modulus
                if (n % testDivisor == 0)
                {
```

```
                    prime = false;
                    break;
                }
                //next divisor
                testDivisor++;
              }

            //is this candidate prime?
            #pragma omp critical
            if (prime)
            {
                count++;
                primes.push_back(n);
            }

            //count the threads in use
            numThreads = omp_get_num_threads();
        }
    }
    return count;
}


int main(int argc, char *argv[])
{
    long first = 0;
    long last = highestPrime;
    std::cout << boost::str( boost::format("Calculating primes in range [%i,%i]\n")
        % first % last);

    timer1.restart();
    long primeCount = findPrimes(0, last);
    double finish = timer1.elapsed();

    primes.sort();

    std::cout << boost::str( boost::format("Found %i primes\n") % primeCount);
    std::cout << boost::str( boost::format("Used %i threads\n") % numThreads);
    std::cout << boost::str( boost::format("Run time = %.8f\n\n") % finish);
```

```
std::cout << "First 100 primes:\n";
int count=0;
BOOST_FOREACH(biglong prime, primes)
{
    count++;
    if (count < 100)
        std::cout << prime << ",";

    else if (count == primeCount-100)
        std::cout << "\n\nLast 100 primes:\n";

    else if (count > primeCount-100)
        std::cout << prime << ",";

}
std::cout << "\n";

system("pause");
return 0;
}
```

We can now compare the two results with the original time and the time for the OpenMP version shown in Figure 3.4. Despite having no optimizations, our

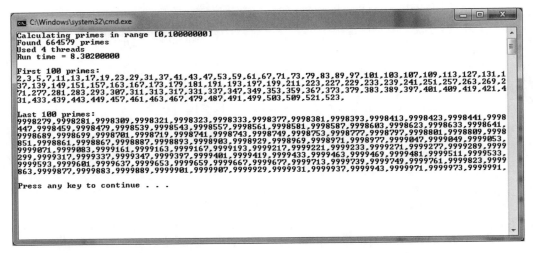

Figure 3.4
Multi-threaded OpenMP version of the *unoptimized* prime number program.

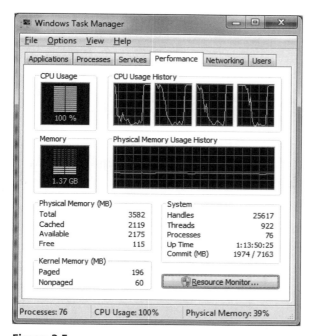

Figure 3.5
OpenMP automatically detects the number of hardware threads available in the CPU and makes use of them.

multi-threaded OpenMP version of the brute force, unoptimized prime number program runs three times faster, shaving the time from 22.5 seconds down to just 8.3! This is due to the number of threads being created automatically by OpenMP. Task Manager is shown in Figure 3.5, showing all four processor cores maxed out by OpenMP while the program is crunching prime numbers.

SUMMARY

OpenMP is a powerful tool for parallel programming, and this chapter has provided a useful introduction to the subject. We will certainly be using OpenMP and its many directives and clauses to optimize game engine code in upcoming chapters. More specifically, a threaded version of the game engine developed in Part II will be threaded with OpenMP in Chapter 18.

REFERENCES

1. "About OpenMP and OpenMP.org"; Feb. 27, 2010. http://openmp.org/wp/about-openmp/.

2. Chapman, B.; Jost, G.; and van der Pas, R. *Using OpenMP: Portable Shared Memory Parallel Programming*. Cambridge: The MIT Press 2007.

3. van der Pas, R. *An Overview of OpenMP 3.0* [PowerPoint slides] 2009. Retrieved from the 2009 International Workshop on OpenMP website: https://iwomp.zih.tu-dresden.de/downloads/2.Overview_OpenMP.pdf.

    "32 OpenMP Traps For C++ Developers"; March 6, 2010. http://www.viva64.com/content/articles/parallel-programming/?f=32_OpenMP_traps.html&lang=en&content=parallel-programming.

    "OpenMP C and C++ Application Program Interface"; March 2002. http://www.openmp.org/mp-documents/cspec20.pdf.

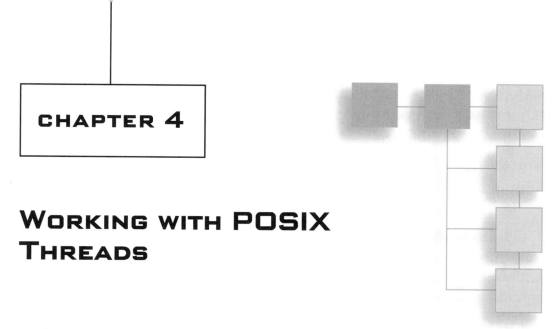

CHAPTER 4

Working with POSIX Threads

In this chapter, you will learn how to create threads using the POSIX threads ("Pthreads") library—a popular cross-platform thread library that is part of the core Linux operating system and available for other platforms such as Windows[1]. A *thread* is a set of instructions—usually running in a while loop within a special thread function—that runs in parallel with other sets of instructions (or threads) in a program. In a multi-core system with a multi-tasking operating system, every program has at least one thread, and it is the job of the operating system to assign each process to one of the processor cores. Unless the operating system—and the processor—has this capability, no amount of threading will improve performance. In the case of a simple processor, such as the Atom found in many netbook PCs, there is only one core available. While a single-core processor may run fast enough, and have enough bandwidth, to handle many threads, the time slicing will cause a greater degradation of system performance as more and more threads are launched. In the case of a single core system, a multi-threaded game engine will possibly run more slowly due to time slicing. We have covered a lot of ground so far, so in this chapter we will take it a bit slower and cover more of the theory behind multi-threaded programming.

This chapter will cover the following topics:

- Thread theory in a nutshell
- Putting POSIX threads to work

- Installing the Pthreads library
- Creating a new thread
- The `thread` function
- Killing a thread
- Mutexes: making data threads safe

INTRODUCING THE POSIX THREADS LIBRARY

Every modern operating system uses threads for essential and basic operation and would not even function without thread support. I will not go into the specific details of POSIX thread programming because we covered general-purpose thread theory in the previous two chapters. The goal of this chapter is to provide a solid overview of the most important features with enough detail to effectively use POSIX threads in a program. Most Linux and UNIX operating system flavors will already have the Pthreads library installed because it is a core feature of the kernel. Windows uses its own multi-threading library, but we will be able to use Pthreads via the SDK files (available in this chapter's resources–www.courseptr.com/downloads). An important thing you should know about the Windows implementation of Pthreads is that it uses Windows threading behind the scenes, so to speak, with function wrappers to make the Windows threading function like POSIX threads. Fortunately, the two are already similar.

Thread Theory in a Nutshell

To be multi-threaded, a program will create at least one thread (running in a unique thread function) that will run in parallel with that program's main loop. Any time a program uses more than one thread, you must take extreme caution when working with data that is potentially shared between threads. It is generally safe for a program to share data with a single thread (although it is not recommended), but when more than one thread is in use, you must use a protection scheme to protect the data from being manipulated by two or more threads at the same time.

To protect data, you can make use of a mutex (a mutual exclusion construct) that will lock data inside a single thread until it is safe to unlock the data again. By "lock," what I mean is, no other thread can proceed beyond the mutex lock source code line until that lock is released. Think of it as a roadblock on an interstate highway—and imagine how much the traffic can become backed up if not used wisely! The locking and unlocking is usually done inside a while loop that runs continuously inside the thread function. Note that if you do not have a loop inside your thread function, it will run once and terminate with the function. The idea is to keep the thread running—doing something—while the main program is doing the delegating work. You should think of a thread as a new employee who has been hired to alleviate the amount of work done by the program (or rather, by the main thread).

We can easily discuss the subject today as if it's just another SDK, but threading was at one time an extraordinary achievement that was every bit as exciting as the first connection in ARPAnet in 1969 or the first working version of UNIX. In the 1980s, parallel programming was as hip as virtual reality, but like the latter, it was not to be a true reality until the early 1990s. *Multi-core programming with threads* is a form of parallel processing that has been effective in modern operating systems. The breakthrough in parallel processing theory came when software engineers realized that the processor is not the focus; rather, software design is.

A single-processor system should be able to run multiple threads. Once that goal was realized, adding two or more processors to a system provided the ability to delegate those threads, and this was a job for the operating system. No longer tasked with designing a parallel-processing architecture in the *hardware*, engineers in both the electronics and software fields abstracted the problem so the two were not reliant upon each other. A single program can run on a motherboard with four CPUs or a single CPU with four or six or more cores, and push all of those cores to the limit—if that single program invokes multiple threads. As such, the programs themselves were treated as single threads. And yet, there can be many single-threaded programs running on our hypothetical multi-core system, and it might not be taxed at all. It depends on what each program is doing. As far as the operating system is concerned, though, there is no difference between a four-processor motherboard and a four-core processor—threads are still delegated to available cores.

Math-intensive processes, such as 3D rendering, can eat a single processor core for breakfast. But with hardware threads and thread support in modern operating systems, programs such as 3D Studio Max, Maya, LightWave, and Photoshop can invoke threads to handle intense processes, such as scene rendering and image manipulation. Suddenly, that hexa-core Mac is able to process a Photoshop image in four seconds, while it might have taken 40 seconds on an old single-core Mac! Why? Threads and multiple processor cores are not limited to just the CPU side of a computer—we can also take advantage of massive threading capabilities in modern GPUs as well (to a much greater extent!) with SDKs like CUDA and Direct Compute.

However, just because a single program is able to share four cores, that doesn't mean each thread is an independent entity. Any global variables in the program (main thread) can be used by the invoked threads as long as care is taken that data is not damaged. Imagine 10 children grasping for an ice cream cone at the same time and you get the picture. What your threaded program must do is isolate the ice cream cone for each child, and only make the ice cream cone available to the others after that child has released it. Massively parallel computing tends to work best on sequential streams of data, which is why GPU computing is based around stream processing[2].

How does this concept of threading relate to processes? Modern operating systems treat each program as a separate process, allocating a certain number of microseconds to each process. This is where we get the term *multi-tasking*; many processes can be run at the same time using a time-slicing mechanism. A process owns a heap (the thing used for global variables and dynamically allocated memory via *new* or *malloc*). The process heap is shared by all the threads in the process. Each thread in the process (the main thread and any additional worker threads you start) gets its own stack (used for local variables). Even though we have multi-core computers today, the operating systems still perform pre-emptive time slicing on all processes.

Putting POSIX Threads to Work

There are two ways to use threads to offload processing from your game loop. The first method is to write a thread function that runs once and then returns. The second method is to write a thread function with its own while loop that runs continually in parallel with your game loop. There are advantages and drawbacks to both methods. The single-run function method uses more processor cycles because the thread function is being called many times per second, but it will result in fewer mutex waits (which happens when the thread is locked by another process). The continually running function with its own while loop is more efficient because it is only called once in order to run in parallel, but the drawbacks are less versatility and more instances of mutex waits. Neither method is better than the other, as both types of thread function will be useful in a game. I tend to favor the single-run thread functions over the embedded loop function method, if only because it allows for smaller, more mission-specific functions. There's no reason why you cannot write *many* single-purpose thread functions that run once depending on the conditions in the game.

Let me give you some examples to help you visualize both scenarios. First, you have a game that creates a thread before launching its own main loop. Inside the thread function, you have programmed it to update all of the sprites in the entity manager. Since the entities are created on the heap with *new*, each entity in the list is really just a pointer. Thus, iterating through the entity list means we go through a list of pointers to gain access to each mesh or sprite object in the list. The thread function runs in a tight loop with no timing whatsoever, so it runs *really* fast. In your game loop, however, each time an entity is updated, there is a call to the update function in your game's source code, and a pointer to the entity is passed to this function each time. Now, if your tightly written thread loop tried to read data in a specific sprite while the function was *writing* data to the same entity, that would crash the program—or lock the thread due to the mutex, which would cause the game to freeze.

Let's take a look at this scenario from the single-run thread function point of view. Let's say we have a list of entities (which can contain sprites, meshes, etc.), which is iterated and a thread function is called to update each entity (with movement, animation, collision detection, and so forth). But *now*, most of that processing is being called from the game loop, not from the thread loop. Whenever we need to update an entity, a thread function is called, and when that update is finished, the thread is terminated. Our game experiences quite a bit of overhead with all of the function calls, but the advantage is that now we can update an entity in the update function without causing a mutex lock. How? If, inside one of the single-run thread functions, we experience a thread lock, that thread will wait until the lock is released, and it will then finish its processing and kill the thread. However, in a tight thread loop, the mutex in the *main program* could be locked instead! This could potentially lock up the game loop. Although the engine's threads would continue to run just fine (hogging the system, so to speak), the game loop that communicates by way of our event function would be interrupted. We can predict this because the game loop has *timing code* in it. That timing code means the game loop can be easily interrupted. The thread loop will have no such timing code, because it is designed to run as fast as possible.

As you can imagine, a lot of thought must be put into a multi-threaded game engine before we just haphazardly create a tight thread function at engine startup and then *assume* that, with our newfound threading power, the engine will run faster. In reality, the thread locks are probably *slowing it down*!

Returning to the subject of single-run thread functions, there is another drawback that I have not mentioned yet. When you create a new thread, the point in the program where the thread was created *continues* to the next statement. The program doesn't need to wait until the thread function returns before it executes the next line. This means we can actually create many threads simultaneously, with each one updating a single object in memory without conflict. This is inevitably faster than a monolithic thread function *if* we have a multi-core processor, since a looping thread will only utilize a single core. Our multiple-thread function call theory would utilize multiple cores, since the operating system decides where threads are run and balances them among all available processor cores.

The drawbacks seem to outweigh the advantages to the single-run threads. Since the threads are being created and destroyed thousands of times per second, the overhead will be high, outweighing any advantages we would otherwise gain by supporting any number of processor cores. In addition, creating and destroying threads repeatedly can cause some instability in the framerate of the game loop, making it difficult to maintain a smooth and reliable core. One alternative is to pre-allocate a *thread pool* and recycle threads when they have completed, so that the overhead of creating and destroying threads is minimized. Another approach is to use thread functions containing while loops to handle updates—one function for rendering, another for collision detection, another for physics, and so on. In any event, experimentation is needed to find the best solution for a given game, as there is no "one size fits all" solution to threading in a game engine.

Installing The Pthreads Library

The Pthreads library is open source, and the current version at the time of this writing is 2.8.0. I have chosen not to distribute the complete sources for Pthreads and have only included the SDK (libs, dlls, and headers). You can download the Pthreads library and find documentation at http://sources.redhat.com/pthreads-win32. I encourage you to browse the site and get the latest version of Pthreads-Win32 from Red Hat. The Pthreads library is composed of three header files, a library file, and a DLL runtime file (which must be distributed with the program's executable). The Pthreads SDK includes these files:

- `pthread.h`
- `sched.h`
- `semaphore.h`
- `pthreadVC2.lib`
- `pthreadVC2.dll`

These files can be copied to your compiler's .\include folder, or you can add a folder to your compiler's include path so that it can find the Pthreads headers (wherever you have copied them to your hard drive).

Advice

Due to the way the Pthreads headers are defined (`sched.h` and `semaphore.h` are included with < > brackets instead of " " quotes), you cannot simply copy the files into your project locally—they must be referenced by your compiler. That means you must add the pthreads-w32-2-8-0-release \Pre-built.2\include and pthreads-w32-2-8-0-releasePre-built.2\lib folders to your compiler's include and library search paths. In Visual C++, that is found under Tools, Options, Projects and Solutions, VC++ Directories.

Second, you must copy the Pthreads library file into your compiler's .\lib folder, or add a library path to your compiler. For Visual C++, the library file is called `pthreadVC2.lib`. You can add it to the list of additional dependencies by its filename or just copy the file into your project's folder.

Third, to run a program compiled with the Pthreads library, you must include the runtime library file `pthreadVC2.dll` with your program's exe file.

Advice

In the book's resource folder (www.jharbour.com/forums or www.courseptr.com/downloads) you will find a folder called .\libraries\pthreads-w32-2-8-0-release that includes ready-to-use headers, libs, and DLLs for Visual C++.

Programming with Pthreads

Because this chapter is covering Pthreads with a hands-on or applied approach, and is not intended to be a comprehensive Pthreads reference, I am going to cover the key functions in this section and let you pursue the full extent of Pthreads on your own using additional references. You will learn enough here to create and destroy threads using Pthreads and to use mutexes, but we will not go into advanced features.

Creating a New Thread

First of all, how do you create a new thread using Pthreads? New threads are created with the `pthread_create` function.

```
int pthread_create (
    pthread_t *tid,
    const pthread_attr_t *attr,
    void *(*start) (void *),
    void *arg);
```

The first parameter is a `pthread_t` struct variable. This struct is large and complex, and you really don't need to know about the internals to use it.

Advice

"Ignorance is bliss," to quote Cipher from *The Matrix*. If you want more information about Pthreads, I encourage you to pick up Butenhof's book *Programming with POSIX Threads* as a reference.

The second parameter is a `pthread_attr_t` struct variable that usually contains attributes for the new thread. This is not usually used, so you can pass NULL to it.

The third parameter is a pointer to the thread function used by this thread for processing. This function should contain its own loop, but should have exit logic for the loop when it's time to kill the thread.

The fourth parameter is a pointer to a numeric value for this thread to uniquely identify it. You can just create an int variable and set it to a value before passing it to pthread_create.

Here's an example of how to create a new thread:

```
int id;
pthread_t pthread0;
int threadid0 = 0;
id = pthread_create(&pthread0, NULL, thread0, (void*)&threadid0);
```

The Thread Function

So you've created this thread, but what about the thread function? Oh, right. Here's an example:

```
void* thread_function(void* data)
{
    int my_thread_id = *((int*)data);
    while(!done)
    {
        //do something!
    }
    return 0;
}
```

Killing a Thread

This brings us to the pthread_exit function, which terminates the thread. Normally, you'll want to call this function only if you need to kill a thread forcefully, since a thread will end automatically when its function returns. Here's the definition for the function:

```
void pthread_exit (void *value_ptr);
```

You can get away with just passing NULL to this function because value_ptr is an advanced topic for gaining more control over the thread.

Mutexes: Making Data Threads Safe

At this point, you can write a multi-threaded program with only pthread_create and a thread function, knowing how to create the function and use it. That is enough if you only want to create worker threads to run inside the process with your program's main thread. But more often than not, you will want to share data with two or more threads. Recall the ice cream cone analogy. Are you sure that new thread won't interfere with any global variables? Have you considered timing? What if you are using a thread for rendering while another thread is writing to the back buffer? Most memory chips cannot read and write data at the same time. It is very likely that you'll update a small portion of the buffer (by drawing a sprite, for instance) while the buffer is being blitted to the screen. The result is some unwanted flicker—yes, even when using a double buffer. That's the best-case scenario—most likely, accessing the same memory will cause the program to crash (i.e., to segfault). What you have here is a situation that is similar to a vertical refresh conflict, only it is occurring in memory rather than directly on the screen. What I am trying to point out is that threads can step on each other's toes, so to speak, if you aren't careful to use a mutex. And, in any event, we can't use multiple threads for rendering with Direct3D so it's a moot point!

A *mutex* is a block used in a thread function to prevent other threads from running until that block is released. Assuming, of course, that all threads use the same mutex, it is possible to use more than one mutex in your program. The easiest way is to create a single mutex, and then block the mutex at the start of each thread's loop, unblocking at the end of the loop. Creating a mutex doesn't require a function; rather, it requires a struct variable. In our simplistic approach here, I'm using only a single mutex for the entire program, but in practice you would want to use many mutexes.

```
//create a new thread mutex to protect variables
pthread_mutex_t threadsafe = PTHREAD_MUTEX_INITIALIZER;
```

This line of code will create a new mutex called `threadsafe` that, when used by all the thread functions, will prevent data read/write conflicts. You must destroy the mutex before your program ends; you can do so using the `pthread_mutex_destroy` function.

```
int pthread_mutex_destroy (pthread_mutex_t *mutex);
```

Here is an example of how it would be used:

```
pthread_mutex_destroy(&threadsafe);
```

Next, you need to know how to lock and unlock a mutex inside a thread function. The `pthread_mutex_lock` function is used to lock a mutex.

```
int pthread_mutex_lock (pthread_mutex_t * mutex);
```

This has the effect of preventing any other threads from locking the same mutex, so any variables or functions you use or call (respectively) while the mutex is locked will be safe from manipulation by any other threads. Basically, when a thread encounters a locked mutex, it waits until the mutex is available before proceeding. (It uses no processor time; it simply waits.)

Here is the unlock function:

```
int pthread_mutex_unlock (pthread_mutex_t * mutex);
```

The two functions just shown will normally return zero if the lock or unlock succeeded immediately; otherwise, a non-zero value will be returned to indicate that the thread is waiting for the mutex. This should not happen for unlocking, only for locking. If you have a problem with pthread_mutex_unlock returning non-zero, it means the mutex was locked while that thread was supposedly in control over the mutex—a bad situation that should never happen. But when it comes to game programming, bad things do often happen while you are developing a new game, so it's helpful to print an error message for any non-zero return.

ThreadDemo Program

We need an example to see how threading works and to see how the Pthreads library is used. The ThreadDemo program is a simple example of Pthreads so you can learn from it.

There are two ways to handle thread synchronization and completion. First, the Pthreads way, is to call pthread_join for every thread we've created, which will cause the main program to pause until all threads have finished and returned from their functions.

```
for (int n = 0; n < THREADS; n++)
    pthread_join(threads[n], 0);
```

When we use this technique, there is no need to keep track of the thread count or wait for the "done" variable to be changed (an imprecise approach to the problem).

Another way to handle thread synchronization with our main program is to keep track of the thread count. Increment a variable when the thread function begins, and decrement it when the thread function is about to end.

In our thread function:

```
thread_counter++;
while( !done )
```

```
{
    ...
}
thread_counter--;
```

In the main function of our program, we can then wait for the thread counter to reach zero before proceeding, as this will mean all worker threads have finished their work.

```
while (thread_counter > 0)
{
    // idle time for any use
}
```

I have left both techniques in the source code listing so you can experiment with them. Using `pthread_join` is the safest approach, but then your main program is basically in a locked state until all threads complete. That might be exactly how you want the program to behave, but it depends on the situation, so knowing about both techniques is helpful.

Figure 4.1 shows the Task Manager while the ThreadDemo program is running.

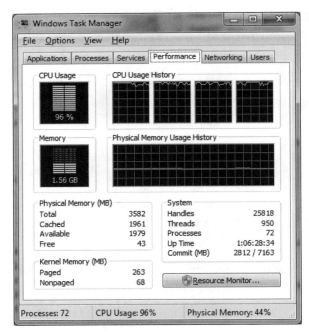

Figure 4.1
Processor core usage in Task Manager while ThreadDemo is running.

ThreadDemo Source Code

```
#include <pthread.h>
#pragma comment(lib,"pthreadVC2.lib")

#include <iostream>
#include <string>
using namespace std;

#include <boost/timer.hpp>

const long MAX = 100 * 1000000;
long counter = 0;

const int THREADS = 8;
pthread_t threads[THREADS];

//create a thread mutex variable
pthread_mutex_t mutex = PTHREAD_MUTEX_INITIALIZER;

bool done = false;
//int thread_counter = 0; //optional use

void* thread_function(void* data)
{
    boost::timer t;
    //thread_counter++;  //optional use
    int id = *((int*)data);
    while( !done )
    {
        //lock the mutex
        pthread_mutex_lock(&mutex);

        counter++;
        if (counter > MAX)
            done = true;

        //unlock the mutex
        pthread_mutex_unlock(&mutex);
    }
    //thread_counter--;  //optional use
```

```cpp
        cout << "thread " << id << " time = " << t.elapsed() << endl;
        return 0;
}

int main(int argc, char argv[])
{
        cout << "Thread Demo" << endl;
        boost::timer timer1;

        //create the thread(s)
        for (int n = 0; n < THREADS; n++)
        {
            cout << "Creating thread " << n << endl;
            int mythread_id = n;
            pthread_create(&threads[n], NULL, thread_function, (void*)&mythread_id);
        }

        cout << "Done creating threads" << endl;

        //now we wait for threads to finish
        cout << "Waiting for threads." << endl;

        //wait for all threads to complete   //first option
        for (int n = 0; n < THREADS; n++)
            pthread_join(threads[n], 0);

// Now in a wait state until all thread functions return

        //while (thread_counter > 0)   //second option
        //{
            //use the idle time
        //}
        pthread_mutex_destroy(&mutex);

        cout << "Counter = " << counter << endl;
        cout << "Run time = " << timer1.elapsed() << endl;
        system("pause");
        return 0;
}
```

Here is the output from the ThreadDemo program with 8 threads. Note that each thread reports about the same runtime, because each thread continues to increment the counter until the threshold is reached. As a result, the final counter value will be a bit higher than the target value while the rest of the threads finish one last loop.

```
Thread Demo
Creating thread 0
Creating thread 1
Creating thread 2
Creating thread 3
Creating thread 4
Creating thread 5
Creating thread 6
Creating thread 7
Done creating threads
Waiting for threads.
thread 3 time = 17.993
thread 7 time = 17.96
thread 6 time = 17.977
thread 2 time = 17.995
thread 1 time = 17.997
thread 5 time = 17.984
thread 0 time = 18
thread 4 time = 17.986
Counter = 100000007
Run time = 18.021
```

Here is the output from the program using only 4 threads. This version is a bit more effective since the PC being used in this example is a quad-core Intel Q6600. If you have a CPU with eight or more hardware threads, such as an Intel Core i7, then you will see an improvement to the 8-thread version of the program.

```
Thread Demo
Creating thread 0
Creating thread 1
Creating thread 2
Creating thread 3
Done creating threads
Waiting for threads.
```

```
thread 0 time = 13.029
thread 2 time = 13.025
thread 1 time = 13.027
thread 3 time = 13.024
Counter = 100000004
Run time = 13.04
```

Comparing Single-thread Results

Now that we have some good data representing multi-threaded results, let's take a look at the output from a single-thread run of the program.

```
Thread Demo
Creating thread 0
Done creating threads
Waiting for threads.
thread 0 time = 4.174
Counter = 100000001
Run time = 4.178
```

Oh no! This result is about two to three times faster than the more highly threaded versions of the ThreadDemo program! And I was feeling pretty confident about the results. This just goes to show that you *must* test your results several ways before deciding on a technique to use. So, why were the threaded results so much slower than a single-core version? The slowdown occurs inside the thread function due to the *mutex locks*. The while loop running inside that thread function is very tight and fast, meaning there are a lot of mutex roadblocks preventing threads from processing the counter variable.

What alternatives are there to this problem? We ran into a similar problem back in the boost::thread chapter, as you may recall. First of all, we are leaving all of the "thinking" in this program to the thread function: counting to 100 million with the conditional logic inside the while loop. It's better if a thread is allowed to run without having to "think" very much. So, what we need to do is split up the problem so that each thread can crunch the numbers exclusively, without sharing or mutex problems. There will be just one time when the mutex is used—to update our global counter variable with the local counter used in the function (without any concern for conflicts). Let's update the code.

```
#include <pthread.h>
#pragma comment(lib,"pthreadVC2.lib")
```

```cpp
#include <iostream>
#include <string>
using namespace std;
#include <boost/timer.hpp>

const long MAX = 100 * 1000000;
long counter = 0;
const int THREADS = 4;
pthread_t threads[THREADS];
pthread_mutex_t mutex = PTHREAD_MUTEX_INITIALIZER;
bool done = false;

void* thread_function(void* data)
{
    boost::timer t;
    int id = *((int*)data);
    long local_counter = 0;

    long range = MAX / THREADS;
    for (long n = 0; n < range; n++)
    {
        local_counter++;
    }

    pthread_mutex_lock(&mutex);

    //update global counter
    counter += local_counter;
    if (counter > MAX) done = true;
    cout << "counter = " << counter << endl;

    pthread_mutex_unlock(&mutex);

    cout << "thread " << id << " time = " << t.elapsed() << endl;
    return 0;
}

int main(int argc, char argv[])
{
    cout << "Thread Demo 2" << endl;
```

```
boost::timer timer1;

//create the thread(s)
for (int id = 0; id < THREADS; id++)
{
    cout << "Creating thread " << id << endl;
    pthread_create(&threads[id], NULL, thread_function, (void*)&id);
}

cout << "Done creating threads" << endl;
cout << "Waiting for threads." << endl;

//wait for all threads to complete
for (int n = 0; n < THREADS; n++)
    pthread_join(threads[n], 0);

pthread_mutex_destroy(&mutex);

cout << "Counter = " << counter << endl;
cout << "Run time = " << timer1.elapsed() << endl;
system("pause");
return 0;
}
```

This new version, called ThreadDemo 2, produces slightly improved results (to put it mildly!). Here is a new 4-thread result that's more realistic since thread lock is not hampering performance. The runtime is 0.077 seconds (77 ms).

```
Thread Demo 2
Creating thread 0
Creating thread 1
Creating thread 2
Creating thread 3
Done creating threads
Waiting for threads.
counter = 25000000
thread 1 time = 0.06
counter = 50000000
thread 2 time = 0.062
counter = 75000000
thread 4 time = 0.058
counter = 100000000
```

```
thread 3 time = 0.065
Counter = 100000000
Run time = 0.077
```

And, for comparison, let's run the 8-thread version with a counter target of 10 billion (up from 100 million). The result is only 1.094 seconds! In this new example, having more threads actually *helped*, because, as you can see, the first few threads finished before the main program had a chance to create all of the threads! What we're seeing here is pipeline optimizations occurring inside the CPU, thanks to an optimizing compiler. Be sure to run your performance code with Release build.

```
Thread Demo 2
Creating thread 0
Creating thread 1
Creating thread 2
Creating thread 3
Creating thread 4
Creating thread 5
Creating thread 6
Creating thread 7
Done creating threads
Waiting for threads.
counter = 176258176
thread 5 time = 0.566
counter = 352516352
thread 8 time = 0.754
counter = 528774528
thread 3 time = 0.791
counter = 705032704
thread 2 time = 0.874
counter = 881290880
thread 8 time = 0.863
counter = 1057549056
thread 8 time = 0.972
counter = 1233807232
thread 1 time = 1.064
counter = 1410065408
thread 8 time = 1.002
Counter = 1410065408
```

Runtime = 1.094

Table 4.1 ThreadDemo Results (Intel Q6600 CPU*)

VERSION	MAX	THREADS	TIME (sec)
global counter	100,000,000	4	13.04
global counter	100,000,000	8	18.021
global counter	**100,000,000**	**1**	**4.178**
local counter	**100,000,000**	**4**	**0.077**
local counter	100,000,000	8	0.092
local counter	100,000,000	1	0.275
local counter	1,000,000,000	4	0.822
local counter	**1,000,000,000**	**8**	**0.741**
local counter	1,000,000,000	1	2.635
local counter	**10,000,000,000**	**4**	**1.028**
local counter	10,000,000,000	8	1.094
local counter	10,000,000,000	1	3.73

*Note: For a precise comparison with other systems, this Core2Quad Q6600 CPU has been overclocked from the base 2.4 to 2.6 GHz.

Table 4.1 shows the results of the program running with various MAX and THREADS values. Included in the table are results for much higher MAX ranges just for a general comparison.

SUMMARY

Writing a multi-threaded game is now even closer to reality with the new knowledge gained in this chapter about Pthreads. Performing a mere accumulation on a variable is hardly a test worthy of benchmark comparison, but the examples were meant to be simple to understand rather than technically intriguing. I recommend performing some real calculations in the thread worker function to put the CPU cores and Pthreads code to the test more effectively. Next, it's up to you to ultimately decide which of the four threading libraries is most effective: Boost threads, OpenMP, Windows threads, or Pthreads? We have yet to cover Windows threads in any detail, so that is the topic for the next chapter.

References

1. "Pthreads-Win32"; http://sourceware.org/pthreads-win32/.

2. "Stream processing"; http://en.wikipedia.org/wiki/Stream_processing.

   Butenhof, David R. *Programming with POSIX Threads*. Unknown City: Addison-Wesley 1997.

   "Pthreads Tutorial"; http://students.cs.byu.edu/~cs460ta/cs460/labs/pthreads.html.

CHAPTER 5

WORKING WITH WINDOWS THREADS

This chapter explores the threading library built into Windows. Using Windows threads is a bit easier than either POSIX threads or Boost threads because Windows threading is already installed with Visual C++ and available via windows.h, so there is no extra effort needed on our part to use Windows threads. We'll see how to create and control a thread in this chapter, which will be familiar to you by now after covering both POSIX threads and Boost threads previously. The differences in the thread support built into Windows is minimal as the same concepts are found here.

Topics covered in this chapter include:

- Exploring Windows threads
- Creating a thread
- Controlling thread execution
- The thread function
- Thread function parameters

EXPLORING WINDOWS THREADS

The Windows Platform SDK and the other support files installed with Visual C++ provide support for threads via just the windows.h header file. We will learn how to invoke a new thread, via a thread function, and control it to a limited degree.

First, let's begin with a simple example to give you a feel for the overall process of using Windows threads.

Quick Example

The simplest example of using a Windows thread involves creating a new thread with the `CreateThread()` function and then calling the `WaitForSingleObject()` function to pause execution of the main program until the thread has finished running (when the `thread` function returns). I always like to see a quick, simple example of a new library or algorithm, so here is one such example for you. We'll go over Windows threads in more detail and cover additional features in the next section.

```
#include <windows.h>
#include <iostream>
DWORD WINAPI threadFunction1( void* data )
{
    std::cout << "threadFunction1 running\n";
    return 0;
}
int main(int argc, char argv[])
{
    HANDLE thread1 = NULL;
    std::cout << "creating thread\n";
    thread1 = CreateThread(NULL,0,&threadFunction1,NULL,0,NULL);
    WaitForSingleObject(thread1,0);
    return 0;
}
```

That quick example produces the following output. However, if the thread starts running before the console finishes printing the text passed to `std::cout`, it's possible that the two lines could be garbled together—this happens frequently when working with threads.

```
creating thread
threadFunction1 running
```

Creating a Thread

The `CreateThread()` function is used to create a thread:

```
CreateThread(
    LPSECURITY_ATTRIBUTES lpThreadAttributes,
```

```
    SIZE_T dwStackSize,
    LPTHREAD_START_ROUTINE lpStartAddress,
    LPVOID lpParameter,
    DWORD dwCreationFlags,
    LPDWORD lpThreadId
);
```

The parameters of `CreateThread()` are explained in the following table.

`lpThreadAttributes`	Security attributes (usually NULL)
`dwStackSize`	Initial stack size (0 for default)
`lpStartAddress`	Address to thread function
`lpParameter`	Pointer to parameter variable passed to function
`dwCreationFlags`	Thread creation flags (usually 0)
`lpThreadId`	Pointer to a variable for the thread id

Every thread needs a `HANDLE` variable (a renamed void* pointer), so this variable must be global or managed by a class.

```
HANDLE thread1 = NULL;
```

If you want to know the identifier value assigned to a new thread, that value is passed back in the last parameter—`threadid`. The data type is `LPDWORD`, which is defined as a `DWORD*`, or unsigned long*.

```
LPDWORD threadid = NULL;
```

Sample usage:

```
thread1 = CreateThread(NULL,0,&threadFunction1,NULL,0,threadid);
```

If the return value (`thread1`) is `NULL`, then an error occurred during the thread creation process. This is rare. About the only thing that could cause an error is a bad memory location specified for the thread function, thread parameter, or thread identifier.

Controlling Thread Execution

The `dwCreationFlags` parameter is of particular interest, since we can use the constant `CREATE_SUSPENDED` to create a thread that starts off in a suspended state, waiting for us to call `ResumeThread()` to allow it to launch. This can be helpful if we want to do any housekeeping before the thread function begins running.

```
DWORD WINAPI ResumeThread(
  HANDLE hThread
);
```

We can control the execution of a thread by using the CREATE_SUSPENDED flag as a parameter when calling CreateThread(). First, we create the new thread:

```
thread1=CreateThread(NULL,0,&threadFunction1,NULL,CREATE_SUSPENDED,threadid);
```

Then we start it running by calling ResumeThread():

```
ResumeThread(thread1);
```

The Thread Function

The thread function starts executing when the thread is created. Normally, a thread function will have some distinct process to run, such as sorting data in a list or reading a file. But often a thread function will contain a while loop and it will continue to run for a longer period in parallel with the main program. When this is the case, we get into difficulties with sharing global variables, which is not permitted—no two threads can access the same memory location at the same time without causing a serious crash (a page fault on most systems).

Here is the definition of a thread function with the correct return type and parameter type. Use the address of your thread function name when creating a new thread. The LPVOID parameter is defined as void*.

```
DWORD WINAPI function( LPVOID data );
```

Thread Function Parameters

We have been passing NULL for the thread function parameter when creating a new thread, but this parameter can be a variable declared as a simple data type or a struct. There are many reasons why you might need to pass data into a thread function: to specify how many items to process, or a pointer to a buffer in memory, for instance. The only real drawback to using parameters with Windows threads is the ugly way in which the parameter data must be created (on the heap), maintained via pointers, and destroyed (from the heap) afterward. In this respect, Windows thread programming is not as convenient as either POSIX or Boost. Here is an example:

```
typedef struct MyParam
{
```

```
    int value1;
    int value2;
} MYPARAM, *PMYPARAM;
```

We can create a variable using this custom struct and pass it to `CreateThread()`, which will make the values available to the `thread` function (as a void* buffer). We must allocate the parameter struct variable on the heap and pass it to the `thread` function as a pointer. This is handled by the `HeapAlloc()` and `HeapFree()` functions.

```
PMYPARAM param;
param=(PMYPARAM)HeapAlloc(GetProcessHeap(),HEAP_ZERO_MEMORY,sizeof(PMYPARAM));
```

When finished with the parameter data, free it with `HeapFree()`:

```
HeapFree(GetProcessHeap(), 0, param);
```

Let's see a complete example:

```cpp
#include <windows.h>
#include <iostream>
#include <string>
#include <iomanip>
using namespace std;

typedef struct MyParam
{
    int value1;
    int value2;
} MYPARAM, *PMYPARAM;

DWORD WINAPI threadFunction1( void* data )
{
    cout << "thread function running\n";

    PMYPARAM param = (PMYPARAM)data;
    cout << "parameter: " << param->value1 << "," << param->value2 << endl;

    cout << "thread function end\n";
    return 0;
}
```

```
int main(int argc, char argv[])
{
    LPDWORD threadid = NULL;
    HANDLE thread1 = NULL;
    PMYPARAM param = NULL;

    param = (PMYPARAM) HeapAlloc( GetProcessHeap(),
                                  HEAP_ZERO_MEMORY,
                                  sizeof(MyParam) );
    param->value1 = 9;
    param->value2 = 800;

    //create thread in suspended state
    thread1 = CreateThread(NULL,0,&threadFunction1,param,CREATE_SUSPENDED,
threadid);
    if (!thread1)
    {
        cout << "Error creating thread\n";
        return 1;
    }
    cout << "thread created: " << &threadid << endl;

    //launch thread
    ResumeThread(thread1);

    WaitForSingleObject(thread1, 500);

    CloseHandle(thread1);
    HeapFree(GetProcessHeap(), 0, param);

    cout << "done\n";
    system("pause");
    return 0;
}
```

The output of this program looks like this:

```
thread created: 0012FE8C
thread function running
parameter: 9,800
thread function end
done
```

Although we aren't doing anything magnificent like solving the largest prime number known to mankind or testing out threaded engine code on an 80-core experimental computer, this chapter does do one thing well—we learned how to create a `thread` function for Windows threads with support for parameters. Now, you may take any of the previous examples and adapt them to Windows threads fairly easily.

Programming Windows threads is a relatively straightforward process since the functions covered in this chapter are part of the Windows SDK and already available in Visual C++ by default. Making use of the Windows threads is not a problem, but we have not covered any of the advanced topics like mutex locking to protect data, as the concept is the same here as it is with POSIX and Boost threads.

SUMMARY

That wraps up Part I and our tour of the four key multi-threading libraries: Boost threads, OpenMP, POSIX threads, and finally, Windows threads. I think it's time to get started working on some very serious game engine code!

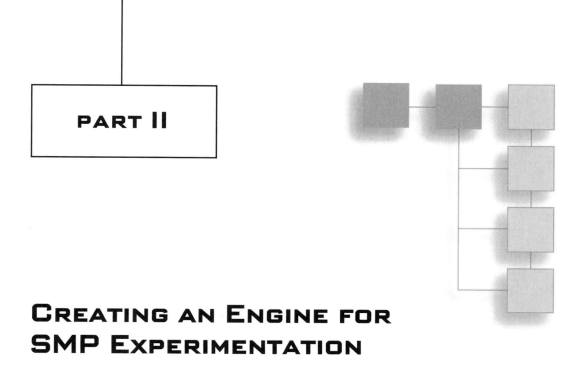

PART II

CREATING AN ENGINE FOR SMP EXPERIMENTATION

The second part of this book is dedicated to the development of a game engine. The engine will feature 3D shader-based rendering, 2D sprite animation, static meshes, hierarchical meshes, mesh rendering, shader-based dynamic lighting, entity management, picking (selecting an object in the scene), and collision detection. We will build each component of the engine one at a time while learning about these advanced topics in Direct3D.

- Chapter 6: Engine Startup
- Chapter 7: Vectors and Matrices
- Chapter 8: Rendering the Scene
- Chapter 9: Mesh Loading and Rendering
- Chapter 10: Advanced Lighting Effects
- Chapter 11: Wrapping the Sky in a Box
- Chapter 12: Environmental Concerns: Recycling Terrain Polygons
- Chapter 13: Skeletal Mesh Animation

- Chapter 14: Sprite Animation and Rasterization
- Chapter 15: Rendering to a Texture
- Chapter 16: Entity Management
- Chapter 17: Picking and Collision Detection

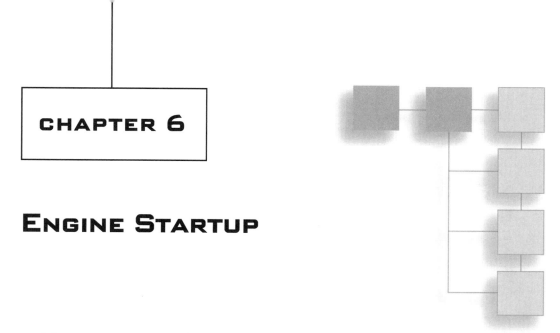

CHAPTER 6

ENGINE STARTUP

Building a game engine from scratch is a lofty goal with the potential to be a great learning experience. Like restoring a car from the frame and body work to the engine and interior, which lends insights into how the car will drive beyond the "road feel" in the steering wheel, designing a game engine from WinMain to the entity manager to the animated hierarchical mesh renderer lends the programmer a unique insight into how his or her games work at a deeply intimate level. Since the engine will be in development for many chapters, we will take the simpler approach by just adding engine source files into each chapter demo individually and forego the process of creating the engine library project (static or DLL) until the last chapter. Having developed all of the demos *with* a separation of the game engine and gameplay code in separate but dependent projects, I can vouch for the positive advantages to using a single project approach to the demos for the time being. For one thing, the engine will be in a state of flux as it is developed over the coming chapters, so at no point will the engine be "finished" until we have covered every topic and built every C++ class needed. In the final chapter, we'll have a final engine project available for further use.

This chapter covers the following topics:

- Why build an engine yourself?
- Creating the engine project
- Engine core system

- Engine rendering system
- Engine support system
- Verifying framerates with FRAPS

WHY BUILD AN ENGINE YOURSELF?

What is the purpose or advantage of a game engine, as opposed to, say, just writing all the code for a game as needed? Why invest all the time in creating a game engine when you could spend that time just writing the game? That is essentially the question we'll try to answer in the pages of this book, beginning in this first chapter in which we'll be building the core code and classes for a new engine.

The simple answer is: You don't need an engine to write a game. But that is a loaded answer because it implies that either 1) The game is very simple, or 2) You already have a lot of code from past projects. The first implication is that you can just write a simple game with DirectX or OpenGL code. The second assumes that you have some code already available, perhaps in a game library—filled with functions you've written and reused. A game library saves a lot of time. For instance, it's a given that you will load bitmap files for use in 2D artwork or 3D textures, and once you've written such a function, you do not want to have to touch it again, because it serves a good purpose. Anytime you have to open up a function and modify it, that's a good sign that it was poorly written in the first place (unless changes were made to underlying functions in an SDK beyond one's control—or perhaps you have gained new knowledge and want to improve your functions).

Advice

It is helpful to decide whether one is interested primarily in *engine* or *gameplay* programming, in order to devote effort into either direction (but not often both). An engine programmer focuses primarily on rendering and optimizations, while a gameplay programmer focuses on artificial intelligence, scripting, event/animation synchronization, user input, and fulfilling design goals.

Valid Arguments in Favor

In my opinion, there are three key reasons why a game engine will help a game development project: teamwork, development tools, and logistics. Let's examine each issue.

- **Teamwork** is much easier when the programmers in a team use a game engine rather than writing their own core game code, because the engine code facilitates standardization across the project. While each programmer has his or her own preferences about how timing should be handled, or how rendering should be done, a game engine with a single high-speed game loop forces everyone on the team to work with the features of the engine. And what of features that are lacking? Usually, one or two team members will be the "engine gurus" who maintain the engine based on the team's needs.

- **Development tools** include the compiler(s) used to build the game code, asset converters and exporters, asset and game level editors, and packaging tools. These types of tools are essential in any game project, and not practical without the use of a game engine. Although many programmers are adept at writing standard C++ code that will build on multiple platforms and compilers, game code usually does not fall into that realm due to its unique requirements (namely, rendering). Cross-compiler support is the ability to compile your game with two or more compilers, rather than just your favorite (such as Visual C++). Supporting multiple render targets (such as Direct3D and OpenGL) is a larger-scale endeavor that is not recommended unless there is a significant market for Mac and Linux systems. Direct3D is the primary renderer used by most game studios today for the Windows platform.

Advice

Writing code that builds on compilers from more than one vendor teaches you to write good, *standards-compliant* code, without ties to a specific platform.

- **Logistics** in a large game project can be a nightmare without some coordinated way to organize the entities, processes, and behaviors in your game. Logistics is the problem of organizing and supporting a large system, and is often used to describe military operations (for example, the logistics of war—equipping, supplying, and supporting troops). The logistics of a game involves managing the characters, vehicles, crafts, enemies, projectiles, and scenery—in other words, the "stuff" in a game. Without a system in place to assist with organizing all of these things, the game's source code and assets can become an unmanageable mess.

Let's summarize all of these points in a simple sentence: A game engine (and all that comes with it) makes it easier to manage the development process of a game project. Contrast that with the problems associated with creating a game from scratch using your favorite APIs, such as Direct3D or OpenGL for graphics, DirectInput or SDL for user input, a networking library such as RakNet, an audio library such as FMOD, and so forth. The logistics of keeping up with the latest updates to all of these libraries alone can be a challenge for an engine programmer. But by wrapping all of these libraries and all of your own custom game code into a game engine, you eliminate the headache of maintaining all of those libraries (including their initialization and shutdown) in each game. The best analogy I can come up with is this: "Rolling your own" game code for each game project is like fabricating your own bricks, forging your own nails, and cutting down your own trees in order to build a single house. Why would you do that?

But perhaps the most significant benefit to wrapping an SDK (such as DirectX) into your own game engine classes is to provide a buffer around unpredictable revisions. Whenever a change occurs in a library (such as Direct3D) that you regularly use in your games, you can accommodate those changes in your engine classes without having to revise any actual *gameplay code* in the process.

Valid Arguments Against

There are many game engines available that a developer can freely (or affordably, at least) put to good use for a game, rather than re-inventing the wheel, so to speak. These engines usually support multiple renderers (OpenGL, Direct3D 9, Direct3D 10, etc.). Examples include:

- **Irrlicht**—"Free Open Source 3D Engine" (http://irrlicht.sourceforge.net)
- **OGRE**—"Open Source 3D Graphics Engine" (http://www.ogre3d.org)
- **Torque by Garage Games** (http://www.torquepowered.com)

Any of these three engines would be a good choice for any aspiring indie game studio, so why would someone want to *try* to create their own engine and try to compete with these well-rounded, feature rich, strongly supported engines with large communities of users? *Touché.*

It's about the learning experience, not about trying to compete with others and outdo them in a foolhardy attempt to gain market share with a new engine. That's not the purpose of building your own engine at all! It's about the journey, the experience gained, the new skills developed, and improving your marketability.

Advice

Building your own game engine is like a car enthusiast building or restoring his own hot rod show car. There is some kinship with professionals like Chip Foose and Jack Roush, but a great chasm of experience and expertise separates a hobbyist from the pros. Do not try to compete. Rather, learn new skills, do your best, and try to enjoy the learning experience!

CREATING THE ENGINE PROJECT

We are going to create the core game engine project in this chapter and then expand it over the next dozen or so chapters to include all of the features we need to build advanced demos, simulations, and games—with the goal of later improving the engine with the threading techniques covered in Part I. Threading will not be weaved into the fabric of the engine from the start—our first goal is to build a stable engine and make it as efficient as possible *before* implementing any thread code. The starting point is the core engine developed in this chapter, which will include WinMain, Direct3D initialization, D3DXSprite initialization, basic game events, timing, and, of course, a game loop. The great thing about doing all of this right now at the beginning is that we will not have to duplicate any of this code in future chapters—it will already be embedded in the game engine. The engine project will remain a standard Win32 executable project, as opposed to a combination library/executable pair, for the sake of simplicity—I want to make the material easy for the reader to get into without logistical issues like solution/project files getting in the way early on. But, all of the source files will easily build inside a Win32 library project just as well (static or DLL, it doesn't matter).

Advice

Most of the source code printed in the book is free of comments to save space (since much of the code is explained in the text), but the comments are in the source code files in the chapter resource files (www.jharbour.com/forum or www.courseptr.com/downloads).

Let's get started creating the engine project so that we'll have a foundation with which to discuss the future design of a multi-threaded engine. The Engine class is embedded in a namespace called Octane. This namespace will contain all engine classes, so there will not be any conflicts with other libraries you may need to use in a game. I will go over the project creation for Visual C++ now for anyone who isn't quite up to the book's recommended reading level, and show which libraries you will need to include in the project, so that you may refer to this chapter again when configuring future projects. We will continue to build on the Engine project in later chapters and the engine will grow.

Advice

Why the namespace "Octane"? *Why not?* It's just a name without any particular meaning, other than being catchy. Go ahead and give your own engine any name you wish. If you are interested in following the development of the engine beyond this book, visit the Google Code website: http://code.google.com/p/octane-engine. Note that the SVN repository for this open source project will *not* conform completely to the code in this book, because the repository is an evolving code base.

Figure 6.1 shows a diagram of the initial design of the engine with each sub-system identified with its component classes. This diagram will be updated as the engine is developed in later chapters.

Advice

I would not expect the reader to type in all of the code for the engine, although there is merit to doing so, as a good learning experience (if one is a bit new to the subject matter). All of the code for every class and program is included in the text, but the reader is encouraged to use the chapter's resource files found at www.jharbour.com/forum or www.courseptr.com/downloads.

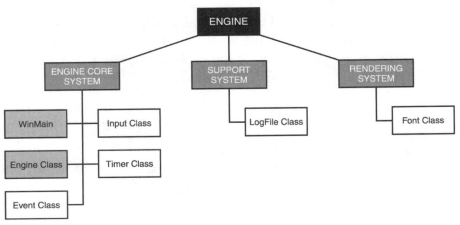

Figure 6.1
Diagram of the engine's design at an early stage of development.

Engine Core System

The engine's core system includes the program entry point (the WinMain function) and core classes not related to rendering. Those classes include the following:

- The Engine class itself, which connects everything together.
- A Timer class, based on boost::timer, used for all timing in the engine core.
- An Input class, based on DirectInput, which provides a clean interface to input devices.
- A base IEvent class and numerous event sub-classes used to generate event messages for user input, pre-set timers, and any custom events.

Advice

This chapter's resource files can be downloaded from www.jharbour.com/forum or www.courseptr.com/downloads. Please note that not every line of code will be in print due to space considerations: only the most important sections of code are covered in each chapter.

The core system makes calls to the following functions, which are declared as extern in Engine.h. Since they are extern, they must be implemented somewhere in the game project (usually that will be the main source code file, main.cpp):

```
bool game_preload();
bool game_init(HWND hwnd);
void game_update( float deltaTime );
void game_render3d();
void game_render2d();
void game_event(IEvent* e);
void game_end();
```

You are welcome to rename them to better suit your own preferences: I offer these function names as merely logical names for their uses. Note that we have no rendering functions defined yet. Though, technically, rendering occurs during the update process, the function calls are made from inside the while loop in WinMain to both the update and rendering functions (which we will go over shortly).

Advice

Since this engine is based on DirectX 9, it goes without saying that the DirectX SDK is required. It can be downloaded from http://msdn.microsoft.com/directx. The latest version at the time of this writing is the June 2010 SDK, which adds support for Visual Studio 2010. The latest version is not needed at all—the code in this book will build with any version of the SDK from 2006 or later.

Entry Point: WinMain

There is quite a bit of dependent code in our first engine source code listing! Herein you will find references from Engine.h (as yet undefined) to Octane:: Timer, Octane::Engine, and the extern-defined functions game_preload(), game_init(), and game_end(). (The update function calls take place inside Engine::Update(), which we'll be covering shortly.) In the chapter project, the following source code may be found in winmain.cpp.

```
#include "stdafx.h"
#include "Engine.h"
using namespace std;

//declare global engine object
std::auto_ptr<Octane::Engine> g_engine(new Octane::Engine);

/**
WndProc - message handler (req'd when user closes window with "X" button)
**/
LRESULT CALLBACK WndProc(HWND hwnd, UINT msg, WPARAM wParam, LPARAM lParam)
{
    if (msg == WM_DESTROY) PostQuitMessage(0);
    return DefWindowProc(hwnd, msg, wParam, lParam);
}

/**
WinMain - entry point of the program
**/
int WINAPI WinMain(HINSTANCE hInstance, HINSTANCE hPrevInstance, LPSTR lpCmdLine,
int nCmdShow)
{
    debug << "WinMain running" << endl;
    srand((unsigned int)time(0));

    //check command line
    debug << "Checking parameters" << endl;
    if ( strlen( lpCmdLine ) > 0 )
    {
        g_engine->setCommandLineParams( lpCmdLine );
```

```
            debug << "Params: " << g_engine->getCommandLineParams() << std::endl;
    }

    //let main program set screen dimensions
    debug << "Calling game_preload" << endl;
    if (!game_preload())
    {
        debug << "Error in game_preload" << endl;
        return 0;
    }

    //initialize the engine
    debug << "Initializing engine" << endl;
    bool res = g_engine->Init(
        hInstance,
        g_engine->getScreenWidth(),     //screen width
        g_engine->getScreenHeight(),    //screen height
        g_engine->getColorDepth(),      //screen depth
        g_engine->getFullscreen());     //screen mode
    if (!res)
    {
        debug << "Error initializing the engine" << endl;
        return 0;
    }

    MSG msg;
    memset(&msg, 0, sizeof(MSG));
    Octane::Timer timer;
    double startTime = timer.getElapsed();

    debug << "Core timer started: " << timer.getElapsed() << endl;
    debug << "Entering while loop" << endl;

    // main message loop
    while (msg.message != WM_QUIT)
    {
        if (PeekMessage(&msg, NULL, 0, 0, PM_REMOVE))
        {
            TranslateMessage(&msg);
            DispatchMessage(&msg);
        }
```

```
        else
        {
            double t = timer.getElapsed();
            float deltaTime = (t - startTime) * 0.001f;
            g_engine->Update( deltaTime );
            startTime = t;
        }
    }

    debug << "Exiting while loop" << endl;
    debug << "Total run time: " << timer.getElapsed() << endl;
    debug << "Freeing game resources" << endl;
    game_end();

    debug << "Shutting down engine" << endl;
    ShowCursor(true);
    return 1;
}
```

Engine Class

One thing that might stand out in the core `Engine` class files is the large list of header `#include` statements. Depending on your C++ programming background, this is either a great idea—or a terrible programming practice. There are two reasons for including all of the needed includes inside the main engine header file.

- It greatly simplifies the task of tracking down the right include file for each engine class, and keeps the code base fairly clean since only the single `#include "Engine.h"` line is needed in all of the support classes in the engine project.

- It has the potential to greatly speed up compile time when using the precompiled header feature of Visual C++. When you have built the engine with your latest game project for the thousandth time and had to wait 30–60 seconds for each build, you will welcome the speed boost that this compiler feature provides.

Below is the `Engine.h` class interface. There are quite a few dependencies—not to worry, they are all provided later in this chapter. You'll note that some Boost headers are included, and that WIN32_LEAN_AND_MEAN has been defined. This define eliminates many of the standard Windows headers and libraries used for application development, including the mmsystem.h file, which contains the reference to an oft-used function called timeGetTime(). If you want to use that instead of boost::timer (see the Timer class later in this chapter), then you can just include mmsystem.h. Personally, though, I recommend using Boost whenever possible, since the C++ standard committee is more reliable than Microsoft.

```
#pragma once

#define WIN32_LEAN_AND_MEAN
#include <windows.h>
#include <iostream>
#include <map>
#include <list>
#include <vector>
#include <string>
#include <sstream>
#include <fstream>
#include <iomanip>
#include <ctime>
#include <cstdio>
#include <cstdlib>
#include <ctime>
#include <cmath>
#include <io.h>
#include <algorithm>
#include <boost/timer.hpp>
#include <boost/foreach.hpp>
#include <boost/format.hpp>

//DirectX headers
#define DIRECTINPUT_VERSION 0x0800
#include <d3d9.h>
#include <d3dx9.h>
#include <dinput.h>

//engine class headers
#include "Timer.h"
```

```
#include "Input.h"
#include "Event.h"
#include "Font.h"
#include "LogFile.h"

//required libraries
#pragma comment(lib,"d3d9.lib")
#pragma comment(lib,"d3dx9.lib")
#pragma comment(lib,"dinput8.lib")
#pragma comment(lib,"xinput.lib")
#pragma comment(lib,"dxguid.lib")
#pragma comment(lib,"winmm.lib")
#pragma comment(lib,"user32.lib")
#pragma comment(lib,"gdi32.lib")

#define VERSION_MAJOR 1
#define VERSION_MINOR 0
#define REVISION 0

//end-user functions
extern bool game_preload();
extern bool game_init(HWND hwnd);
extern void game_update( float deltaTime );
extern void game_render3d();
extern void game_render2d();
extern void game_event(Octane::IEvent* e);
extern void game_end();

LRESULT CALLBACK WndProc(HWND hwnd, UINT msg, WPARAM wParam, LPARAM lParam);

namespace Octane
{
    //helper function to convert values to string format
    template <class T>std::string static ToString(const T & t, int places = 2)
    {
        std::ostringstream oss;
        oss.precision(places);
        oss.setf(std::ios_base::fixed);
        oss << t;
        return oss.str();
    }
```

```
class Engine
{
private:
    std::string p_commandLineParams;
    int p_versionMajor, p_versionMinor, p_revision;
    HWND p_windowHandle;
    LPDIRECT3D9 p_d3d;
    LPDIRECT3DDEVICE9 p_device;
    LPD3DXSPRITE p_spriteObj;
    std::string p_apptitle;
    bool p_fullscreen;
    int p_screenwidth;
    int p_screenheight;
    int p_colordepth;
    bool p_pauseMode;
    Timer p_coreTimer;
    long p_coreFrameCount;
    long p_coreFrameRate;
    Timer p_screenTimer;
    long p_screenFrameCount;
    long p_screenFrameRate;
    Timer timedUpdate;
    D3DCOLOR p_backdropColor;

    //primary surface pointers used when restoring render target
    LPDIRECT3DSURFACE9 p_MainSurface;
    LPDIRECT3DSURFACE9 p_MainDepthStencilSurface;

    Input *p_input;
    void updateKeyboard();
    void updateMouse();

public:
    Engine();
    virtual ~Engine();
    bool Init(HINSTANCE hInstance, int width, int height,
        int colordepth, bool fullscreen);
    void Update(float deltaTime);
    void Message(std::string message, std::string title = "Engine");
    void fatalError(std::string message, std::string title = "FATAL ERROR");
    void Shutdown();
```

```
void clearScene(D3DCOLOR color);
void setIdentity();
void setSpriteIdentity();
int Release();
void savePrimaryRenderTarget();
void restorePrimaryRenderTarget();

//accessor/mutator functions expose the private variables
bool isPaused() { return p_pauseMode; }
void setPaused(bool value) { p_pauseMode = value; }

LPDIRECT3D9 getObject() { return p_d3d; }
  LPDIRECT3DDEVICE9 getDevice() { return p_device; }
  LPD3DXSPRITE getSpriteObj() { return p_spriteObj; }

void setWindowHandle(HWND hwnd) { p_windowHandle = hwnd; }
HWND getWindowHandle() { return p_windowHandle; }

std::string getAppTitle() { return p_apptitle; }
void setAppTitle(std::string value) { p_apptitle = value; }

int getVersionMajor() { return p_versionMajor; }
int getVersionMinor() { return p_versionMinor; }
int getRevision() { return p_revision; }
std::string getVersionText();

long getCoreFrameRate() { return p_coreFrameRate; };
long getScreenFrameRate() { return p_screenFrameRate; };

void setScreen(int w,int h,int d,bool full);
int getScreenWidth() { return p_screenwidth; }
void setScreenWidth(int value) { p_screenwidth = value; }
int getScreenHeight() { return p_screenheight; }
void setScreenHeight(int value) { p_screenheight = value; }
int getColorDepth() { return p_colordepth; }
void setColorDepth(int value) { p_colordepth = value; }
bool getFullscreen() { return p_fullscreen; }
void setFullscreen(bool value) { p_fullscreen = value; }

D3DCOLOR getBackdropColor() { return p_backdropColor; }
void setBackdropColor(D3DCOLOR value) { p_backdropColor = value; }
```

```
        //command line params
        std::string getCommandLineParams() { return p_commandLineParams; }
        void setCommandLineParams(std::string value) { p_commandLineParams =
value; }

        //event system
        void raiseEvent(IEvent*);

    }; //class
}; //namespace

//define the global engine object (visible everywhere!)
//extern Octane::Engine* g_engine;
extern std::auto_ptr<Octane::Engine> g_engine;
```

Following is the Engine.cpp class implementation, with all of the engine
initialization, updating, and rendering code.

```
#include "stdafx.h"
#include "Engine.h"
using namespace std;

namespace Octane
{
    Engine::Engine()
    {
        p_apptitle = "Octane Engine";
        p_screenwidth = 640;
        p_screenheight = 480;
        p_colordepth = 32;
        p_fullscreen = false;
        p_device = NULL;
        p_coreFrameCount = 0;
        p_coreFrameRate = 0;
        p_screenFrameCount = 0;
        p_screenFrameRate = 0;
        p_backdropColor = D3DCOLOR_XRGB(0,0,80);
        p_windowHandle = 0;
        p_pauseMode = false;
```

```
    p_versionMajor = VERSION_MAJOR;
    p_versionMinor = VERSION_MINOR;
    p_revision = REVISION;
    p_commandLineParams = "";

    //null render target variables
    p_MainSurface = 0;
    p_MainDepthStencilSurface = 0;

    //window handle must be set later on for DirectX
    p_windowHandle = 0;
}

Engine::~Engine()
{
    delete p_input;
    if (p_device) p_device->Release();
    if (p_d3d) p_d3d->Release();
}

std::string Engine::getVersionText()
{
    std::ostringstream s;
    s << "Octane Engine v" << p_versionMajor << "."
        << p_versionMinor << "." << p_revision;
    return s.str();
}

void Engine::Message(std::string message, std::string title)
{
    MessageBox(0, message.c_str(), title.c_str(), 0);
}

void Engine::setScreen(int w,int h,int d,bool full)
{
    setScreenWidth(w);
    setScreenHeight(h);
    setColorDepth(d);
    setFullscreen(full);
}
```

```cpp
bool Engine::Init(HINSTANCE hInstance, int width, int height,
    int colordepth, bool fullscreen)
{
    //get window caption string from engine
    string title;
    title = g_engine->getAppTitle();

    //set window dimensions
    RECT windowRect;
    windowRect.left = 0;
    windowRect.right = g_engine->getScreenWidth();
    windowRect.top = 0;
    windowRect.bottom = g_engine->getScreenHeight();

  //create the window class structure
    WNDCLASSEX wc;
    memset(&wc, 0, sizeof(WNDCLASS));
    wc.cbSize = sizeof(WNDCLASSEX);
    wc.style         = CS_HREDRAW | CS_VREDRAW;
    wc.lpfnWndProc   = (WNDPROC)WndProc;
    wc.hInstance     = hInstance;
    wc.lpszClassName = title.c_str();
      wc.hCursor       = LoadCursor(NULL, IDC_ARROW);
      wc.cbClsExtra    = 0;
      wc.cbWndExtra    = 0;
      wc.hIcon         = 0;
      wc.hIconSm       = 0;
      wc.hbrBackground = 0;
      wc.lpszMenuName  = 0;

    //set up the window with the class info
    RegisterClassEx(&wc);

    //set up the screen in windowed or fullscreen mode?
    DWORD dwStyle, dwExStyle;
    if (g_engine->getFullscreen())
    {
        DEVMODE dm;
        memset(&dm, 0, sizeof(dm));
        dm.dmSize = sizeof(dm);
        dm.dmPelsWidth = g_engine->getScreenWidth();
```

```
        dm.dmPelsHeight = g_engine->getScreenHeight();
        dm.dmBitsPerPel = g_engine->getColorDepth();
        dm.dmFields = DM_BITSPERPEL | DM_PELSWIDTH | DM_PELSHEIGHT;

        if (ChangeDisplaySettings(&dm,CDS_FULLSCREEN)!=DISP_CHANGE_
SUCCESSFUL)
        {
            debug << "Display mode change failed" << std::endl;
            g_engine->setFullscreen(false);
        }
        dwStyle = WS_POPUP;
        dwExStyle = WS_EX_APPWINDOW;
    }
    else {
        dwStyle = WS_OVERLAPPEDWINDOW | WS_VISIBLE;
        dwExStyle = WS_EX_APPWINDOW | WS_EX_WINDOWEDGE;
    }

    //adjust window to true requested size
    AdjustWindowRectEx(&windowRect, dwStyle, FALSE, dwExStyle);

    //create the program window
    int wwidth = windowRect.right - windowRect.left;
    int wheight = windowRect.bottom - windowRect.top;

    debug << "Screen size: " << width << "," << height << endl;
    debug << "Creating program window" << endl;

    HWND hWnd = CreateWindowEx( 0,
        title.c_str(), //window class
        title.c_str(), //title bar
        dwStyle |
        WS_CLIPCHILDREN |
        WS_CLIPSIBLINGS, //window styles
        0, 0, //x,y coordinate
        wwidth, //width of the window
        wheight, //height of the window
        0, //parent window
        0, //menu
        hInstance, //application instance
        0 ); //window parameters
```

```
//was there an error creating the window?
if (!hWnd)
{
    debug << "Error creating program window" << endl;
    return 0;
}

//display the window
ShowWindow(hWnd, SW_SHOW);
UpdateWindow(hWnd);

//save window handle in engine
g_engine->setWindowHandle(hWnd);

debug << "Creating Direct3D object" << endl;

//initialize Direct3D
p_d3d = Direct3DCreate9(D3D_SDK_VERSION);
if (p_d3d == NULL) {
    return 0;
}

//get system desktop color depth
D3DDISPLAYMODE dm;
p_d3d->GetAdapterDisplayMode(D3DADAPTER_DEFAULT, &dm);

//set configuration options for Direct3D
D3DPRESENT_PARAMETERS d3dpp;
ZeroMemory(&d3dpp, sizeof(d3dpp));
d3dpp.Windowed = (!fullscreen);
d3dpp.SwapEffect = D3DSWAPEFFECT_DISCARD;
d3dpp.EnableAutoDepthStencil = 1;
d3dpp.AutoDepthStencilFormat = D3DFMT_D24S8;
d3dpp.Flags = D3DPRESENTFLAG_DISCARD_DEPTHSTENCIL;
d3dpp.PresentationInterval    = D3DPRESENT_INTERVAL_IMMEDIATE;
d3dpp.BackBufferFormat = dm.Format;
d3dpp.BackBufferCount = 1;
d3dpp.BackBufferWidth = width;
d3dpp.BackBufferHeight = height;
d3dpp.hDeviceWindow = p_windowHandle;
d3dpp.MultiSampleType = D3DMULTISAMPLE_NONE;
```

```
debug << "Creating Direct3D device" << endl;

//create Direct3D device (hardware T&L)
p_d3d->CreateDevice(
    D3DADAPTER_DEFAULT,
    D3DDEVTYPE_HAL,
    p_windowHandle,
    D3DCREATE_HARDWARE_VERTEXPROCESSING,
    &d3dpp,
    &p_device);

//if hardware T&L failed, try software
if (p_device == NULL)
{
    debug << "Hardware vertex option failed! Trying software..." << endl;

    p_d3d->CreateDevice(
        D3DADAPTER_DEFAULT,
        D3DDEVTYPE_HAL,
        p_windowHandle,
        D3DCREATE_SOFTWARE_VERTEXPROCESSING,
        &d3dpp,
        &p_device
    );
    if (p_device == NULL)
    {
        debug << "Software vertex option failed; shutting down." << endl;
        return 0;
    }
    else {
        debug << "Software vertex processing" << endl;
    }
}
else {
    debug << "Hardware vertex processing" << endl;
}

debug << "Creating 2D renderer" << endl;
```

```
    //initialize 2D renderer
    HRESULT result = D3DXCreateSprite(p_device, &p_spriteObj);
    if (result != D3D_OK)
    {
        debug << "D3DXCreateSprite failed" << endl;
        return 0;
    }

    //initialize directinput
    debug << "Init input system" << endl;
    p_input = new Input(getWindowHandle());

    debug << "Calling game_init(" << getWindowHandle() << ")" << endl;

    //call game initialization extern function
    if (!game_init(getWindowHandle()))     return 0;

    debug << "Engine init succeeded" << endl;

    return 1;
}


/**
Resets 3D transforms by setting the identity matrix
**/
void Engine::setIdentity()
{
    D3DXMATRIX identity;
    D3DXMatrixIdentity(&identity);
    g_engine->getDevice()->SetTransform(D3DTS_WORLD, &identity);
}


/**
Resets sprite transforms by setting the identity matrix
**/
void Engine::setSpriteIdentity()
{
    D3DXMATRIX identity;
    D3DXMatrixIdentity(&identity);
    g_engine->getSpriteObj()->SetTransform(&identity);
}
```

```
/**
Saving and restoring the render target is used when rendering to a texture
**/
void Engine::savePrimaryRenderTarget()
{
    //save primary rendering & depth stencil surfaces
    p_device->GetRenderTarget( 0, &p_MainSurface );
    p_device->GetDepthStencilSurface( &p_MainDepthStencilSurface );
}
void Engine::restorePrimaryRenderTarget()
{
    //restore normal render target
    p_device->SetRenderTarget( 0, p_MainSurface );
    p_device->SetDepthStencilSurface( p_MainDepthStencilSurface );
}


void Engine::clearScene(D3DCOLOR color)
{
    p_device->Clear(0, NULL,
        D3DCLEAR_TARGET | D3DCLEAR_ZBUFFER,
        color, 1.0f, 0);
}


void Engine::Update( float elapsedTime )
{
    static float accumTime=0;

    //calculate core framerate
    p_coreFrameCount++;
    if (p_coreTimer.Stopwatch(1000))
    {
        p_coreFrameRate = p_coreFrameCount;
        p_coreFrameCount = 0;
    }

    //fast update
    game_update( elapsedTime );

    //60fps = ~16 ms per frame
    if (!timedUpdate.Stopwatch(16))
```

```
        {
            //free the CPU for 1 ms
            timedUpdate.Rest(1);
        }
        else
        {
            //calculate real framerate
            p_screenFrameCount++;
            if (p_screenTimer.Stopwatch(1000))
            {
                p_screenFrameRate = p_screenFrameCount;
                p_screenFrameCount = 0;
            }

            //update input devices
            p_input->Update();
            updateKeyboard();
            updateMouse();

            //begin rendering
            if (p_device->BeginScene() == D3D_OK)
            {
                g_engine->clearScene(p_backdropColor);

                game_render3d();

                //2d rendering
                p_spriteObj->Begin(D3DXSPRITE_ALPHABLEND);

                game_render2d();

                p_spriteObj->End();

                p_device->EndScene();
                p_device->Present(0,0,0,0);
            }
        }
    }
}

void Engine::updateMouse()
```

```
{
    static int oldPosX = 0;
    static int oldPosY = 0;

    //check mouse buttons
    for (int n=0; n<4; n++)
    {
        if (p_input->GetMouseButton(n))
        {
            //launch event
            raiseEvent( new MouseClickEvent( n ) );
        }
    }

    //check mouse position
    int posx = p_input->GetMousePosX();
    int posy = p_input->GetMousePosY();
    if (posx != oldPosX || posy != oldPosY)
    {
        oldPosX = p_input->GetMousePosX();
        oldPosY = p_input->GetMousePosY();
        //launch event
        raiseEvent( new MouseMoveEvent(   posx, posy ) );
    }

    //check mouse motion
    int deltax = p_input->GetMouseDeltaX();
    int deltay = p_input->GetMouseDeltaY();
    if (deltax != 0 || deltay != 0 )
    {
        //launch event
        raiseEvent( new MouseMotionEvent( deltax, deltay ) );
    }

    //check mouse wheel
    int wheel = p_input->GetMouseDeltaWheel();
    if (wheel != 0)
    {
        //launch event
        raiseEvent( new MouseWheelEvent( wheel ) );
    }
}
```

```
void Engine::updateKeyboard()
{
    static char old_keys[256];

    for (int n=0; n<255; n++) {
        //check for key press
        if (p_input->GetKeyState(n) & 0x80)
        {
            old_keys[n] = p_input->GetKeyState(n);
            //launch event
            raiseEvent( new KeyPressEvent( n ) );
        }
        //check for release
        else if (old_keys[n] & 0x80)
        {
            old_keys[n] = p_input->GetKeyState(n);
            //launch event
            raiseEvent( new KeyReleaseEvent( n ) );
        }
    }
}

void Engine::Shutdown()
{
    PostQuitMessage(0);
}

void Engine::raiseEvent(IEvent* e)
{
    game_event(e);
    delete e;
}

} //namespace
```

Timer Class

Timing in the engine core is handled by the `Timer` class, which is based on `boost::timer`, part of the standard C++ Boost library (or, perhaps I should say, *soon* to be standard, since C++0x has not been formally adopted yet). The current standard is still C++03, but the new standard is expected to be voted on by the SC22-WG21 committee during 2010[1].

Advice

It's always a dicey proposition to begin using a new language feature before it has been officially recognized, as is the case with Boost. It is possible that `boost::timer` will become `std::timer`, and that similar Boost features that we've used in this book (such as `boost::thread`) will be similarly changed. However, the C++0x standard has been in the works for several years already and is quite reliable at this point. As usual, if any changes impact the source code, an errata with code updates will be available at http://www.jharbour.com/forum.

Fortunately, as we have already learned, there is a great advantage to writing wrapper classes around key engine core and rendering SDKs and APIs (such as Direct3D and Boost). There is very little pure Boost code used in the engine. Rather, what you will find are classes such as Timer, which wraps `boost::timer` into a nicely managed package. Thus, if anything changes in `boost::timer`, only the Timer class will need to be modified, while the rest of the engine (and game code) will be unaffected.

Timing in the core engine is based on some assumptions (which you are welcome to change to suit your own engine goals). Here are the assumptions I made when designing the core timing of the engine:

- Frame "updates" should not be time limited in any way, to provide maximum performance for time-critical processes like collision detection and physics.

- A "delta time" millisecond timer, maintained by the core engine, is passed to the update function so that individual processes and entities can handle timing independently without needing a timer function.

- Rendering always takes place at a fixed 60 fps. Trying to render at any higher rate is just a waste of CPU cycles (which has the detrimental effect of bogging down the core update). Although some monitors can operate at 70 Hz or higher frequencies, 60 Hz is the standard for game rendering.

Here is the `Timer.h` class interface:

```
#pragma once
#include "Engine.h"
#include <boost/timer.hpp>
namespace Octane
{
    class Timer
    {
    private:
        boost::timer p_timer;
        double timer_start;
        double stopwatch_start;

    public:
        Timer(void);
        ~Timer(void);
        double getElapsed();
        void Rest(double ms);
        void Reset();
        bool Stopwatch(double ms);
    };
};
```

Below is the `Timer.cpp` class implementation. The most important function is `getElapsed()`. Although `boost::timer` returns a floating-point value (where the decimal part represents milliseconds), our `getElapsed()` function multiplies this by 1,000 to arrive at a straight millisecond timer (returned as a double). This timer starts at zero when the class instantiates. To retrieve the elapsed seconds, just divide by 1,000.

```
#include "stdafx.h"
#include "Engine.h"
#include <boost/timer.hpp>

namespace Octane
{
    Timer::Timer(void)
    {
        Reset();
    }
```

```
Timer::~Timer(void) {}
double Timer::getElapsed()
{
    double elapsed = p_timer.elapsed() * 1000;
    return elapsed;
}

void Timer::Rest(double ms)
{
    double start = getElapsed();
    while (start + ms > getElapsed())
    {
        Sleep(1);
    }
}

void Timer::Reset()
{
    stopwatch_start = getElapsed();
}

bool Timer::Stopwatch(double ms)
{
    if ( getElapsed() > stopwatch_start + (double)ms )
    {
        Reset();
        return true;
    }
    else return false;
}
};
```

Input Class

Getting input from the user is as important as rendering (as far as gameplay is concerned), but this subject does not often get as much attention because, frankly, it just doesn't change very often. We're going to use DirectInput to get input from the keyboard and the mouse in this chapter. DirectInput hasn't changed in many years and is still at version 8.1. Contrast that with the huge changes taking place with Direct3D every year! Although we can use a joystick, it's such a non-standard device for the PC that it's not worth the effort—unless you are a flight sim fan, in which case, you might want to support a joystick! Just note that most PC gamers prefer a keyboard and mouse. If you want to support an Xbox 360 controller, you can look into the XInput library, which is now packaged with the DirectX SDK (as well as included with XNA Game Studio).

The keyboard is the standard input device, even for games that don't specifically use it, so it is a given that your games must support a keyboard one way or another. If nothing else, you should allow the user to exit your game or at least bring up an in-game menu by pressing the Escape key (that's the standard). The DirectInput library file is called `dinput8.lib`.

Once you have created a DirectInput keyboard device, you can then initialize the keyboard handler to prepare it for input. The next step is to set the keyboard's data format, which instructs DirectInput how to pass the data back to your program. It is abstracted in this way because there are hundreds of input devices on the market with myriad features, so there has to be a uniform way to read them all.

After you have written a handler for the keyboard, the mouse is a bit easier to deal with because the DirectInput object will already exist. The code to initialize and poll the mouse is very similar to the keyboard code. Below is an `Input` class, which handles both the keyboard and mouse. First is the `Input.h` class interface:

```
#pragma once

#include "Engine.h"

namespace Octane
{
    class Input
    {
    private:
        HWND window;
        IDirectInput8 *di;
        IDirectInputDevice8 *keyboard;
        char keyState[256];
        IDirectInputDevice8 *mouse;
        DIMOUSESTATE mouseState;
        POINT position;
```

```
public:
    Input( HWND window );
    virtual ~Input();
    void Update();
    char GetKeyState(int key) { return keyState[key]; }
    long GetMousePosX() { return position.x; }
    long GetMousePosY() { return position.y; }
    int GetMouseButton( char button );
    long GetMouseDeltaX() { return mouseState.lX; }
    long GetMouseDeltaY() { return mouseState.lY; }
    long GetMouseDeltaWheel() { return mouseState.lZ; }
    };
};
```

Next is the `Input.cpp` class implementation. The keyboard and mouse devices are created and initialized, and polling functions are provided. Since the mouse events supplied to us by DirectInput only produce mouse motion ("mickeys") rather than an actual X,Y position on the screen, we need to use a couple of helper functions to actually get the mouse position on the screen—or, more accurately, in the bounds of the window. That is done with the `GetCursorPos()` and `ScreenToClient()` functions, which you will see in the code listing.

```cpp
#include "Engine.h"

namespace Octane
{
    Input::Input( HWND hwnd )
    {
        //save window handle
        window = hwnd;

        //create DirectInput object
        DirectInput8Create( GetModuleHandle(NULL),
            DIRECTINPUT_VERSION, IID_IDirectInput8, (void**)&di, NULL );

        //initialize keyboard
        di->CreateDevice(GUID_SysKeyboard, &keyboard, NULL);
        keyboard->SetDataFormat( &c_dfDIKeyboard );
        keyboard->SetCooperativeLevel( window,
            DISCL_FOREGROUND | DISCL_NONEXCLUSIVE );
        keyboard->Acquire();
```

```
    //clear key array
    memset(keyState, 0, 256);

    //initialize mouse
    di->CreateDevice(GUID_SysMouse, &mouse, NULL);
    mouse->SetDataFormat(&c_dfDIMouse);
    mouse->SetCooperativeLevel(window,
        DISCL_FOREGROUND | DISCL_NONEXCLUSIVE);
    mouse->Acquire();
}

Input::~Input()
{
    di->Release();
    keyboard->Release();
    mouse->Release();
}

void Input::Update()
{
    //poll state of the keyboard
    keyboard->Poll();
    if (!SUCCEEDED(keyboard->GetDeviceState(256,(LPVOID)&keyState)))
    {
        //keyboard device lost, try to re-acquire
        keyboard->Acquire();
    }

    //poll state of the mouse
    mouse->Poll();
    if (!SUCCEEDED( mouse->GetDeviceState(
        sizeof(DIMOUSESTATE),&mouseState)) )
    {
        //mouse device lost, try to re-acquire
        mouse->Acquire();
    }

    //get mouse position on screen (not DirectInput)
    GetCursorPos(&position);
    ScreenToClient(window, &position);
}
```

```
int Input::GetMouseButton( char button )
{
    return (mouseState.rgbButtons[button] & 0x80);
}
};
```

Handling Engine Events

The IEvent class defines an interface for the event system in the engine, which is used for all user input and other purposes (such as automatic timing). In the past I have used individual event functions for every type of event (such as mouse_click, key_down, and so on). A single event handler function and support classes is a much cleaner way to process events in the engine. And, as an added bonus, event classes and functions are more thread friendly, since we can queue events and make the handler thread safe (if needed).

We'll start with an abstract class called IEvent. This class is used to create small sub-classed event classes for each type of event. At this point, all we're using the event system for are user input events (key presses, mouse movement, etc.). Here is the Event.h base class interface:

```
#pragma once

#include "Engine.h"

namespace Octane
{
    class IEvent {
    protected:
        int id;
    public:
        IEvent();
        virtual ~IEvent(){}
        int getID() { return id; }
    };
```

The base IEvent class provides only the event identifier; it is up to the subclasses to define additional data needed for each unique event. Here is an enumeration that describes the events currently in use:

```
enum eventtype {
    EVENT_TIMER = 10,
```

```
        EVENT_KEYPRESS = 20,
        EVENT_KEYRELEASE = 30,
        EVENT_MOUSECLICK = 40,
        EVENT_MOUSEMOTION = 50,
        EVENT_MOUSEWHEEL = 60,
        EVENT_MOUSEMOVE = 70,
    };
```

Each event sub-class is derived from IEvent, and identified by one of the above EVENT_ enumerated constant values. Below are the event sub-classes currently defined to handle the user input events (and you will expect to see this grow as new engine events are needed).

```
class KeyPressEvent : public IEvent {
public:
    int keycode;
    KeyPressEvent( int key );
};

class KeyReleaseEvent : public IEvent {
public:
    int keycode;
    KeyReleaseEvent( int key );
};

class MouseClickEvent : public IEvent {
public:
    int button;
    MouseClickEvent( int btn );
};

class MouseMotionEvent : public IEvent {
public:
    int deltax,deltay;
    MouseMotionEvent( int dx, int dy );
};

class MouseWheelEvent : public IEvent {
public:
    int wheel;
    MouseWheelEvent( int wheel );
};
```

```
        class MouseMoveEvent : public IEvent {
        public:
            int posx, posy;
            MouseMoveEvent( int px, int py );
        };
};
```

Here is the Event.cpp class implementation. The various event classes are much easier to use as individual classes rather than as a single large class with support for any type of event using properties and methods. Also, we must be mindful that these events will be fired off *frequently* from user input alone, not to mention future events like automatic timers and entity events like collisions.

```
#include "Engine.h"

namespace Octane
{
    IEvent::IEvent()
    {
        id = 0;
    }

    KeyPressEvent::KeyPressEvent(int key)
    {
        id = EVENT_KEYPRESS;
        keycode = key;
    }

    KeyReleaseEvent::KeyReleaseEvent(int key)
    {
        id = EVENT_KEYRELEASE;
        keycode = key;
    }

    MouseClickEvent::MouseClickEvent(int btn)
    {
        id = EVENT_MOUSECLICK;
        button = btn;
    }

    MouseMotionEvent::MouseMotionEvent( int dx, int dy )
```

```
    {
        id = EVENT_MOUSEMOTION;
        deltax = dx;
        deltay = dy;
    }

    MouseWheelEvent::MouseWheelEvent( int whl )
    {
        id = EVENT_MOUSEWHEEL;
        wheel = whl;
    }

    MouseMoveEvent::MouseMoveEvent( int px, int py )
    {
        id = EVENT_MOUSEMOVE;
        posx = px;
        posy = py;
    }
};
```

Engine Rendering System

The engine's rendering system is centered around the Direct3D functions BeginScene() and EndScene(), plus Present(). All rendering takes place within the block of code bounded by these function calls, and no rendering can occur anywhere else in the code. Between the BeginScene() and EndScene() function calls, you will perform all 3D rendering of the scene and all entity meshes. In addition, all 2D rendering takes place within an inner block of code bounded by ID3DXSprite::Begin() and ID3DXSprite::End(). Over time, the rendering system will expand to include 2D components such as sprites and GUI controls, and 3D components such as terrain, environments, and animated characters. This rendering code has already been implemented, and we'll be creating new things to render in upcoming chapters.

Font Class

One of the most crucial features of a game engine is the ability to display text on the screen, also called *text output*. This is important because this font system is used in most games for the graphical user interface (GUI), so it needs to be functional and fast. The Font class provides an interface to the ID3DXFont class in the Direct3DX library for basic font-based text output using any standard Windows TrueType font and point size.

We will use a function called D3DXCreateFontIndirect() to create the font and prepare it for printing out text. But before doing that, we must first set up the properties desired for the font using the D3DXFONT_DESC structure. Printing text is done with the ID3DXFont::DrawText() function.

```
#pragma once
#include "Engine.h"
namespace Octane
{
    class Font {
    private:
        LPD3DXFONT fontObj;

    public:
        Font(std::string name, int size);
        ~Font();
        void Print(int x, int y, std::string text, D3DCOLOR color=0xffffffff);
        int getTextWidth(std::string text);
        int getTextHeight(std::string text);
    };
};
```

ID3DXFont has the ability to render text into a rectangle with word wrapping, which could be very useful in a GUI textbox or label control. Normally, the rectangle is defined with a width and height of zero, so no boundary is used at all. But if you specify a width and height, and use the DT_CALCRECT option, then DrawText will do automatic word wrapping! Below is the Font.cpp class implementation.

```
#include "stdafx.h"
#include "Engine.h"
using namespace std;

namespace Octane
{
    Font::Font(string name, int pointsize)
    {
```

```
        fontObj = NULL;
        D3DXFONT_DESC fontDesc = {
            pointsize,                  //height
            0,                          //width
            0,                          //weight
            0,                          //miplevels
            false,                      //italic
            DEFAULT_CHARSET,            //charset
            OUT_TT_PRECIS,              //output precision
            CLIP_DEFAULT_PRECIS,        //quality
            DEFAULT_PITCH,              //pitch and family
            " "
        };
        strcpy(fontDesc.FaceName, name.c_str());

        D3DXCreateFontIndirect(g_engine->getDevice(), &fontDesc, &fontObj);
}


Font::~Font()
{
    fontObj->Release();
}


void Font::Print(int x, int y, string text, D3DCOLOR color)
{
    //figure out the text boundary
    RECT rect = { x, y, 0, 0 };
    fontObj->DrawText( NULL, text.c_str(), text.length(),
        &rect, DT_CALCRECT, color);

    //print the text
    fontObj->DrawText( g_engine->getSpriteObj(), text.c_str(),
        text.length(), &rect, DT_LEFT, color);
}


int Font::getTextWidth(std::string text)
{
    RECT rect = { 0, 0, 0, 0 };
    fontObj->DrawText( NULL, text.c_str(), text.length(), &rect,
        DT_CALCRECT, 0xffffffff);
```

```
            return rect.right;
    }

    int Font::getTextHeight(std::string text)
    {
        RECT rect = { 0, 0, 0, 0 };
        fontObj->DrawText( NULL, text.c_str(), text.length(), &rect,
            DT_CALCRECT, 0xffffffff);
        return rect.bottom;
    }

};
```

Engine Support System

The engine support system will start by including a debugging tool that no programmer should be able to go without—a log file with basic std::cout-style functionality for quickly and effortlessly sending debug data out to a text file.

Logging the engine's processes is a helpful feature for debugging the engine components once it reaches a certain high level of complexity. It is also helpful to log output to assist when tracking down the cause of an unexpected game crash, so the ability to send output to a log file goes beyond mere engine debugging: it becomes a valuable aid for developers when a user reports a problem. Here is an example of what the log produces during a typical run of the engine (from the First Engine Demo project coming up). Any time something goes wrong, just take a look at the output.txt log file to see quickly where to go in the code to resolve it. By all means, add more debugging output to increase the amount of information, but you do not want to log anything from inside the game loop—just startup and shutdown processes.

```
WinMain running
Checking parameters
Calling game_preload
Initializing engine
Screen size: 800,600
Creating program window
Creating Direct3D object
Creating Direct3D device
Hardware vertex processing
```

```
Creating 2D renderer
Init input system
Calling game_init(00D50846)
Engine init succeeded
Core timer started: 0
Entering while loop
Exiting while loop
Total run time: 2594
Freeing game resources
Shutting down engine
```

The LogFile class is not complete at present. At any time that you would like to see more custom data sent out to the log file, go ahead and add new overloads to the operator≪() function, as the current crop of overloads support only a handful of simple data types. I would expect the log to support vectors, perhaps even matrices, if the need to debug such information is deemed necessary. However, you would not want to send any log output from inside the while loop—including inside any of the updating or rendering functions; not only would that kill the game's framerate, but it would fill the file very quickly with millions of lines of text.

Advice

Most runtime errors occur during program startup (including asset loading) and program shutdown.

The LogFile.h class interface follows.

```
#pragma once
#include "Engine.h"
namespace Octane
{
    class LogFile
    {
    public:
        LogFile();
        ~LogFile();
        void Print(std::string s);
        void Print(char c[]);
        std::ofstream& operator≪(char c[]);
```

```
            std::ofstream& operator≪(std::string s);
            std::ofstream& operator≪(double d);
            std::ofstream& operator≪(float f);
            std::ofstream& operator≪(int i);
            std::ofstream& operator≪(bool b);
        };
    };
static Octane::LogFile debug;
```

Here is the LogFile.cpp class implementation:

```
#include "Engine.h"
using namespace std;

std::ofstream out("output.txt");

namespace Octane
{
    LogFile::LogFile() {}
    LogFile::~LogFile()
    {
        if (out.good()) out.close();
    }
    void LogFile::Print(string s)
    {
        out ≪ s ≪ endl;
    }
    void LogFile::Print(char c[])
    {
        out ≪ c ≪ endl;
    }
    std::ofstream& LogFile::operator≪(char c[])
    {
        out ≪ c;
        return out;
    }
    std::ofstream& LogFile::operator≪(string s)
    {
        out ≪ s;
        return out;
    }
    std::ofstream& LogFile::operator≪(double d)
```

```
        {
            out << d;
            return out;
        }
        std::ofstream& LogFile::operator<<(float f)
        {
            out << f;
            return out;
        }
        std::ofstream& LogFile::operator<<(int i)
        {
            out << i;
            return out;
        }
        std::ofstream& LogFile::operator<<(bool b)
        {
            if (b) out << "True";
            else out << "False";
            return out;
        }
};
```

First Engine Demo

To illustrate the functionality of the initial version of this new engine, we'll write a short program that uses all of the new classes, including the event system, to print user input events to the screen. Figure 6.2 shows the output of this program.

```
#include "Engine.h"
using namespace std;
using namespace Octane;

Font *font=NULL;
int keypresscode=0;
int keyreleasecode=0;
int mousebutton=0;
int movex=0,movey=0;
int posx=0,posy=0;
int wheel=0;
float delta=0;
```

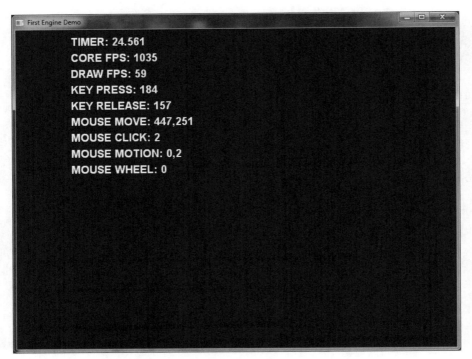

TIMER: 24.561
CORE FPS: 1035
DRAW FPS: 59
KEY PRESS: 184
KEY RELEASE: 157
MOUSE MOVE: 447,251
MOUSE CLICK: 2
MOUSE MOTION: 0,2
MOUSE WHEEL: 0

Figure 6.2
The First Engine Demo program.

```
//these functions are not used at this time
void game_render3d() {}
void game_end() {}

bool game_preload()
{
    g_engine->setAppTitle("First Engine Demo");
    g_engine->setScreen(800,600,32,false);
    return true;
}

bool game_init(HWND hwnd)
{
    font = new Font("Arial Bold",30);
    if (!font)
```

```
        {
            debug << "Error creating font" << endl;
            return false;
        }
        return true;
}


void game_update( float deltaTime )
{
    delta = deltaTime;
}


void game_render2d()
{
    ostringstream os;
    os.imbue(std::locale("english-us"));
    os << "DELTA: " << Octane::ToString(delta,4) << endl;
    os << "CORE FPS: " << g_engine->getCoreFrameRate() << endl;
    os << "SCREEN FPS: " << g_engine->getScreenFrameRate() << endl;
    os << "KEY PRESS: " << keypresscode << endl;
    os << "KEY RELEASE: " << keyreleasecode << endl;
    os << "MOUSE MOVE: " << posx << "," << posy << endl;
    os << "MOUSE CLICK: " << mousebutton << endl;
    os << "MOUSE MOTION: " << movex << "," << movey << endl;
    os << "MOUSE WHEEL: " << wheel << endl;
    font->Print(100,20,os.str());

    mousebutton = 0;
    wheel = 0;
}


void game_event( IEvent* e )
{
    switch( e->getID() )
    {
        case EVENT_KEYPRESS:
        {
            KeyPressEvent* kpe = (KeyPressEvent*) e;
            keypresscode = kpe->keycode;
            if (keypresscode == DIK_ESCAPE)
```

```
                g_engine->Shutdown();
            break;
        }
        case EVENT_KEYRELEASE:
        {
            KeyReleaseEvent* kre = (KeyReleaseEvent*) e;
            keyreleasecode = kre->keycode;
            break;
        }
        case EVENT_MOUSEMOVE:
        {
            MouseMoveEvent* mme = (MouseMoveEvent*) e;
            posx = mme->posx;
            posy = mme->posy;
            break;
        }
        case EVENT_MOUSECLICK:
        {
            MouseClickEvent* mce = (MouseClickEvent*) e;
            mousebutton = mce->button + 1;
            break;
        }
        case EVENT_MOUSEMOTION:
        {
            MouseMotionEvent* mme = (MouseMotionEvent*) e;
            movex = mme->deltax;
            movey = mme->deltay;
            break;
        }
        case EVENT_MOUSEWHEEL:
        {
            MouseWheelEvent* mwe = (MouseWheelEvent*) e;
            wheel = mwe->wheel;
            break;
        }
    }
}
```

Not bad for a complete Windows program with a Direct3D device, text output, a core update timer, a screen refresh timer, a real-time loop, user input support, an event handler, and logging! This is definitely not your usual "Hello World" example.

ENUMERATING VIDEO MODES

Although not built into the engine core at this point, it may be helpful to have a list of known video modes that are supported on any given PC. For instance, if you want to run your code in high-definition widescreen format (1920×1080), it's foolhardy to just hard code the resolution because it simply won't run on a PC that does not support such exotic video hardware. However, there *is* a way to determine whether a desired video mode is supported—by having the Direct3D device enumerate the video modes. Figure 6.3 shows an example of an enumerated list of modes being printed out.

```
D3DDISPLAYMODE  mode;
int adapters = g_engine->getObject()->GetAdapterCount();
for (int i=0; i < adapters; ++i)
```

Figure 6.3
Supported video modes are enumerated by Direct3D.

```
    {
        UINT modes = g_engine->getObject()->GetAdapterModeCount(i, D3DFMT_X8R8G8B8);
        for (int n=0; n < modes; ++n)
        {
            g_engine->getObject()->EnumAdapterModes(i, D3DFMT_X8R8G8B8, n, &mode);
            //these properties represent a supported mode:
            //   mode.Width
            //   mode.Height
            //   mode.Format
            //   mode.RefreshRate
        }
    }
}
```

ENUMERATING MULTI-SAMPLING SUPPORT

Direct3D can detect the multi-sampling modes supported by the video hardware in a PC with the help of a function called CheckDeviceMultiSample-Type(). By iterating from D3DMULTISAMPLE_2_SAMPLES (the first one) through D3DMULTISAMPLE_16_SAMPLES (the last one), we can determine whether each multi-sample type is supported in the system. First, we can check for full 32-bit support with the option D3DFMT_X8R8G8B8; if that fails, we'll try D3DFMT_D24S8 (which should be supported on all video cards). Figure 6.4 shows the output of enumerated modes reported by Direct3D on a GeForce 8800GT video card.

```
int start = D3DMULTISAMPLE_2_SAMPLES;
int end = D3DMULTISAMPLE_16_SAMPLES;

for (int n=start; n < end; n++)
{
    D3DMULTISAMPLE_TYPE mst = (D3DMULTISAMPLE_TYPE)n;
    DWORD quality=0;

    if(SUCCEEDED(
    g_engine->getObject()->CheckDeviceMultiSampleType(
        D3DADAPTER_DEFAULT,
        D3DDEVTYPE_HAL,
        D3DFMT_X8R8G8B8,
        true,
        mst,
```

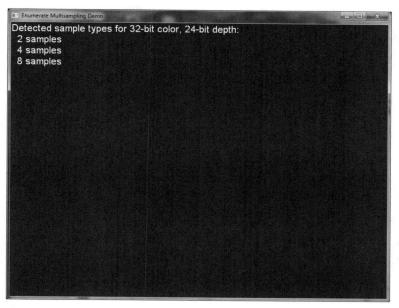

Figure 6.4
Supported multi-sampling modes are enumerated by Direct3D.

```
            &quality )))
    {
        if (SUCCEEDED(
            g_engine->getObject()->CheckDeviceMultiSampleType(
                D3DADAPTER_DEFAULT,
                D3DDEVTYPE_HAL,
                D3DFMT_D24S8,
                true,
                mst,
                &quality )))
        {
            //Set Direct3D presentation parameters:
            //  params.MultiSampleType = mst;
            //  params.MultiSampleQuality = quality-1;

            //  n = valid multi-sample rate
        }
    }
}
```

Verifying Framerates with FRAPS

There is a great little tool available called FRAPS that can calculate and display the framerate of a Direct3D program running, as well as capture video and screenshots. The trial version of FRAPS can be downloaded for free from http://www.fraps.com. Registering the software will eliminate a watermark embedded in captured videos as well as support video captures of more than 30 seconds in length. Many *World of Warcraft* players use FRAPS to record their best dungeon raids to put up on YouTube, but we can use it to capture our awesome Direct3D demos running in all their glory.

As shown in Figure 6.5, the FPS settings in FRAPS provides a way to customize the position of the framerate overlay and optionally output statistical information into CSV formatted files (readable by Excel, but basically just text). Figure 6.6 shows the FRAPS framerate overlay displayed on the First Engine Demo program. If you are concerned about FRAPS slowing down the performance of your demo, you can set FRAPS to only update the display once per second rather than every frame.

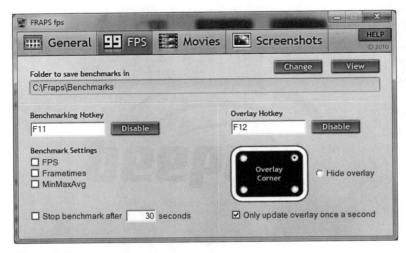

Figure 6.5
The framerate overlay options in FRAPS.

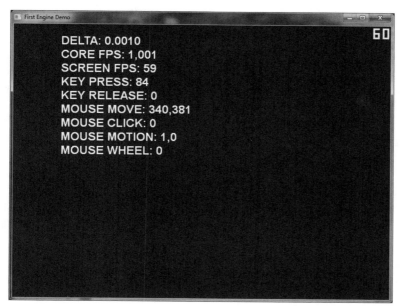

Figure 6.6
Our First Engine Demo with FRAPS framerate overlay displayed in the upper-right.

SUMMARY

We've made huge progress in this chapter! This wraps up the initial functionality of the new engine. Although it has meager rendering capabilities at this stage, all of the important core features are present in the engine already, including an event handler, timing, and text output. The rendering code is already present, as is the sprite renderer, and these components are simply waiting for something to render. In the chapters to come, we will fill in asset loading, mesh and sprite rendering and animation, texture manipulation, shader effects, and all of the features one would expect in a serious engine.

REFERENCES

1. Stroustrup, Bjarne. *C++0x FAQ.* 2010. Retrieved March 13, 2010, from C++0x FAQ website: http://www2.research.att.com/~bs/C++0xFAQ.html.

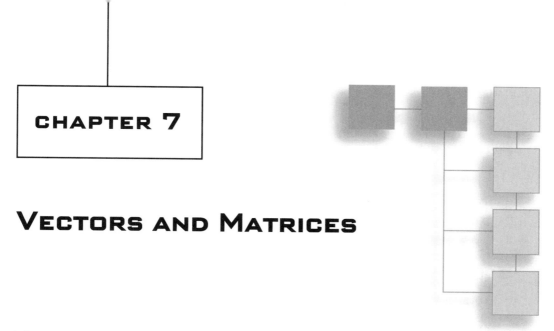

CHAPTER 7

VECTORS AND MATRICES

The most useful thing we will need in order to manipulate game objects effectively is a vector. A *vector* is a mathematical construct that can represent two different things—a point or a direction. A vector is not merely a point, nor is it merely a direction; otherwise, we would use one term or the other to describe it. However, we can use a vector to represent simple points, or positions, for game entities such as sprites and meshes, and another vector to represent a direction. A vector with its own properties that work with common math functions will be incredibly helpful. We will be able to give a game entity important properties such as position, direction, and velocity, as well as calculate the trajectory to a target, the normal angle of a polygon, and other helpful functions (some of which we may not need but which are available nonetheless). We will use the vector classes (listed in the following section) and a new math class to do the "heavy lifting" for upcoming game entity classes (namely, objects based on sprites and meshes).

This chapter covers some basic math functions that will improve the support library within the game engine. First, we will look at linear velocity, then we'll examine a more advanced technique for calculating the angle between two points (which is helpful when targeting an enemy in a game or for moving a sprite along a path set by waypoints). Note that this chapter is not about the theory behind any of these math functions, nor does this text attempt to derive any of the math functions—we are simply coding some of the more common math functions into our game engine.

This chapter covers the following topics:

- Understanding vectors
- Direct3D vectors
- `Vector` classes
- Linear velocity
- Angle to target
- `Math` class
- Math vector demo
- Zero and identity matrices
- Matrix operations
- Direct3D matrices
- Matrix transforms
- Math matrix demo

VECTORS AND POINTS

First, let's discuss what a vector is and what it is used for. A vector is a geometrical object that has two properties: length and direction. The length of a vector represents its strength or power depending on the context. If we treat a ray of sunlight as a vector, then the length of the vector represents the brightness of the light. If we treat wind as a vector, then the length of the vector may represent the speed of the wind. Technically, or rather, mathematically, a vector does not have a position. But from a game development perspective, we sort of *abuse* a vector by also using it for position, which is technically an incorrect usage. It is more accurate to refer to position with a *point*, not a *vector*. Futhermore, a math major will identify a vector as a single-column matrix as shown in Figure 7.1. We could treat a vector as a one-column matrix and just derive a vector and a matrix from a base *matrix column*, but the goal in graphics programming is not always to represent things in mathematical terms, but in terms that work better in the context of rendering. For our purposes, a 1×3 matrix *is* a vector with properties X, Y, Z.

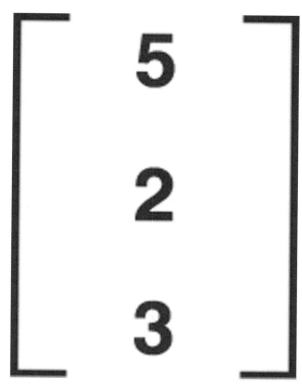

Figure 7.1
A vector is a single-column matrix.

Advice

We will not be using *correct* math terminology and formulas to represent equations and concepts in this chapter, because most non-math majors tend to gloss over formal math representations. I recommend a good math tutorial website in the References at the end of the chapter that will bring you up to speed on these concepts in short order.

Understanding Vectors

A point, or position, will never have a length or direction—it is simply a location in Cartesian space. A point may be represented with either two axes (X, Y) or three axes (X, Y, Z). It takes two points to produce one vector. The difference between the two points—also called the *displacement*—is the vector. Another common concept in computer graphics is the *transformation*, usually in reference to a matrix. A transform is the resulting point from adding a vector to a starting point, which can be either 2D or 3D. So, for a simple demonstration, take the point P(1,1) and vector V(5,3): adding them together, the translation = P + V, or (1,1) + (5,3). The translation for X is 1 + 5 = 6, and for Y is 1 + 3 = 4, for a target point of (6,4). That's all there is to translation, and you can see that it is closely tied to both points and vectors. The other common transforms (rotation and scaling) are variations of this familiar theme with points and vectors.

Advice

This chapter's resource files can be downloaded from www.jharbour.com/forum or www.courseptr.com/downloads. Please note that not every line of code will be in print due to space considerations: the most important sections of code are covered in each chapter while the logistical code is found in the chapter resource files.

Direct3D Vectors

The DirectX SDK defines two primary vector structures, each with many manipulation functions (which we will mostly ignore): D3DXVECTOR2 and D3DXVECTOR3. You may use either the custom vector classes or DirectX vectors, but it is better to abstract an engine's classes to protect them from future changes in an SDK (such as DirectX).

We will be creating a pair of versatile vector classes with inherent properties and functions to make it easy to copy, multiply, add, and perform other basic operations to vectors (and points). Since most of the DirectX matrix and vector classes and related functions treat vectors interchangeably with points, we will just do the same to be consistent.

Vector2 Class

Both the Vector2 and Vector3 classes are found in the Vector.h interface and Vector.cpp implementation files. Both vector classes can copy from a D3DXVECTOR2 or a D3DXVECTOR3, as well as convert to those DirectX classes. Following is the class interface definition for Vector2 :

```
class Vector2
{
public:
    double x, y;
```

```
    virtual ~Vector2() {}
    Vector2();
    Vector2(const Vector2& V);
    Vector2(double x, double y);
    Vector2(int x, int y);
    Vector2(const D3DXVECTOR2& dv);
    Vector2(const D3DXVECTOR3& dv);
    Vector2& operator=( const Vector2& V);

    //manipulation functions
    void Set(double x1,double y1);
    void Set(const Vector2& V);
    double getX() { return x; }
    void setX(double value) { x = value; }
    double getY() { return y; }
    void setY(double value) { y = value; }
    void Move( double mx,double my );
    void operator+=(const Vector2& V);
    void operator-=(const Vector2& V);
    void operator*=(const Vector2& V);
    void operator/=(const Vector2& V);
    Vector2 operator/(const double& d);
    bool operator==( const Vector2& V ) const;
    bool operator!=( const Vector2& V ) const;

    //exporters to Direct3D vectors
    D3DXVECTOR3 ToD3DXVECTOR3();
    D3DXVECTOR2 ToD3DXVECTOR2();
};
```

Here is the Vector2 class implementation, which is also found in the Vector.cpp file (with the Vector3 class):

```
Vector2::Vector2()
{
    x = y = 0;
}

Vector2::Vector2( const Vector2& V )
{
    *this = V;
}
```

```
Vector2::Vector2( double x, double y )
{
    Set( x, y );
}

Vector2::Vector2( int x, int y )
{
    Set((double)x,(double)y);
}

Vector2::Vector2(const D3DXVECTOR2& dv)
{
    x=dv.x; y=dv.y;
}

Vector2::Vector2(const D3DXVECTOR3& dv)
{
    x=dv.x; y=dv.y;
}

Vector2& Vector2::operator=( const Vector2& V)
{
    Set( V );
    return *this;
}

void Vector2::Set( double x1,double y1 )
{
    x=x1; y=y1;
}

void Vector2::Set( const Vector2& V)
{
    x=V.x; y=V.y;
}

void Vector2::Move( double mx,double my )
{
    x+=mx; y+=my;
}
```

```cpp
void Vector2::operator+=(const Vector2& V)
{
    x+=V.x; y+=V.y;
}

void Vector2::operator-=(const Vector2& V)
{
    x-=V.x; y-=V.y;
}

void Vector2::operator*=(const Vector2& V)
{
    x*=V.x; y*=V.y;
}

void Vector2::operator/=(const Vector2& V)
{
    x/=V.x; y/=V.y;
}

Vector2 Vector2::operator/(const double& d)
{
    Vector2 v( x/d, y/d );
    return v;
}

//equality operator comparison includes double rounding
bool Vector2::operator==( const Vector2& V ) const
{
    return (
        ((((V.x - 0.0001f) < x) && (x < (V.x + 0.0001f))) &&
        ((((V.y - 0.0001f) < y) && (y < (V.y + 0.0001f)))) );
}

//inequality operator
bool Vector2::operator!=( const Vector2& V ) const
{
    return (!(*this == V));
}
```

```
D3DXVECTOR3 Vector2::ToD3DXVECTOR3()
{
    return D3DXVECTOR3( (float)x, (float)y, 0.0f );
}

D3DXVECTOR2 Vector2::ToD3DXVECTOR2()
{
    return D3DXVECTOR2( (float)x, (float)y );
}
```

Vector3 Class

Also found in the Vector.h file is the Vector3 class interface:

```
class Vector3
{
public:
    double x, y, z;

    virtual ~Vector3() {}
    Vector3();
    Vector3(const Vector3& V);
    Vector3(double x, double y, double z);
    Vector3(int x, int y, int z);
    Vector3(const D3DXVECTOR2& dv);
    Vector3(const D3DXVECTOR3& dv);
    Vector3& operator=( const Vector3& V);


    //manipulation functions
    void Set(double x1,double y1,double z1);
    void Set(const Vector3& V);
    double getX() { return x; }
    void setX(double value) { x = value; }
    double getY() { return y; }
    void setY(double value) { y = value; }
    double getZ() { return z; }
    void setZ(double value) { z = value; }
    void Move( double mx,double my,double mz);
    void operator+=(const Vector3& V);
    void operator-=(const Vector3& V);
    void operator*=(const Vector3& V);
```

```
    void operator/=(const Vector3& V);
    Vector3 operator/(const double& d);
    bool operator==( const Vector3& V ) const;
    bool operator!=( const Vector3& V ) const;

    //exporters to Direct3D vectors
    D3DXVECTOR3 ToD3DXVECTOR3();
    D3DXVECTOR2 ToD3DXVECTOR2();
};
```

Also in the `Vector.cpp` source code file is the `Vector3` class implementation:

```
Vector3::Vector3()
{
    x = y = z = 0;
}

Vector3::Vector3( const Vector3& V )
{
    *this = V;
}

Vector3::Vector3( double x, double y, double z )
{
    Set( x, y, z );
}

Vector3::Vector3( int x, int y, int z)
{
    Set((double)x,(double)y,(double)z);
}

Vector3::Vector3(const D3DXVECTOR2& dv)
{
    x=dv.x; y=dv.y; z=0.0;
}

Vector3::Vector3(const D3DXVECTOR3& dv)
{
    x=dv.x; y=dv.y; z=dv.z;
}
```

```
//assignment operator
Vector3& Vector3::operator=( const Vector3& V)
{
    Set(V);
    return *this;
}

void Vector3::Set( double x1,double y1,double z1 )
{
    x=x1; y=y1; z=z1;
}

void Vector3::Set( const Vector3& V)
{
    x=V.x; y=V.y; z=V.z;
}

void Vector3::Move( double mx,double my,double mz)
{
    x+=mx; y+=my; z+=mz;
}

void Vector3::operator+=(const Vector3& V)
{
    x+=V.x; y+=V.y; z+=V.z;
}

void Vector3::operator-=(const Vector3& V)
{
    x-=V.x; y-=V.y; z-=V.z;
}

void Vector3::operator*=(const Vector3& V)
{
    x*=V.x; y*=V.y; z*=V.z;
}

void Vector3::operator/=(const Vector3& V)
{
    x/=V.x; y/=V.y; z/=V.z;
}
```

```
Vector3 Vector3::operator/(const double& d)
{
    Vector3 v( x/d, y/d, z/d );
    return v;
}


//equality operator comparison includes rounding
bool Vector3::operator==( const Vector3& V ) const
{
    return (
        (((V.x - 0.0001f) < x) && (x < (V.x + 0.0001f))) &&
        (((V.y - 0.0001f) < y) && (y < (V.y + 0.0001f))) &&
        (((V.z - 0.0001f) < z) && (z < (V.z + 0.0001f))) );
}


//inequality operator
bool Vector3::operator!=( const Vector3& V ) const
{
    return (!(*this == V));
}

D3DXVECTOR3 Vector3::ToD3DXVECTOR3()
{
    return D3DXVECTOR3( (float)x, (float)y, (float)z);
}

D3DXVECTOR2 Vector3::ToD3DXVECTOR2()
{
    return D3DXVECTOR2( (float)x, (float)y );
}
```

MATH FUNCTIONS

We're going to create a new Math class to provide reusable functions for vectors and matrices. The Math class provides reusable functions that could be implemented in the other classes (Vector2, etc.), but we want to define these functions as static and keep the data types as lightweight as possible. The math functions will be overloaded in some cases with various parameters to support both the

`Vector2` and `Vector3` classes and some intrinsic data types. Here are some of the calculations the new `Math` class will provide:

- Distance
- Length
- Dot product
- Cross product
- Normal
- Radian conversion
- Degree conversion
- Linear velocity
- Angle-to-target vector

We'll gloss over the more mundane (but still very important) functions and jump right into an explanation of the two more valuable ones: linear velocity and angle-to-target vector.

Advice

I found the following website to be a helpful reference for the math behind computer graphics concepts such as points, lines, vectors, and matrices: http://programmedlessons.org/VectorLessons/vectorIndex.html.

Linear Velocity

Have you ever wondered how some shooter-style games are able to fire projectiles (be they bullets, missiles, plasma bolts, phaser beams, or what have you) at any odd angle away from the player's ship, as well as at any angle from enemy sprites? These projectiles are moving using velocity values (for X and Y) that are based on the object's direction (or angle) of movement. Given any angle, we can calculate the velocity needed to move in precisely that direction. This applies to aircraft, sea vessels, spacecraft, as well as projectiles, missiles, lasers, plasma bolts, or any other object that needs to move at a given angle (presumably toward a target).

The X velocity of a game entity can be calculated for any angle, and that value is then multiplied by the speed at which you want the object to move in the given direction. The `LinearVelocityX` function (below) automatically orients the angle to quadrant four of the Cartesian coordinate system and converts the angle from degrees to radians. Since the cosine function gives us the *horizontal* value of a point on a circle, we use cosine to calculate the X velocity as if we were drawing a circle based on a small radius.

```
double Math::linearVelocityX(double angle)
{
    angle -= 90;
    if (angle < 0) angle = 360 + angle;
    return cos( toRadians( angle ) );
}
```

Likewise for the Y velocity value, we use the Y position on the edge of a circle (based on radius) for the calculation using the sine function.

```
double Math::linearVelocityY(double angle)
{
    angle -= 90;
    if (angle < 0) angle = 360 + angle;
    return sin( toRadians( angle ) );
}
```

As it turns out, the "velocity" of an object based on an angle—that is, its linear velocity—is simply the same pair of X,Y values that would be calculated when tracing the boundary of a circle (based on a radius).

Angle to Target

Calculating the angle from one point to another (as in the case where one sprite is targeting another) is extremely useful (if not crucial) in most games. Imagine you are working on a real-time strategy game. You must program the game so that the player can select units with the mouse and right-click a target location where the unit must move to. Even a simple process like that requires a calculation—between the unit's location and the selected target location in the game. In the space shooter genre, in order to fire at the player's ship, enemies must be able to face the player to fire in the correct direction. I could provide you with many more examples, but I suspect you get the point. The key to this important need is a calculation that I like to call *angle to target*.

The calculation is very simple—about as simple as calculating angular velocity, which is much simpler than the `Distance` function. We need to use another trigonometry function this time: `atan2()`. This is a standard C math library function that calculates the arctangent of two deltas—first the Y delta, then the X delta. A *delta* is the difference between two values. For our purposes here, we need to get the delta of both X and Y for two points. For instance, if Point A is located at X1,Y1, and Point B is located at X2,Y2, then we can calculate the delta of the two points like so:

```
deltaX = X2 - X1
deltaY = Y2 - Y1
```

The `atan2()` function requires the `deltaY` first, then the `deltaX` parameter. Here is the `AngleToTarget` method as it appears in the `Math` class:

```
double Math::angleToTarget(double x1, double y1, double x2, double y2)
{
    double deltaX = (x2-x1);
    double deltaY = (y2-y1);
    return atan2(deltaY,deltaX);
}
```

I have coded an overloaded version of this function so you can pass `Vector3` values:

```
double Math::angleToTarget(Vector3& A,Vector3& B)
{
    return angleToTarget(A.getX(),A.getY(),B.getX(),B.getY());
}
```

Math Class Header

Here is the header for the `Math` class with some constants pre-defined for convenience:

```
#pragma once
#include "stdafx.h"
#include "Vector.h"
namespace Octane
{
    const double PI = 3.1415926535;
    const double PI_over_180 = PI / 180.0f;
    const double PI_under_180 = 180.0f / PI;
```

```
class Math
{
public:
    static double toDegrees(double radian);
    static double toRadians(double degree);
    static double wrapAngleDegs(double degs);
    static double wrapAngleRads(double rads);
    static double wrapValue(double value, double min, double max);
    static double Limit(double value, double min, double max); //***addition
    static double linearVelocityX(double angle);
    static double linearVelocityY(double angle);
    static Vector2 linearVelocity(double angle);
    static double angleToTarget(double x1,double y1,double x2,double y2);
    static double angleToTarget(Vector3& source,Vector3& target);
    static double angleToTarget(Vector2& source,Vector2& target);
    static double Distance(double x1,double y1,double z1, double x2,double
y2,double z2);
    static double Distance(double x1,double y1,double x2,double y2);
    static double Distance(Vector3& A, Vector3& B);
    static double Distance(Vector2& A, Vector2& B);
    static double Length(double x,double y,double z);
    static double Length(double x,double y);
    static double Length(Vector3& V);
    static double Length(Vector2& V);
    static double dotProduct(double x1,double y1,double z1,double x2,
double y2,double z2);
    static double dotProduct(double x1,double y1,double x2,double y2);
    static double dotProduct(Vector3& A, Vector3& B);
    static double dotProduct(Vector2& A, Vector2& B);
    static Vector3 crossProduct(double x1,double y1,double z1,double x2,
double y2,double z2);
    static Vector3 crossProduct(Vector3& A, Vector3& B);
    static Vector3 Normal(double x,double y,double z);
    static Vector3 Normal(Vector3& V);
    };
};
```

Math Class Implementation

Now we can go over the code for the Math implementation file. The Math class includes the angular velocity and angle-to-target functions, which I will explain in detail in subsequent sections of the chapter.

```
#include "stdafx.h"
#include "Engine.h"
namespace Octane
{
    double Math::toDegrees(double radians)
    {
        return radians * PI_under_180;
    }

    double Math::toRadians(double degrees)
    {
        return degrees * PI_over_180;
    }

    double Math::wrapAngleDegs(double degs)
    {
        double result = fmod(degs, 360.0);
        if (result < 0) result += 360.0f;
        return result;
    }

    double Math::wrapAngleRads(double rads)
    {
        double result = fmod(rads, PI);
        if (result < 0) result += PI;
        return result;
    }

    double Math::wrapValue(double value, double min, double max)
    {
        if (value < min) value = max;
        else if (value > max) value = min;
        return value;
    }

    double Math::Limit(double value, double min, double max)
    {
        if (value < min) value = min;
        else if (value > max) value = max;
        return value;
    }
```

```
/**
Calculate X velocity based on degree angle
**/
double Math::linearVelocityX(double angle)
{
    angle -= 90;
    if (angle < 0) angle = 360 + angle;
    return cos( toRadians( angle ) );
}


/**
Calculate Y velocity based on degree angle
**/
double Math::linearVelocityY(double angle)
{
    angle -= 90;
    if (angle < 0) angle = 360 + angle;
    return sin( toRadians( angle ) );
}


/**
Calculate Vector velocity based on degree angle
**/
Vector2 Math::linearVelocity(double angle)
{
    double vx = linearVelocityX(angle);
    double vy = linearVelocityY(angle);
    return Vector2(vx,vy);
}

double Math::angleToTarget(double x1,double y1,double x2,double y2)
{
    double deltaX = (x2-x1);
    double deltaY = (y2-y1);
    return atan2(deltaY,deltaX);
}

double Math::angleToTarget(Vector3& A, Vector3& B)
{
    return angleToTarget(A.getX(),A.getY(),B.getX(),B.getY());
}
```

```
double Math::angleToTarget(Vector2& A, Vector2& B)
{
    return angleToTarget(A.getX(),A.getY(),B.getX(),B.getY());
}

double Math::Distance( double x1,double y1,double z1,
    double x2,double y2,double z2 )
{
    double deltaX = (x2-x1);
    double deltaY = (y2-y1);
    double deltaZ = (z2-z1);
    return sqrt(deltaX*deltaX + deltaY*deltaY + deltaZ*deltaZ);
}


double Math::Distance( double x1,double y1,double x2,double y2 )
{
    double deltaX = (x2-x1);
    double deltaY = (y2-y1);
    return sqrt(deltaX*deltaX + deltaY*deltaY);
}

double Math::Distance( Vector3& A, Vector3& B )
{
    return Distance(A.getX(),A.getY(),A.getZ(),
        B.getX(),B.getY(),B.getZ());
}

double Math::Distance( Vector2& A, Vector2& B )
{
    return Distance(A.getX(),A.getY(), B.getX(),B.getY());
}

double Math::Length(double x,double y,double z)
{
    return sqrt(x*x + y*y + z*z);
}

double Math::Length(double x,double y)
{
    return sqrt(x*x + y*y);
}
```

```cpp
double Math::Length(Vector3& V)
{
    return Length(V.getX(),V.getY(),V.getZ());
}

double Math::Length(Vector2& V)
{
    return Length(V.getX(),V.getY());
}

double Math::dotProduct(double x1,double y1,double z1,
    double x2,double y2,double z2)
{
    return (x1*x2 + y1*y2 + z1*z2);
}

double Math::dotProduct(double x1,double y1,double x2,double y2)
{
    return (x1*x2 + y1*y2);
}

double Math::dotProduct( Vector3& A, Vector3& B )
{
    return dotProduct(A.getX(),A.getY(),A.getZ(),
        B.getX(),B.getY(),B.getZ());
}

double Math::dotProduct( Vector2& A, Vector2& B )
{
    return dotProduct(A.getX(),A.getY(),B.getX(),B.getY());
}

Vector3 Math::crossProduct( double x1,double y1,double z1,
    double x2,double y2,double z2)
{
    double nx = (y1*z2)-(z1*y2);
    double ny = (z1*y2)-(x1*z2);
    double nz = (x1*y2)-(y1*x2);
    return Vector3(nx,ny,nz);
}
```

```
Vector3 Math::crossProduct( Vector3& A, Vector3& B )
{
    return crossProduct(A.getX(),A.getY(),A.getZ(),B.getX(),B.getY(),
B.getZ());
}

Vector3 Math::Normal(double x,double y,double z)
{
    double length = Length(x,y,z);
    if (length != 0) length = 1 / length;
    double nx = x*length;
    double ny = y*length;
    double nz = z*length;
    return Vector3(nx,ny,nz);
}

Vector3 Math::Normal(Vector3& V)
{
    return Normal(V.getX(),V.getY(),V.getZ());
}
};
```

Now that you have the Math class available, you can begin exploring its features in a more convenient way (as opposed to writing examples with C++ functions, and then porting them to the class afterward—you can now just defer to the class directly).

Math Vector Demo

Let's run the new Math and Vector classes through a few tests to make sure they're working as expected. This is always a good idea before plugging a new module or class into the engine (and assuming it works without testing). Figure 7.2 shows the output of the Math Vector Demo program. Toward the end of the code listing, I have retained the unused events for reference, since we have not used the event system since it was created in the previous chapter.

```
#include "Engine.h"
#include "Vector.h"
#include "Math.h"
using namespace std;
using namespace Octane;
```

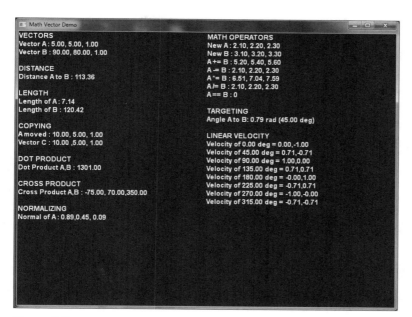

Figure 7.2
This program demonstrates the Math and Vector classes.

```
Font *font=NULL;
float elapsed=0.0f;

//unused functions
void game_render3d() {}

bool game_preload()
{
    g_engine->setAppTitle("Math Vector Demo");
    g_engine->setScreen(800,600,32,false);
    return true;
}

bool game_init(HWND hwnd)
{
    font = new Font("Arial Bold",18);
    if (!font)
    {
        debug << "Error creating font" << endl;
```

```
            return false;
        }
        return true;
}

void game_end()
{
    if (font) delete font;
}

void game_update( float elapsedTime )
{
    elapsed = elapsedTime;
}

void game_render2d()
{
    std::ostringstream out;
    out.setf(ios::fixed);
    out << setprecision(2);

    out << "VECTORS" << endl;
        Vector3 A(5,5,1);
    out << "Vector A : " <<
        A.getX() << ", " << A.getY() << ", " << A.getZ() << endl;

        Vector3 B(90,80,1);
    out << "Vector B : " <<
        B.getX() << ", " << B.getY() << ", " << B.getZ() << endl;

    out << endl << "DISTANCE" << endl;
    out << "Distance A to B : " << Math::Distance( A, B ) << endl;

    out << endl << "LENGTH" << endl;
    out << "Length of A : " << Math::Length(A) << endl;
    out << "Length of B : " << Math::Length(B) << endl;

    out << endl << "COPYING" << endl;
        A.Move(5, 0, 0);
```

```
out << "A moved : " <<
    A.getX() << ", " << A.getY() << ", " << A.getZ() << endl;


    Vector3 C = A;
out << "Vector C : " <<
    C.getX() << " ," << C.getY() << ", " << C.getZ() << endl;


out << endl << "DOT PRODUCT" << endl;
out << "Dot Product A,B : " << Math::dotProduct(A,B) << endl;


out << endl << "CROSS PRODUCT" << endl;
Vector3 D = Math::crossProduct(A,B);
out << "Cross Product A,B : " <<
    D.getX() << ", " << D.getY() << "," << D.getZ() << endl;


out << endl << "NORMALIZING" << endl;
D = Math::Normal(A);
out << "Normal of A : " <<
    D.getX() << "," << D.getY() << ", " << D.getZ() << endl;


font->Print(0, 0, out.str() );

//start second column
out.str("");
out << "MATH OPERATORS" << endl;
    A.Set(2.1,2.2,2.3);
    B.Set(3.1,3.2,3.3);
out << "New A : " <<
    A.getX() << ", " << A.getY() << ", " << A.getZ() << endl;
out << "New B : " <<
    B.getX() << ", " << B.getY() << ", " << B.getZ() << endl;


    A += B;
out << "A += B : " <<
    A.getX() << ", " << A.getY() << ", " << A.getZ() << endl;


    A -= B;
out << "A -= B : " <<
    A.getX() << ", " << A.getY() << ", " << A.getZ() << endl;
```

```
            A *= B;
    out << "A *= B : " <<
        A.getX() << ", " << A.getY() << ", " << A.getZ() << endl;


            A /= B;
    out << "A /= B : " <<
        A.getX() << ", " << A.getY() << ", " << A.getZ() << endl;

    out << "A == B : " << (A == B) << endl;

    out << endl << "TARGETING" << endl;
    double angle = Math::angleToTarget( A, B );
        out << "Angle A to B: " << angle << " rad ("
        << Math::toDegrees(angle) << " deg)" << endl;


    out << endl << "LINEAR VELOCITY" << endl;
        for (angle=0; angle<360; angle+=45)
    {
        double x = Math::linearVelocityX(angle);
        double y = Math::linearVelocityY(angle);
            out << "Velocity of " << angle <<
            " deg = " << x << "," << y << endl;
    }

    font->Print(400, 0, out.str() );
}

void game_event( IEvent* e )
{
    switch( e->getID() )
    {
        case EVENT_KEYPRESS:
        {
            KeyPressEvent* evt = (KeyPressEvent*) e;
            if (evt->keycode == DIK_ESCAPE)
                g_engine->Shutdown();
            break;
        }
    }
}
```

MATRICES

All 3D graphics calculations can be done with trigonometry, but using sine and cosine functions to calculate angles is very slow compared to matrix math. In simple terms, a *matrix* is a rectangular (that is, 2D) array of numbers.[1] According to Wolfram, a *matrix* is "a concise and useful way of uniquely representing and working with *linear transformations*." The matrix is an important concept in linear algebra, first formulated by mathematicians Sylvester and Cayley in the nineteenth century. A game programmer who has never benefitted from a linear algebra course might have assumed that matrices were a recent invention!

A matrix represents a system of equations, where each system (or sequence) is represented by a row in the matrix. If we use a one-dimensional matrix row such as:

[10, 18, 47, 12]

and perform the same calculation on each matrix element (say, multiplying by 2), that might be represented as:

[10*2, 18*2, 47*2, 12*2] = [20, 36, 94, 24]

Figure 7.3 shows a typical 4×4 matrix. Most math references will refer to a 3×3 matrix, and this is indeed the type of matrix needed to perform a single transform (such as translation or rotation). But in 3D graphics programming we use a 4×4 matrix because it can represent more than one transform at a time: translation *and* rotation *and* scaling, if desired. Each value within the matrix is called a *matrix element*.

A matrix is composed of any number of columns and rows (Figure 7.4), but we most commonly use a 3×3 or 4×4 matrix for 3D graphics transforms. To get the orientation correct: An *m X n* matrix consists of *m* rows and *n* columns. Figure 7.5 shows a 3×4 matrix.

Zero and Identity Matrices

Addition and subtraction of matrices is done with the help of a zero matrix. Just like adding zero to any real number results in an unchanged number, so to does adding or subtracting a matrix from a zero matrix result in the original *unchanged*

Figure 7.3
A 4 × 4 matrix is used for fast 3D transform calculations.

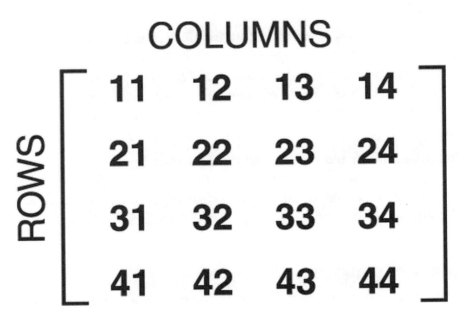

Figure 7.4
A matrix is described in terms of *rows X columns*.

Figure 7.5
This 3 × 4 matrix has *3 rows* and *4 columns*.

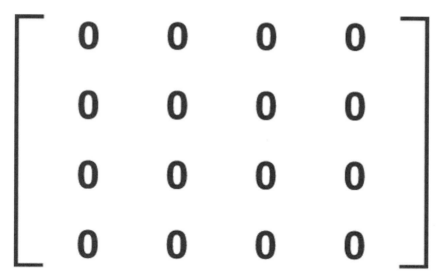

Figure 7.6
A zero matrix is a matrix with all elements set to zero.

matrix. Think of this as a *starting point* when performing addition or subtraction operations on a matrix. Remember, a matrix represents a system, or sequence, of equations. Figure 7.6 shows an illustration of a zero matrix.

An *identity matrix* (Figure 7.7) is used for multiplication and division operations, representing a value of 1 for such calculations (similar to the zero matrix

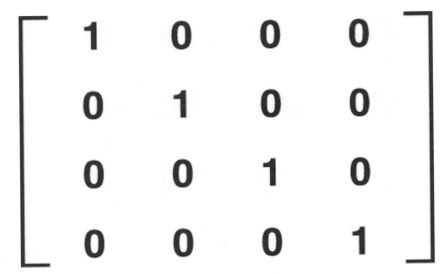

Figure 7.7
An identity matrix is used to reset transformations.

when performing addition and subtraction of matrices). An identity matrix is filled with zeroes, except for the diagonal from upper left to lower right, represented by matrix elements 11, 22, 33, 44. We use an identity matrix to reset any existing transformations back to the origin (0, 0, 0). Every 3D transform must start with the identity matrix, otherwise transforms become additive!

For example, imagine you are rendering a mesh at position (10, 10, 0) in 3D space. From a default camera in a left-handed coordinate system, the object would be located near the upper-left part of the camera's viewport. Now, suppose you render *another* object at (−10, 10, 0), *without* using an identity matrix to reset the transforms currently in place. Instead of actually moving to (−10, 10, 0) in the scene, the object will be positioned *relative* to the *last* transform, which was at (10, 10, 0), where the first mesh is located. That results in a position of:

$$(10, 10, 0) + (-10, 10, 0) = (10 + -10, 10 + 10, 0 + 0) = (0, 20, 0)$$

which is not at all what one might have expected!

Matrix Operations

A matrix can be modified by any mathematical operation with any real number or any other matrix. To be consistent, be sure to only perform operations on matrices with the same dimensions, or you may get unexpected results. Think of a 4×4 matrix as an *encoded* transform containing (potentially) the translation, rotation, *and* scaling matrices. We could use a 4×4 matrix to represent the transforms of anything—a mesh, an entire environment, or a light, or even a camera. All operations involving a real number are performed on all of the elements inside the matrix. For example:

[2.0, 5.0, 9.0, 3.0] * 0.5 = [1.0, 2.5, 4.5, 1.5]

The same process occurs for all of the matrix elements, although this example only illustrates one row.

Operations can also be performed between two matrices. One of the most common is matrix multiplication. We multiply two matrices together to *combine* them. For instance, when passing a matrix to an effect for rendering (i.e., the vertex and pixel shaders), the *world, view,* and *projection* matrices are often passed together in one combined matrix. (Granted, for best performance, all three are passed so the GPU can combine them, but bear with me for this *fixed function pipeline* illustration.)

`MatrixWVP = WorldMatrix * ViewMatrix * ProjectionMatrix;`

Another typical use for matrix multiplication is combining the transforms of an object before it is transformed and rendered:

`WorldMatrix = RotationMatrix * ScalingMatrix * TranslateMatrix;`

If `RotationMatrix` = [2, 3, 1, 5] (simplified for illustration—assume there are 4 rows), and `ScalingMatrix` = [8, 3, 9, 4], then:

[2, 3, 1, 5] * [8, 3, 9, 4] = [2*8, 3*3, 1*9, 5*4] = [16, 9, 9, 20]

This combined matrix is then multiplied by the next matrix in the calculation. If `TranslateMatrix` = [0, 10, 10, −5], then:

[16, 9, 9, 20] * [0, 10, 10, −5] = [16*0, 9*10, 9*10, 20*−5] = [0, 90, 90, −100]

The resulting combined matrix for a mesh, or camera, or any other use in the 3D scene, is called the "world matrix." The "world matrix" just represents the current transformation. In this example:

`WorldMatrix` = [0, 90, 90, −100]

The same premise for matrix multiplication holds true for addition, subtraction, division, and any other mathematical operation performed between two matrices.

Direct3D Matrices

If you want to write your own matrix code, you can still work within D3D by passing a D3DXMATRIX to any Direct3D functions that need it (like an effect). The DirectX SDK defines a D3DMATRIX struct in the d3dx9math.h header file like so:

```
typedef struct _D3DMATRIX {
    union {
        struct {
            float           _11, _12, _13, _14;
            float           _21, _22, _23, _24;
            float           _31, _32, _33, _34;
            float           _41, _42, _43, _44;

        };
        float m[4][4];
    };
} D3DMATRIX;
```

This is the base struct for handling matrices in Direct3D. Another data type called D3DXMATRIX extends D3DMATRIX by adding calculations with overloaded math operators and other conveniences. By inheriting these features from D3DXMATRIX, we do not need to code them on our own, but doing so would be a good learning experience! (Especially considering that D3DX no longer exists in DirectX 10 and 11.)

```
typedef struct D3DXMATRIX : public D3DMATRIX
{
public:
    D3DXMATRIX() {};
    D3DXMATRIX( CONST FLOAT * );
    D3DXMATRIX( CONST D3DMATRIX& );
    D3DXMATRIX( CONST D3DXFLOAT16 * );
    D3DXMATRIX( FLOAT _11, FLOAT _12, FLOAT _13, FLOAT _14,
                FLOAT _21, FLOAT _22, FLOAT _23, FLOAT _24,
                FLOAT _31, FLOAT _32, FLOAT _33, FLOAT _34,
                FLOAT _41, FLOAT _42, FLOAT _43, FLOAT _44 );


    // access grants
    FLOAT& operator () ( UINT Row, UINT Col );
    FLOAT  operator () ( UINT Row, UINT Col ) const;
```

```
    // casting operators
    operator FLOAT* ();
    operator CONST FLOAT* () const;

    // assignment operators
    D3DXMATRIX& operator *= ( CONST D3DXMATRIX& );
    D3DXMATRIX& operator += ( CONST D3DXMATRIX& );
    D3DXMATRIX& operator -= ( CONST D3DXMATRIX& );
    D3DXMATRIX& operator *= ( FLOAT );
    D3DXMATRIX& operator /= ( FLOAT );

    // unary operators
    D3DXMATRIX operator + () const;
    D3DXMATRIX operator - () const;

    // binary operators
    D3DXMATRIX operator * ( CONST D3DXMATRIX& ) const;
    D3DXMATRIX operator + ( CONST D3DXMATRIX& ) const;
    D3DXMATRIX operator - ( CONST D3DXMATRIX& ) const;
    D3DXMATRIX operator * ( FLOAT ) const;
    D3DXMATRIX operator / ( FLOAT ) const;

    friend D3DXMATRIX operator * ( FLOAT, CONST D3DXMATRIX& );

    BOOL operator == ( CONST D3DXMATRIX& ) const;
    BOOL operator != ( CONST D3DXMATRIX& ) const;

} D3DXMATRIX, *LPD3DXMATRIX;
```

Of particular interest are the overloaded constructors, including this one:

```
D3DXMATRIX( FLOAT _11, FLOAT _12, FLOAT _13, FLOAT _14,
            FLOAT _21, FLOAT _22, FLOAT _23, FLOAT _24,
            FLOAT _31, FLOAT _32, FLOAT _33, FLOAT _34,
            FLOAT _41, FLOAT _42, FLOAT _43, FLOAT _44 );
```

Using this D3DXMATRIX constructor with your own Matrix class, as well as the *float m[4][4]* array and the individual float properties _11, _12, _13, etc., it's entirely possible to write your own matrix code and then just convert to and from the Direct3D matrix data types (preferably with inline code for best performance).

Matrix Transforms

When we have a way to easily print out the values in a matrix, things get really interesting (from a learning point of view). We can actually see what all of the values are after performing various transformations!

When a translation transformation is calculated, and the results stored in a matrix, the X,Y,Z values for the new position are stored in matrix elements 14, 24, and 34 (see Figure 7.8).

For a scaling transformation, the result is stored in matrix elements 11, 22, and 33 (see Figure 7.9).

A rotation transformation affects more than just three matrix elements. Rotating on the X-axis affects elements 22, 23, 32, and 33. Rotating on the Y-axis affects elements 11, 13, 31, and 33. Rotating on the Z-axis affects elements 22, 23, 32, and 33. (See Figure 7.10.) While we can derive which matrix elements are being modifed by observing the element values after performing transformations on the matrix, we really do not know from this exactly what's happening. Tables 7.1, 7.2, and 7.3 show the actual content of a matrix after each transformation is

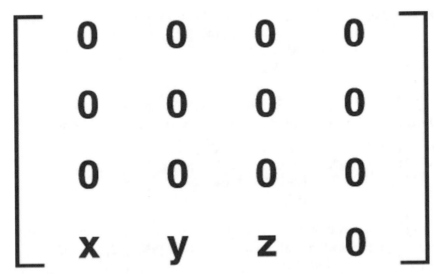

Figure 7.8
A translation transformation affects matrix elements 14, 24, 34.

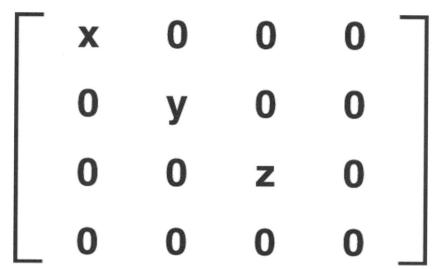

Figure 7.9
A scaling transformation affects matrix elements 11, 22, 33.

Figure 7.10
A rotation transformation affects matrix elements 11, 13, 22, 23, 31, 32, and 33.

Table 7.1 X rotation matrix

	C1	C2	C3	C4
R1	1	0	0	0
R2	0	$\cos(\theta)$	$-\sin(\theta)$	0
R3	0	$\sin(\theta)$	$\cos(\theta)$	0
R4	0	0	0	1

Table 7.2 Y rotation matrix

	C1	C2	C3	C4
R1	$\cos(\theta)$	0	$-\sin(\theta)$	0
R2	0	1	0	0
R3	$\sin(\theta)$	0	$\cos(\theta)$	0
R4	0	0	0	1

Table 7.3 Z rotation matrix

	C1	C2	C3	C4
R1	$\cos(\theta)$	$-\sin(\theta)$	0	0
R2	$\sin(\theta)$	$\cos(\theta)$	0	0
R3	0	0	1	0
R4	0	0	0	1

calculated (for rotations X, Y, and Z, respectively). You'll note that all three would fit inside a 3 × 3 matrix, but by using a 4 × 4 we can combine rotation with the other transformations[2].

Matrix Struct

We're going to start with a meager `Matrix` struct and then expand it in the future as needed. For now, all we need to do is extend the base `D3DXMATRIX` and our own `Matrix` struct can then be passed to Direct3D functions without the need for typecasting or conversion functions. We don't necessarily want to replicate all of the functionality in D3DXMATRIX immediately, because that could lead to bugs in our rendering code later. We *will* probably want to replace all of the D3DX functions with our own eventually. What we *do* want is to learn, and as long as performance is not impaired, it's okay to replace some of the basic D3DX matrix code with our own right now.

You might be wondering, why use a struct, instead of a class? Good question! The reason is, D3DXMATRIX is a struct, and we want to just inherit its properties and functions without reinventing the wheel all at once. Later on, perhaps this will evolve into a full class.

Advice

If you want to examine the code for most of the calculations performed on Direct3D matrices, take a look at the d3dx9math.inl file from the downloads found at www.jharbour.com/forum or www.courseptr.com/downloads.

Identity Matrix

Let's start with an identity matrix function. Since D3DX exposes functions such as D3DXMatrixIdentity, we can code it into our class internally and bypass the D3DX function. Here is the D3DX version:

```
D3DXINLINE D3DXMATRIX* D3DXMatrixIdentity( D3DXMATRIX *pOut )
{
    pOut->m[0][1] = pOut->m[0][2] = pOut->m[0][3] =
    pOut->m[1][0] = pOut->m[1][2] = pOut->m[1][3] =
    pOut->m[2][0] = pOut->m[2][1] = pOut->m[2][3] =
    pOut->m[3][0] = pOut->m[3][1] = pOut->m[3][2] = 0.0f;
    pOut->m[0][0] = pOut->m[1][1] = pOut->m[2][2] = pOut->m[3][3] = 1.0f;
    return pOut;
}
```

Our own version looks almost identical (because the float m[][] array is shared):

```
void Matrix::setIdentity()
{
    //set most elements to zero
    m[0][1] = m[0][2] = m[0][3] =
    m[1][0] = m[1][2] = m[1][3] =
```

```
    m[2][0] = m[2][1] = m[2][3] =
    m[3][0] = m[3][1] = m[3][2] = 0.0f;

    //set diagonals 11,22,33,44 to one
    m[0][0] = m[1][1] = m[2][2] = m[3][3] = 1.0f;
}
```

Zero Matrix

The zero matrix can be easily set by just setting all of the matrix elements to zero, like so:

```
void Matrix::setZero()
{
    Fill( 0.0f );
}
void Matrix::Fill( float value )
{
    m[0][0] = m[0][1] = m[0][2] = m[0][3] =
    m[1][0] = m[1][1] = m[1][2] = m[1][3] =
    m[2][0] = m[2][1] = m[2][2] = m[2][3] =
    m[3][0] = m[3][1] = m[3][2] = m[3][3] = value;
}
```

Matrix Struct Interface

We can now create a fairly well-balanced Matrix structure with quite a bit of added functionality beyond its parent, D3DXMATRIX. I have included rudimentary copy constructors and assignment operators for various data types and rudimentary transformation functions. The idea is to reduce calls to D3DX functions from inside the engine code and roll at least the most commonly used ones into struct functions.

Advice

When building a struct or class that will see frequent but short lifetimes, it's recommended that you not write any code as *inline* inside the interface/header file because that code is allocated with the struct or class definition every time it is instantiated. On the other hand, functions implemented in a separate .cpp file are *called*, not actually stored inside the instantiated object. This struct definition below has quite a few functions but it is still extremely lightweight.

```
struct Matrix : public D3DXMATRIX
  {
  public:
      Matrix();
      Matrix( const Matrix& );
      Matrix( const D3DXMATRIX& );
      Matrix& operator=( const Matrix& );
      Matrix& operator=( const D3DXMATRIX& );
      void setZero();
      void setIdentity();
      void Fill( int );
      void Fill( float );
      void Fill( double );
      void Translate( float x, float y, float z );
      void Translate( Vector3& );
      void rotateYawPitchRoll( float x, float y, float z );
      void rotateYawPitchRoll( Vector3& );
      void rotateX( float );
      void rotateY( float );
      void rotateZ( float );
      void Scale( float x, float y, float z );
      void Scale( Vector3& );
  };
```

Matrix Struct Implementation

The implementation is found in the source code file `Matrix.cpp`, which will belong in the engine's *support module*. As you can see from the code, we're still highly coupled with D3DX, but that's to be expected (and desired) during the early stages of the engine's development. Let's not reinvent the wheel just for the sake of doing everything on our own! There are some things we simply do not have time (let alone knowledge and experience) to implement on our own—and to try is wasteful.

```
Matrix::Matrix() : D3DXMATRIX() { }

Matrix::Matrix(const Matrix& M) : D3DXMATRIX(M)
{
    *this = M;
}
```

```
Matrix::Matrix( const D3DXMATRIX& M ) : D3DXMATRIX(M)
{
    *this = M;
}


Matrix& Matrix::operator=( const Matrix& M )
{
    memcpy( m, &M.m, sizeof(float)*16 );
    return *this;
}


Matrix& Matrix::operator=( const D3DXMATRIX& M )
{
    memcpy( m, &M.m, sizeof(float)*16 );
    return *this;
}


void Matrix::setZero()
{
    Fill( 0.0f );
}


void Matrix::setIdentity()
{
    //set most elements to zero
    m[0][1] = m[0][2] = m[0][3] =
    m[1][0] = m[1][2] = m[1][3] =
    m[2][0] = m[2][1] = m[2][3] =
    m[3][0] = m[3][1] = m[3][2] = 0.0f;

    //set diagonals 11,22,33,44 to one
    m[0][0] = m[1][1] = m[2][2] = m[3][3] = 1.0f;
}


void Matrix::Fill( int value )
{
    Fill( (float) value );
}
```

```
void Matrix::Fill( float value )
{
    m[0][0] = m[0][1] = m[0][2] = m[0][3] =
    m[1][0] = m[1][1] = m[1][2] = m[1][3] =
    m[2][0] = m[2][1] = m[2][2] = m[2][3] =
    m[3][0] = m[3][1] = m[3][2] = m[3][3] = value;
}

void Matrix::Fill( double value )
{
    Fill ((float) value );
}

void Matrix::Translate( float x, float y, float z )
{
    D3DXMatrixTranslation( (D3DXMATRIX*) this, x, y, z );
}

void Matrix::Translate( Vector3& V )
{
    Translate( (float)V.x, (float)V.y, (float)V.z );
}

void Matrix::rotateYawPitchRoll( float x, float y, float z )
{
    D3DXMatrixRotationYawPitchRoll( (D3DXMATRIX*) this, x, y, z);
}

void Matrix::rotateYawPitchRoll( Vector3& V )
{
    rotateYawPitchRoll( (float)V.x, (float)V.y, (float)V.z );
}

void Matrix::rotateX( float x )
{
    D3DXMatrixRotationX( (D3DXMATRIX*) this, x );
}

void Matrix::rotateY( float y )
{
    D3DXMatrixRotationY( (D3DXMATRIX*) this, y );
}
```

```
void Matrix::rotateZ( float z )
{
    D3DXMatrixRotationX( (D3DXMATRIX*) this, z );
}

void Matrix::Scale( float x, float y, float z )
{
    D3DXMatrixScaling( (D3DXMATRIX*) this, x, y, z );
}

void Matrix::Scale( Vector3& V )
{
    Scale( (float)V.x, (float)V.y, (float)V.z );
}
```

Math Matrix Demo

The Math Matrix Demo (see Figure 7.11) shows how to use the new Matrix struct. As discussed earlier, Matrix extends D3DXMATRIX, so we'll be able to make use of any intrinsic helper functions inside D3DXMATRIX, as well as the grandparent D3DMATRIX struct's matrix elements (_11, _12, etc.).

```
#include "stdafx.h"
#include "Engine.h"
#include "Vector.h"
#include "Matrix.h"
using namespace std;
using namespace Octane;

Font *font=NULL;

bool game_preload()
{
    g_engine->setAppTitle("Math Matrix Demo");
    g_engine->setScreen(1024,768,32,false);
    return true;
}

bool game_init(HWND hwnd)
{
    font = new Font("Arial Bold",18);
```

Figure 7.11
The Math Matrix Demo demonstrates our new custom `Matrix` code.

```
    if (!font)
    {
        debug << "Error creating font" << endl;
        return false;
    }
    return true;
}

void game_end()
{
    if (font) delete font;
}

void game_update( float elapsedTime ) { }
void game_render3d() {}
```

```cpp
std::string Vector2ToString( Vector2& V )
{
    ostringstream out;
    out << V.getX() << ", " << V.getY();
    return out.str();
}

std::string Vector3ToString( Vector3& V )
{
    ostringstream out;
    out << V.getX() << ", " << V.getY() << ", " << V.getZ();
    return out.str();
}

std::string MatrixToString( D3DXMATRIX& M )
{
    ostringstream out;
    out << M._11 << ", " << M._12 << ", " << M._13 << ", "
        << M._14 << endl;
    out << M._21 << ", " << M._22 << ", " << M._23 << ", "
        << M._24 << endl;
    out << M._31 << ", " << M._32 << ", " << M._33 << ", "
        << M._34 << endl;
    out << M._41 << ", " << M._42 << ", " << M._43 << ", "
        << M._44;
    return out.str();
}

void game_render2d()
{
    std::ostringstream out;
    out.setf(ios::fixed);
    out << setprecision(2);

    Matrix A;
    A.setIdentity();
    A *= 1.25f;
    out << "Matrix A * 1.25 = " << endl <<
        MatrixToString(A) << endl << endl;

    Matrix B;
```

```
B.Fill( 12.875 );
out << "Matrix B = " << endl << MatrixToString(B) <<
    endl << endl;


A += B;
out << "Matrix A + B = " << endl << MatrixToString(A) <<
    endl << endl;


Matrix C = B * 2.75;
out << "Matrix C = B * 2.75 : " << endl << MatrixToString(C) <<
    endl << endl;


D3DXMATRIX D;
D3DXMatrixRotationX( &D, 3.14f );


//instantiating a Matrix on the heap
Matrix *E = new Matrix( D );
out << "Matrix E = D (D3DXMATRIX copy) : " << endl <<
    MatrixToString( *E ) << endl << endl;


E->setIdentity();
E->Translate( 1, -2, 3 );
out << "E->Translate(1,-2,3) = " << endl <<
    MatrixToString( *E ) << endl << endl;


font->Print(0, 0, out.str() );


//start second column
out.str("");


E->Scale( 1, -2, 3 );
out << "E->Scale(1,-2,3) = " << endl << MatrixToString( *E ) <<
    endl << endl;


E->rotateX( 1 );
out << "E->RotateX(1) = " << endl << MatrixToString( *E ) <<
    endl << endl;


E->rotateY( -2 );
out << "E->RotateY(-2) = " << endl << MatrixToString( *E ) <<
    endl << endl;
```

```
    E->rotateZ( 3 );
    out << "E->RotateZ(3) = " << endl << MatrixToString( *E ) <<
        endl << endl;

    E->rotateYawPitchRoll( 1, -2, 3 );
    out << "E->RotateYawPitchRoll(1,-2,3) = " << endl <<
        MatrixToString( *E ) << endl << endl;

    delete E;

    font->Print(400, 0, out.str() );
}

void game_event( IEvent* e )
{
    switch( e->getID() )
    {
        case EVENT_KEYPRESS:
        {
            KeyPressEvent* evt = (KeyPressEvent*) e;
            if (evt->keycode == DIK_ESCAPE)
                g_engine->Shutdown();
            break;
        }
    }
}
```

SUMMARY

That wraps up our math chapter! Does it seem like we've been learning just about everything there is to learn about 3D graphics and rendering without actually rendering anything? I concur! But these are all important topics or prerequisites to an effective knowledge base about rendering techniques, so that when we do start working with animated bone meshes and environmental collision, we'll understand at least some of the math behind it all.

REFERENCES

1. Pipho, Evan. *Focus On 3D Models*. Cincinnati: Premier Press. 2003.

   "Wolfram MathWorld"; http://mathworld.wolfram.com/.

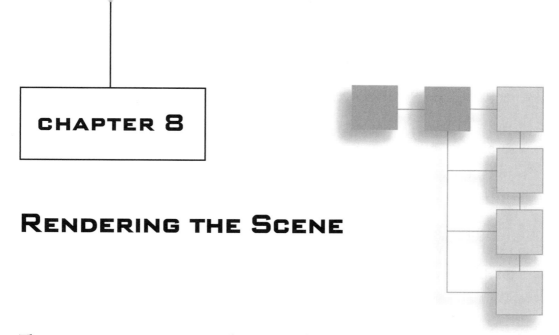

CHAPTER 8

RENDERING THE SCENE

The two most important considerations when writing a renderer for the first time are the *camera* and the *light source*. If either of these is set improperly, you might see nothing on the screen and incorrectly assume that nothing is being rendered. In fact, something *is* often being rendered even when you don't see anything, but due to the camera's orientation or the lighting conditions of the scene, you might not see anything. Remember those two issues while you peruse the code in this chapter.

The camera determines what you see on the screen. The camera may be *positioned* anywhere in 3D space, as well as *pointed* in any direction in 3D space. The camera defines the viewport of a 3D environment—what the player can see. A lot of settings go into the setup of the camera's view to determine how the scene will be rendered on the screen. The viewport itself is set up in a matrix that represents the *view*. The projection of that viewport onto the screen is also a matrix, which represents the *projection*. These two matrices—*view* and *projection*—determine what appears in the scene and how it is presented on the screen.

Rendering is the process of transforming an entity's transformation data into a visual representation. I hesitate to use the terms "two-dimensional" or "three-dimensional" explicitly, because it's possible to render in more ways than what is viewed through a computer monitor.

This chapter will cover the following topics:

- View matrix
- Projection matrix
- World matrix
- Rendering a basic scene
- Loading an effect file
- Ambient wireframe shader
- Matrix inverse/transpose
- Directional lighting

THE CAMERA (VIEW AND PROJECTION MATRICES)

There are 360 degrees in a circle, which is equivalent to $2 * \pi$ radians (not to be confused with the very similar calculation for the *circumference* of a circle, which is $C = 2\pi r$). You can calculate the number of degrees in one radian with $360/(2\pi)$, which is approximately 57.2958. Likewise, we can calculate the number of radians in a degree with $(2\pi)/360$.

1 radian = 57.2958 degrees

1 degree = 0.0175 radians

But if you want to be as accurate as possible (albeit with a slight loss of performance), calculating the conversions with as much precision as possible will net better results:

degrees = radians * (360 / (2 * 3.1415926535))

radians = degrees * ((2 * 3.1415926535) / 360)

This problem can be simplified without losing any precision. A quicker (and easier to remember) solution for converting from radians to degrees is to multiply the radian value by $180 / \pi$. Conversely, to convert from degrees to radians, multiply degrees by $\pi / 180$. In the Math class, these were pre-calculated into static variables called PI_UNDER_180 and PI_OVER_180, respectively.

degrees = radians * (180 / 3.1415926535)

radians = degrees * (3.1415926535 / 180)

The View Matrix

You may be wondering: what's the relation between this discussion of degree and radian conversions and the camera in a 3D renderer? Believe it or not, they are related. The *field of view* is the angle size for the viewport that is "seen" by the camera and sent to the projection matrix. We start with a new matrix, which is then filled by the function D3DXMatrixLookAtLH, which creates a view based on the left-handed coordinate viewpoint (where the Z-axis increases toward the camera, decreases away from it). There are three properties needed: the position of the camera as a vector, the target or "look at" position, and the "up direction," which is constant. If you want to see what values this function fills into the matrix, use the MatrixToString() function presented in the previous chapter with some traceable values, such as 5.55, 6.66, and 7.77, for some of the vector properties to see where they end up in the matrix. If you can figure this out, then you can replace the D3DX function with one of your own and embed it inside the Matrix class. Finally, since the updir property never changes, it is declared directly as a D3DXVECTOR3 so no conversion is needed from our own Vector3 class.

```
Matrix matrixView;
matrixView.setIdentity();
Vector3 position = Vector3( 0.0f, 0.0f, 10.0f );
Vector3 target = Vector3( 0.0f, 0.0f, 0.0f );
updir = D3DXVECTOR3( 0.0f, 1.0f, 0.0f );
D3DXMatrixLookAtLH(&matrixView, &pos, &target, &updir);
```

Any time the position or target of the camera changes, this matrix will need to be re-created by calling D3DXMatrixLookAtLH() again, which is why this code will be found inside the Camera::Update() function in the Camera class.

The Projection Matrix

The projection (also referred to as *perspective*) matrix determines how the scene is transferred from the camera to the frame buffer and ultimately to the screen. To be more specific, the projection matrix determines how the viewport is rasterized onto a 2D monitor, based on properties such as the field of view, aspect ratio (width to height), and the camera's near and far clipping ranges Hence, the term "projection," an analogy for the way a film projector displays a film onto a theater screen (an apt comparison because that is essentially what is happening). While your game might have many cameras, it will usually have only one "projector" or projection matrix.

The ratio property should reflect the horizontal and vertical scaling you wish to see in the viewport, which is usually a width-to-height ratio of 1.33 (which is nominal for the standard resolutions of 640x480, etc.). You will want to change this assumption if targeting a widescreen display.

The field of view property determines how wide of an angle the camera should have when rendering a snapshot of the scene (which is then passed to the projection matrix). Since 2π radians is one complete circle, it is common to use one-fourth π or 45 degrees, but I encourage you to experiment.

```
float ratio = 640 / 480;
float fieldOfView = PI / 4.0f;
```

As mentioned earlier, unless these properties change there is no reason to recalculate the projection matrix. There are some cases where you will want a different projection, such as with a sniper rifle scope or fisheye view. In those cases, I recommend just using multiple projection matrices, like multiple cameras, to handle those situations without needing to recalculate. Granted, a matrix is only a 4x4 array, so these calculations are not going to slow down the framerate much, but every little optimization over the long run does add up.

Camera Class

The Camera class incorporates the view and projection matrices as its primary function, but it also needs to provide basic camera positioning and orientation functions. At minimum, you will want to move the camera to track an object and cause the target position to move along with the camera's position. These features are not difficult to implement at all, but we aren't quite ready to build a first-person camera just yet—see the section on that topic later in this chapter.

Advice

This chapter's resource files can be downloaded from www.jharbour.com/forum or www.courseptr. com/downloads. Please note that not every line of code will be in print due to space considerations: only the most important sections of code are covered in each chapter.

```
class Camera
{
private:
    Matrix p_matrixProj;
```

```
        Matrix p_matrixView;
        Matrix p_matrixRot;
        D3DXVECTOR3 p_updir;

        Vector3 p_position;
        Vector3 p_rotation;
        Vector3 p_target;

        double p_nearRange;
        double p_farRange;
        double p_aspectRatio;
        double p_fov;
public:
        Camera(void);
        ~Camera(void);
        void setPerspective(double fov, double aspectRatio, double nearRange,
            double farRange);
        Matrix getProjMatrix() { return p_matrixProj; }
        Matrix getViewMatrix() { return p_matrixView; }

        //camera position helpers
        Vector3 getPosition() { return p_position; }
        void setPosition(double x, double y, double z);
        void setPosition(Vector3 vector) { p_position = vector; }

        void setRotation(double x,double y,double z);
        void setRotation(Vector3 vector) { p_rotation = vector; }

        //camera lookat helpers
        Vector3 getTarget() { return p_target; }
        void setTarget(Vector3 value) { p_target = value; }
        void setTarget(double x, double y, double z)
        {
            p_target.x = (float)x;
            p_target.y = (float)y;
            p_target.z = (float)z;
        }

        void Update();
        void Rotate(double x, double y, double z);
```

```
    void Look(double x, double y, double z);
    void Move(double x, double y, double z);
};
```

The Camera class's implementation adds helper functions to assist with camera movement in addition to the projection matrix and view matrix code already covered. As usual, the peripheral code (headers, namespace definitions, etc.) has been omitted to save space—these are just the class methods found in the Camera.cpp file.

```
Camera::Camera(void)
{
    //create default perspective matrix
    p_position = Vector3(0.0f,0.0f,10.0f);
    p_updir = D3DXVECTOR3(0.0f,1.0f,0.0f);
    double ratio = 640 / 480;
    setPerspective( Octane::PI / 4.0f, ratio, 1.0f, 10000.0f);

    //create default view matrix
    this->Update();
}

Camera::~Camera(void){}

void Camera::setPerspective(double fov, double aspectRatio,
    double nearRange, double farRange)
{
    p_fov = fov;
    p_aspectRatio = aspectRatio;
    p_nearRange = nearRange;
    p_farRange = farRange;

    //set the camera's perspective matrix
    D3DXMatrixPerspectiveFovLH(&this->p_matrixProj, (float)p_fov,
        (float)p_aspectRatio, (float)p_nearRange, (float)p_farRange);
}

void Camera::Update()
{
    //create the view matrix
    D3DXVECTOR3 pos = p_position.ToD3DXVECTOR3();
```

```
    D3DXVECTOR3 target = p_target.ToD3DXVECTOR3();
    D3DXMatrixLookAtLH(&p_matrixView, &pos, &target, &p_updir);
}

//set specific position values
void Camera::setPosition(double x, double y, double z)
{
    p_position.x = (float)x;
    p_position.y = (float)y;
    p_position.z = (float)z;
}

//set specific rotation values
void Camera::setRotation(double x, double y, double z)
{
    p_rotation.x = (float)x;
    p_rotation.y = (float)y;
    p_rotation.z = (float)z;

    //update rotation matrix
    D3DXMatrixRotationYawPitchRoll(&p_matrixRot, (float)p_rotation.x,
        (float)p_rotation.y, (float)p_rotation.z);
}

//adjust rotation relative to current rotation values
void Camera::Rotate(double x, double y, double z)
{
    p_rotation.x += (float)x;
    p_rotation.y += (float)y;
    p_rotation.z += (float)z;
}

//relative adjustment to lookat target
void Camera::Look(double x, double y, double z)
{
    p_target.x += (float)x;
    p_target.y += (float)y;
    p_target.z += (float)z;
}
```

```
//relative adjustment to both position and target
void Camera::Move(double x, double y, double z)
{
    p_position.x += (float)x;
    p_position.y += (float)y;
    p_position.z += (float)z;

    p_target.x += (float)x;
    p_target.y += (float)y;
    p_target.z += (float)z;
}
```

THE SCENE (WORLD MATRIX)

We have already learned to use the view and projection matrices in order to create a camera viewport in the scene. The third matrix that completes this trio is the *world matrix*. So called because it represents transformations that take place in the game world, or 3D world, or 3D scene—depending on the narrator. The *world matrix* is a reusable matrix for rendering every object in the scene, one at a time. This matrix does not represent the whole "world" (that is, the whole scene), but rather is used to fill in the "world" or scene with all of the objects with which it is comprised. Individual game objects—terrain, trees, buildings, vehicles, people, alien characters, spaceships, planets, and so on—may or may not have their own internal matrices to represent the transformation of each object. More often, the object has properties such as position, rotation, and scaling, which are then used to *create* the matrix as that entity is being rendered.

Rendering a Basic Scene

Back in Chapter 6, we wrote the basic Direct3D rendering code in the Octane engine's primary source code file (Engine.cpp) in a function called Engine::Update(). Here it is again for reference:

```
void Engine::Update( float elapsedTime )
{
    static float accumTime=0;

    p_coreFrameCount++;
    if (p_coreTimer.Stopwatch(1000))
    {
```

```
        p_coreFrameRate = p_coreFrameCount;
        p_coreFrameCount = 0;
    }

    game_update( elapsedTime );

    if (!timedUpdate.Stopwatch(16))
    {
        timedUpdate.Rest(1);
    }
    else
    {
        p_screenFrameCount++;
        if (p_screenTimer.Stopwatch(1000))
        {
            p_screenFrameRate = p_screenFrameCount;
            p_screenFrameCount = 0;
        }

        p_input->Update();
        updateKeyboard();
        updateMouse();

        if (p_device->BeginScene() == D3D_OK)
        {
            g_engine->clearScene(p_backdropColor);
            game_render3d();
            p_spriteObj->Begin(D3DXSPRITE_ALPHABLEND);
            game_render2d();
            p_spriteObj->End();
            p_device->EndScene();
            p_device->Present(0,0,0,0);
        }
    }
}
```

There are three important function calls in the `Engine::Update` function:

- `game_update(float deltaTime)`
- `game_render3d()`
- `game_render2d()`

These three functions bring our game code to life by allowing us to update everything in each frame (running at the core clock speed of the CPU), and to render the 3D scene, and then to do any 2D sprite drawing (such as text output) as needed. There is no facility here for effect/shader-based rendering, so we'll address that issue now.

We need to add shader-based rendering to the `Engine::Update` function via the `game_render3d()` function. Since the Direct3D rendering block is already being handled for us in the `Engine::Update()` function, all we need to do on the "front end," so to speak, is invoke the effect's own functions and perform rendering of a mesh. To start an effect, we first use the `ID3DXEffect::Begin()` function, and then finish rendering with `ID3DXEffect::End()`. Within the Begin/End block is a call to `BeginPass()` and `EndPass()`.

This example assumes that there is only one pass in the current technique, and that is how it's coded in the `Effect` class later in this chapter. If you have any effects that do render with multiple passes, then it will be a rather simple matter to modify the class to take into account multiple passes as this code suggests:

```
UINT passes;
effect->Begin(&passes, 0);
effect->BeginPass(0);
...
effect->EndPass();
effect->End();
```

This effect rendering pipeline is repeated for every mesh in the scene, with each mesh being rendered individually with the appropriate effect, and all taking place within the Direct3D rendering pipeline. But, since each mesh will need to be rendered with its own textures, we will have to embed the effect code inside the mesh rendering function. (More on this in Chapter 9, "Mesh Loading and Rendering.")

Loading an Effect File

An effect file has an extension of .fx and contains one or more rendering techniques, each of which will have a vertex shader function and usually a pixel shader function as well. While it's possible to render a mesh entirely with vertex lighting, the result is never going to be as good as the quality achieved with a pixel shader—or *fragment program*. In order to load an effect file, we'll use another

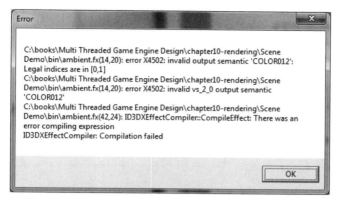

Figure 8.1
Shader errors are quite detailed and helpful to the developer.

D3DX structure called ID3DXEffect, or the pointer version, LPD3DXEFFECT. An ID3DXBuffer variable is also used to detect error messages generated while the effect file is being compiled. These errors are quite detailed, specifying the line number and position in the effect file where an error occurred! Figure 8.1 shows a sample shader compile error message.

```
ID3DXEffect* effect = 0;
ID3DXBuffer *errors = 0;
```

The D3DXCreateEffectFromFile function is used to load an effect file. Of all the parameters in this function definition, we need concern ourselves with only four—the Direct3D device, the effect filename, the effect object pointer, and the errors object pointer.

```
D3DXCreateEffectFromFile(
    g_engine->getDevice(),    //Direct3D device
    filename.c_str(),         //effect filename
    0,                        //macros
    0,                        //includes
    D3DXSHADER_DEBUG,         //flags
    0,                        //pool
    &p_effect,                //effect pointer
    &errors );                //error text
```

Effect File Structure

Every effect file will have at least three global variables or properties that must be set in C++ code for the effect to render anything: a View matrix, a

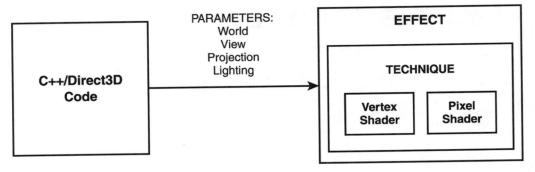

Figure 8.2
Parameters define how shader functions will manipulate vertices and render pixels.

Projection matrix, and a World matrix. For every mesh rendered in a scene, the transformation of that mesh, along with the camera's view and projection matrices, are passed as parameters to the effect. A matrix is defined in an effect with the `float4x4` data type:

```
float4x4 World;
float4x4 View;
float4x4 Projection;
```

Parameters such as these are used to communicate information from the CPU to the GPU (i.e., from your C++ code to the shader functions in the effect file). See Figure 8.2.

An effect file may define more than one technique, but at least one must be defined. The technique specifies the vertex shader and pixel shader functions that are to be used for the technique, along with any special rendering parameters. It is entirely possible to use just one effect file with many dozens of techniques and vertex/pixel shader functions within, but since that combined code would be a bit difficult to maintain I recommend using one effect file per technique until you are fully confident in your shader programming skill.

```
technique Ambient
{
    pass P0
    {
        VertexShader = compile vs_2_0 VertexShaderFunction();
```

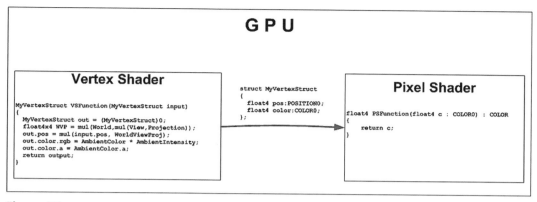

Figure 8.3
A custom struct is the glue between the vertex shader and pixel shader.

```
        PixelShader   = compile ps_2_0 PixelShaderFunction();
        CullMode = none;
        FillMode = wireframe;
    }
}
```

Our simple ambient color effect is about as pathetic as a renderer can get! But it's a step in the learning process and demonstrates basic shader programming in its simplest form. The "Ambient" technique defined two functions: VertexShaderFunction and PixelShaderFunction. Normally, a technique will specify vertex and pixel shader functions that are named according to their function, like a diffuse light shader or a normal mapping shader.

Within the GPU, the vertex shader is always invoked first, which is why it's possible to render a mesh with just vertex lighting and no pixel lighting. Figure 8.3 shows the relationship between vertex shader and pixel shader. As the illustration suggests, the output from the vertex shader becomes the input to the pixel shader, defined as a custom struct created by the programmer.

Microsoft introduced the concept of a *geometry shader* in DirectX 10 (with obvious collaboration with NVIDIA and ATI). A geometry shader receives input from the vertex shader, and has the ability to add *new vertices* and *entire meshes* to the scene before passing the rendering task on to the pixel shader. See Figure 8.4.

The vertex shader can receive individual parameters, but it's far more convenient to use a custom struct with those parameters defined within, because this

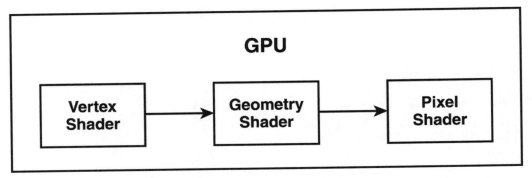

Figure 8.4
A GPU that supports DirectX 10 and later will also have a geometry shader.

struct is often used for the output of the vertex shader (which becomes the input parameter of the pixel shader).

```
struct MyVertexStruct
{
    float4 position   : POSITION0;
    float4 color : COLOR0;
};
```

The job of the vertex shader is to manipulate vertices—*not* to render, which is solely the job of the pixel shader (or fragment program as it is often called). The vertex shader function takes as input the incoming position of a vertex as a vector (with an X,Y,Z component). This vector is combined through multiplication with the World, View, and Projection matrices, all of which are similarly multiplied together to arrive at a combined matrix used to transform the vertex. Any vertex *color* value is simply passed on to the pixel shader unchanged. Likewise, when applying a texture to a mesh, the pixels of the texture that are mapped onto the mesh are passed straight through the vertex shader on to the pixel shader where each pixel of the texture is combined with the lighting to arrive at a combined color value.

```
MyVertexStruct VertexShaderFunction( MyVertexStruct input_param )
{
    MyVertexStruct output = (MyVertexStruct)0;

    //combine world + view + projection matrices
```

```
    float4x4 WorldViewProj = mul(World,mul(View,Projection));

    //translate the current vertex
    output.position = mul(input_param.position, WorldViewProj);

    output.color.rgb = AmbientColor * AmbientIntensity;
    output.color.a = AmbientColor.a;

    return output;
}
```

This pixel shader function simply renders the vertex color passed to it as a passthrough, without performing any processing on the pixels itself. The result is a rendered mesh with only vertex coloring and lighting.

```
float4 PixelShaderFunction(float4 c : COLOR0) : COLOR
{
    return c;
}
```

Sample Effect File

The following code listing belongs to the ambient.fx file included in the project for this chapter. This effect only defines an ambient color and ambient intensity for rendering, which will cause any mesh rendered with it to appear washed out in whatever ambient color it is set to. Since the full ambient has no discernable faces, with no light source, the mesh is poorly defined, so the FillMode property in this effect's technique has been set to wireframe. This basic effect source code is a good starting point if you're new to shader programming since the addition of lighting code tends to increase its complexity very quickly.

```
// Basic ambient light shader with no texture support
float4x4 World;
float4x4 View;
float4x4 Projection;
float4 AmbientColor : AMBIENT = float4(1.0,1.0,1.0,1.0);
float AmbientIntensity = 1.0;

struct MyVertexStruct
{
    float4 position  : POSITION0;
```

```
    float4 color : COLOR0;
};

MyVertexStruct VertexShaderFunction( MyVertexStruct input_param )
{
    MyVertexStruct output = (MyVertexStruct)0;

    //combine world + view + projection matrices
    float4x4 WorldViewProj = mul(World,mul(View,Projection));

    //translate the current vertex
    output.position = mul(input_param.position, WorldViewProj);

    output.color.rgb = AmbientColor * AmbientIntensity;
    output.color.a = AmbientColor.a;

    return output;
}

float4 PixelShaderFunction(float4 c : COLOR0) : COLOR
{
    return c;
}

technique Ambient
{
    pass P0
    {
        VertexShader = compile vs_2_0 VertexShaderFunction();
        PixelShader  = compile ps_2_0 PixelShaderFunction();
        FillMode = wireframe;
    }
}
```

Effect Class

We need a wrapper class to handle all of the effect file loading and rendering functions with the use of properties to centralize all of the shader processing in one place. We can also take advantage of function overloading to support many types of parameters. The three main matrices that must be passed to every effect (World, View, Projection) are supported with their own custom functions with optional parameter names. Depending on the effect file, these names are likely to never be the same unless one programmer is writing them (which we can't just assume). To change the defaults from "World," "View," and "Projection," you can pass the necessary string to the setWorldMatrix(), setViewMatrix(), and setProjectionMatrix() functions, respectively. Below is the header file for a new Effect class that will encapsulate ID3DXEffect.

```
class Effect
{
private:
    LPD3DXEFFECT p_effect;

public:
    Effect();
    ~Effect();
    LPD3DXEFFECT getObject() { return p_effect; }
    bool Load(std::string filename);
    void setTechnique(std::string technique);
    void setViewMatrix(D3DXMATRIX matrix,
        std::string fxViewParam = "View");
    void setProjectionMatrix(D3DXMATRIX matrix,
        std::string fxProjParam = "Projection");
    void setWorldMatrix(D3DXMATRIX matrix,
        std::string fxWorldParam = "World");

    void setParam(std::string name, D3DXMATRIX matrix);
    void setParam(std::string name, LPDIRECT3DTEXTURE9 texture);
    void setParam(std::string name, LPDIRECT3DCUBETEXTURE9 cubeTexture);
    void setParam(std::string name, D3DXVECTOR4 vector);
    void setParam(std::string name, D3DXVECTOR3 vector);
    void setParam(std::string name, Vector3 vector);
    void setParam(std::string name, float f);

    bool Begin();
    void End();
};
```

The implementation of the Effect class follows next.

```
Effect::Effect()
{
    p_effect = NULL;
}
```

```cpp
Effect::~Effect()
{
    if (p_effect) p_effect->Release();
}

bool Effect::Load(std::string filename)
{
    ID3DXBuffer *errors = 0;
    D3DXCreateEffectFromFile( g_engine->getDevice(), filename.c_str(),
        0, 0, D3DXSHADER_DEBUG, 0, &p_effect, &errors);
    if (errors) {
        MessageBox(0, (char*)errors->GetBufferPointer(), 0, 0);
        return false;
    }
    return true;
}

void Effect::setTechnique(std::string technique)
{
    p_effect->SetTechnique(technique.c_str());
}

void Effect::setViewMatrix(D3DXMATRIX matrix, std::string fxViewParam)
{
    p_effect->SetMatrix( fxViewParam.c_str(), &matrix );
}

void Effect::setProjectionMatrix(D3DXMATRIX matrix, std::string fxProjParam)
{
    p_effect->SetMatrix( fxProjParam.c_str(), &matrix );
}

void Effect::setWorldMatrix(D3DXMATRIX matrix, std::string fxWorldParam)
{
    p_effect->SetMatrix( fxWorldParam.c_str(), &matrix );
}

bool Effect::Begin()
{
    if (!p_effect) return false;
```

```
    UINT passes;
    p_effect->Begin(&passes, 0);
    if (passes == 0) return false;
    p_effect->BeginPass(0);
    return true;
}

void Effect::End()
{
    if (!p_effect) return;
    p_effect->EndPass();
    p_effect->End();
}

void Effect::setParam( std::string name, D3DXMATRIX matrix )
{
    p_effect->SetMatrix( name.c_str(), &matrix );
}

void Effect::setParam( std::string name, LPDIRECT3DTEXTURE9 texture )
{
    p_effect->SetTexture( name.c_str(), texture );
}

void Effect::setParam( std::string name, LPDIRECT3DCUBETEXTURE9 cubeTexture )
{
    p_effect->SetTexture( name.c_str(), cubeTexture );
}

void Effect::setParam( std::string name, D3DXVECTOR4 vector)
{
    p_effect->SetVector( name.c_str(), &vector );
}

void Effect::setParam( std::string name, D3DXVECTOR3 vector )
{
    D3DXVECTOR4 v;
    v.x = vector.x;
    v.y = vector.y;
    v.z = vector.z;
```

```
    v.w = 0;
    p_effect->SetVector( name.c_str(), &v );
}

void Effect::setParam( std::string name, Vector3 vector )
{
    D3DXVECTOR4 v;
    v.x = (float) vector.x;
    v.y = (float) vector.y;
    v.z = (float) vector.z;
    v.w = 0;
    p_effect->SetVector( name.c_str(), &v );
}

void Effect::setParam( std::string name, float f )
{
    p_effect->SetFloat( name.c_str(), f );
}
```

Rendering a Stock Mesh

The D3DX library provides us with six stock meshes for experimentation and testing purposes, although you could use them in a game if that would fulfill a gameplay design goal. The stock meshes are:

Stock Shape	D3DX Function
Torus	D3DXCreateTorus
Sphere	D3DXCreateSphere
Cube	D3DXCreateBox
Teapot	D3DXCreateTeapot
Cylinder	D3DXCreateCylinder
Text	D3DXCreateText

The parameters for each function are self-explanatory. In some cases, we are given the option of specifying how detailed a shape will be based on the number of rows, columns, sides, etc. One of my favorites is the torus, which looks like a large donut or ring (see Figure 8.5).

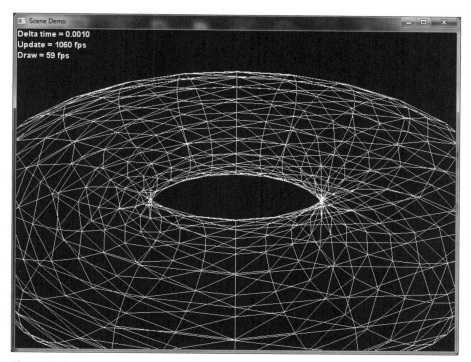

Figure 8.5
Wireframe render of the stock torus mesh.

Advice

There's one unusual mesh that you can create with the D3DX library—D3DXCreateText. Specify the TrueType font name and a mesh will be created containing a representation of the text you wish to render in 3D. The only drawback is that this function requires a GDI+ device context that must be created beforehand, and after the mesh has been created this device context must be freed, which is a very slow process. But for special-purpose rendering needs, such as a high-score screen or custom effects rendered on the title screen of a game, this may provide some intriguing possibilities.

```
HDC hdc = CreateCompatibleDC(0);
HFONT hfont;
hfont=CreateFont(0,0,0,0,FW_NORMAL, false, false, false, DEFAULT_CHARSET,
    OUT_DEFAULT_PRECIS, CLIP_DEFAULT_PRECIS, DEFAULT_QUALITY,
    VARIABLE_PITCH|FF_MODERN, "Tahoma");
SelectObject(hdc,hfont);
D3DXCreateText(g_engine->getDevice(),hdc,"3D Text",0,1.0f,&text,0,0);
DeleteObject(hfont);
DeleteDC(hdc);
```

Ambient Wireframe Shader Demo

The following program demonstrates the Ambient.fx effect with the FillMode property set to *wireframe*. You may selectively swap one type of mesh for another to see the sphere, teapot, cylinder, cube, or torus by making minor changes to the code.

```cpp
#include "stdafx.h"
#include "Engine.h"
using namespace std;
using namespace Octane;

LPD3DXMESH torus;
LPD3DXMESH sphere;
LPD3DXMESH cube;
LPD3DXMESH teapot;
LPD3DXMESH cylinder;
Matrix matWorld;
Font* font=NULL;
Camera* camera=NULL;
Effect* effect=NULL;
float deltaTime=0;

bool game_preload()
{
    g_engine->setAppTitle("Ambient Wireframe Shader Demo");
    g_engine->setScreen(800,600,32,false);
    return true;
}

bool game_init(HWND hwnd)
{
    font = new Font("Arial Bold",18);
    if (!font)
    {
        debug << "Error creating font" << endl;
        return false;
    }

    //g_engine->setBackdropColor(D3DCOLOR_XRGB(0,250,250));

    //create a camera
```

```
        camera = new Camera();
        camera->setPosition(0, 0.0, 10.0);
        camera->setTarget(0,0,0);

        //load the ambient.fx effect
        effect = new Effect();
        if (!effect->Load("ambient.fx"))
        {
            MessageBox(hwnd, "Error loading ambient.fx", "Error",0);
            return false;
        }

        matWorld.setIdentity();

        //create stock meshes
        D3DXCreateTorus(g_engine->getDevice(), 2.0f, 4.0f, 20, 20, &torus, NULL);
        D3DXCreateTeapot(g_engine->getDevice(), &teapot, NULL);
        D3DXCreateSphere(g_engine->getDevice(), 2.0f, 10, 10, &sphere, NULL);
        D3DXCreateBox(g_engine->getDevice(), 2.0f, 2.0f, 2.0f, &cube, NULL);
        D3DXCreateCylinder(g_engine->getDevice(), 2.0f, 2.0f, 3.0f, 10, 10,
            &cylinder, NULL);


        return true;
}

void game_render3d()
{
    //effect->setTechnique("Ambient");
    effect->setViewMatrix( camera->getViewMatrix(), "View");
    effect->setProjectionMatrix( camera->getProjMatrix(), "Projection");


    //draw the cube
    {
        static float rot = 0;
        rot += 0.01f;
        matWorld.rotateX(rot);
        effect->Begin();
        effect->setWorldMatrix( (D3DXMATRIX) matWorld , "World");
```

```cpp
        //choose which mesh to render here
        torus->DrawSubset(0);
        //cube->DrawSubset(0);
        //sphere->DrawSubset(0);
        //teapot->DrawSubset(0);
        //cylinder->DrawSubset(0);
        effect->End();
    }
}

void game_end()
{
    if (font) delete font;
    if (effect) delete effect;
    if (camera) delete camera;
    torus->Release();
    teapot->Release();
    cube->Release();
    sphere->Release();
    cylinder->Release();
}

void game_update( float dltTime )
{
    deltaTime = dltTime;

    camera->Update();

    //move the torus mesh in a circular pattern
    static float x = 0.0f;
    static float y = 0.0f;
    static float z = 0.0f;
    static float angle = 0.0f;
}

void game_render2d()
{
    std::ostringstream out;
    out.setf(ios::fixed);
    out << setprecision(4);
```

```
        out << "Delta time = " << deltaTime << endl;
        out << "Update = " << g_engine->getCoreFrameRate() << " fps" << endl;
        out << "Draw = " << g_engine->getScreenFrameRate() << " fps";

        font->Print(0,0,out.str());
}


void game_event( IEvent* e )
{
    switch( e->getID() )
    {
        case EVENT_KEYPRESS:
        {
            KeyPressEvent* evt = (KeyPressEvent*) e;
            if (evt->keycode == DIK_ESCAPE) g_engine->Shutdown();
            break;
        }
        case EVENT_MOUSEMOTION:
        {
            MouseMotionEvent* evt = (MouseMotionEvent*)e;
            camera->Look( evt->deltax/100.0f, evt->deltay/100.0f, 0 );
            break;
        }
        case EVENT_MOUSEWHEEL:
        {
            MouseWheelEvent* evt = (MouseWheelEvent*) e;
            camera->Move(0, 0, (float)(-evt->wheel/200.0f) );
            break;
        }
    }
}
```

DIFFUSE LIGHTING

The ambient light shader in the previous example of this chapter was designed for illustration, meant to be easy to understand, but it is not very useful for a game. To correctly render a mesh we need to add a light source so that the mesh can reflect light realistically (while our ambient demo did no such reflection and could only really be seen in wireframe mode).

Diffuse light is light that is spread out or scattered over an area (such as the faces of a mesh), or light that is dim or bright depending on the type of surface it is shining on. While ambient light appears to reflect evenly from all surfaces, diffuse light lacks that perfect conciseness, which is precisely why it is a superior form of lighting. In a sense, all light other than ambient may be considered diffuse, but it is most often referred to as light from a directional light source.

Directional Light

A directional light mimics sunlight, in that rays appear to come from an infinitely far light source, are emitted parallel to each other, and strike an object or scene uniformly from that direction without any apparent radiant source (such as a light bulb or spotlight). Directional light will, therefore, appear to reflect on all objects in a scene uniformly (as long as every object is rendered with the directional light applied).

To render a mesh with a directional light, in addition to the usual World/View/Projection matrices, we must also supply a vector to the light source, the light's color and intensity, and an inverse/transposed matrix. When calculating the lighting on the faces of a mesh we must calculate the normal and the light intensity. The normal is calculated from an inverse/transposed version of the World matrix. The light intensity is calculated by taking the dot product of the normal.

Matrix Inverse/Transpose

Calculating the inverse of a matrix is rather complex, involving some derivation that is beyond the scope of this book. In brief, the inverse of a matrix is such that when matrix A is inverted to B, both A times B and B times A will equal the identity matrix. As a result of the theory required to explain inverting a matrix, this is a calculation we cannot easily detach from the D3DX library at this time without further research. What we can do, however, is make use of the `D3DXMatrixInverse` function to perform this calculation.

Transposing a matrix involves shifting the rows 90 degrees into the columns as illustrated in Figure 8.6. We can calculate the transposed matrix with the function `D3DXMatrixTranspose`.

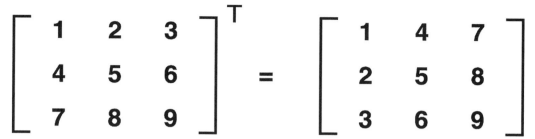

Figure 8.6
Transposing a matrix.

Both the matrix inverse and transpose are needed to calculate how light will affect the faces of a mesh, taking into account the position of a light source. Assuming your world matrix represents the transforms for a given mesh, then this code will perform the calculation:

```
D3DXMATRIX inverse, wit;
D3DXMatrixInverse( &inverse, 0, &world );
D3DXMatrixTranspose( &wit, &inverse );
```

Both of these functions return the calculated matrix as a return value as well as passing the result back through the reference parameter, so the result can be carried on to a calling function. If you wish, you may combine the function calls like so:

```
D3DXMatrixTranspose(&wit,D3DXMatrixInverse(&inverse,0,&world));
```

And, finally, assuming our effect has a global property so named, we can pass the inverted/transposed World matrix to the effect via our setParam() function:

```
effect->setParam( "WorldInverseTranspose", wit );
```

Advice

You will probably not want to calculate inverse/transpose inside your shader because those calculations will be repeated for every vertex and potentially every pixel being rendered. Instead, calculate the inverse/transpose once in the CPU and pass that calculation on to the effect for an entire mesh.

Vector A = (1,2,3)
Vector B = (4,5,6)

$$A \cdot B = A.x * B.x + A.y + A.z * B.z)$$
$$A \cdot B = 1 * 4 + 2 * 5 + 3 * 6$$
$$A \cdot B = 4 + 10 + 18$$
$$A \cdot B = 32$$

Figure 8.7
Calculating the dot product of two vectors.

Dot Product

To calculate a dot product, the X,Y,Z properties of two vectors are multiplied by each other, and those products are then added together. The name "dot product" comes from the dot that is used to represent the calculation. Figure 8.7 shows an example of calculating using dot product.

Directional Light Shader

This effect source code adds a few more global properties compared to the previous ambient effect, to take into account directional lighting. Now we have these globals:

Data Type	Global Name
float4x4	World
float4x4	View
float4x4	Projection
float4x4	WorldInverseTranspose
float3	LightVector
float4	LightColor
float	LightPower

It's important to take note of these global properties because they must be set correctly in our source code—and case sensitivity must be observed.

```
float4x4 World;
float4x4 View;
float4x4 Projection;
float4x4 WorldInverseTranspose;

float3 LightVector = float3(0, 0, 1);
float4 LightColor = float4(1,1,1,1);
float LightPower = 0.6;

struct MyVertexInput
{
    float4 position  : POSITION;
    float2 texcoord : TEXCOORD0;
    float4 normal : NORMAL;
};
struct MyVertexOutput
{
    float4 position : POSITION;
    float2 texcoord : TEXCOORD0;
    float4 color : COLOR0;
};

MyVertexOutput VertexShaderFunction( MyVertexInput input_param )
{
    MyVertexOutput output = (MyVertexOutput)0;

    //transform
    float4x4 viewProj = mul(View,Projection);
    float4x4 WorldViewProj = mul(World,viewProj);
    output.position = mul(input_param.position, WorldViewProj);

    //lighting
    float4 normal = mul( input_param.normal, WorldInverseTranspose );
    float intensity = dot( normal, LightVector );
    output.color = saturate( LightColor * LightPower * intensity );

    return output;
}
```

```
float4 PixelShaderFunction(MyVertexOutput input_param) : COLOR0
{
    float4 light = saturate( input_param.color + LightColor * LightPower );
    return light;
}

technique DirectionalLight
{
    pass P0
    {
        vertexShader = compile vs_2_0 VertexShaderFunction();
        pixelShader  = compile ps_2_0 PixelShaderFunction();
    }
}
```

Directional Light Demo

We have covered quite a bit of new material on diffuse lighting, and our first experiment is with a directional light source (the most common form of lighting after ambient). This example required quite a bit more work beyond the ambient light demo presented earlier in the chapter, including an inverse/transposed World matrix and properties for the directional light source (position vector, intensity value, and color value). Figure 8.8 shows the somewhat overused teapot mesh with a green directional light illuminating it.

This program has some interactivity programmed in. By pressing the up/down arrows, you can rotate the mesh. The left/right arrows will rotate the light source around the scene (or more accurately, rotate the normalized vector pointing at the directional light). The +/− keys on the numeric keypad increase and decrease the light intensity, respectively. The R, G, B, and A keys on the keyboard adjust the color values used for the directional light's color. Figure 8.9 shows another stock mesh being rendered.

Engine Enhancement: Color Class

We're going to need a new feature in the engine to make working with colored lighting more effective. The Direct3D color macros and functions could not be much more confusing to the uninitiated. At best you are likely to get the integer and floating-point color macros confused; at worst, nothing but a black scene will reward you for your hard work. A new Color class will alleviate these

Figure 8.8
Directional lighting on a stock mesh with interactive controls.

difficulties by abstracting color at a more basic level—just dealing with the basic
four color components: Red, Green, Blue, Alpha. Here is the class definition:

```
class Color
{
public:
    float r,g,b,a;
    virtual ~Color();
    Color();
    Color( const Color& color );
    Color(int R,int G,int B,int A);
    Color(float R,float G,float B,float A);
    Color& Color::operator=(const Color& c);

    void Set(int R,int G,int B,int A);
    void Set(float R,float G,float B,float A);
```

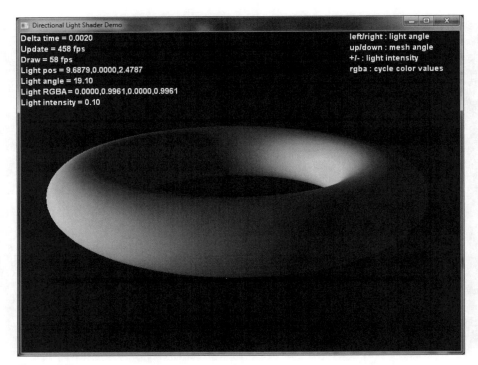

Directional Light Shader Demo

Figure 8.9
The familiar torus mesh is rendered with a directional light shader.

```
    //D3D compatibility
    D3DCOLOR ToD3DCOLOR();
    //shader compatibility
    D3DXVECTOR4 ToD3DXVECTOR4();
};
```

The class implementation will be a good starting point for what will eventually become a robust `Color` class that will replace all direct-coded Direct3D color macros (such as the ubiquitous `D3DCOLOR_ARGB` macro—yes, it's a macro, not a function, declared with a #define). In addition to providing a conversion to a `D3DCOLOR` value, also included is a conversion to a `D3DXVECTOR4`, which is used to pass the color to a shader. Once again, this is the code solely for the `Color` class, not the complete listing from the file, so headers and namespaces are omitted.

```
Color::~Color() { }

Color::Color()
```

```
{
    r=g=b=a=1.0f;
}

Color::Color( const Color& color )
{
    *this = color;
}

Color::Color(int R,int G,int B,int A)
{
    Set(R,G,B,A);
}

Color::Color(float R,float G,float B,float A)
{
    Set(R,G,B,A);
}

Color& Color::operator=( const Color& color )
{
    Set(color.r,color.g,color.b,color.a);
    return *this;
}

/**
Convert 0-255 color values to 0.0-1.0 range
**/
void Color::Set(int R,int G,int B,int A)
{
    r = (float)R/256.f;
    g = (float)G/256.f;
    b = (float)B/256.f;
    a = (float)A/256.f;
}

void Color::Set(float R,float G,float B,float A)
{
    r=R; g=G; b=B; a=A;
}
```

```
/**
Convert from our 0.f-1.f color values to 0-255 based D3DCOLOR
**/
D3DCOLOR Color::ToD3DCOLOR()
{
    D3DCOLOR color = D3DCOLOR_COLORVALUE(r,g,b,a);
    return color;
}


/**
Convert to a D3DXVECTOR4 for use by shader code
**/
D3DXVECTOR4 Color::ToD3DXVECTOR4()
{
    D3DXVECTOR4 v4(r,g,b,a);
    return v4;
}
```

Now that we have a useful Color class available, we can begin overloading functions that previously supported only D3DCOLOR. For instance, in Engine.h, we can overload setBackdropColor() to support a Color parameter:

```
void setBackdropColor(Color value)
{
    p_backdropColor = value.ToD3DCOLOR();
}
```

Another change we can make is to the Font class. Previously, the Print function had a D3DCOLOR parameter with a default value. We'll remove the default and add an overloaded function with a default Color parameter instead:

```
void Font::Print(int x, int y, string text, D3DCOLOR color)
{
    RECT rect = { x, y, 0, 0 };
    fontObj->DrawText( NULL, text.c_str(), text.length(), &rect,
        DT_CALCRECT, color);
    fontObj->DrawText( g_engine->getSpriteObj(), text.c_str(),
        text.length(), &rect, DT_LEFT, color);
}

void Font::Print(int x, int y, std::string text, Color color)
{
```

```
    Print(x, y, text, color.ToD3DCOLOR());
}
```

Directional Light Demo Source

Let's now go over the source code for this slightly more complex example. Since we now have quite a few new shader parameters to pass, a detailed analysis of the source code is needed at this stage. Later examples might gloss over these details once they have been sufficiently explained. First, we'll begin with the program's header code which contains the global variables. Of particular interest here is the use of many high-level engine classes with fewer and fewer Direct3D-specific constructs in use. Our examples will become even more abstracted with each new chapter.

```
#include "Engine.h"
using namespace std;
using namespace Octane;

LPD3DXMESH torus;
LPD3DXMESH sphere;
LPD3DXMESH cube;
LPD3DXMESH teapot;
LPD3DXMESH cylinder;
Matrix matWorld;
Font* font=NULL;
Camera* camera=NULL;
Effect* effect=NULL;

Vector3 lightVector;
Color lightColor;
float lightAngle=0;
float lightPower=0.1f;
float objectAngle=0;
float deltaTime=0;

bool game_preload()
{
    g_engine->setAppTitle("Directional Light Shader Demo");
    g_engine->setScreen(800,600,32,false);
    return true;
}
```

There's quite a bit of new code in the initialization function that demands an explanation. First, we create a font like usual, but now we're also creating a camera using the new Camera class. The camera is very easy to initilaize since only the position and target (or *look at* point) are needed here. Next, an effect file is loaded (directional_light.fx), and then the sample meshes are created. You may render any of these meshes you wish, as all are created and destroyed by the program but not all are used.

```
bool game_init(HWND hwnd)
{
    font = new Font("Arial Bold",18);
    if (!font)
    {
        debug << "Error creating font" << endl;
        return false;
    }

    //create a camera
    camera = new Camera();
    camera->setPosition(0, 0.0, 5.0);
    camera->setTarget(0,0,0);


    //load the ambient.fx effect
    effect = new Effect();
    if (!effect->Load("directional_light.fx"))
    {
        MessageBox(hwnd, "Error loading directional_light.fx", "Error",0);
        return false;
    }

    matWorld.setIdentity();
    lightColor.Set(0,255,0,255);

    //create stock meshes
    D3DXCreateTorus(g_engine->getDevice(), 0.3f, 1.0f, 80, 80, &torus, 0);
    D3DXCreateTeapot(g_engine->getDevice(), &teapot, 0);
    D3DXCreateSphere(g_engine->getDevice(), 1.0f, 80, 80, &sphere, 0);
    D3DXCreateBox(g_engine->getDevice(), 1.0f, 1.0f, 1.0f, &cube, 0);
    D3DXCreateCylinder(g_engine->getDevice(),1.0f,1.0f,3.0f,80,80,&cylinder,0);
```

```
    return true;
}
```

Rendering is slightly more complex than the ambient light demo covered earlier. We've already gone over the new shader globals that are required for directional lighting, and now those parameters are actually used as the mesh is being rendered. Although you can render two or more of the meshes with this example, since we are only modifying the world matrix once—to represent transforms—the shapes will all draw over each other. If you want to see more than one shape in the scene, you will have to create a new transform and render them separately, each in a new effect rendering block.

```
void game_render3d()
{
    effect->setTechnique("DirectionalLight");
    effect->setViewMatrix( camera->getViewMatrix(), "View");
    effect->setProjectionMatrix( camera->getProjMatrix(), "Projection");

    //draw the mesh
    {
        matWorld.rotateX(objectAngle);
        effect->Begin();
        effect->setWorldMatrix( (D3DXMATRIX) matWorld , "World");


        //calculate combined inverse transpose matrix
        D3DXMATRIX inverse, wit;
        D3DXMatrixInverse( &inverse, 0, &matWorld );
        D3DXMatrixTranspose( &wit, &inverse );
        effect->setParam( "WorldInverseTranspose", wit );

        //move the light source
        lightVector.x = cosf(lightAngle) * 10.0f;
        lightVector.y = 0.0f;
        lightVector.z = sinf(lightAngle) * 10.0f;
        effect->setParam("LightVector", lightVector);

        //set the light intensity
        lightPower = Math::Limit(lightPower, 0.0, 1.0);
        effect->setParam("LightPower", lightPower);
```

```
        //set the light color
        lightColor.r = Math::wrapValue(lightColor.r, 0.0, 1.0);
        lightColor.g = Math::wrapValue(lightColor.g, 0.0, 1.0);
        lightColor.b = Math::wrapValue(lightColor.b, 0.0, 1.0);
        lightColor.a = Math::wrapValue(lightColor.a, 0.0, 1.0);
        effect->setParam("LightColor", lightColor.ToD3DXVECTOR4() );


        //choose one mesh to render here
        torus->DrawSubset(0);
        //cube->DrawSubset(0);
        //sphere->DrawSubset(0);
        //teapot->DrawSubset(0);
        //cylinder->DrawSubset(0);
        effect->End();
    }
}

void game_end()
{
    if (font) delete font;
    if (effect) delete effect;
    if (camera) delete camera;
    torus->Release();
    teapot->Release();
    cube->Release();
    sphere->Release();
    cylinder->Release();
}

void game_update( float dltTime )
{
    deltaTime = dltTime;
    camera->Update();
}

void game_render2d()
{
    std::ostringstream out;
    out.setf(ios::fixed);
```

```cpp
        out << setprecision(4);

        out << "Delta time = " << deltaTime;
        font->Print(0,0,out.str());

        out.str("");
        out << "Update = " << g_engine->getCoreFrameRate() << " fps";
        font->Print(0,20,out.str());

        out.str("");
        out << "Draw = " << g_engine->getScreenFrameRate() << " fps";
        font->Print(0,40,out.str());

        out.str("");
        out << "Light pos = " << lightVector.x << "," << lightVector.y
            << "," << lightVector.z;
        font->Print(0,60,out.str());

        font->Print(0,80,"Light angle = " + Octane::ToString(lightAngle));

        out.str("");
        out << "Light RGBA = " << lightColor.r << "," << lightColor.g
            << "," << lightColor.b << "," << lightColor.a;
        font->Print(0,100,out.str());


        font->Print(0,120,"Light intensity = "+Octane::ToString(lightPower));

        int w = g_engine->getScreenWidth();
        font->Print(w-200,0,"left/right : light angle");
        font->Print(w-200,20,"up/down : mesh angle");
        font->Print(w-200,40,"+/- : light intensity");
        font->Print(w-200,60,"rgba : cycle color values");
}

void game_event( IEvent* e )
{
    switch( e->getID() )
    {
        case EVENT_KEYPRESS:
        {
```

```
            KeyPressEvent* evt = (KeyPressEvent*) e;
            switch(evt->keycode)
            {
                case DIK_ESCAPE: g_engine->Shutdown(); break;

                //left/right arrow keys rotate light source
                case DIK_LEFT: lightAngle -= 0.1f; break;
                case DIK_RIGHT: lightAngle += 0.1f; break;

                //up/down arrow keys rotate the mesh
                case DIK_UP: objectAngle -= 0.02f; break;
                case DIK_DOWN: objectAngle += 0.02f; break;

                //+/- keys change light power
                case DIK_NUMPADPLUS: lightPower += 0.01f; break;
                case DIK_NUMPADMINUS: lightPower -= 0.01f; break;

                //rgba keys cycle color values
                case DIK_R: lightColor.r += 0.01f; break;
                case DIK_G: lightColor.g += 0.01f; break;
                case DIK_B: lightColor.b += 0.01f; break;
                case DIK_A: lightColor.a += 0.01f; break;
            }
            break;
        }
        case EVENT_MOUSEMOTION:
        {
            MouseMotionEvent* evt = (MouseMotionEvent*)e;
            camera->Look( evt->deltax/100.0f, evt->deltay/100.0f, 0 );
            break;
        }
        case EVENT_MOUSEWHEEL:
        {
            MouseWheelEvent* evt = (MouseWheelEvent*) e;
            camera->Move(0, 0, (float)(-evt->wheel/200.0f) );
            break;
        }
    }
}
```

SUMMARY

This hefty chapter covered a lot of ground, as a full-blown effect-based renderer was added to the engine! While ambient wireframe and colored directional light shaders are nothing to jump up and down with excitement over, they do have their uses, and it has been extremely helpful to start with these very basic examples for anyone who is new to shader programming. One of the most important components of rendering is missing, though—*textured meshes*. I did not get into texture mapping in this chapter because it requires a loaded mesh with defined textures, which we'll get into in the next chapter.

REFERENCES

"Dot product"; http://en.wikipedia.org/wiki/Dot_product.

"Inverse"; http://en.wiktionary.org/wiki/inverse_matrix.

"Transpose"; http://en.wikipedia.org/wiki/Transpose.

Gilbert Strang; MIT; Video lecture on matrix multiplication: http://ocw.mit.edu/OcwWeb/Mathematics/18-06Spring-2005/VideoLectures/detail/lecture03.htm.

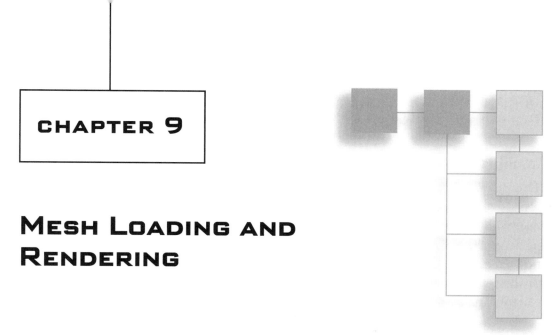

CHAPTER 9

MESH LOADING AND RENDERING

This chapter adds to the code base begun in the previous chapter on shader-based lighting with some new techniques, such as texture-mapped lighting shaders, while exploring basic mesh loading and rendering.

The following topics are covered in this chapter:

- .X Files
- Mesh class
- Textured ambient light rendering
- Lighting texture-mapped meshes
- Textured directional light shader

MESH LOADING AND RENDERING

Now we need to write the code for a new class that will load up a mesh from a .X file, because in order to explore texturing we cannot use the stock meshes generated by the D3DXCreate? functions. There are two ways to load a mesh with Direct3D—either as a hierarchical mesh with bone data and animation or as a simple static mesh without these features. We'll begin by writing a simple mesh loader that will not handle bone or animation data, and then return to these subjects in Chapter 13 and go over them with the full treatment. At this point,

I'm more concerned with shader code to light the scene, and we just need meshes to test our lighting effects.

.X Files

The primary way to get a mesh asset into the Direct3D rendering pipeline is by way of the .X file format. This is the standard Direct3D mesh file format, but it is not widely supported among the popular modeling and animation software packages (3DS Max and Maya being the most popular). There are exceptions, however. The Game Creators (www.thegamecreators.com) sell a number of products that work well with the native .X mesh file format, including Cartography Shop (Figure 9.1) and 3D World Studio.

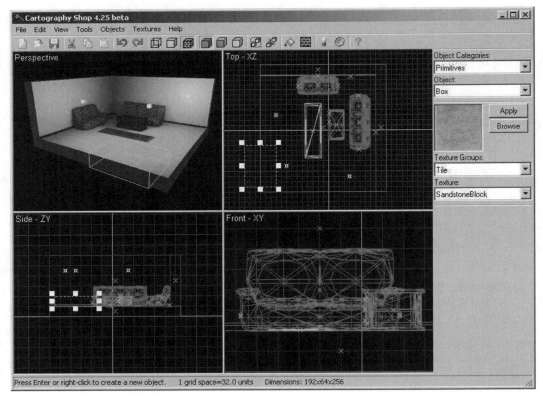

Figure 9.1
Cartography Shop is a *freeware* modeling package that can export directly to the .X format.

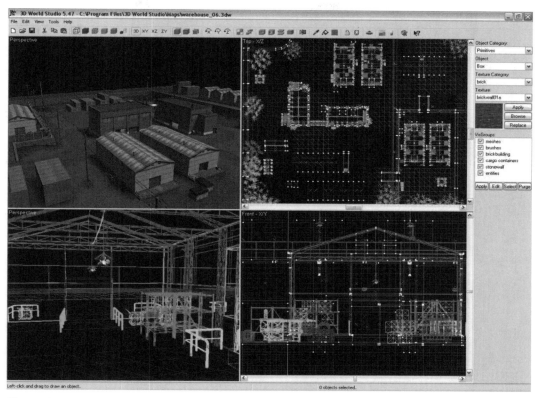

Figure 9.2
3D World Studio is an affordable modeling program with terrific features.

3D World Studio (http://leadwerks.com) is a great little environment modeling package. With a price tag of only $50, it will import *and* export files in the .X format, as well as other popular formats such as *Half-Life* and *Quake 3* files. See Figure 9.2 for a screenshot.

Whether you create your own game level and character mesh assets or use free assets from one of the many resources on the web that share Half-Life, Quake III, 3DS, or DirectX mesh files, you will need to ultimately convert them to the .X format for use in a Direct3D-based engine such as Octane (until such time that you are willing and/or able to write reader code to support those file formats internally). Later in this chapter is an example that renders a crate mesh, which is just a cube and a wooden crate texture that is repeated on all six sides. Figure 9.3 shows the crate mesh in the DirectX Viewer.

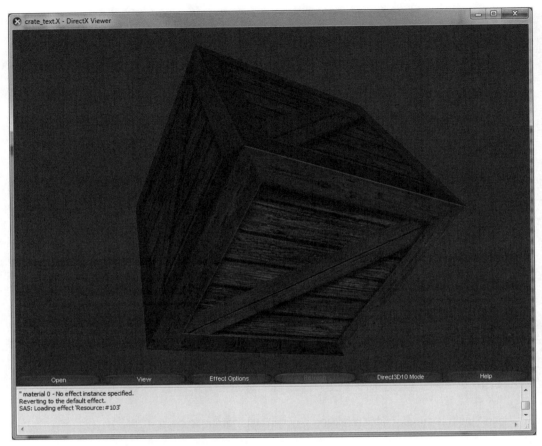

Figure 9.3
A wooden crate mesh rendered by the DirectX Viewer utility.

Some .X files contain ASCII text, which is readable and editable, while some .X mesh files are binary and cannot be edited by hand, only with a modeling package that supports it (such as 3D World Studio).

Crate Mesh Internals

Below are the contents of the crate.x file, which I have renamed to crate_text.x in the upcoming textured directional light demo. After the templates, you will see the first Material definition, which contains vertex colors and a texture filename. Beyond that is a single-frame animation set containing the crate vertex and face definitions. Take note of the Mesh section itself, which contains the vertices. The values, or extents, in this mesh are quite large, in the range of −25 to 50. This tells me that the scenes this crate were designed for are also quite large in scale. It is perfectly acceptable to use dimensions for the crate in 3D space on the order of −1 to +1, if the environment is similarly scaled. When you have a really huge mesh like this, however, be sure to scale back your camera's position to take it into account or you may assume that the mesh is not being rendered—when, in fact, it is just not showing up because the camera resides inside it!

```
xof 0303txt 0032
template FVFData {
 <b6e70a0e-8ef9-4e83-94ad-ecc8b0c04897>
 DWORD dwFVF;
 DWORD nDWords;
 array DWORD data[nDWords];
}
template EffectInstance {
 <e331f7e4-0559-4cc2-8e99-1cec1657928f>
 STRING EffectFilename;
 [...]
}
template EffectParamFloats {
 <3014b9a0-62f5-478c-9b86-e4ac9f4e418b>
 STRING ParamName;
 DWORD nFloats;
 array FLOAT Floats[nFloats];
}
template EffectParamString {
 <1dbc4c88-94c1-46ee-9076-2c28818c9481>
 STRING ParamName;
 STRING Value;
}
template EffectParamDWord {
 <e13963bc-ae51-4c5d-b00f-cfa3a9d97ce5>
 STRING ParamName;
 DWORD Value;
}

Material PDX01_-_Default {
 1.000000;1.000000;1.000000;1.000000;;
 3.200000;
```

```
 0.000000;0.000000;0.000000;;
 0.000000;0.000000;0.000000;;
 TextureFilename {
   "crate.tga";
 }
}


Frame Box01 {
FrameTransformMatrix {
 1.000000,0.000000,0.000000,0.000000,
 0.000000,1.000000,0.000000,0.000000,
 0.000000,0.000000,1.000000,0.000000,
 0.000000,0.000000,0.000000,1.000000;;
 }

Mesh   {
 20;
 -25.000000;-25.000000;0.000000;,
 25.000000;-25.000000;0.000000;,
 -25.000000;25.000000;0.000000;,
 25.000000;25.000000;0.000000;,
 -25.000000;-25.000000;50.000000;,
 25.000000;-25.000000;50.000000;,
 -25.000000;25.000000;50.000000;,
 25.000000;25.000000;50.000000;,
 -25.000000;-25.000000;0.000000;,
 25.000000;-25.000000;0.000000;,
 25.000000;-25.000000;50.000000;,
 -25.000000;-25.000000;50.000000;,
 25.000000;25.000000;0.000000;,
 25.000000;-25.000000;50.000000;,
 25.000000;25.000000;0.000000;,
 -25.000000;25.000000;0.000000;,
 -25.000000;25.000000;50.000000;,
 25.000000;25.000000;50.000000;,
 -25.000000;25.000000;0.000000;,
 -25.000000;-25.000000;50.000000;;
 12;
 3;0,2,3;,
 3;3,1,0;,
```

```
 3;4,5,7;,
 3;7,6,4;,
 3;8,9,10;,
 3;10,11,8;,
 3;1,12,7;,
 3;7,13,1;,
 3;14,15,16;,
 3;16,17,14;,
 3;18,0,19;,
 3;19,6,18;;

MeshNormals  {
 6;
 0.000000;0.000000;-1.000000;,
 0.000000;0.000000;1.000000;,
 0.000000;-1.000000;0.000000;,
 1.000000;0.000000;0.000000;,
 0.000000;1.000000;0.000000;,
 -1.000000;0.000000;0.000000;;
 12;
 3;0,0,0;,
 3;0,0,0;,
 3;1,1,1;,
 3;1,1,1;,
 3;2,2,2;,
 3;2,2,2;,
 3;3,3,3;,
 3;3,3,3;,
 3;4,4,4;,
 3;4,4,4;,
 3;5,5,5;,
 3;5,5,5;;
}

MeshMaterialList  {
 1;
 12;
 0,0,0,0,0,0,
 0,0,0,0,0,0;
 { PDX01_-_Default }
}
```

```
MeshTextureCoords   {
 20;
 1.000000;1.000000;,
 0.000000;1.000000;,
 1.000000;0.000000;,
 0.000000;0.000000;,
 0.000000;1.000000;,
 1.000000;1.000000;,
 0.000000;0.000000;,
 1.000000;0.000000;,
 0.000000;1.000000;,
 1.000000;1.000000;,
 1.000000;0.000000;,
 0.000000;0.000000;,
 1.000000;1.000000;,
 0.000000;0.000000;,
 0.000000;1.000000;,
 1.000000;1.000000;,
 1.000000;0.000000;,
 0.000000;0.000000;,
 0.000000;1.000000;,
 1.000000;0.000000;;
  }
 }
}
```

Why would one want to manually edit a mesh file such as this? There are some advantages to knowing what the internal structure of a .X file looks like. Since all .X files have this basic structure, it should be possible to write your own function to read in a .X file, in either text mode or binary. Note that each structure begins with a counter to tell you how many values are following in the file; this counter value will make loading a .X file that much easier, as long as your loading function looks for blocks without expecting them in any particular order, since the .X format does not define a rigid, sequential format. Seeing the file laid out on the page like this also helps to visualize how you might work with mesh data in your own game engine, perhaps with the use of your own custom data format (along with a converter for .X, of course!).

Asteroid Mesh Internals

Now let's look at a less uniform mesh that is not quite as clean-cut as a boxy crate—an asteroid with a lot of jagged edges. Figure 9.4 shows the asteroid mesh in the DirectX Viewer utility. I'll skip most of the definitions for the mesh since it's quite lengthy, and I just want you to see what the mesh's internal composition looks like.

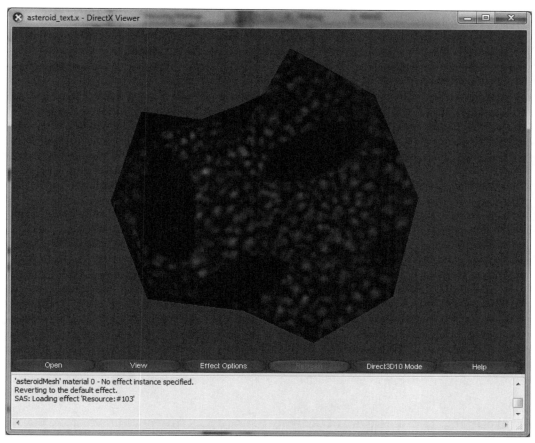

Figure 9.4
An asteroid mesh rendered by the DirectX Viewer utility.

```
xof 0303txt 0032

Frame asteroidFrame
{
    FrameTransformMatrix
    {
        1.000000,0.000000,0.000000,0.000000,
        0.000000,1.000000,0.000000,0.000000,
        0.000000,0.000000,1.000000,0.000000,
        0.000000,0.000000,0.000000,1.000000;;
    }

    Mesh asteroidMesh
    {
        42;
        -1.390577;0.143709;-0.362994;,
        -0.422214;0.193709;-2.100000;,
        -1.743692;2.443709;-1.771478;,
        -0.422214;4.056703;-2.418363;,
        1.099265;2.443709;-1.771478;,

            .
            .
            .

        MeshNormals
        {
            42;
            -0.188146;0.299602;-0.935328;,
            -0.530179;0.069419;-0.845039;,
            -0.143705;-0.158832;-0.976791;,
            0.292207;0.687314;-0.664991;,
            0.058945;0.370537;-0.926945;,

                .
                .
                .
        }

        MeshTextureCoords
        {
            42;
```

```
        0.375672;0.480374;,
        0.489480;0.474513;,
        0.334171;0.210774;,
        0.489480;0.021703;,
        0.668293;0.210774;,
            .
            .
            .
    }

MeshMaterialList
{
    1;
    80;
    0,0,0,0,
        .
        .
        .


    Material Material01
    {
        0.800000;0.800000;0.800000;1.000000;;
        0.000000;
        0.000000;0.000000;0.000000;;
        0.000000;0.000000;0.000000;;

        TextureFileName
        {
            "asteroidTex.dds";
        }
    }
  }
 }
}
```

Mesh Class

We're going to quickly go over a `Mesh` class that encapsulates the best Direct3D can give us with regard to mesh loading and rendering support at this point. I will assume that either you are already familiar with this code or you have another reference available, because we aren't going to discuss every line of code. We'll be exploring hierarchical mesh rendering and animation later (see Chapter 13), so that subject is deferred until then. At this point, all we need is basic mesh loading and rendering without support for bones or animation frames.

Advice

This chapter's resource files can be downloaded from www.jharbour.com/forum or www.courseptr. com/downloads. Please note that not every line of code will be in print due to space considerations: only the most important sections of code are covered in each chapter.

```
class Mesh
{
private:
    LPD3DXMESH mesh;
    D3DMATERIAL9* materials;
    DWORD material_count;
    LPDIRECT3DTEXTURE9* textures;

    Vector3 position;
    Vector3 rotation;
    Vector3 scale;

    Matrix matWorld;
    Matrix matTranslate;
    Matrix matRotate;
    Matrix matScale;

    Effect *p_effect;

public:
    Mesh(void);
    virtual ~Mesh(void);

    bool Load(char *filename, bool computeNormals=false);
    bool findFile(std::string *filename);
    bool doesFileExist(std::string &filename);
    void splitPath(std::string& inputPath, std::string* pathOnly,
        std::string* filenameOnly);
```

```
void Update(float deltaTime);
void Render();
void Render( Effect *effect, std::string fxTextureParam="Texture" );
void setEffect(Effect* effect) { p_effect = effect; }

Matrix getMatrix() { return matWorld; }
void setMatrix(Matrix matrix) { matWorld = matrix; }
void setMatrix(D3DXMATRIX matrix) { matWorld = (Matrix) matrix; }
LPD3DXMESH getMesh() { return mesh; }
virtual int getFaceCount();
virtual int getVertexCount();

void createTorus(float innerRadius = 0.5f, float outerRadius = 1.0f,
    int sides = 20, int rings = 20);
void createCylinder(float radius1, float radius2, float length,
    int slices, int stacks);
void createSphere(double radius = 0.1f, int slices = 10, int stacks = 10);
void createCube(double width = 1.0f, double height = 1.0f,
    double depth = 1.0f);
void createTeapot();

void Transform();
void Rotate(Vector3 rot);
void Rotate(double x,double y,double z);
void setPosition(Vector3 pos) { position = pos; }
void setPosition(double x,double y,double z);
Vector3 getPosition() { return position; }
void setRotation(Vector3 rot) { rotation = rot; }
void setRotation(double x,double y,double z);
Vector3 getRotation() { return rotation; }
void setScale(Vector3 value) { scale = value; }
void setScale(double x,double y,double z);
void setScale(double value);
Vector3 getScale() { return scale; }};
```

Here is the source code for the Mesh class's implementation, found in the Mesh .cpp file. The basic mesh at this point pretty much just handles loading, transforms, and rendering, so the code is on the short side. It's a good idea to keep basic mesh and complex hierarchical mesh code separate, because the latter requires a lot more memory and you may not want that complexity for rendering simple meshes like rocks or grass on a hillside.

```
Mesh::Mesh()
{
    mesh = 0;
    materials = 0;
    material_count = 0;
    textures = 0;
    position = Vector3(0.0f,0.0f,0.0f);
    rotation = Vector3(0.0f,0.0f,0.0f);
    scale = Vector3(1.0f,1.0f,1.0f);
}

Mesh::~Mesh(void)
{
    if (materials != NULL) delete[] materials;

    //remove textures from memory
    if (textures != NULL) {
        for( DWORD i = 0; i < material_count; i++)
        {
            if (textures[i] != NULL)
                textures[i]->Release();
        }
        delete[] textures;
    }

    if (mesh != NULL) mesh->Release();
}

int Mesh::getFaceCount()
{
    return mesh->GetNumFaces();
}

int Mesh::getVertexCount()
{
    return mesh->GetNumVertices();
}
```

```
void Mesh::createTorus(float innerRadius, float outerRadius,
    int sides, int rings)
{
    D3DXCreateTorus(g_engine->getDevice(), innerRadius, outerRadius,
        sides, rings, &mesh, NULL);
}

void Mesh::createCylinder(float radius1, float radius2, float length,
    int slices, int stacks)
{
    D3DXCreateCylinder(g_engine->getDevice(), radius1, radius2,
        length, slices, stacks, &mesh, NULL);
}

void Mesh::createSphere(double radius, int slices, int stacks)
{
    D3DXCreateSphere(g_engine->getDevice(), (float)radius, slices,
        stacks, &mesh, NULL);
}

void Mesh::createCube(double width, double height, double depth)
{
    D3DXCreateBox(g_engine->getDevice(), (float)width, (float)height,
        (float)depth, &mesh, NULL);
}

void Mesh::createTeapot()
{
    D3DXCreateTeapot(g_engine->getDevice(), &mesh, NULL);
}


void Mesh::splitPath(string& inputPath, string* pathOnly,
    string* filenameOnly)
{
    string fullPath( inputPath );
    replace( fullPath.begin(), fullPath.end(), '\\', '/' );
    string::size_type lastSlashPos = fullPath.find_last_of('/');

    // check for there being no path element in the input
```

```
    if (lastSlashPos == string::npos)
    {
        *pathOnly="";
        *filenameOnly = fullPath;
    }
    else {
        if (pathOnly) {
            *pathOnly = fullPath.substr(0, lastSlashPos);
        }
        if (filenameOnly)
        {
            *filenameOnly = fullPath.substr(
                lastSlashPos + 1,
                fullPath.size() - lastSlashPos - 1 );
        }
    }
}

bool Mesh::doesFileExist(string &filename)
{
    return (_access(filename.c_str(), 0) != -1);
}

bool Mesh::findFile(string *filename)
{
    if (!filename) return false;

    //since the file was not found, try removing the path
    string pathOnly;
    string filenameOnly;
    splitPath(*filename,&pathOnly,&filenameOnly);

    //is file found in current folder, without the path?
    if (doesFileExist(filenameOnly))
    {
        *filename=filenameOnly;
        return true;
    }

    //not found
```

```
        return false;
}

bool Mesh::Load(char* filename, bool computeNormals)
{
    HRESULT result;
    LPD3DXBUFFER matbuffer;
    LPD3DXMATERIAL d3dxMaterials;

    //load mesh from the specified file
    result = D3DXLoadMeshFromX(
        filename,                 //filename
        D3DXMESH_SYSTEMMEM,       //mesh options
        g_engine->getDevice(),    //Direct3D device
        NULL,                     //adjacency buffer
        &matbuffer,               //material buffer
        NULL,                     //special effects
        &material_count,          //number of materials
        &mesh);                   //resulting mesh

    if (result != D3D_OK)   {
        return false;
    }

    //extract material properties and texture names from material buffer
    d3dxMaterials = (LPD3DXMATERIAL)matbuffer->GetBufferPointer();
    materials = new D3DMATERIAL9[material_count];
    textures  = new LPDIRECT3DTEXTURE9[material_count];

    //create the materials and textures
    for(DWORD i=0; i < material_count; i++)
    {
        //grab the material
        materials[i] = d3dxMaterials[i].MatD3D;

        //load texture(s)
        textures[i] = NULL;
        if (d3dxMaterials[i].pTextureFilename != NULL)
        {
            string filename = d3dxMaterials[i].pTextureFilename;
```

```
            if( findFile(&filename) )
            {
                //load texture file specified in .x file
                result = D3DXCreateTextureFromFile(g_engine->getDevice(),
                    filename.c_str(), &textures[i]);
                if (result != D3D_OK) return false;

                //verify texture header
                if (textures[i]->GetType() != D3DRTYPE_TEXTURE)
                    return false;
            }
        }
    }

    //done using material buffer
    matbuffer->Release();

    if (computeNormals)
    {
        HRESULT res = D3DXComputeNormals( mesh, NULL );
        if (res != S_OK)
        {
            debug << "Mesh::CreateSphere: Error computing normals\n";
        }
    }

    return true;
}

void Mesh::Update(float deltaTime)
{
    Transform();}
```

Now we come to the Mesh::Render function. Although we are not doing anything as fancy as hierarchical rendering or animation yet, our mesh still requires an effect for rendering. While there are many ways to go about this, from passing the mesh to the effect to using a global effect pointer, this function uses an effect passed as a parameter to render the mesh. Note the calls to effect->Begin() and effect->End()—this means that you should not call these functions when calling Mesh::Draw() since they are already being called. (Again, please note that this is not the complete source code from the `Mesh.cpp` file, just the class methods.)

```cpp
void Mesh::Render()
{
    Render( p_effect, "Texture" );
}


void Mesh::Render( Effect *effect, std::string fxTextureParam )
{
    p_effect = effect;
    p_effect->setWorldMatrix( matWorld );
    p_effect->Begin();

    if (material_count == 0)
    {
        mesh->DrawSubset(0);
    }
    else {
        //draw each mesh subset
        for( DWORD i=0; i < material_count; i++ )
        {
            // set the texture used by this face
            if (textures[i])
            {
                p_effect->setParam( fxTextureParam, (textures[i]) );
            }

            // Draw the mesh subset
            mesh->DrawSubset( i );
        }
    }

    p_effect->End();
}

void Mesh::Transform()
{
    //set rotation matrix
    double x = D3DXToRadian(rotation.x);
    double y = D3DXToRadian(rotation.y);
```

```
        double z = D3DXToRadian(rotation.z);
        D3DXMatrixRotationYawPitchRoll(&matRotate, (float)x, (float)y,
            (float)z);

        //set scaling matrix
        D3DXMatrixScaling(&matScale, (float)scale.x, (float)scale.y,
            (float)scale.z);

        //set translation matrix
        D3DXMatrixTranslation(&matTranslate, (float)position.x,
            (float)position.y, (float)position.z);

        //transform the mesh
        matWorld = matRotate * matScale * matTranslate;
}

void Mesh::setPosition(double x,double y,double z)
{
        position = Vector3((float)x,(float)y,(float)z);
}

void Mesh::Rotate(Vector3 rot)
{
        Rotate(rot.x,rot.y,rot.z);
}

void Mesh::Rotate(double x,double y,double z)
{
        rotation.x += (float)x;
        rotation.y += (float)y;
        rotation.z += (float)z;
}

void Mesh::setRotation(double x,double y,double z)
{
        rotation = Vector3((float)x,(float)y,(float)z);
}
```

```
void Mesh::setScale(double x,double y,double z)
{
    scale = Vector3((float)x,(float)y,(float)z);
}

void Mesh::setScale(double value)
{
    scale.x = scale.y = scale.z = value;
}
```

Textured Ambient Light Rendering

Now that we have the crucial building blocks ready, let's do some texture-mapped rendering with a shader! The basic ambient light shader from the previous chapter was about as crude a renderer as they come, resulting in a totally washed out mesh. By using a texture-mapped mesh, you can actually use an ambient-lit object for something useful in a scene, although with obvious lack of true lighting support.

Textured Ambient Light Shader

The new `ambient.fx` effect will now support a texture map, and therefore it will need a sampler struct. Also, the technique has been renamed to "Ambient Textured," so be sure to use that technique name when using this effect file. Since texture mapping and the sampler are described below in the section on textured directional light rendering, I'll forego an explanation of how it works until then. In the meantime, note the differences in bold text.

```
float4x4 World;
float4x4 View;
float4x4 Projection;
float4 AmbientColor : AMBIENT = float4(1,1,1,1);
float AmbientIntensity = 1;
texture Texture;

struct MyVertexStruct
{
    float4 position  : POSITION0;
    float4 texcoord : TEXCOORD0;
};
```

```
MyVertexStruct VertexShaderFunction( MyVertexStruct input_param )
{
    //create struct variable to return
    MyVertexStruct output = (MyVertexStruct)0;

    //combine world + view + projection matrices
    float4x4 viewProj = mul(View,Projection);
    float4x4 WorldViewProj = mul(World,viewProj);

    //translate the current vertex
    output.position = mul(input_param.position, WorldViewProj);

    //set texture coordinates
    output.texcoord = input_param.texcoord;

    return output;
}

sampler MySampler = sampler_state
{
    texture = <Texture>;
};

float4 PixelShaderFunction(float2 texcoord : TEXCOORD0) : COLOR
{
    return ( tex2D( MySampler,texcoord ) * AmbientColor * AmbientIntensity);
}

technique AmbientTextured
{
    pass P0
    {
        vertexShader = compile vs_2_0 VertexShaderFunction();
        pixelShader  = compile ps_2_0 PixelShaderFunction();
    }
}
```

Testing the Textured Ambient Shader

To put the new textured ambient effect to the test, we need a real mesh file since the stock meshes will no longer work. As you may recall, the meshes generated

Figure 9.5
Apache helicopter rendered with the `ambient_textured.fx` effect. Mesh courtesy of www.geo-metricks.com.

by the `D3DXCreate` functions do not have texture coordinates in their vertex format definitions. Instead, we'll start using meshes loaded from .X files, starting with our first real-world example: a U.S. Army AH-64 Apache helicopter. Figure 9.5 shows the output of this demo.

```
#include "stdafx.h"
#include "Engine.h"
#include "Mesh.h"
#include "Effect.h"

using namespace std;
using namespace Octane;
```

```
Font* font=NULL;
Camera* camera=NULL;
Effect* effect=NULL;
Mesh* mesh;

float objectAngle=0;
float deltaTime=0;

bool game_preload()
{
    g_engine->setAppTitle("Ambient Textured Shader Demo");
    g_engine->setScreen(800,600,32,false);
    return true;
}

bool game_init(HWND hwnd)
{
    font = new Font("Arial Bold",18);
    if (!font)
    {
        debug << "Error creating font" << endl;
        return false;
    }

    //create a camera
    camera = new Camera();
    camera->setPosition(0, 2.0, 10.0);
    camera->setTarget(0,0,0);

    //load the ambient.fx effect
    effect = new Effect();
    if (!effect->Load("ambient_textured.fx"))
    {
        MessageBox(hwnd, "Error loading ambient_textured.fx", "Error",0);
        return false;
    }

    //create sphere
    mesh = new Mesh();
    mesh->Load("apache.x");
```

```
    mesh->setScale(0.01f);
    mesh->setRotation(0, -90, 0);

    return true;
}


void game_render3d()
{
    effect->setTechnique("AmbientTextured");
    effect->setViewMatrix( camera->getViewMatrix(), "View");
    effect->setProjectionMatrix( camera->getProjMatrix(), "Projection");
    effect->setWorldMatrix( (D3DXMATRIX) mesh->getMatrix(), "World");
    mesh->Render( effect, "Texture" );
}


void game_end()
{
    if (font) delete font;
    if (effect) delete effect;
    if (camera) delete camera;
    if (mesh) delete mesh;
}


void game_update( float dltTime )
{
    deltaTime = dltTime;
    camera->Update();
    mesh->Rotate( 20.0 * deltaTime, 0, 0 );
    mesh->Transform();
}


void game_render2d()
{
    std::ostringstream out;
    out.setf(ios::fixed);
    out << setprecision(4);

    out << "Delta time = " << deltaTime;
    font->Print(0,0,out.str());
```

```cpp
        out.str("");
        out << "Update = " << g_engine->getCoreFrameRate() << " fps";
        font->Print(0,20,out.str());

        out.str("");
        out << "Draw = " << g_engine->getScreenFrameRate() << " fps";
        font->Print(0,40,out.str());
}


void game_event( IEvent* e )
{
    switch( e->getID() )
    {
        case EVENT_KEYPRESS:
        {
            KeyPressEvent* evt = (KeyPressEvent*) e;
            switch(evt->keycode)
            {
                case DIK_ESCAPE: g_engine->Shutdown(); break;
            }
            break;
        }
        case EVENT_MOUSEMOTION:
        {
            MouseMotionEvent* evt = (MouseMotionEvent*)e;
            camera->Look(evt->deltax/100.0f, evt->deltay/100.0f, 0);
            break;
        }
        case EVENT_MOUSEWHEEL:
        {
            MouseWheelEvent* evt = (MouseWheelEvent*) e;
            camera->Move(0, 0, (float)(-evt->wheel/200.0f) );
            break;
        }

    }

}
```

Texture Class

Having now used a texture to render a mesh, we come upon the need for a new class to help with texture management, as far as allocating and freeing memory, loading a bitmap into a texture, or even creating a texture in memory for various rendering effects (such as mirrors and rendering of vector shapes). Our Texture class will, at minimum, load a bitmap and make the IDirect3DTexture9 object visible to any other class or engine resource that needs it. Let's begin with the class's definition. Note the two private surface objects—renderDepthStencilSurface and renderSurface. These are needed when we want to create a texture in memory and use it as a render target (which will be covered later).

```cpp
class Texture
{
private:
    LPDIRECT3DSURFACE9 renderDepthStencilSurface;
    LPDIRECT3DSURFACE9 renderSurface;
public:
    Texture();
    ~Texture();
    bool Create(int width,int height);
    bool Load(std::string filename, Color transcolor = Color(255,0,255,0));
    bool Save(std::string filename, _
        D3DXIMAGE_FILEFORMAT format = D3DXIFF_BMP);
    void Release();

    bool createRenderTarget(int width,int height);
    bool renderStart(bool clear = true, bool sprite = true,
        Color clearColor = Color(255,0,255,0));
    bool renderStop(bool sprite = true);

    LPDIRECT3DTEXTURE9 getTexture() { return texture; }
    int getWidth();
    int getHeight();
    RECT getBounds();

    LPDIRECT3DTEXTURE9 texture;
    D3DXIMAGE_INFO info;
};
```

Now we'll go over the implementation for the Texture class. There are some functions in the class that will not be used immediately—namely, the render target code—but we will be using these features soon enough, and it's handy to keep the code for working with textures as render targets all inside the Texture class.

```
Texture::Texture()
{
    texture = NULL;
    renderDepthStencilSurface = NULL;
    renderSurface = NULL;
}


Texture::~Texture()
{
    Release();
}


int Texture::getWidth()
{
    return info.Width;
};


int Texture::getHeight()
{
    return info.Height;
};


RECT Texture::getBounds()
{
    RECT rect = {0, 0, getWidth()-1, getHeight()-1};
    return rect;
}


bool Texture::Load(std::string filename, Color transcolor)
{
    //standard Windows return value
    HRESULT result;
```

```
    //get width and height from bitmap file
    result = D3DXGetImageInfoFromFile(filename.c_str(), &info);
    if (result != D3D_OK)
    {
        texture = NULL;
        return false;
    }

    //create the new texture by loading a bitmap image file
    D3DXCreateTextureFromFileEx(
        g_engine->getDevice(),  //Direct3D device object
        filename.c_str(),       //bitmap filename
        info.Width,             //bitmap image width
        info.Height,            //bitmap image height
        1,                      //mip-map levels (1 for no chain)
        D3DPOOL_DEFAULT,        //the type of surface (standard)
        D3DFMT_UNKNOWN,         //surface format (default)
        D3DPOOL_DEFAULT,        //memory class for the texture
        D3DX_DEFAULT,           //image filter
        D3DX_DEFAULT,           //mip filter
        transcolor.ToD3DCOLOR(), //color key for transparency
        &info,                  //bitmap file info (from loaded file)
        NULL,                   //color palette
        &texture );             //destination texture

    //make sure the bitmap textre was loaded correctly
    if (result != D3D_OK)
    {
        texture = NULL;
        return false;
    }

    return true;
}

void Texture::Release()
{
    if (texture) texture->Release();
    if (renderDepthStencilSurface)
        renderDepthStencilSurface->Release();
```

```
        if (renderSurface) renderSurface->Release();
}

bool Texture::Create(int width,int height)
{
    //if texture is already in use, first deallocate memory
    if (texture)
    {
        texture->Release();
        texture = NULL;
    }

    HRESULT r;
    r = D3DXCreateTexture(g_engine->getDevice(), width, height, 1,
        D3DUSAGE_DYNAMIC, D3DFMT_A8R8G8B8, D3DPOOL_DEFAULT, &texture);
    if (r != D3D_OK)
    {
        texture = NULL;
        return false;
    }

    //save texture info
    info.Width = width;
    info.Height = height;
    info.Format = D3DFMT_A8R8G8B8;

    return true;
}

bool Texture::createRenderTarget(int width,int height)
{
    //if texture is already in use, first deallocate memory
    if (texture)
    {
        texture->Release();
        texture = NULL;
    }

    //create the render target surface, depth stencil
    g_engine->getDevice()->CreateTexture( width, height, 1,
```

```
            D3DUSAGE_RENDERTARGET, D3DFMT_A8R8G8B8, D3DPOOL_DEFAULT,
            &texture, NULL );
        g_engine->getDevice()->CreateDepthStencilSurface( width, height,
            D3DFMT_D16, D3DMULTISAMPLE_NONE, 0, false,
            &renderDepthStencilSurface, NULL );
        texture->GetSurfaceLevel( 0, &renderSurface );

        //save texture info
        info.Width = width;
        info.Height = height;
        info.Format = D3DFMT_A8R8G8B8;

        return true;
}


/**
    Used only when texture is a render target
    and never when the primary device is rendering!
**/
bool Texture::renderStart(bool clear, bool sprite, Color clearColor)
{
    g_engine->getDevice()->SetRenderTarget(0, renderSurface);
    g_engine->getDevice()->SetDepthStencilSurface(renderDepthStencilSurface);
    if (clear)
    {
        g_engine->getDevice()->Clear( 0, NULL, D3DCLEAR_TARGET,
            clearColor.ToD3DCOLOR(), 1.0f, 0 );
    }
    g_engine->getDevice()->BeginScene();

    if (sprite)
        g_engine->getSpriteObj()->Begin(D3DXSPRITE_ALPHABLEND);

    D3DXMATRIX identity;
    D3DXMatrixIdentity(&identity);
    g_engine->getSpriteObj()->SetTransform(&identity);

    return true;
}
```

```
/**
    Used only when texture is a render target
    and never when the primary device is rendering!
**/
bool Texture::renderStop(bool sprite)
{
    if (sprite)
        g_engine->getSpriteObj()->End();

    g_engine->getDevice()->EndScene();
    return true;
}


/**
    Saves a texture in memory to a file.
    Supports TGA, JPG, PNG, DDS, BMP (default).
**/
bool Texture::Save(std::string filename, _D3DXIMAGE_FILEFORMAT format)
{
    if (texture)
    {
        D3DXSaveTextureToFile(filename.c_str(),format,texture,NULL);
        return true;
    }
    else
        return false;
}
```

Lighting Texture-Mapped Meshes

A mesh must have a vertex format that supports the UV coordinates of a texture map, without which the texture cannot be rendered or *wrapped* around the vertices of a mesh. The D3DXCreate-based meshes do not have UV-mapped vertices so the best we can do with them is basic lighting, as you learned in the previous chapter. You can do a lot with just materials, but a texture adds a serious dose of realism to a scene, without which a scene will look like an old virtual reality game from the early '90s, the likes of which were popularized in many "VR" movies of the time: Stephen King's *Lawnmower Man*; Keanu Reaves as *Johnny Mnemonic*; Denzel Washington in *Virtuosity*; and let us not forget the

Figure 9.6
Light cycles in *TRON 2.0*.

mother of all VR movies, *TRON* (released in 1982 and quite revolutionary for its time). Figure 9.6 shows a screenshot of *TRON 2.0*, the video game released to favorable review in 2003 by developer Monolith Productions.

Although the environment in this screenshot shows multiple levels above and below the translucent floor, the light cycle and its barrier were rendered with vertex coloring only, and little or no vertex color shading, with hard-edged shadows. The film was remarkable for the time period—remember, this was 1976, close to the time IBM released the first IBM PC (4 MHz, 64KB of RAM, 4-color CGA graphics, and a floppy drive). The Cray-1 supercomputer (see Figure 9.7) used to render portions of the film cost about $8 million, had a single-core microprocessor with an operating clock frequency of 80 MHz, containing 200,000 transistors, achieved 100 million operations per second

Figure 9.7
Cray-1 supercomputer, circa 1976–1980.

through supercooling. (It was, therefore, not unlike the overclocked PCs built by game PC hobbyists.) In comparison, an Apple iPhone (or the similarly equipped iPod Touch and iPad) has far superior performance today with several hundred *million* transistors in its 1 GHz CPU and 200 MHz PowerVR SGX 53 GPU. These specifications are actually *meager* today, and yet an iPad is more than capable of rendering a film like TRON in real time (see Figure 9.8).

Advice

Ken Perlin, creator of the Perlin noise library (libnoise) widely used to generate realistic textures, won an academy award for his revolutionary texturing code, which resulted from his work on the first *TRON* film while he was with MAGI (Mathematics Application Group, Inc.). My team used Perlin to generate planet textures for the real-time rotating planets in *Starflight—The Lost Colony* (www.starflightgame.com), so I can vouch for how incredibly useful it is.

Figure 9.8
Apple iPad, circa 2010.

High-performance, real-time textured rendering has really only been around for the last decade, since around 1999 when NVIDIA released the GeForce 256, the world's first GPU with full transform and lighting built into the hardware. (Of course, there were competitors, such as 3Dfx and ATI, who some may claim produced the first true "GPU," but NVIDIA is credited with coining the term and revolutionizing the PC graphics industry through new technology, such as shaders.) I find that reminiscing a bit, delving into nostalgia, fosters an enormous amount of enthusiasm within me for any game or simulation I may be working on!

Textured Directional Light Shader

Now we are going to revisit the directional light shader introduced in the previous chapter, but with the new addition of texture support. Directional lights are peculiar in that you specify the direction of the light, but not its source position. The directional light emits parallel light rays from a distant source that you need not specify. This vector is referred to as a normal vector because it points in the desired direction and has a length of 1.0. You can create a normal vector using the `Normalize` function on an existing vector with length, which results in a vector pointing in the desired direction but with a length of 1.0. Why must the length of a normalized vector be 1.0? Because when that vector is multiplied by another vector or matrix, the product results in only a direction vector.

Texture mapping is done by the pixel shader, which receives the color value for each pixel of each face (i.e., polygon) that is rendered by the GPU. When a vertex color comes into the pixel shader via the input parameter (see the `MyVertexInput` struct), the pixel shader must then combine the incoming vertex color with the directional light color and combine those with the pixel color from the supplied texture. The pixels of a texture are retrieved with a *sampler*, which returns the pixel color of the texture at each point as the face is being lit and rendered, pixel by pixel. The sampler just forwards the texture to be used, while the GPU does the work of

```
sampler MySampler = sampler_state
{
    texture = <Texture>;
};
```

The pixel shader function uses the sampler when calculating the per-pixel lighting for a face as it is being rendered. The `tex2D` function has two parameters—the name of the sampler, and the texture coordinate for each point. We need only tell the GPU *how* to render each pixel, while the actual processing of each pixel on each face is handled automatically.

```
float4 PixelShaderFunction(MyVertexOutput input) : COLOR0
{
    float4 light = saturate( input.color + LightColor * LightPower );
    return ( tex2D( MySampler, input.texcoord ) * light );
}
```

Our directional light shader now needs to support texture mapping, which raises an important concern: If the shader tries to render a mesh with a null texture (i.e., your code does not pass the texture properly), then the mesh will render in black. Why? Because, in the pixel shader, the texture sampler is *multiplied* with the incoming vertex color in addition to the light color and intensity; if the texture sampler is null or zero, it will wipe out all lighting for the mesh.

Although this issue could be resolved with intelligent code in our Mesh class, it would be better to add some error-handling code or, better yet, an optional technique in the effect file that will handle both material-based meshes and texture-mapped meshes. Let's focus on just the textured version for now, to eliminate confusion since you can refer to the previous chapter for the materials-only directional light shader. We'll revisit the combined effect later. The differences between this version and the one presented in the previous chapter are highlighted in bold text.

```
float4x4 World;
float4x4 View;
float4x4 Projection;
float4x4 WorldInverseTranspose;
texture Texture;

float3 LightVector = float3(0, 0, 1);
float4 LightColor = float4(1,1,1,1);
float LightPower = 0.1;

struct MyVertexInput
{
    float4 position  : POSITION;
    float2 texcoord : TEXCOORD0;
    float4 normal : NORMAL;
};
struct MyVertexOutput
{
    float4 position : POSITION;
    float2 texcoord : TEXCOORD0;
    float4 color : COLOR0;
};

MyVertexOutput VertexShaderFunction( MyVertexInput input )
{
    MyVertexOutput output = (MyVertexOutput)0;

    //transform
    float4x4 viewProj = mul(View,Projection);
    float4x4 WorldViewProj = mul(World,viewProj);
    output.position = mul(input.position, WorldViewProj);
```

```
    //lighting
    float4 normal = mul( input.normal, WorldInverseTranspose );
    float intensity = dot( normal, LightVector );
    output.color = saturate( LightColor * LightPower * intensity );
    output.texcoord = input.texcoord;

    return output;
}


sampler MySampler = sampler_state
{
    texture = <Texture>;
};


float4 PixelShaderFunction(MyVertexOutput input) : COLOR0
{
    float4 light = saturate( input.color + LightColor * LightPower );
    return ( tex2D( MySampler, input.texcoord ) * light );
}


technique DirectionalTextured
{
    pass P0
    {
        vertexShader = compile vs_2_0 VertexShaderFunction();
        pixelShader  = compile ps_2_0 PixelShaderFunction();
    }
}
```

Now let's test this new effect with an example program that demonstrates a texture-mapped mesh with a directional light shining on it. This program is a bit different from the directional light demo in the previous chapter. In addition to texture support, this version loads a mesh from a .X file rather than using a stock mesh created in memory. Figure 9.9 shows the output of the textured directional light shader demo. Like the example in the previous chapter, the mesh can be rotated with the up/down keys, while the light source can be moved with the left/right keys, and there are some other controls for the light color and intensity as well.

Figure 9.9
Wooden crate mesh lit with a textured directional light shader.

```
#include "Engine.h"
#include "Mesh.h"
#include "Effect.h"
using namespace std;
using namespace Octane;

Font* font=NULL;
Camera* camera=NULL;
Effect* effect=NULL;
Mesh* mesh;

Vector3 lightVector;
Color lightColor;
```

```
float lightAngle=90;
float lightPower=0.1f;
float objectAngle=0;
float deltaTime=0;

void game_end()
{
    if (font) delete font;
    if (effect) delete effect;
    if (camera) delete camera;
    if (mesh) delete mesh;
}


bool game_preload()
{
    g_engine->setAppTitle("Textured Directional Light Shader Demo");
    g_engine->setScreen(800,600,32,false);
    return true;
}


bool game_init(HWND hwnd)
{
    font = new Font("Arial Bold",18);
    if (!font)
    {
        debug << "Error creating font" << endl;
        return false;
    }

    //create a camera
    camera = new Camera();
    camera->setPosition(0, 5.0, 10.0);
    camera->setTarget(0,3.0,0);

    //load the ambient.fx effect
    effect = new Effect();
    if (!effect->Load("directional_textured.fx"))
    {
        debug << "Error loading effect file\n";
```

```
            return false;
        }
        effect->setTechnique("DirectionalTextured");

        lightColor.Set(255,255,255,255);

        //create sphere
        mesh = new Mesh();
        mesh->Load("crate_text.x");
        mesh->setRotation(0, -90, 0);
        mesh->setScale(0.08);


        return true;
}

void game_render3d()
{
        effect->setViewMatrix( camera->getViewMatrix(), "View" );
        effect->setProjectionMatrix( camera->getProjMatrix(), "Projection" );
        effect->setWorldMatrix( (D3DXMATRIX) mesh->getMatrix(), "World" );
        //mesh->Render( effect, "Texture" );


        //calculate combined inverse transpose matrix
        D3DXMATRIX inverse, wit;
        D3DXMatrixInverse( &inverse, 0, (D3DXMATRIX*) &mesh->getMatrix() );
        D3DXMatrixTranspose( &wit, &inverse );
        effect->setParam( "WorldInverseTranspose", wit );

        //move the light source
        lightVector.x = cosf(lightAngle) * 10.0f;
        lightVector.y = 0.0f;
        lightVector.z = sinf(lightAngle) * 10.0f;
        effect->setParam("LightVector", lightVector);

        //set the light intensity
        lightPower = Math::Limit(lightPower, 0.0, 1.0);
        effect->setParam("LightPower", lightPower);
```

```
        //set the light color
        lightColor.r = Math::wrapValue(lightColor.r, 0.0, 1.0);
        lightColor.g = Math::wrapValue(lightColor.g, 0.0, 1.0);
        lightColor.b = Math::wrapValue(lightColor.b, 0.0, 1.0);
        lightColor.a = Math::wrapValue(lightColor.a, 0.0, 1.0);
        effect->setParam("LightColor", lightColor.ToD3DXVECTOR4() );

        mesh->Render( effect, "Texture" );
}



void game_update( float dltTime )
{
        deltaTime = dltTime;
        camera->Update();

        mesh->Rotate(objectAngle, 0, 0);
        mesh->Transform();
}


//
void game_render2d()
{
        std::ostringstream out;
        out.setf(ios::fixed);
        out << setprecision(4);

        out << "Delta time = " << deltaTime << endl;
        out << "Update = " << g_engine->getCoreFrameRate() << " fps\n";
        out << "Draw = " << g_engine->getScreenFrameRate() << " fps\n";
        out << "Light pos = " << lightVector.x << "," << lightVector.y << ","
            << lightVector.z << endl;
        out << "Light angle = " << lightAngle << endl;
        out << "Light RGBA = " << lightColor.r << "," << lightColor.g << ","
            << lightColor.b << "," << lightColor.a << endl;
        out << "Light intensity = " << lightPower << endl;
        font->Print(0,0,out.str());
```

```
    int w = g_engine->getScreenWidth();
    font->Print(w-200,0,"left/right : light angle");
    font->Print(w-200,20,"up/down : mesh angle");
    font->Print(w-200,40,"+/- : light intensity");
    font->Print(w-200,60,"rgba : cycle color values");
}


void game_event( IEvent* e )
{
    switch( e->getID() )
    {
        case EVENT_KEYPRESS:
        {
            KeyPressEvent* evt = (KeyPressEvent*) e;
            switch(evt->keycode)
            {
                case DIK_ESCAPE: g_engine->Shutdown(); break;

                //left/right arrow keys rotate light source
                case DIK_LEFT: lightAngle -= 0.1f; break;
                case DIK_RIGHT: lightAngle += 0.1f; break;

                //up/down arrow keys rotate the mesh
                case DIK_UP: objectAngle -= 0.02f; break;
                case DIK_DOWN: objectAngle += 0.02f; break;

                //+/- keys change light power
                case DIK_NUMPADPLUS: lightPower += 0.01f; break;
                case DIK_NUMPADMINUS: lightPower -= 0.01f; break;

                //rgba keys cycle color values
                case DIK_R: lightColor.r += 0.01f; break;
                case DIK_G: lightColor.g += 0.01f; break;
                case DIK_B: lightColor.b += 0.01f; break;
                case DIK_A: lightColor.a += 0.01f; break;

            }
            break;
        }
```

```
        case EVENT_MOUSEMOTION:
        {
            MouseMotionEvent* evt = (MouseMotionEvent*)e;
            camera->Look( evt->deltax/100.0f, evt->deltay/100.0f, 0 );
            break;
        }
        case EVENT_MOUSEWHEEL:
        {
            MouseWheelEvent* evt = (MouseWheelEvent*) e;
            camera->Move(0, 0, (float)(-evt->wheel/200.0f) );
            break;
        }
    }

}
```

Summary

We now have the ability to load and render a simple mesh with several types of lighting, which is a good addition to our engine's rendering system that was started in the previous chapter (with materials-based effects). The next chapter goes into more detail by describing how to render with point lights and spotlights, which are quite a bit more difficult than a directional light, but extremely important for any renderer! Following that, we have two more chapters on rendering to address terrain and hierarchical (i.e., "skeleton") mesh animation.

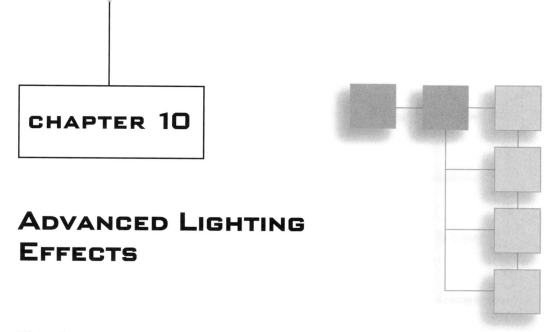

CHAPTER 10

Advanced Lighting Effects

This chapter continues the study of shader-based lighting with some new, advanced lighting effects such as point lights, spotlights, and specular reflection, which dramatically improves the appearance and realism of a mesh.

The following topics are covered in this chapter:

- Textured point light shader
- Textured spotlight shader
- Specular reflection shader
- Textured specular reflection shader

Textured Point Light Shader

When transitioning from a somewhat mundane (and common) directional light to a more exotic light source such as a point light, a shift to per-pixel lighting is essential in order for the light source to illuminate a mesh properly. Since the lighting can be subtle, the next two examples will use a white background so that the lighting on the mesh can be seen on the printed page. The point light source shader will take a few steps beyond the directional light shader, adding light properties that will be used more commonly, such as the ambient lighting level, as well as specular (reflectivity).

Point Lights

A point light is a single light source that emits in all directions like a light bulb. You set the position, color, and attenuation, which is the amount of a decrease in light over distance. The range is the maximum distance that the light will illuminate your 3D objects. Positioning the light source (as a vector), setting its light range, and setting its light strength or power is all there is to a point light— it will light up every mesh within range.

Advice

This chapter's resource files can be downloaded from www.jharbour.com/forum or www.courseptr. com/downloads. Please note that not every line of code will be in print due to space considerations: only the most important sections of code are covered in each chapter.

We begin with the global variable definitions in the effect file. The usual `float4x4` matrices are found here: `World`, `View`, `Projection`, and `WorldInverse-Transpose`, as well as the usual `Texture` variable. For the specific variables needed for the point light, we have `float3 LightPosition` and `float LightRadius`. Those are the most important variables in the point light shader. The remaining ones will differ based on the type of rendering desired. In the case of our example here, we'll be rendering with specular highlights added to the diffuse and ambient values.

```
float4x4 World;
float4x4 View;
float4x4 Projection;
float4x4 WorldInverseTranspose;
texture Texture;

float3 LightPosition;
float LightRadius;

float4 GlobalAmbient;
float4 AmbientMaterial;
float4 AmbientLightColor;

float4 DiffuseMaterial;
float4 DiffuseLight;
```

```
float4 SpecularMaterial;
float4 SpecularLight;

float MaterialSheen;
```

The texture sampler now has some additional quality-setting properties, which are part of the HLSL sampler feature set, and include the `magfilter`, `minfilter`, and `mipfilter`—all of which define how anti-aliasing of lines is performed—as well as texture coordinate options.

```
//Texture sampler
sampler2D TextureSampler = sampler_state
{
    texture = <Texture>;
    magfilter = LINEAR;
    minfilter = LINEAR;
    mipfilter = LINEAR;
    addressU = mirror;
    addressV = mirror;
};
```

Our shader calculates quite a few variables internally, so there will be more properties in the output struct than the input struct—which needs to supply only the position, surface normal, and texture coordinate. Output adds diffuse and specular light levels, view direction (which determines the specular highlight angle), and source light direction.

```
struct VS_INPUT
{
    float3 Position : POSITION0;
    float3 Normal : NORMAL;
    float2 TexCoord : TEXCOORD0;
};

struct VS_OUTPUT
{
    float4 Position : POSITION0;
    float2 TexCoord : TEXCOORD0;
    float3 Normal : TEXCOORD2;
    float3 ViewDir : TEXCOORD3;
    float3 LightDirection : TEXCOORD4;
```

```
    float4 Diffuse : COLOR0;
    float4 Specular : COLOR1;
};
```

Now we come to the vertex shader function, which accepts the input struct as a parameter and returns the output struct (which is passed on to the pixel shader as input). The usual calculations are performed on the `World`, `View`, `Projection`, and `inverse/transform` matrices, and the light source and specular highlight calculations are done to the output variable.

```
VS_OUTPUT vertexShader(VS_INPUT IN)
{
    VS_OUTPUT OUT;
    float4x4 worldViewProjection = mul(mul(World, View), Projection);
    float3 WorldPosition = mul(float4(IN.Position, 1.0f), World).xyz;
    OUT.Position = mul(float4(IN.Position, 1.0f), worldViewProjection);
    OUT.TexCoord = IN.TexCoord;
    OUT.ViewDir = LightPosition - WorldPosition;
    OUT.LightDirection = (LightPosition - WorldPosition) / LightRadius;
    OUT.Normal = mul(IN.Normal, (float3x3)WorldInverseTranspose);
    OUT.Diffuse = DiffuseMaterial * DiffuseLight;
    OUT.Specular = SpecularMaterial * SpecularLight;
    return OUT;
}
```

The pixel shader function is up next. We have quite a bit more code in the pixel shader this time around because we want a smooth transition from the center of the specular highlight to its outer edges, while the vertex shader produces only face-level lighting without smooth gradients. The pixel shader function accepts the output struct from the vertex shader and calculates normals—for the vertex, light direction, view direction, and combined result. Next, dot product is used to produce that gradient blend around the specular highlight to produce a high-quality light reflection based on the light position and view direction (which comes from the camera). Finally, each pixel is lit using the Phong method by adding the ambient, light attenuation, and specular values to arrive at a final color value. This is passed to the part of the GPU that draws pixels.

```
float4 pixelShader(VS_OUTPUT IN) : COLOR
{
```

```
        float Attenuation = saturate(1.0f -
            dot(IN.LightDirection, IN.LightDirection));
        //Finds normals of the vertex normal, light direction,
        //view direction, and combined light and view direction.
        float3 N = normalize(IN.Normal);
        float3 L = normalize(IN.LightDirection);
        float3 V = normalize(IN.ViewDir);
        float3 H = normalize(L + V);

        //find saturated dot product of the light direction
        //normal and the combined light and view direction normal
        float NDotL = saturate(dot(N, L));
        float NDotH = saturate(dot(N, H));

        //find the gloss factor of the specular property
        float Power = (NDotL == 0.0f) ? 0.0f : pow(NDotH, MaterialSheen);

        //calculates the color and amount of the vertexes pixels
        //lighting by using a modified Phong method
        float4 color = (AmbientMaterial * (GlobalAmbient +
            (Attenuation * AmbientLightColor))) +
            (IN.Diffuse * NDotL * Attenuation) +
            (IN.Specular * Power * Attenuation);

        //Returns pixel color modified by lighting color and amount.
        return color * tex2D(TextureSampler, IN.TexCoord);
}

technique TexturedPointLight
{
    pass P0
    {
        VertexShader = compile vs_2_0 vertexShader();
        PixelShader = compile ps_2_0 pixelShader();
    }
}
```

Textured Point Light Shader Demo

The Textured Point Light Shader Demo has quite a few more new parameters to contend with than any previous program, but the end result is a much higher

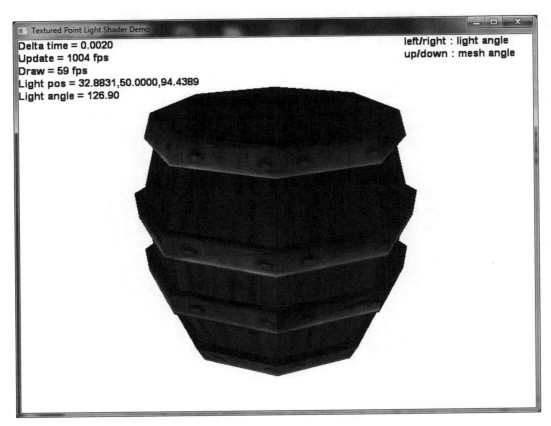

Figure 10.1
The Textured Point Light Shader Demo.

quality render. Figure 10.1 shows the output from the program. Use the left and right arrow keys to rotate the light source around the barrel mesh to see how the dynamic lighting looks!

```cpp
#include "Engine.h"
using namespace std;
using namespace Octane;

Mesh* barrel;
Font* font=NULL;
Camera* camera=NULL;
```

```
Effect* effect=NULL;

Vector3 lightVector;
Color globalAmbient = Color(0.1f,0.1f,0.1f,1.0f);
Color ambientMaterial = Color(0.1f,0.1f,0.1f,1.0f);
Color ambientLightColor = Color(1.0f,1.0f,1.0f,1.0f);
Color diffuseMaterial = Color(1.0f,1.0f,1.0f,1.0f);
Color diffuseLight = Color(1.0f,1.0f,1.0f,1.0f);
Color specularMaterial = Color(0.1f,0.1f,0.1f,1.0f);
Color specularLight = Color(1,1,1,1);

D3DCOLOR BLACK = D3DCOLOR_XRGB(0,0,0);
float lightAngle=90;
float objectAngle=90;
float deltaTime=0;

bool game_preload()
{
    g_engine->setAppTitle("Textured Point Light Shader Demo");
    g_engine->setScreen(800,600,32,false);
    return true;
}

bool game_init(HWND hwnd)
{
    g_engine->setBackdropColor(D3DCOLOR_RGBA(255,255,255,255));
    font = new Font("Arial Bold",20);
    if (!font)
    {
        debug << "Error creating font" << endl;
        return false;
    }

    //create a camera
    camera = new Camera();
    camera->setPosition(0, 0, 100.0);
    camera->setTarget(0,0,0);

    //load the ambient.fx effect
    effect = new Effect();
```

```
        if (!effect->Load("point_light.fx"))
        {
            debug << "Error loading point_light.fx" << endl;
            return false;
        }
        effect->setTechnique("TexturedPointLight");

        //load the mesh
        barrel = new Mesh();
        barrel->Load("barrel.x");

        return true;
}

void game_render3d()
{
        effect->setViewMatrix( camera->getViewMatrix());
        effect->setProjectionMatrix( camera->getProjMatrix());


        //draw the mesh
        {
            barrel->setRotation(0,objectAngle,0);
            barrel->Transform();
            effect->setWorldMatrix( (D3DXMATRIX) barrel->getMatrix());

            //calculate combined inverse transpose matrix
            D3DXMATRIX inverse, wit;
            D3DXMatrixInverse( &inverse, 0, (D3DXMATRIX*)&barrel->getMatrix() );
              D3DXMatrixTranspose( &wit, &inverse );
            effect->setParam( "WorldInverseTranspose", wit );

            //move the light source
            lightVector.x = cosf(lightAngle) * 100.0f;
            lightVector.y = 50.0f;
            lightVector.z = sinf(lightAngle) * 100.0f;
            effect->setParam("LightPosition", lightVector);

            effect->setParam("LightRadius", 200);
            effect->setParam("GlobalAmbient", globalAmbient.ToD3DXVECTOR4());
```

```
            effect->setParam("AmbientMaterial", ambientMaterial.ToD3DXVECTOR4());
            effect->setParam("AmbientLightColor",ambientLightColor.ToD3DXVECTOR4());
            effect->setParam("DiffuseMaterial",diffuseMaterial.ToD3DXVECTOR4());
            effect->setParam("DiffuseLight",diffuseLight.ToD3DXVECTOR4());
            effect->setParam("SpecularMaterial",specularMaterial.ToD3DXVECTOR4());
            effect->setParam("SpecularLight",specularLight.ToD3DXVECTOR4());
            effect->setParam("MaterialSheen", 50.0f);

            barrel->Render( effect );
        }
}

void game_end()
{
    if (font) delete font;
    if (effect) delete effect;
    if (camera) delete camera;
    if (barrel) delete barrel;
}

void game_update( float dltTime )
{
    deltaTime = dltTime;
    camera->Update();
}

void game_render2d()
{
    std::ostringstream out;
    out.setf(ios::fixed);
    out << setprecision(4);
    out << "Delta time = " << deltaTime << endl;
    out << "Update = " << g_engine->getCoreFrameRate() << " fps\n";
    out << "Draw = " << g_engine->getScreenFrameRate() << " fps\n";
    out << "Light pos = " << lightVector.x << "," << lightVector.y
        << "," << lightVector.z << endl;
    out << "Light angle = " << lightAngle << endl;
    font->Print(0,0,out.str(),BLACK);
```

```cpp
        int w = g_engine->getScreenWidth();
        font->Print(w-200,0,"left/right : light angle",BLACK);
        font->Print(w-200,20,"up/down : mesh angle",BLACK);
}

void game_event( IEvent* e )
{
    switch( e->getID() )
    {
        case EVENT_KEYPRESS:
        {
            KeyPressEvent* evt = (KeyPressEvent*) e;
            switch(evt->keycode)
            {
                case DIK_ESCAPE: g_engine->Shutdown(); break;

                //left/right arrow keys rotate light source
                case DIK_LEFT: lightAngle -= 0.1f; break;
                case DIK_RIGHT: lightAngle += 0.1f; break;

                //up/down arrow keys rotate the mesh
                case DIK_UP: objectAngle -= 1.0f; break;
                case DIK_DOWN: objectAngle += 1.0f; break;
            }
            break;
        }
        case EVENT_MOUSEMOTION:
        {
            MouseMotionEvent* evt = (MouseMotionEvent*)e;
            camera->Look( evt->deltax/100.0f, evt->deltay/100.0f, 0 );
            break;
        }
        case EVENT_MOUSEWHEEL:
        {
            MouseWheelEvent* evt = (MouseWheelEvent*) e;
            camera->Move(0, 0, (float)(-evt->wheel/200.0f) );
            break;
        }
```

SPECULAR REFLECTION SHADER

We have been using a specular effect in the last two examples to improve the appearance of the point light and spotlight, but with all of the other types of lighting also being used in those examples, it's not clear what exactly the specular effect adds to the render on its own, so we'll go over specular reflection now with a pair of smaller demos. The first one renders a high-poly asteroid mesh without its texture, since the first `specular.fx` file ignores the texture map, resulting in a *chrome-like* effect. The second example renders the same mesh with its texture for a brightly polished look that is quite remarkable. Figure 10.2 shows the first example that renders a material-only mesh.

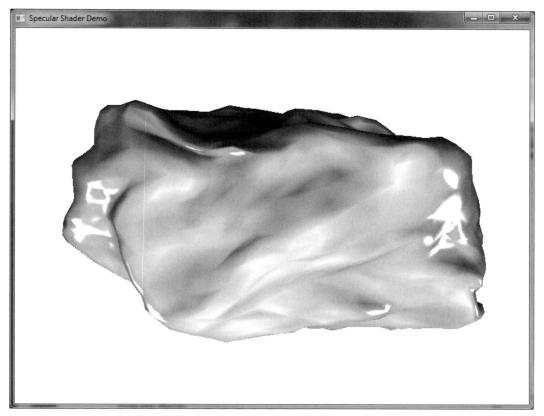

Figure 10.2
This mesh is being rendered with a specular shader that gives it a reflective quality.

There are so few parameters needed this time, illustrating the value of setting initial values for the global properties in an effect file, since that allows the effect to function with minimal input from the C++ side (in the event that you forget to pass a particular parameter). The specular reflection shader uses a dot product calculation to create a reflective highlight based on the light source and the view position.

Some of the globals in the effect file will be familiar to you by now, such as the usual world, view, projection, world inverse transform, ambient, and so on. Where the specular effect comes in is with the shininess, specular color, and specular intensity properties. I encourage you to tweak these values to see what interesting changes you can create in the rendered mesh. The shininess property, for instance:

```
float4x4 World;
float4x4 View;
float4x4 Projection;
float4x4 WorldInverseTranspose;

float4 AmbientColor = float4(1, 1, 1, 1);
float AmbientIntensity = 0.01;

float3 DiffuseLightDirection = float3(0, 0, 1);
float4 DiffuseColor = float4(1, 1, 1, 1);
float DiffuseIntensity = 1;

float Shininess = 100;
float4 SpecularColor = float4(1, 1, 1, 1);
float SpecularIntensity = 1;
float3 ViewVector = float3(1, 0, 0);

struct VertexShaderInput
{
    float4 Position : POSITION0;
    float4 Normal : NORMAL0;
};

struct VertexShaderOutput
{
    float4 Position : POSITION0;
```

```
    float4 Color : COLOR0;
    float3 Normal : TEXCOORD0;
};

VertexShaderOutput VertexShaderFunction(VertexShaderInput input)
{
    VertexShaderOutput output;

    float4 worldPosition = mul(input.Position, World);
    float4 viewPosition = mul(worldPosition, View);
    output.Position = mul(viewPosition, Projection);

    float4 normal = normalize(mul(input.Normal, WorldInverseTranspose));
    float lightIntensity = dot(normal, DiffuseLightDirection);
    output.Color = saturate(DiffuseColor * DiffuseIntensity *
        lightIntensity);

    output.Normal = normal;

    return output;
}

float4 PixelShaderFunction(VertexShaderOutput input) : COLOR0
{
    float3 light = normalize(DiffuseLightDirection);
    float3 normal = normalize(input.Normal);
    float3 r = normalize(2 * dot(light, normal) * normal - light);
    float3 v = normalize(mul(normalize(ViewVector), World));
    float dotProduct = abs(dot(r, v));

    float4 specular = SpecularIntensity * SpecularColor
        * max(pow(dotProduct, Shininess), 0) * length(input.Color);

    return saturate(input.Color + AmbientColor *
        AmbientIntensity + specular);
}

technique Specular
{
    pass Pass1
```

```
    {
        VertexShader = compile vs_2_0 VertexShaderFunction();
        PixelShader = compile ps_2_0 PixelShaderFunction();
    }
}
```

Specular Light Demo

The source code for this program is similar to the previous program but with the addition of the texture property, which is now actually used by the effect.

```
#include "Engine.h"
using namespace Octane;

//game objects
Effect* effect=NULL;
Camera* camera=NULL;
Mesh* mesh=NULL;

bool game_preload()
{
    g_engine->setAppTitle("Specular Shader Demo");
    g_engine->setScreen(800,600,32,false);
    g_engine->setBackdropColor( D3DCOLOR_XRGB(255,255,255) );
    return true;
}

bool game_init(HWND)
{
    srand(time(NULL));

    //set the camera and perspective
    camera = new Camera();
    camera->setPosition(0.0f, 3.0f, 6.0f);
    camera->setTarget(0.0f, 0.0f, 0.0f);
    camera->Update();

    //create effect object
    effect = new Effect();
    if (!effect->Load("specular.fx"))
    {
```

```
            debug << "Error loading effect\n";
            return false;
    }

    //load the mesh
    mesh = new Mesh();
    if (!mesh->Load("AST_02.x"))
    {
        debug << "Error loading mesh file\n";
        return false;
    }
    mesh->setScale(0.05f,0.05f,0.05f);
    mesh->Rotate( 0, -90.0f, 0 );

    return true;
}

void game_render3d()
{
    mesh->Rotate( 1.0f,0.0f,0.0f);
    mesh->Transform();

    effect->setProjectionMatrix( camera->getProjMatrix() );
    effect->setViewMatrix( camera->getViewMatrix() );
    effect->setWorldMatrix( mesh->getMatrix() );

    D3DXMATRIX wit;
    D3DXMatrixInverse( &wit, 0, &mesh->getMatrix() );
    D3DXMatrixTranspose( &wit, &wit );
    effect->setParam( "WorldInverseTranspose", wit );

    mesh->Render( effect );
}

void game_update(float deltaTime) { }

void game_end()
{
    if (camera) delete camera;
    if (mesh) delete mesh;
```

```
        if (effect) delete effect;
}

void game_keyRelease (int key)
{
        if (key == DIK_ESCAPE) g_engine->Shutdown();
}
void game_render2d(){}

void game_event( IEvent* e )
{
        switch( e->getID() )
        {
                case EVENT_KEYPRESS:
                {
                        KeyPressEvent* evt = (KeyPressEvent*) e;
                        switch(evt->keycode)
                        {
                                case DIK_ESCAPE: g_engine->Shutdown(); break;
                        }
                        break;
                }
                case EVENT_MOUSEMOTION:
                {
                        MouseMotionEvent* evt = (MouseMotionEvent*)e;
                        camera->Look( evt->deltax/100.0f, evt->deltay/100.0f, 0 );
                        break;
                }
                case EVENT_MOUSEWHEEL:
                {
                        MouseWheelEvent* evt = (MouseWheelEvent*) e;
                        camera->Move(0, 0, (float)(-evt->wheel/200.0f) );
                        break;
                }
        }}
```

Textured Specular Reflection

Now, comparing the material-based specular shader with the textured version
(see below), we can see that very little change is needed: just the addition of the
texture sampler, one new property in the input and output structs. Figure 10.3

Figure 10.3
The textured version.

shows the textured version. The source code for the textured specular demo is unchanged from the non-textured version, so we'll forego a duplication of the code here and just present the textured specular reflection shader.

```
float4x4 World;
float4x4 View;
float4x4 Projection;
float4x4 WorldInverseTranspose;
texture Texture;

float4 AmbientColor = float4(1, 1, 1, 1);
float AmbientIntensity = 0.01;
float3 DiffuseLightDirection = float3(1, 1, 1);
```

```
float4 DiffuseColor = float4(1, 1, 1, 1);
float DiffuseIntensity = 0.9f;
float Shininess = 10;
float4 SpecularColor = float4(1, 1, 1, 1);
float SpecularIntensity = 1;
float3 ViewVector = float3(1, 1, 1);

sampler2D textureSampler =
sampler_state {
    Texture = (Texture);
    MagFilter = Linear;
    MinFilter = Linear;
    AddressU = Clamp;
    AddressV = Clamp;
};

struct VertexShaderInput
{
    float4 Position : POSITION0;
    float4 Normal : NORMAL0;
    float2 TextureCoordinate : TEXCOORD0;
};

struct VertexShaderOutput
{
    float4 Position : POSITION0;
    float4 Color : COLOR0;
    float3 Normal : TEXCOORD0;
    float2 TextureCoordinate : TEXCOORD1;
};

VertexShaderOutput VertexShaderFunction(VertexShaderInput input)
{
    VertexShaderOutput output;

    float4 worldPosition = mul(input.Position, World);
    float4 viewPosition = mul(worldPosition, View);
    output.Position = mul(viewPosition, Projection);

    float4 normal = normalize(mul(input.Normal, WorldInverseTranspose));
```

```
    float lightIntensity = dot(normal, DiffuseLightDirection);
    output.Color = saturate(DiffuseColor * DiffuseIntensity * lightIntensity);

    output.Normal = normal;
    output.TextureCoordinate = input.TextureCoordinate;

    return output;
}

float4 PixelShaderFunction(VertexShaderOutput input) : COLOR0
{
    float3 light = normalize(DiffuseLightDirection);
    float3 normal = normalize(input.Normal);
    float3 r = normalize(2 * dot(light, normal) * normal - light);
    float3 v = normalize(mul(normalize(ViewVector), World));
    float dotProduct = abs(dot(r, v));

    float4 specular = max(pow(dotProduct, Shininess), 0) *
        length(input.Color) * SpecularIntensity * SpecularColor;

    float4 textureColor = tex2D(textureSampler, input.TextureCoordinate);
    textureColor.a = 1;

    return saturate(textureColor * (input.Color) +
        AmbientColor * AmbientIntensity + specular);
}

technique Specular
{
    pass Pass1
    {
        VertexShader = compile vs_2_0 VertexShaderFunction();
        PixelShader = compile ps_2_0 PixelShaderFunction();
    }
}
```

Summary

Lighting is a monumental challenge when we're considering the features for a game engine's rendering system, as you have seen in the pages of this chapter! While the concepts behind lighting are not *complex*, implementing a directional light, spotlight, and point light in GPU code can be *complicated*. What often surprises many engine or renderer programmers is how unique (and uniquely demanding) each game's shader requirements are. While there are some concepts that do see re-use, such as the usual diffuse/directional light shader, most techniques will change to meet the needs of each scene in a game, because an innovative designer does not want his or her game to look like all the rest, and everyone knows that whiz-bang glowing fireballs alone do not sell! (On the contrary, such is now assumed as a baseline.)

CHAPTER 11

WRAPPING THE SKY IN A BOX

The environment of a game can vary widely from one game genre to the next, from an outer space environment (like in the phenomenally uber-classic *Homeworld*), which is usually just a large sky sphere with a space scene texture and various asteroids and planets in the vicinity, to the typical outdoor game world comprised of heightmap terrain (like the world in *World of Warcraft*), to a common indoor theme for first-person shooters (like *Doom III*). In this chapter, we will see how to create a skybox and how to apply it to an outer space scene, while relegating the indoor and outdoor environment demos for upcoming chapters.

This chapter covers the following topics:

- Skybox or skysphere?
- Creating a custom skybox
- Skybox class
- Skybox shader
- Mountain skybox demo
- Space skybox demo

BUILDING A SKYBOX

The first step toward creating an environment that *grabs* the player with a strong suspension of disbelief (where one forgets he or she is actually playing a game and becomes engrossed in the story, much like the experience while reading a great novel) is to add a skybox. A *skybox* is a cube mesh (or a sphere in the case of a sky *sphere*) that surrounds the camera at all times. But, rather than rendering a skybox *within* the scene, it *wraps* around the entire scene. Therefore, the surface normals for a skybox must be directed inward from the inside of the cube, rather than pointing outward on the outer faces of the cube as is normally done to light a normal mesh. A skybox moves *with* the camera to create the illusion of distance. This is crucial! To fool the player's eyes into believing they are really in a larger environment surrounded by stars, or mountains (as are typical for most games), the skybox must move with the camera, giving the impression that it does not move at all.

Skybox or Skysphere?

Advice

Although it may seem that a sphere map would produce better results due to its higher number of faces, a cube map is actually preferred because it works better with lower-resolution textures and renders a higher quality surface when using algorithmically generated textures.

The preferred way to professionally render a skybox or skysphere is with a cube texture, a self-contained texture file that must be generated with a custom tool such as the DirectX Texture Tool (look in the DirectX SDK in your Start Menu). This is one of the least user-friendly utilities ever created, so don't expect to get much practical use out of it. Think of a cube texture as a paper cube with the sides unfolded to make a cross shape, like the one in Figure 11.1.

The reason why I dislike the cube texture approach to rendering a skybox is because I have no control over the cube texture (or at least not without much effort), while a simpler mesh of a cube with six texture files is more easily modifiable, giving us more control over exactly which mesh is being rendered on which side. After loading the mesh and the six textures, we can also modify each individual texture in memory if needed—or replace the textures on the fly. One nice effect is to adjust the ambient light intensity when rendering the skybox to reflect daytime or nighttime in the scene.

One thing to note about a skybox: it will *never* encompass the entire scene. That's right; the skybox does not need to be larger than all of the geometry in the scene! But, won't the geometry intersect with the skybox unless it is really large?

Figure 11.1
A cube texture is a single texture that wraps a cube with a different image on each of the six sides.

Yes, quite simply. The trick is not to make the skybox really huge, but instead to screw with the Z-buffer. Strangely enough, we can just turn off the Z-buffer for the skybox and turn it back on for everything else. Therefore, even if you have a scene that stretches from virtual horizon to virtual horizon, encompassing thousands of units in 3D space, while the skybox is only $10 \times 10 \times 10$ units, it will still appear to be a vast distance away.

Advice

Due to the advanced render states needed to render a skybox or skysphere with a shader, our skybox will render around the origin with only trivial geometry in the scene. The skybox developed in this chapter *can* be transformed to move with the camera. When rendering a small skybox "around" a normal scene in a game, be sure to disable z-buffering before rendering the skybox, and then re-enable z-buffering again afterward.

Another way to create a skybox is with a mesh already modeled with the normals correctly set on the inside of the faces and the texture filenames specified inside the .X file. This is certainly the easiest type of skybox to create—just load the mesh, increase its scale, and render with any fixed function or

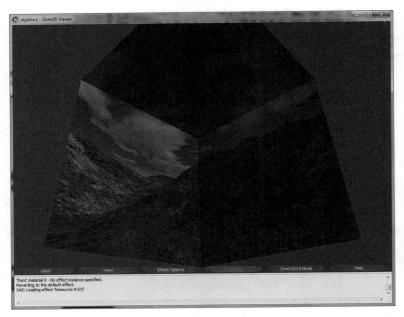

Figure 11.2
Note how the inverse normals cause the faces to reflect light from *inside* the skybox.

programmable pipeline code. Figure 11.2 shows a sample skybox mesh rendered by the DirectX Viewer.

There is a third approach to creating a skybox: generating our own vertex buffer for a cube mesh and applying textures manually. This is the most *educational* way to create a skybox, but certainly not the *easiest* or even necessarily the best method. Doing something from scratch does afford a learning experience, but often at the expense of performance and quality. In this case, there's no harm in generating your own vertex buffer for a skybox.

Creating a Custom Skybox

Skybox meshes are fairly easy to come by, and that is the approach you may want to take with your own engine—by just loading a mesh with the internal normals and textures already built in. However, we don't want to rely entirely on someone else's skybox mesh, so we'll also see how to create a skybox vertex buffer with texture coordinates in the FVF so we can generate a mesh with

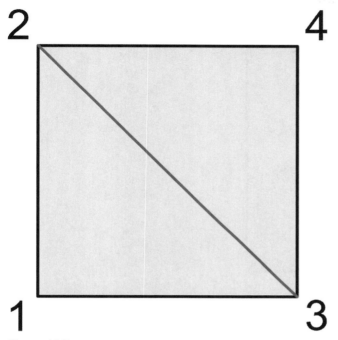

Figure 11.3
Each side of the skybox cube is made of a quad with two faces and four vertices in this counter-clockwise order.

desired dimensions as needed. Why? Because I just like to torture myself with more work than is actually necessary, with the goal of achieving awesomeness. (Oh, gee, I made a cube!)

Our generated cube mesh will have four vertices per side, arranged as shown in Figure 11.3. We will need six sides for the cube, each comprised of four vertices containing position and texture coordinate values. The upper-left corner of a side will have a UV texture coordinate of (0,0), while the lower-right corner will have a UV of (1,1), as shown in Figure 11.4.

Advice

This chapter's resource files can be downloaded from www.jharbour.com/forum or www.courseptr.com/downloads. Please note that not every line of code will be in print due to space considerations: only the most important sections of code are covered in each chapter.

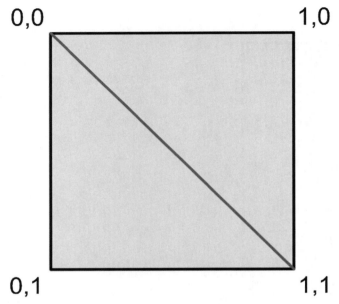

Figure 11.4
The UV texture coordinates for the quad wrap one entire texture to cover one side of the cube mesh.

Skybox Class

This Skybox class should meet our needs:

```
class Skybox
{
    private:
        Texture* textures[6];
        ID3DXMesh *mesh;
    public:
        Skybox(void);
        virtual ~Skybox(void);
        bool Create( std::string sharedFilename );
        void Render();
};
```

The Skybox class maintains its own internal vertex buffer via ID3DXMesh. The vertex buffer is filled with vertices that describe the shape of a cube with position and texture coordinate properties. Here is the code listing for the Skybox class and its supporting code. Note that, as usual, the headers and namespaces have been omitted to save space.

```
const int SKYBOX_FVF = D3DFVF_XYZ | D3DFVF_TEX1;

struct SkyboxVertex
{
    float x, y, z;
    float u, v;
    SkyboxVertex(float _x, float _y, float _z, float _u, float _v)
    {
        x = _x;
        y = _y;
        z = _z;
        u = _u;
        v = _v;
    }
};

Skybox::Skybox(void)
{
    mesh = NULL;

    for (int n=0; n<6; n++)
        textures[n] = NULL;
}

Skybox::~Skybox(void)
{
    //delete the textures
    for (int n = 0; n < 6; n++)
    {
        if (textures[n])
        {
            delete textures[n];
            textures[n] = NULL;
        }
    }

    //delete mesh
    if(mesh) mesh->Release();
}

bool Skybox::Create( std::string sharedFilename )
{
```

```
std::string prefix[] = {"U_", "F_", "B_", "R_", "L_", "D_"};

//set texture mapping sampler states
for(int i=0; i<4; i++)
{
    g_engine->getDevice()->SetSamplerState(
        i, D3DSAMP_MAGFILTER, D3DTEXF_LINEAR);
    g_engine->getDevice()->SetSamplerState(
        i, D3DSAMP_MINFILTER, D3DTEXF_LINEAR);
    g_engine->getDevice()->SetSamplerState(
        i, D3DSAMP_MIPFILTER, D3DTEXF_POINT);
}

//release textures if already in memory
for (int n=0; n<6; n++)
{
    if (textures[n])
    {
        delete textures[n];
        textures[n] = NULL;
    }
}
//re-create any null texture
for (int n=0; n<6; n++)
{
    if (!textures[n])
        textures[n] = new Texture();
}

//load skybox textures
bool res = true;
for(int n=0; n<6; n++)
{
    string fn = prefix[n] + sharedFilename;
    if (!textures[n]->Load(fn.c_str()))
    {
        debug << "Skybox: Error loading " << fn << endl;
          return false;
    }
}
```

```cpp
//create mesh
D3DXCreateMeshFVF(12, 24, D3DXMESH_MANAGED, SKYBOX_FVF,
    g_engine->getDevice(), &mesh);

//create vertices
SkyboxVertex* v = 0;
mesh->LockVertexBuffer(0,(void**)&v);

{
    float size = 4000.0f;

    //up face
    v[0]  = SkyboxVertex( size, size,  size, 0.f, 0.f);
    v[1]  = SkyboxVertex(-size, size,  size, 1.f, 0.f);
    v[2]  = SkyboxVertex( size, size, -size, 0.f, 1.f);
    v[3]  = SkyboxVertex(-size, size, -size, 1.f, 1.f);

    //front face
    v[4]  = SkyboxVertex(-size,  size, size, 0.f, 0.f);
    v[5]  = SkyboxVertex( size,  size, size, 1.f, 0.f);
    v[6]  = SkyboxVertex(-size, -size, size, 0.f, 1.f);
    v[7]  = SkyboxVertex( size, -size, size, 1.f, 1.f);

    //back face
    v[8]  = SkyboxVertex( size,  size, -size, 0.f, 0.f);
    v[9]  = SkyboxVertex(-size,  size, -size, 1.f, 0.f);
    v[10] = SkyboxVertex( size, -size, -size, 0.f, 1.f);
    v[11] = SkyboxVertex(-size, -size, -size, 1.f, 1.f);

    //right face
    v[12] = SkyboxVertex(-size,  size, -size, 0.f, 0.f);
    v[13] = SkyboxVertex(-size,  size,  size, 1.f, 0.f);
    v[14] = SkyboxVertex(-size, -size, -size, 0.f, 1.f);
    v[15] = SkyboxVertex(-size, -size,  size, 1.f, 1.f);

    //left face
    v[16] = SkyboxVertex(size,  size,  size, 0.f, 0.f);
    v[17] = SkyboxVertex(size,  size, -size, 1.f, 0.f);
    v[18] = SkyboxVertex(size, -size,  size, 0.f, 1.f);
    v[19] = SkyboxVertex(size, -size, -size, 1.f, 1.f);
```

```cpp
        //down face
        v[20] = SkyboxVertex( size, -size, -size, 0.f, 0.f);
        v[21] = SkyboxVertex(-size, -size, -size, 1.f, 0.f);
        v[22] = SkyboxVertex( size, -size,  size, 0.f, 1.f);
        v[23] = SkyboxVertex(-size, -size,  size, 1.f, 1.f);
    }

    mesh->UnlockVertexBuffer();

    //calculate indices
    unsigned short* indices = 0;
    mesh->LockIndexBuffer(0,(void**)&indices);

    int index = 0;
    for(int quad=0;quad<6;quad++)
    {
        //first face
        indices[index++] = quad * 4;
        indices[index++] = quad * 4 + 1;
        indices[index++] = quad * 4 + 2;

        //second Face
        indices[index++] = quad * 4 + 1;
        indices[index++] = quad * 4 + 3;
        indices[index++] = quad * 4 + 2;
    }

    mesh->UnlockIndexBuffer();

    //set each quad to its sub mesh
    unsigned long *att = 0;
    mesh->LockAttributeBuffer(0,&att);
    for(int i=0;i<12;i++)
        att[i] = i / 2;
    mesh->UnlockAttributeBuffer();

    return true;
}

void Skybox::Draw()
{
    //save render states
```

```
g_engine->getDevice()->SetRenderState(D3DRS_LIGHTING, false);
g_engine->getDevice()->SetRenderState(D3DRS_ZWRITEENABLE, false);
g_engine->getDevice()->SetRenderState(D3DRS_ZENABLE, false);
g_engine->getDevice()->SetSamplerState(
    0, D3DSAMP_ADDRESSU, D3DTADDRESS_CLAMP);
g_engine->getDevice()->SetSamplerState(
    0, D3DSAMP_ADDRESSV, D3DTADDRESS_CLAMP);


//render the skybox
for ( int n = 0; n < 6; n++ )
{
    g_engine->getDevice()->SetTexture(0,textures[n]->getTexture());
    mesh->DrawSubset(n);
}


//restore render states
g_engine->getDevice()->SetRenderState(D3DRS_LIGHTING, true);
g_engine->getDevice()->SetRenderState(D3DRS_ZWRITEENABLE, true);
g_engine->getDevice()->SetRenderState(D3DRS_ZENABLE, true);
g_engine->getDevice()->SetSamplerState(
    0, D3DSAMP_ADDRESSU, D3DTADDRESS_WRAP);
g_engine->getDevice()->SetSamplerState(
    0, D3DSAMP_ADDRESSV, D3DTADDRESS_WRAP);
}
```

Skybox Shader

The shader we'll use to render a skybox is not a "skybox shader," but really just an improved version of the old ambient.fx file we've been using for the last few chapters. The improvements include support for a texture and, of course, a sampler. It's the sampler that is of particular interest (which we'll address in the next section).

```
float4x4 World;
float4x4 View;
float4x4 Projection;
float4 AmbientColor = float4(1.0,1.0,1.0,1);
float AmbientIntensity = 1;
texture Texture;
```

```
struct MyVertexStruct
{
    float4 position   : POSITION0;
    float4 texcoord : TEXCOORD0;
};

MyVertexStruct VertexShaderFunction( MyVertexStruct input )
{
    //create struct variable to return
    MyVertexStruct output = (MyVertexStruct)0;

    //combine world + view + projection matrices
    float4x4 viewProj = mul(View,Projection);
    float4x4 WorldViewProj = mul(World,viewProj);

    //translate the current vertex
    output.position = mul(input.position, WorldViewProj);

    //set texture coordinates
    output.texcoord = input.texcoord;

    return output;
}

sampler TextureSampler =
sampler_state
{
    texture = <Texture>;
    minfilter = linear;
    magfilter = linear;
    mipfilter = point;
    addressu = clamp;
    addressv = clamp;
};

float4 PixelShaderFunction(float2 texcoord : TEXCOORD0) : COLOR
{
    return ( tex2D( TextureSampler,texcoord ) * AmbientColor * AmbientIntensity);
}

technique Ambient
```

```
{
    pass P0
    {
        vertexShader = compile vs_2_0 VertexShaderFunction();
        pixelShader  = compile ps_2_0 PixelShaderFunction();
    }
}
```

Advice

When rendering the skybox, it may be helpful to create a separate Camera object since the projection matrix has to be changed a bit for the skybox—specifically, the field of view (FOV) is changed from the usual π * 0.25f to π * 0.4f (or roughly twice the normal value). Also, when rendering a skybox, the Z-buffer needs to be disabled so that the skybox will be rendered behind all other geometry in the scene.

Mountain Skybox Demo

When building your own skybox by creating a cube at runtime, it's important to pay attention to the ordering of the cube face textures, as they must be named correctly as well as put into the correct order. You may change the default prefixes used by modifying the prefix array in Skybox::Create:

```
std::string prefix[] = {"U_", "F_", "B_", "R_", "L_", "D_"};
```

Here is the order of the skybox textures:

1. Up (or top) (U_)

2. Forward (F_)

3. Backward (B_)

4. Right (R_)

5. Left (L_)

6. Down (or bottom) (D_)

Our sample program to demonstrate the Skybox class is shown in Figure 11.5 with the provided skybox textures for this project. You may purchase a huge assortment of skyboxes and skyspheres for a very affordable price from The Game Creators (www.thegamecreators.com).

Textures courtesy of www.TheGameCreators.com.

Figure 11.5
Realistic-looking environments like this can be created with TerraGen (www.planetside.co.uk).

Now, this is a very nice-looking skybox, thanks to the use of high-quality, 1024 × 1024, seamless textures (courtesy of The Game Creators). But with a simple change to the sampler, we can seriously screw up the skybox. What we need to happen is for the seams to blend together nicely so that no line is visible between the seams, which reveals our secret—that the skybox is not a true scene of distant mountains but just a sort of magic trick with z-buffering and a cube with some nice textures applied to its inner surface. No, we don't want to reveal that to the player at all! But that is what will happen without proper sampler settings. Here again is the sample for reference, which renders the skybox with nice, clean, blended edges.

```
sampler TextureSampler = sampler_state
{
    texture = <Texture>;
    minfilter = linear;
    magfilter = linear;
    mipfilter = point;
```

Figure 11.6
Seamless textures used to render the mountain skybox.

```
    addressu = clamp;
    addressv = clamp;
};
```

Figure 11.6 shows the textures used in the Mountain Skybox Demo program.

Here is the source code for the Mountain Skybox Demo, which just renders a simple skybox with mouse look: support. There is still a small amount of skybox camera code in the main program, but since this is likely to change in every game based on preferences, it is best left out of the Skybox class.

```cpp
#include "Engine.h"
#include "Skybox.h"
using namespace Octane;
using namespace std;

//game objects
Font* font=NULL;
Effect* effect=NULL;
Skybox* skybox=NULL;
Camera* camera=NULL;
```

```
Matrix matWorld;
Vector3 mouseRotate;
D3DXVECTOR3 focus;

void game_end()
{
    if (camera) delete camera;
    if (effect) delete effect;
    if (skybox) delete skybox;
    if (font) delete font;
}

bool game_preload()
{
    g_engine->setAppTitle("Mountain Skybox Demo");
    g_engine->setScreen(1024,768,32,false);
    g_engine->setBackdropColor( D3DCOLOR_XRGB(10,10,20) );
    return true;
}

bool game_init(HWND hwnd)
{
    //create a font
    font = new Font("Arial",14);

    //create the skybox camera
    camera = new Camera();

    //create effect object
    effect = new Effect();
    if (!effect->Load("ambient.fx"))
    {
        debug << "Error loading effect\n";
        return false;
    }

    //create a skybox
    skybox = new Skybox();
    if (!skybox->Create( "mtns.jpg" ))
    {
        debug << "Error creating skybox\n";
```

```
            return false;
        }

        matWorld.setIdentity();
        mouseRotate = Vector3(0,0,0);

        return true;
    }


    void game_render3d()
    {
        //calculate normalized lookat vector for the skybox
        D3DXMATRIX r;
        D3DXMatrixRotationYawPitchRoll(&r, mouseRotate.y, mouseRotate.x,
    mouseRotate.z);
        focus = D3DXVECTOR3(1.0f, 0.0f, 0.0f);
        D3DXVec3TransformNormal(&focus, &focus, &r);
        D3DXVec3Normalize(&focus, &focus);

        //set camera perspective to render skybox
        camera->setPosition(0,0,0);
        camera->setTarget(focus.x, focus.y, focus.z);
        camera->setPerspective( Octane::PI * 0.4f, 1.33333f, 0.01f, 10000.0f );
        camera->Update();

        //send transforms to shader
        matWorld.setIdentity();
        effect->setWorldMatrix( matWorld );
        effect->setViewMatrix( camera->getViewMatrix() );
        effect->setProjectionMatrix( camera->getProjMatrix() );

        //render the skybox
        effect->Begin();
        skybox->Render();
        effect->End();

        //restore normal camera perspective
        camera->setPerspective( Octane::PI / 4.0f, 1.33333f, 0.01f, 10000.0f );
        camera->setPosition(0,0,-200);
        camera->setTarget(0,0,0);
```

```
        camera->Update();
}

void game_update(float deltaTime) { }

void game_render2d()
{
    ostringstream out;
    out << "Core: " << g_engine->getCoreFrameRate() << endl;
    out << "Camera: " << focus.x << "," << focus.y << ","
        << focus.z << endl;
    font->Print(0,0, out.str());
}

void game_event( IEvent* e )
{
    switch( e->getID() )
    {
        case EVENT_KEYPRESS:
        {
            KeyPressEvent* evt = (KeyPressEvent*) e;
            switch(evt->keycode)
            {
                case DIK_ESCAPE: g_engine->Shutdown(); break;
            }
            break;
        }
        case EVENT_MOUSEMOTION:
        {
            MouseMotionEvent* evt = (MouseMotionEvent*)e;
            mouseRotate.y += (evt->deltax) * 0.001f;
            mouseRotate.z -= (evt->deltay) * 0.001f;
            break;
        }
    }
}
```

Space Skybox Demo

Lets try a different skybox, this time with a seamless space texture, shown in Figure 11.7. Unfortunately, our Skybox class does not have the ability to create an entire

Figure 11.7
A seamless texture containing a space scene.

skybox with just a single texture—at present, that is. It seems fairly useful to add this as a feature to the class so that there is not a waste of memory as is currently the case. Even though we're using just one texture for all six sides of the skybox, that one texture file has been copied into six filenames with the appropriate prefixes for all of the sides. May be a future feature to consider adding!

The Space Skybox Demo is a step beyond the previous example, as we now have an example of how to render geometry in addition to the skybox. In this example, shown in Figure 11.8, an asteroid mesh is being transformed and rendered in addition to the skybox, both using an ambient shader—although you are welcome to try different effect files! As this example illustrates, we can add any number of meshes to the scene after rendering the skybox. However, in this simplistic example, if the scene is too large then z-buffering will need to be disabled when rendering the skybox mesh. The code related to the asteroid is highlighted in bold in the following listing.

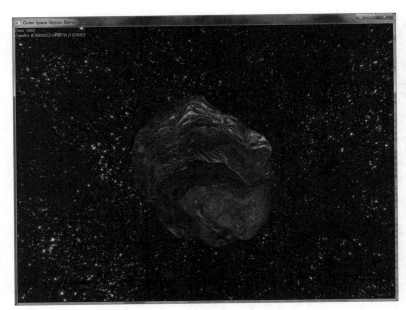

Figure 11.8
The Space Skybox Demo features some geometry in the scene along with the skybox.

```
#include "Engine.h"
#include "Skybox.h"
using namespace Octane;
using namespace std;

//game objects
Skybox* skybox=NULL;
Font* font=NULL;
Effect* effect=NULL;
Camera* camera=NULL;
Mesh* asteroid=NULL;
Matrix matWorld;
Vector3 mouseRotate;
D3DXVECTOR3 focus;

void game_end()
{
    if (skybox) delete skybox;
    if (font) delete font;
```

```
    if (effect) delete effect;
    if (camera) delete camera;
    if (asteroid) delete asteroid;
}

bool game_preload()
{
    g_engine->setAppTitle("Outer Space Skybox Demo");
    g_engine->setScreen(1024,768,32,false);
    g_engine->setBackdropColor( D3DCOLOR_XRGB(10,10,20) );
    return true;
}

bool game_init(HWND hwnd)
{
    //create a font
    font = new Font("Arial",14);

    //create the skybox camera
    camera = new Camera();

    //create effect object
    effect = new Effect();
    if (!effect->Load("ambient.fx"))
    {
        debug << "Error loading effect\n";
        return false;
    }

    asteroid = new Mesh();
    if (!asteroid->Load("AST_02.x"))
    {
        debug << "Error loading asteroid\n";
        return false;
    }
    asteroid->setScale(0.1);

    //create a skybox
    skybox = new Skybox();
    if (!skybox->Create( "space.bmp" ))
```

```
        {
            debug << "Error creating skybox\n";
            return false;
        }

        matWorld.setIdentity();
        mouseRotate = Vector3(0,0,0);

        return true;
    }

    void game_render3d()
    {
        //calculate normalized lookat vector for the skybox
        D3DXMATRIX r;
        D3DXMatrixRotationYawPitchRoll(&r,
            mouseRotate.y, mouseRotate.x, mouseRotate.z);
        focus = D3DXVECTOR3(1.0f, 0.0f, 0.0f);
        D3DXVec3TransformNormal(&focus, &focus, &r);
        D3DXVec3Normalize(&focus, &focus);

        //set camera for skybox rendering
        camera->setPosition(0,0,0);
        camera->setTarget(focus.x, focus.y, focus.z);
        camera->setPerspective(Octane::PI * 0.4f,1.33333f,0.01f,10000.0f);
        camera->Update();

        //send matrices to shader
        matWorld.setIdentity();
        effect->setWorldMatrix( matWorld );
        effect->setViewMatrix( camera->getViewMatrix() );
        effect->setProjectionMatrix( camera->getProjMatrix() );

        //render the skybox
        effect->Begin();
        skybox->Render();
        effect->End();

        //set perspective to normal
        camera->setPerspective(Octane::PI / 4.0f,1.33333f,0.01f,10000.0f);
```

```cpp
    camera->setPosition(0,0,-20);
    camera->setTarget(0,0,0);
    camera->Update();

    //rotate the asteroid
    asteroid->setPosition(0,0,0);
    asteroid->Rotate(0.1f,0,0);
    asteroid->Transform();

    //send matrices to shader
    effect->setWorldMatrix( matWorld );
    effect->setViewMatrix( camera->getViewMatrix() );
    effect->setProjectionMatrix( camera->getProjMatrix() );

    //render the asteroid
    asteroid->Render(effect);
}

void game_update(float deltaTime) { }

void game_render2d()
{
    ostringstream out;
    out << "Core: " << g_engine->getCoreFrameRate() << endl;
    out << "Camera: " << focus.x << "," << focus.y << ","
        << focus.z << endl;

    font->Print(0,0, out.str());

}

void game_event( IEvent* e )
{
    switch( e->getID() )
    {
        case EVENT_KEYPRESS:
        {
            KeyPressEvent* evt = (KeyPressEvent*) e;
            switch(evt->keycode)
            {
```

```
                    case DIK_ESCAPE: g_engine->Shutdown(); break;
                }
                break;
            }
            case EVENT_MOUSEMOTION:
            {
                MouseMotionEvent* evt = (MouseMotionEvent*)e;
                mouseRotate.y += (evt->deltax) * 0.001f;
                mouseRotate.z -= (evt->deltay) * 0.001f;
                break;
            }
        }
    }
}
```

Summary

As you can see from the example code here, a skybox is not at all difficult to implement, but it sure does produce awe-inspiring results and improve realism in the scene! The skybox is an important part of the suspension of disbelief that you *always* want to give the players of your games. Give them that treat of an alternate reality from the difficulties of life for a few minutes or hours and they will come to love your game (without perhaps quite knowing exactly why). An immersive environment is only part of a great game; of course, great gameplay is the most important consideration, but a great game is made up of many smaller parts, each of which must be *just right* to grab the players and suck them in to your alternate world.

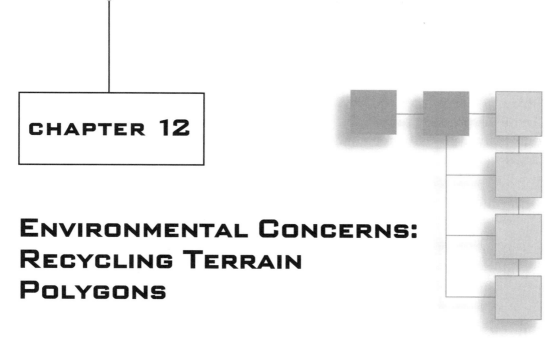

CHAPTER 12

ENVIRONMENTAL CONCERNS: RECYCLING TERRAIN POLYGONS

A terrain system is a crucial component of any would-be game engine when the designer has a goal of being taken seriously. Nearly every game genre (in 3D at least) will require a game world of some type, even if the gameplay takes place primarily indoors. In this chapter, we'll study the fundamentals of heightmap-based terrain rendering with height data being procedurally generated with the Perlin noise library (libnoise). As it turns out, Perlin has applications far beyond terrain texture and height data generation—Perlin can be used to generate realistic textures for many different types of scenes, which greatly expands on an engine's capabilities. But an outdoor terrain is not always relevant for some game genres, particularly games set in outer space! So, we'll explore some of the environments likely to be rendered by our engine with a consideration for what types of objects we'll need for such environments.

This chapter will cover the following topics:

- Outer space environments
- Indoor/outdoor environments
- Creating terrain
- Heightmap terrain generation
- Walking on terrain

Outer Space Environments

An outer space environment is perhaps the most difficult type to define because each game will be different, and so there is never a definable "outer space" scene that will be reusable enough to be shared by several games, unless they are all from the same game series. One of the earliest successful games set in outer space is *Wing Commander*: collectively, the original game, the many sequels, the *film*, and several spin-offs (including *Privateer* and *Armada*—see Figure 12.1). These games were created by Richard Garriott's studio, Origin Systems, founded primarily around his *Ultima* series with some great successes and innovations in the early 1990s, as well as the highly successful *Ultima Online* MMORPG in the late 1990s. For the *Wing Commander* universe, the team developed a game engine called *RealSpace*, and it was used successfully for many more games over the years, such as *Strike Commander* and *Pacific Strike*.[1]

A completely new engine was created for *Wing Commander: Prophesy* (Figure 12.2), released in 1997 to rave reviews for its engaging story, the return of some beloved characters, and a quality 3D engine with high-resolution graphics. *Prophesy* was slated to be a new spin-off series in the *Wing Commander* universe, but instead it was a one-off. Despite the successes of Origin Systems (later acquired by Electronic Arts and renamed to ORIGIN),

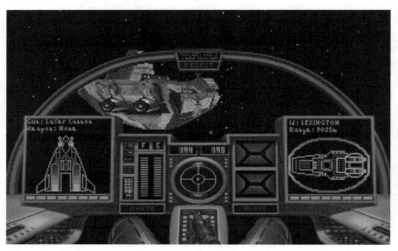

Figure 12.1
Wing Commander Armada by Origin Systems.

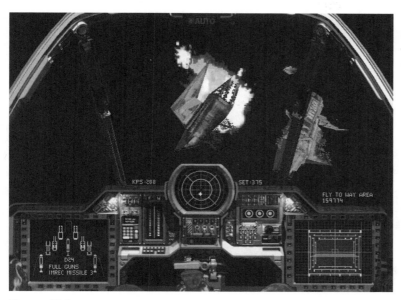

Figure 12.2
Wing Commander: Prophesy by ORIGIN.

sales for its games declined in the early 2000s and the studio was closed by EA in 2004, ending a two-decade long success story for a studio that *invented* many of the game genres we still enjoy today.

Another well-loved and recognized game that takes place entirely in outer space is *Homeworld* (Figure 12.3), published by Sierra in 1999, developed by Relic Entertainment. This classic also fostered its own series with an expansion called *Cataclysm*, and then a much more complex and less enjoyable *Homeworld 2* was released in 2003 by THQ, Inc. At its core, *Homeworld* is an RTS game, with a compelling story wrapped around its RTS gameplay. Fans of science fiction are drawn to the gameplay because of its "tried and true" but cliché plot: "You are lost in space and need to find your way home," or the more sanguine "Your home has been destroyed by aliens, so you must seek out a new home world." However, the gameplay is so intense that an all-too-familiar premise for the plot actually does work quite well.

An outer space environment will usually be a wide-open area bounded by a skybox with a texture depicting a starfield or other stellar bodies, with view frustum clipping as an optimization in the scene manager.

Figure 12.3
The epic sci-fi outer space game of *Homeworld* received stellar reviews for its gorgeous scenes.

INDOOR/OUTDOOR ENVIRONMENTS

An indoor environment usually takes place entirely inside the walls of a building or castle or other structure, often with windows showing an outdoor scene the player usually cannot reach. A good example of this comes from the genre-defining *Quake* by id Software, and more so in *Quake II*, shown in Figure 12.4 (although *Quake II* did have some hybrid indoor/outdoor scenes). Another genre-perfecting game, *Unreal Tournament* by Epic Games, and the many new versions up to the current *Unreal Tournament 3*, may be considered a hybrid since it supports seamless indoor and outdoor environments. Figure 12.5 shows a "mod" of *Unreal Tournament 2004* called *COR* (Counter Organic Revolution), created by UAT students (see www.corproject.com).

CREATING TERRAIN

While game engines were once designed to function in a limited gameplay area, such as inside an indoor level, and optimized for that type of gameplay due to slow processors and limited video cards, most engines today make no such distinction and are able to render a scene for any genre with stable performance.

Figure 12.4
Quake II perfected the networked indoor deathmatch genre at the time.

Figure 12.5
Counter Organic Revolution (COR) is a UT 2004 mod created by UAT students.

Indeed, game developers today can even write lazy code without optimization (the "brute force" approach), with decent results thanks to high-performance chips in even the most average PC. (Of course, neither you nor I would ever write sloppy code just because the CPU and GPU are fast, as there are always new polygons eager to be rendered!)

Nearly every technology in game development today was built in pyramidal style on the work of those who have come before, which means almost every algorithm and function used to render something was developed and used and improved by many people. For a young technology like game development, the earliest pioneers are almost all still alive today, which means they are aware of how game development has evolved after having been there at the start—indeed, for having been part of that beginning. The terrain code in this chapter is largely credited to the work of Carl Granberg, who himself borrowed code from others and improved upon it. (See *Programming an RTS Game with Direct3D*, published by Charles River Media in 2006—and be sure to get the author's latest sources that support Visual C++ 2008.) Likewise, I have improved upon Granberg's work by incorporating a new random generation system (based on Perlin noise) to replace his custom random terrain generator.

Advice

This chapter's resource files (including the Perlin library) can be downloaded from www.jharbour.com/forum or www.courseptr.com/downloads. Please note that not every line of code will be in print due to space considerations: only the most important sections of code are covered in each chapter.

Perlin Noise

Perlin is the name of a world-famous noise generation library used to produce unique patterns of random number sequences. This library was named for its creator, Ken Perlin, who won an Academy Award for his work on texture generation for Disney's movie, *TRON*. We'll be using this open source library—which is called "libnoise" (http://libnoise.sourceforge.net)—to generate our random terrain. The Perlin noise library (see Table 12.1) is comprised of a number of header files, but we need only be concerned with two: `noise.h` and `noiseutils.h`. To use libnoise, we will add `libnoise.lib` to our project's linker options (via a `#pragma`) and add `noiseutils.cpp` to the project as well.

Table 12.1 Perlin Noise SDK

libnoise.lib	Compiled noise library (add to project folder)
libnoise.dll	Compiled noise dll (add to output folder)
noiseutils.h	Support header (add to sources folder)
noiseutils.cpp	Support code (add to sources folder)
noise.h	Primary noise header (add the whole .\noise folder to sources folder)

The Perlin noise library is very easy to use (fortunately for us!) and can generate just a simple, basic array of float values for a heightmap, which can then be copied over to our terrain's heightmap. Or, the height data can be saved as a bitmap and written out to a file. Figure 12.6 shows an example heightmap texture generated procedurally by libnoise.

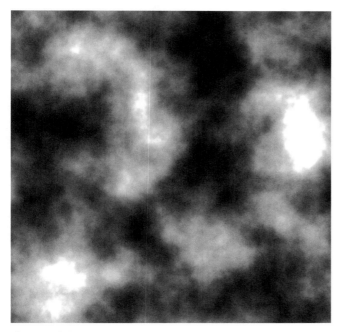

Figure 12.6
Heightmap terrain texture generated by Perlin noise library.

Heightmap and Texture Generation

This versatile library can also generate seamless textures for use in a scene, such as wood, stone, marble, and clouds. Imagine generating all of the textures you need for a game based entirely on script descriptions of the type of textures needed for each mesh! Suppose you have a mesh of a picnic table for an outdoor scene: perhaps you might describe the texture used for the picnic table in script code, and then have Perlin generate that texture based on its name. Suppose your engine also knows how to generate a great number of textures on the fly from pre-programmed Perlin noise configurations. Another feature of Perlin is the ability to generate tiled texture maps, allowing for seamless and potentially endless random textures in a certain direction, with the same textures produced again if your game characters move back in the way they came. Imagine generating millions of square miles of terrain to simulate a truly gigantic game world, all without requiring a level designer to create the data by hand. These ideas are all entirely possible—and *are* done in many engines already.

First, assuming we have included the libnoise support files needed to compile with the library, we start by creating a `noise::module::Perlin` variable and initializing it with the desired texture generation properties:

```
module::Perlin perlin;
perlin.SetSeed( seed );
perlin.SetFrequency( frequency );
perlin.SetOctaveCount( octaves );
perlin.SetPersistence( persistence );
```

There are three key properties used to customize the random numbers generated by Perlin:

- Frequency
- Persistence
- Octaves

Frequency   The first property, frequency, is the most important one to consider as it determines what the overall texture will look like. Frequency determines the number of "bumps" in the texture, with 0.0 being perfectly smooth and 10.0 looking almost like white noise. Most of the time you will want to use a value in the range of 0.2 to 3.0 for terrain, depending on the size of the game world.

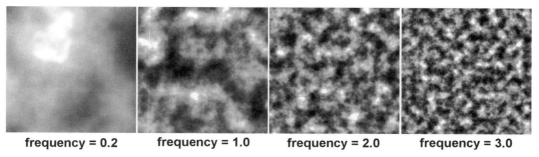

frequency = 0.2   frequency = 1.0   frequency = 2.0   frequency = 3.0

Figure 12.7
Frequency determines the bumpiness of the generated texture.

Figure 12.8
Comparison of heightmap textures generated with low and high *frequencies*.

Figure 12.7 shows the textures generated with different frequency values, while Figure 12.8 shows the scene view.

Persistence   The second property, persistence, also contributes to how smooth or bumpy the terrain will look, as it affects the way bumps in the terrain flow together. Or, looking at it from a different perspective, persistence determines how much one hill or valley flows into or out of those nearest to it. A very low persistence of 0.1 has almost no effect, while a value of 0.9 causes the image to scatter toward white noise—which may be exactly what you want, depending on the desired scene for a game world. Figure 12.9 shows results for several persistence values, while Figure 12.10 shows the output at two extremes.

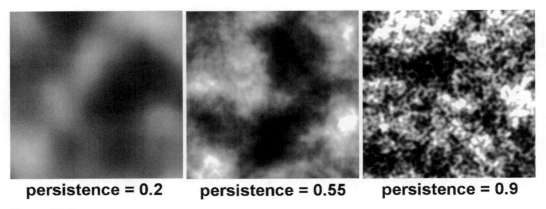

persistence = 0.2   persistence = 0.55   persistence = 0.9

Figure 12.9
Persistence determines how well the bumps in the texture flow together.

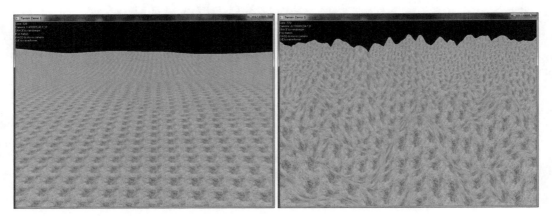

Figure 12.10
Comparison of heightmap textures generated with low and high *persistence*.

Octaves   The third property, octaves, determines how many passes or levels of randomness a texture is given during its construction. An octave setting of 1.0 results in a texture with just the raw frequency and persistence properties determining how it turns out. An octave setting of 10.0 results in highly complex randomness added to the base frequency- and persistence-defined shape of the texture. Think of the octave passes as a way to add more detail to the existing shape of the terrain or texture, without changing the overall shape of the hills and valleys. Figure 12.11 shows the textures generated by two different octaves,

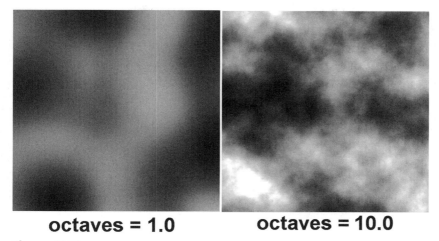

octaves = 1.0   **octaves = 10.0**

Figure 12.11
The number of Octaves represents the number of detail passes used to add more complexity.

Figure 12.12
The rendered scene with terrain reflecting the heightmaps.

while Figure 12.12 shows the rendered scene with terrain reflecting those heightmaps.

Now that we have the `Perlin` object initialized properly with the desired properties, the next step is to create a `NoiseMap` object that will contain the texture data that will ultimately be used as the height data for our terrain.

```
noise::utils::NoiseMap noiseMap;
```

The type of texture we need is for a regular plane. Perlin has support for seamless texture generation and can even generate sphere textures with the correct stretching applied to the poles so the texture looks correct wrapped on a sphere. (We used this technique in *Starflight—The Lost Colony* [www .starflightgame.com] to generate random planets.)

```
noise::utils::NoiseMapBuilderPlane heightMapBuilder;
```

Next, we tell our heightmap object to use the `Perlin` object for it's random algorithms, set the destination to the noise map object, and set the width and height of the data set.

```
heightMapBuilder.SetSourceModule( perlin );
heightMapBuilder.SetDestNoiseMap( noiseMap );
heightMapBuilder.SetDestSize( width, length );
```

Finally, we have to tell the heightmap object where on the Cartesian coordinate system it should base its calculations for tiling purposes. Tiling is an advanced feature that I won't get into here because we just don't need it, but I encourage you to look into it if you want to generate a huge game world without consuming huge amounts of memory. After setting the bounds to the upper-right quadrant, we can then build the random data.

```
heightMapBuilder.SetBounds( 0.0, 5.0, 0.0, 5.0 );
heightMapBuilder.Build();
```

At this point, we have the data needed to apply height data to a terrain vertex buffer. To get at the data, access the `GetValue()` function in `NoiseMap`.

```
float value = noiseMap.GetValue(x,z);
```

The value coming from Perlin will be fairly small, so it's normally multiplied by the desired height value to bring the terrain up from the sub-1.0 range into a tangible height.

Finally, if you would like to save the height data to a texture, libnoise can do that as well. Just to be clear, it's normal to add the "noise" namespace to simplify variable declarations, so I'll include it here for reference.

```
using namespace noise;
utils::RendererImage renderer;
utils::Image image;
renderer.SetSourceNoiseMap(noiseMap);
```

```
renderer.SetDestImage(image);
renderer.Render();
utils::WriterBMP writer;
writer.SetSourceImage (image);
writer.SetDestFilename("texture.bmp");
writer.WriteDestFile();
```

Terrain Generation

A terrain system is basically a vertex buffer filled with two-triangle quads that
share four vertices. The vertex buffer has a defined flexible vertex format (FVF)
with vertex position, texture coordinates, and lighting normal angles supported.

```
TERRAIN_FVF = D3DFVF_XYZ | D3DFVF_NORMAL | D3DFVF_TEX1;
```

The texture coordinate property tells me that the terrain requires at least one
texture to render properly. We could generate the ground textures needed here
with Perlin very easily, but texture theory is a bit beyond the goals for this
chapter so I have just selected three interesting textures that will make the
terrain look vaguely like an alien world with a curious pattern in greens and
browns. We will supply the terrain system with three textures to accommodate
three height levels (water, grass, and hills).

Our height data is nothing more complex than an array of floats initialized to
zero:

```
heightMap = new float[width * length];
memset(heightMap, 0, sizeof(float)*width*length);
```

What you do with heightMap after this point will be based on the type of
environment needed for the game's genre! We've seen how to generate height
data from Perlin, but the real question is this: how do you go from a bunch of
floats to a rendered terrain mesh?

First, to build the terrain system's vertex buffer we will use patches that will
simplify texture mapping and also divide the terrain system into a grid, which
will also be helpful for gameplay code. Assuming width and length represent the
dimensions of the terrain (oriented "flat" on the Z-axis, out and away from the
origin), we can divide up the terrain system into a series of patches, each
represented by a rectangle or quad.

```
for (int y=0;y<numPatches;y++)
{
    for (int x=0;x<numPatches;x++)
    {
        RECT r = {
            (int)(x * (width - 1) / (float)numPatches),
            (int)(y * (length - 1) / (float)numPatches),
            (int)((x+1) * (width - 1) / (float)numPatches),
            (int)((y+1) * (length - 1) / (float)numPatches)
        };
        Patch *p = new Patch();
        p->CreateMesh(*heightMap, r);
        patches.push_back(p);
    }
}
```

For each patch, a mesh is created with the `D3DXCreateMeshFVF` function, which generates a mesh based on a defined FVF format (in this case, we'll be using `TERRAIN_FVF`, previously defined). The heightmap data is then used to build the vertex buffer.

```
TerrainVertex* ver = 0;
mesh->LockVertexBuffer(0,(void**)&ver);
for(int z=source.top,z0=0; z<=source.bottom; z++,z0++)
    for(int x=source.left,x0=0; x<=source.right; x++,x0++)
    {
        D3DXVECTOR3 pos = D3DXVECTOR3(
            (float)x,
            hm.heightMap[x + z * hm.width],
            (float)-z);
        D3DXVECTOR2 uv = D3DXVECTOR2(x * 0.2f, z * 0.2f);
        ver[z0 * (width + 1) + x0] = TerrainVertex(pos, uv);
    }
mesh->UnlockVertexBuffer();
```

Afterward, an index buffer and attributes are added to improve rendering performance. After the vertex buffer has been filled with height data, and the vertices positioned correctly into patch-based quads, then the whole thing is normalized with `D3DXComputeNormals`. Regarding the attributes, this is an important section of the code because it determines which texture is used on the terrain based on height. Take a look at the `if` statement, currently with hard-coded ranges. The water level is at a height of 0.0, while the grass level goes up to 60% of the height, and the final 40% of the terrain is set to the final texture (normally granite or other rocky-looking texture). A good improvement to this code will be to make those ranges definable, and perhaps even add in support for more than just three.

```
for(int z = source.top; z < source.bottom; z++)
    for(int x = source.left; x < source.right; x++)
    {
        //calculate vertices based on height
        int subset;
        if (hm.heightMap[x + z * hm.width] == 0.0f)
            subset = 0;
        else if (hm.heightMap[x+z*hm.width] <= hm.maxHeight*0.6f)
            subset = 1;
        else subset = 2;

        att[a++] = subset;
        att[a++] = subset;
    }
```

Terrain Class

The snippets of code presented thus far will be easier to re-use in the form of a class—namely, the Terrain class, which is now part of the Octane engine if you peruse the projects included with this chapter. This Terrain class makes use of two helper structs (Heightmap and Patch) to help manage heightmap and mesh generation for the terrain.

```
#include "..\Engine\Engine.h"
struct TerrainVertex
{
    D3DXVECTOR3 position, normal;
    D3DXVECTOR2 uv;

    TerrainVertex(){}
    TerrainVertex(D3DXVECTOR3 pos, D3DXVECTOR2 texuv)
    {
        position = pos;
        uv = texuv;
        normal = D3DXVECTOR3(0.0f, 1.0f, 0.0f);
    }
};
```

```
struct Heightmap
{
    int width,length;
    float maxHeight;
    float *heightMap;

    Heightmap(int _width, int _length, float _depth);
    ~Heightmap();
    void Release();
    bool CreateRandom(int seed, float frequency, float persistence,
        int octaves, bool water=false);
};

struct Patch
{
    ID3DXMesh *mesh;

    Patch();
    ~Patch();
    void Release();
    bool CreateMesh(Heightmap &hm, RECT source);
    void Render(int texture);
};

class Terrain
{
    private:
        int p_width,p_length;
        int p_numPatches;
        int p_maxHeight;
        Heightmap *p_heightMap;
        std::vector<Patch*> p_patches;
        std::vector<IDirect3DTexture9*> p_textures;
    public:
        Terrain();
        virtual ~Terrain();
        void Init(int width,int length,int depth,std::string tex1,
            std::string tex2,std::string tex3);
        void Flatten(float height);
        void CreateRandom(float freq=0.8f, float persist=0.5f,
```

```
            int octaves=5, bool water=false);
        void Render( Octane::Effect *effect );
        void BuildHeightmap();
        int getWidth() { return p_width; }
        int getLength() { return p_length; }
        float getHeight(int x,int z);
        void Release();
};
```

The terrain system is actually comprised of three components, as you saw in the header listing: the `Heightmap` and `Patch` structs and the `Terrain` class. It is possible to combine all into just the `Terrain` class but the functionality of the terrain system is cleaner in these separate parts (using helper structs for each component of the terrain system). First, let's see how the `Heightmap` struct works.

```
const DWORD TERRAIN_FVF = D3DFVF_XYZ | D3DFVF_NORMAL | D3DFVF_TEX1;

Heightmap::Heightmap(int _width, int _length, float _depth)
{
    try
    {
        width = _width;
        length = _length;
        maxHeight = _depth;

        heightMap = new float[width * length];
        memset(heightMap, 0, sizeof(float)*width*length);
    }
    catch(...)
    {
        debug << "Error creating Heightmap";
    }
}

Heightmap::~Heightmap()
{
    Release();
}

void Heightmap::Release()
{
```

```cpp
    if (heightMap != NULL) delete [] heightMap;
    heightMap = NULL;
}

bool Heightmap::CreateRandom(int seed, float frequency, float persistence, int
octaves, bool water)
{
    //init perlin noise library
    module::Perlin perlin;
    perlin.SetSeed( seed );
    perlin.SetFrequency( frequency );
    perlin.SetOctaveCount( octaves );
    perlin.SetPersistence( persistence );

    //build the heightmap
    utils::NoiseMap noiseMap;
    utils::NoiseMapBuilderPlane heightMapBuilder;
    heightMapBuilder.SetSourceModule( perlin );
    heightMapBuilder.SetDestNoiseMap( noiseMap );
    heightMapBuilder.SetDestSize( width, length );
    heightMapBuilder.SetBounds( 0.0, 5.0, 0.0, 5.0 );
    heightMapBuilder.Build();

    //copy Perlin generated height data to our heightmap
    for(int z=0; z<length; z++)
    {
        for(int x=0; x<width; x++)
        {
            //get height value from perlin
            float value = noiseMap.GetValue(x,z) * maxHeight;

            //cap negatives to 0 for water
            if (water)
            {
                if (value < 0.0f) value = 0.0f;
            }

            //copy height data to our terrain
            heightMap[x + z * width] = value;
        }
    }
```

```
        return true;
}
```

Now we have the `Patch` struct with its primary purpose of housing the mesh data for the terrain system. The entire terrain system is made up of these patches, and this is the object actually drawing when the terrain is rendered.

```
Patch::Patch()
{
    mesh = NULL;
}
Patch::~Patch()
{
    Release();
}

void Patch::Release()
{
    if(mesh != NULL)
        mesh->Release();
    mesh = NULL;
}

bool Patch::CreateMesh(Heightmap &hm, RECT source)
{
    if(mesh != NULL)
    {
        mesh->Release();
        mesh = NULL;
    }

    try
    {
        int width = source.right - source.left;
        int height = source.bottom - source.top;
        int nrVert = (width + 1) * (height + 1);
        int nrTri = width * height * 2;

        if(FAILED(D3DXCreateMeshFVF(nrTri, nrVert, D3DXMESH_MANAGED,
            TERRAIN_FVF, g_engine->getDevice(), &mesh)))
        {
```

```
        debug << "Error creating patch mesh\n";
        return false;
    }

    //create terrain vertices
    TerrainVertex* ver = 0;
    mesh->LockVertexBuffer(0,(void**)&ver);
    for(int z=source.top, z0 = 0;z<=source.bottom;z++, z0++)
        for(int x=source.left, x0 = 0;x<=source.right;x++, x0++)
        {
            D3DXVECTOR3 pos = D3DXVECTOR3(
                (float)x,
                hm.heightMap[x + z * hm.width],
                (float)-z);
            D3DXVECTOR2 uv = D3DXVECTOR2(x * 0.2f, z * 0.2f);
            ver[z0 * (width + 1) + x0] = TerrainVertex(pos, uv);
        }
    mesh->UnlockVertexBuffer();

    //calculate terrain indices
    WORD* ind = 0;
    mesh->LockIndexBuffer(0,(void**)&ind);
    int index = 0;

    for(int z=source.top, z0 = 0;z<source.bottom;z++, z0++)
        for(int x=source.left, x0 = 0;x<source.right;x++, x0++)
        {
            //triangle 1
            ind[index++] =   z0   * (width + 1) + x0;
            ind[index++] =   z0   * (width + 1) + x0 + 1;
            ind[index++] = (z0+1) * (width + 1) + x0;

            //triangle 2
            ind[index++] = (z0+1) * (width + 1) + x0;
            ind[index++] =   z0   * (width + 1) + x0 + 1;
            ind[index++] = (z0+1) * (width + 1) + x0 + 1;
        }

    mesh->UnlockIndexBuffer();
```

```
        //set attributes
        DWORD *att = 0, a = 0;
        mesh->LockAttributeBuffer(0,&att);

        for(int z=source.top;z<source.bottom;z++)
            for(int x=source.left;x<source.right;x++)
            {
                //calculate vertices based on height
                int subset;
                if (hm.heightMap[x + z * hm.width] == 0.0f)
                    subset = 0;
                else if (hm.heightMap[x + z * hm.width]
                    <= hm.maxHeight * 0.6f)
                    subset = 1;
                else subset = 2;

                att[a++] = subset;
                att[a++] = subset;
            }

        mesh->UnlockAttributeBuffer();

        //compute normal for the terrain
        D3DXComputeNormals(mesh, NULL);
    }
    catch(...)
    {
        debug << "Error creating patch mesh\n";
        return false;
    }

    return true;
}

void Patch::Render(int texture)
{
    if (mesh != NULL)
        mesh->DrawSubset(texture);
}
```

Finally, we have the `Terrain` class, which wraps up the `Heightmap` and `Patch` data with some high-level functions to make terrain initialization and configuration relatively easy from the calling code.

```
Terrain::Terrain()
{
    p_heightMap = NULL;
}

Terrain::~Terrain()
{
    Release();
}

void Terrain::Init(int width,int length,int depth,std::string tex1,
    std::string tex2,std::string tex3)
{
    p_width = width;
    p_length = length;
    p_maxHeight = depth;
    p_numPatches = 3;
    p_heightMap = NULL;
    CreateRandom(0.8f, 0.5f, 5, false);

    //load terrain textures
    IDirect3DTexture9* levels[3];
    for (int n=0; n<3; n++)
        levels[n] = NULL;

    D3DXCreateTextureFromFile(g_engine->getDevice(),tex1.c_str(),&levels[0]);
    D3DXCreateTextureFromFile(g_engine->getDevice(),tex2.c_str(),&levels[1]);
    D3DXCreateTextureFromFile(g_engine->getDevice(),tex3.c_str(),&levels[2]);

    for (int n=0; n<3; n++)
        p_textures.push_back( levels[n] );
}

void Terrain::Release()
{
    for(int i=0;i<(int)p_patches.size();i++)
```

```
        if(p_patches[i] != NULL)
            p_patches[i]->Release();

    p_patches.clear();

    if(p_heightMap != NULL)
    {
        p_heightMap->Release();
        delete p_heightMap;
        p_heightMap = NULL;
    }
}

void Terrain::Flatten(float height)
{
    float* hm = p_heightMap->heightMap;
    for(int y=0;y<p_length;y++)
    {
        for(int x=0;x<p_width;x++)
        {
            hm[x + y * p_width] = height;
        }
    }
    BuildHeightmap();
}

void Terrain::CreateRandom(float freq,float persist,int octaves,bool water)
{
    try
    {
        //recreate heightmap array
        Release();
        p_heightMap = new Heightmap(p_width,p_length,(float)p_maxHeight);

        //fill heightmap with generated data
        p_heightMap->CreateRandom(rand()%1000, freq, persist, octaves, water);
        BuildHeightmap();
    }
    catch(...)
    {
```

```
            debug ≪ "Error creating random terrain\n";
        }
}


void Terrain::BuildHeightmap()
{
    try
    {
        //free any old patches
        for(int i=0;i<(int)p_patches.size();i++)
            if(p_patches[i] != NULL)
                p_patches[i]->Release();
        p_patches.clear();

        if (p_heightMap == NULL) return;

        //(re)create patch meshes
        for (int y=0;y<p_numPatches;y++)
        {
            for (int x=0;x<p_numPatches;x++)
            {
                RECT r = {
                    (int)(x * (p_width - 1) / (float)p_numPatches),
                    (int)(y * (p_length - 1) / (float)p_numPatches),
                    (int)((x+1) * (p_width - 1) / (float)p_numPatches),
                    (int)((y+1) * (p_length - 1) / (float)p_numPatches)
                };

                Patch *p = new Patch();
                p->CreateMesh(*p_heightMap, r);
                p_patches.push_back(p);
            }
        }
    }
    catch(...)
    {
        debug ≪ "Error creating terrain grid\n";
    }
}
```

```
void Terrain::Render( Octane::Effect *effect )
{
    for(int t=0;t<3;t++)
    {
        effect->setParam("Texture", p_textures[t]);

        effect->Begin();

        for(int i=0;i<(int)p_patches.size();i++)
            p_patches[i]->Render(t);

        effect->End();
    }
}

float Terrain::getHeight(int x,int z)
{
    float* hm = p_heightMap->heightMap;

    if (x < 0 || x > p_width) return 0;
    if (z < 0 || z > p_length) return 0;

    try
    {
        float height = hm[x + z * p_width];
        return height;
    }
    catch(...)
    {
        return 0.0f;
    }
}
```

Terrain Demo

The Terrain Demo program will show how easy it is to use the `Terrain` class to generate and render a terrain system using either all default properties or with custom-defined properties. Figure 12.13 shows a view of the program running. If you want to render the terrain with water (or at least using the first texture—you

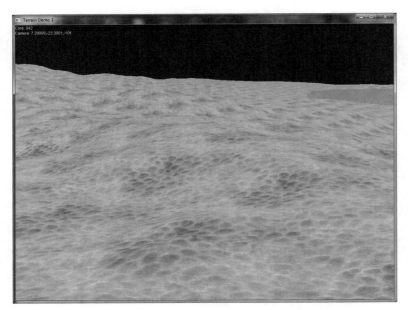

Figure 12.13
The Terrain Demo shows how to use the new Terrain class with Perlin-based heightmap generation.

may pass a different texture if you wish), you will want to set the parameters to
Terrain::CreateRandom() rather than just leaving them to their defaults.

```
#include "Engine.h"
#include "Terrain.h"
using namespace Octane;
using namespace std;

Font* font=NULL;
Effect* effect=NULL;
Camera* camera=NULL;
Matrix matWorld;
Vector3 mouseRotate;
Terrain* terrain;

void game_end()
{
    if (terrain) delete terrain;
    if (camera) delete camera;
    if (effect) delete effect;
```

```
        if (font) delete font;
}

bool game_preload()
{
    g_engine->setAppTitle("Terrain Demo");
    g_engine->setScreen(1024,768,32,false);
    g_engine->setBackdropColor(D3DCOLOR_XRGB(30,0,30));
    return true;
}

bool game_init(HWND hwnd)
{
    font = new Font("Arial",14);

    camera = new Camera();
    camera->setPosition(0,10,10);
    camera->setTarget(0,10,0);

    effect = new Effect();
    if (!effect->Load("ambient.fx"))
    {
        debug << "Error loading effect\n";
        return false;
    }

    //create terrain
    terrain = new Terrain();
    terrain->Init(512, 512, 40, "water.bmp","slime2.bmp","slime1.bmp");

    return true;
}

void game_render3d()
{
    effect->setTechnique("Ambient");
    effect->setViewMatrix( camera->getViewMatrix() );
    effect->setProjectionMatrix( camera->getProjMatrix() );

    //set shader world matrix to terrain position
    matWorld.setIdentity();
```

```
    matWorld.Translate( -terrain->getWidth()/2,0,0 );
    effect->setWorldMatrix( matWorld );

    //render the terrain
    terrain->Render( effect );
}

void game_update(float deltaTime)
{
    camera->Update();
}

void game_render2d()
{
    ostringstream out;
    out << "Core: " << g_engine->getCoreFrameRate() << endl;
    out << "Camera: " << camera->getTarget().x << ","
                      << camera->getTarget().y << ","
                      << camera->getTarget().z << endl;
    out << "SPACE to randomize" << endl;
    out << "F to flatten" << endl;
    out << "WASD to move camera" << endl;
    out << "Q/E to raise/lower" << endl;

    font->Print(0,0, out.str());

}

void game_event( IEvent* e )
{
    switch( e->getID() )
    {
        case EVENT_KEYPRESS:
        {
            KeyPressEvent* evt = (KeyPressEvent*) e;
            switch(evt->keycode)
            {
                case DIK_ESCAPE: g_engine->Shutdown(); break;
                case DIK_SPACE:
                    terrain->CreateRandom(0.8f,0.5f,5,true);
                    break;
```

```
            case DIK_F: terrain->Flatten(1); break;
            case DIK_W: camera->Move(0,0,-1.0); break;
            case DIK_S: camera->Move(0,0,1.0); break;
            case DIK_A: camera->Move(1.0,0,0); break;
            case DIK_D: camera->Move(-1.0,0,0); break;
            case DIK_Q: camera->Move(0,1.0,0); break;
            case DIK_E: camera->Move(0,-1.0,0); break;
        }
        break;
    }
    case EVENT_MOUSEMOTION:
    {
        MouseMotionEvent* evt = (MouseMotionEvent*)e;
        double dx = -evt->deltax / 100.0;
        double dy = -evt->deltay / 100.0;
        camera->Look(dx, dy, 0);
        break;
    }
}}
```

WALKING ON TERRAIN

Generating and rendering terrain is one thing (and it looks nice!), but it's useless if we don't have the capability to actually walk on it. That is already built into the Terrain class by way of its internal heightmap array, but we need to get at that array data and determine the height of the terrain at any given X,Z position over it. Getting that data is simply a matter of retrieving the heightmap value, but the real trick is aligning our game's meshes with the terrain's position in the scene. If you position the terrain at its default location, with it positioned in the first quadrant (of an X,Z Cartesian coordinate system), then Z decreases away from the camera, while X decreases to the right. So, positive X will move objects into the terrain, while negative X would move objects in the wrong direction. Likewise, transforming an object into the negative Z will move it deeper into the terrain.

Calculating Height

Therefore, to transform an object onto the terrain and calculate its height at that given value, it's best to leave the terrain at its original position, focused on the

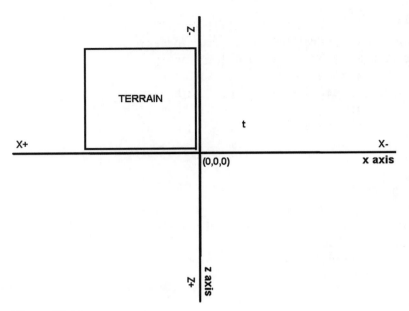

Figure 12.14
The terrain mesh is positioned into Z-, X+, in quadrant one by default.

origin and expanding forward and to the left (see Figure 12.14). The `Terrain::getHeight()` function retrieves the height value at a given X,Z position in the terrain's heightmap. Following is a simplified version of the function as it appears in the `Terrain` class code listing.

```
float Terrain::getHeight(int x,int z)
{
    float* hm = p_heightMap->heightMap;
    if (x < 0 || x > p_width) return 0;
    if (z < 0 || z > p_length) return 0;
    try
    {
        float height = hm[x + z * p_width];
        return height;
    }
    catch(...)
    {
        return 0.0f;
    }
}
```

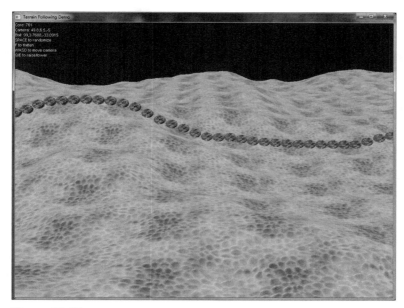

Figure 12.15
The sphere meshes are "walking" the terrain as a line to demonstrate heightmap following.

Terrain Following Demo

The Terrain Following Demo project helps to illustrate terrain following in a very simple way, but the simplicity of this demo helps greatly to understand how the terrain system is oriented and how objects may follow the heightmap correctly. Figure 12.15 shows the program. Note that a string of spheres is moving in sync on the Z-axis, forward and backward across the terrain, and adjusting their heights to match the heightmap value in the terrain at each sphere's X,Z position over the terrain.

```
#include "Engine.h"
#include "Terrain.h"
using namespace Octane;
using namespace std;

Font* font=NULL;
Effect* effect=NULL;
Camera* camera=NULL;
Matrix matWorld;
Vector3 mouseRotate;
Terrain* terrain=NULL;
```

```cpp
Mesh* ball=NULL;
Texture* fire=NULL;
float ballVel = -6.0f;
Vector3 balls[100];

void game_end()
{
    if (fire) delete fire;
    if (ball) delete ball;
    if (terrain) delete terrain;
    if (camera) delete camera;
    if (effect) delete effect;
    if (font) delete font;
}

bool game_preload()
{
    g_engine->setAppTitle("Terrain Following Demo");
    g_engine->setScreen(1024,768,32,false);
    g_engine->setBackdropColor(D3DCOLOR_XRGB(30,30,0));
    return true;
}

bool game_init(HWND hwnd)
{
    font = new Font("Arial",14);

    effect = new Effect();
    if (!effect->Load("ambient.fx"))
    {
        debug << "Error loading effect\n";
        return false;
    }

    //create terrain
    terrain = new Terrain();
    terrain->Init(100, 100, 5, "slime2.bmp","slime2.bmp","slime2.bmp");

    //create ball mesh
    ball = new Mesh();
    ball->Load("ball.x");
```

```
        ball->setPosition(50,0,0);
        ball->setScale(0.5);

        fire = new Texture();
        fire->Load("fire.jpg");

        for (int n=0; n<100; n++)
        {
            balls[n].x = n;
            balls[n].y = 0;
            balls[n].z = 0;
        }

        camera = new Camera();
        camera->setPosition( 50,10,10 );
        camera->setTarget( 50,10,0 );

        return true;
}

void game_render3d()
{
        effect->setTechnique("Ambient");
        effect->setViewMatrix( camera->getViewMatrix() );
        effect->setProjectionMatrix( camera->getProjMatrix() );

        //render the terrain
        matWorld.setIdentity();
        effect->setWorldMatrix( matWorld );
        terrain->Render( effect );

        //render the balls
        for (int n=0; n<100; n++)
        {
            ball->setPosition(balls[n]);
            ball->Transform();
            effect->setWorldMatrix(ball->getMatrix());
            effect->setParam("Texture", fire->getTexture());
            ball->Draw(effect);
        }
}
```

```cpp
void game_update(float deltaTime)
{
    camera->Update();

    //move the balls
    for (int n=0; n<100; n++)
    {
        balls[n].z += ballVel * deltaTime;

        int size = terrain->getLength();
        if (balls[n].z < -size || balls[n].z > 0)
        {
            ballVel *= -1;
            balls[n].z += ballVel * deltaTime;
        }

        int actualx = balls[n].x;
        int actualz = -balls[n].z;
        balls[n].y = terrain->getHeight(actualx,actualz) + 1.0f;
    }
}

void game_render2d()
{
    ostringstream out;
    out << "Core: " << g_engine->getCoreFrameRate() << endl;
    out << "Camera: " << camera->getTarget().x << ","
                      << camera->getTarget().y << ","
                      << camera->getTarget().z << endl;
    out << "Ball: " << ball->getPosition().x << ","
                    << ball->getPosition().y << ","
                    << ball->getPosition().z << endl;
    out << "SPACE to randomize" << endl;
    out << "F to flatten" << endl;
    out << "WASD to move camera" << endl;
    out << "Q/E to raise/lower" << endl;

    font->Print(0,0, out.str());
}
```

```
void game_event( IEvent* e )
{
    switch( e->getID() )
    {
        case EVENT_KEYPRESS:
        {
            KeyPressEvent* evt = (KeyPressEvent*) e;
            switch(evt->keycode)
            {
                case DIK_ESCAPE: g_engine->Shutdown(); break;
                case DIK_SPACE:
                    terrain->CreateRandom(0.5f,0.5f,5,false);
                    break;
                case DIK_F: terrain->Flatten(1); break;
                case DIK_W: camera->Move(0,0,-1.0); break;
                case DIK_S: camera->Move(0,0,1.0); break;
                case DIK_A: camera->Move(1.0,0,0); break;
                case DIK_D: camera->Move(-1.0,0,0); break;
                case DIK_Q: camera->Move(0,1.0,0); break;
                case DIK_E: camera->Move(0,-1.0,0); break;
            }
            break;
        }
        case EVENT_MOUSEMOTION:
        {
            MouseMotionEvent* evt = (MouseMotionEvent*)e;
            double dx = -evt->deltax / 100.0;
            double dy = -evt->deltay / 100.0;
            camera->Look(dx, dy, 0);
            break;
        }
    }
}
```

Summary

This chapter has been one of the most productive as far as contributing toward actually creating a game environment, while all prior chapters have been building block chapters in nature, providing services needed up to this point just to get a rudimentary scene to render. One limitation of this terrain system is the use of square textured patches with no multi-texturing to smooth over the sharp edges. From a certain vantage point, it looks okay, but up close it might resemble a checkerboard. Applying blended textures over the seams would solve the problem and dramatically improve the appearance of the terrain. Another way to improve quality is to use a shader other than ambient—specular, for instance, would look really nice. I encourage you to explore these possibilities. Although we can't do all of these things in a single chapter, they are being explored as the engine continues to evolve beyond the version shared here. Visit the forum at www.jharbour.com/forum to learn about new things happening.

REFERENCES

1. "Graphics Engine: RealSpace"; Moby Games. http://www.mobygames.com/game-group/graphics-engine-realspace.

2. Granberg, Carl. *Programming an RTS Game with Direct3D*. Charles River Media, 2006.

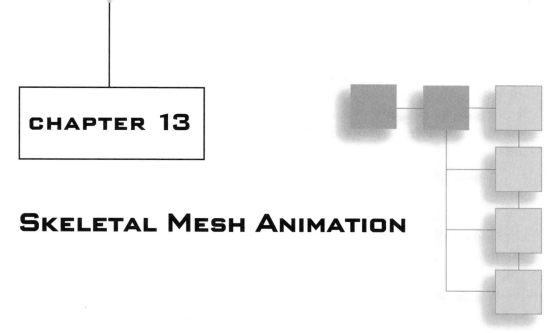

CHAPTER 13

SKELETAL MESH ANIMATION

This chapter builds upon the material covered previously on simple mesh loading and rendering (see Chapter 9, "Mesh Loading and Rendering," for more information), extending into full hierarchical mesh loading, rendering, and animating. We will build a new C++ class for the engine called BoneMesh, a subclass of Mesh, taking advantage of the existing transforms already supported in the parent class. There's a lot of code required to load a hierarchical mesh, which is far more complicated than dealing with simple meshes, so we will need to cover this subject thoroughly. A helper class is required when loading a hierarchical mesh, which does all of the memory allocation and deallocation of data in memory, but once we have written that code it will be highly reusable.

This chapter covers the following topics:

- Hierarchical mesh structure
- Asset pipeline
- Bone structure
- Loading a skeletal mesh
- Mesh file differences
- Allocating the hierarchy
- Rendering a skeletal mesh
- Animating a skeletal mesh

HIERARCHICAL MESH STRUCTURE

The .X mesh format supports both simple, fixed meshes—already seen—as well as the more modern hierarchical, animated meshes, which we learn to use in this chapter. We will use a different means to load the two different types of mesh even though the same .X file type continues to be used.

A static mesh (like a rock) is loaded with the function D3DXLoadMeshFromX(). If you pass a .X file to this function containing a bone hierarchy and animation frames, it will still be able to load the more complex mesh but will only "see" the starting vertex positions and the first frame. Figure 13.1 shows just such an example—a skeleton mesh with a sword and shield (sub-meshes), and vertex animation frames, none of which can be rendered when loaded with the simple D3DXLoadMeshFromX() function.

An animated mesh (like a biped human or quadruped creature) is loaded with a different function: D3DXLoadHierarchyFromX(). While the previous function still

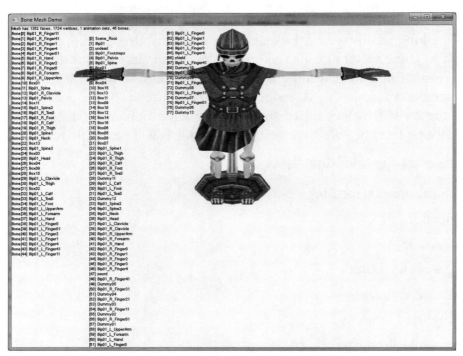

Figure 13.1
The default positions of the sub-meshes in a hierarchical .X model file.

required that we post-process the mesh information in order to parse the materials and texture filenames, it was a straightforward process with a reasonable amount of code. Unfortunately, the same cannot be said of hierarchical mesh loading. The hierarchy consists of frames with matrix and mesh data for different parts of the model and a bone or skeleton structure that is not rendered but still found inside the mesh hierarchy, with each node in the hierarchy called a "frame." Skinning the model involves transforming the matrix for each subsequent part of the model relative to its parent frame, which causes the "body parts" to move with the bones.

Asset Pipeline

A hierarchical mesh contains a bone structure with a root bone. Moving a root bone will cause all attached frames to move with it. You can move the entire mesh by moving the root. The bone hierarchy is also used to animate the mesh with baked-in animation frames. A bone structure is also required when using a physics system (for the so-called "ragdoll physics" often applied to game characters). The way animation is created is usually with live motion capture. Motion capture ("mo-cap") data is usually shared by many meshes in a game, and generic libraries of mo-cap animations are recycled. Some game engines will dynamically use mo-cap data to animate characters. Other game engines will "bake" the mo-cap animation directly into the mesh as key frame data—the most common technique, and the one we will use.

Advice

Baking animation data into a mesh is a job for a modeling/animation professional, where mo-cap data is applied to a model. The process is called "rigging," and seems to bring the model to life. In a native model file, with the two most common software packages being 3ds Max and Maya, the rigged character and animation are stored in their raw formats for later editing and any additional tweaking as needed. When the animations are approved by a project lead, then the animated model is "baked"—that is, the animation frames with the animation are saved to an output file, such as our familiar .X file format. This overall process—modeling, motion capture, rigging, baking, exporting—is called the "asset pipeline." In a professional game development environment, tools are built to automate the asset pipeline as much as possible, since it is otherwise a very manual, time-consuming process. Exporters are written for the modeling software, and tools are written to convert the assets into a format used by the game engine.

The animation system of a game engine will usually "interpolate" from one frame to the next to produce quality animations. Although the asset pipeline should streamline the process of getting assets to the renderer as quickly and easily as possible, that doesn't change the fact that an animator is working with digital data. But, the world is an analog place, so if you want characters to have realistic behaviors, they cannot be animated and rendered purely from the digital files they are stored in—the *precision* of the digital data is too perfect to simulate a real world. That precision must be smoothed out into an analog form that is more lifelike than the typical robot movements of a non-interpolated character. (No matter how skillful a modeler/animator is, it's impossible to make a digital animation look perfect; to do so would require tens of thousands of frames and *huge* asset files.)

In other words, even a hierarchical mesh has baked-in animation data, which makes it somewhat similar to the structure of a non-bone (but animated) mesh. The main advantage of a hierarchical mesh is the ability to manipulate it with a physics system and transform the bone structure with a vertex shader. In contrast, the vertex data in a non-bone mesh cannot be manipulated in the GPU with a shader because each frame is an individual static mesh—the faces of such a mesh are simply rendered.

The Bone Structure

Figure 13.2 shows the bone hierarchy of a human skeleton with the outline of skin, which is comparable to the structure of a skeletal mesh. Like this human skeleton, the bones of a model are not just figurative, but located inside the model.

You *can* iterate the hierarchy when transforming and rendering the mesh without knowing the bone names. Also, any one mesh can be attached to any other mesh at its pivot point. These child meshes will be treated as a part of the parent mesh, but can still be identified by name. You could, for instance, swap weapons in a game character from a spear to a sword by locating the name of the character's hand and first detaching the old weapon, then attaching the new one. The weapon, once attached to the character's hand, can be removed since it too can be identified by name.

If we had a 3D model of the human body, it might be divided into head, body, arms, and legs. The body might be the top frame with each part in frames below defining their own matrix and mesh data. The frame matrix provides the offset position and orientation from the body matrix. When the object is transformed

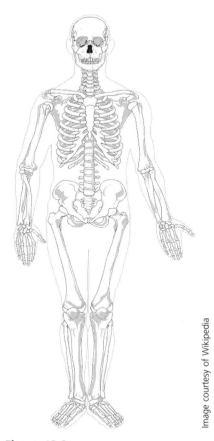

Image courtesy of Wikipedia

Figure 13.2
The skeletal structure of a hierarchical mesh has "skin" parts attached to the "bone" parts, like this illustration of a human body.

(that is, positioned in the scene) the first frame (known as the root) is moved to the desired position. This is where you want the whole object to be located. By transforming the entire model from the root first, all of the child and sibling objects in the hierarchy will move too—literally with a transformed matrix for each frame.

When rendering the mesh, a similar process takes place—the root frame is rendered, and all children and siblings of every node under the root are recursively rendered (if they have an associated mesh—and not every node does). In other words, we need to move the hand with the forearm, the forearm with the shoulder, and the shoulder with the neck. To do that, we have to multiply the matrix of a node by its parent so that it will "follow along." This combining of matrices is already common fare due to the previous chapter that manipulated matrices extensively in order to build a terrain system.

LOADING A SKELETAL MESH

Ideally, we would like to have the following features for a mesh rendering and animation system, but a practical approach will likely skip some of the more challenging features in order to first get an animated bone mesh up on the screen, with advanced features to come later.

- Load a hierarchical mesh file
- Maintain the bone hierarchy
- Perform animation
- Interpolate between frames
- Transition between animations
- Render the mesh with skinning

The .X file format supports both simple, static meshes, and the more complex hierarchical "bone/skeletal" type meshes. Previously, we used D3DXLoadMeshFromX to load a simple mesh from a .X file. Now we will use a more complex function to load a hierarchical mesh: D3DXLoadMeshHierarchyFromX. In either case, the mesh data inside a .X file can be loaded by either function, but transforming, animating, and rendering a hierarchical mesh requires new functions and classes beyond the single function call needed for a simple mesh. Figure 13.3 shows a diagram of the hierarchical structure of a biped character. In this figure, the pelvis is the root of the hierarchy, with Neck, Left Hip, and Right Hip being the highest-level child nodes of Pelvis, and siblings with each other. Head is a child of Neck. However, Left Upper Arm is the *parent* of Left Lower Arm, not a sibling.

Advice

The importance of child and sibling nodes to the structure will be obvious when we go over the source code that recursively parses the hierarchy.

Next, in Figure 13.4, the nodes are arranged in the order they are processed when the model is being transformed and rendered. This view makes it easier to see the

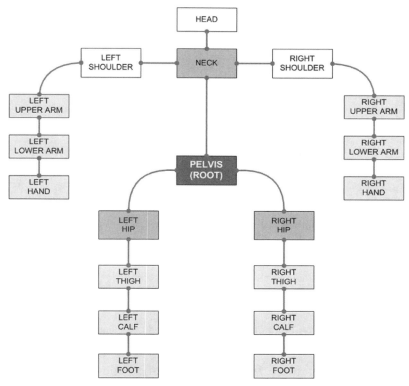

Figure 13.3
An illustration of the hierarchical structure of a biped character, showing the root and first three high-level nodes (Neck, Left Hip, Right Hip).

hierarchical structure in a top-down fashion. Although Neck is higher than Head, it is not more important; this hierarchy simply reflects the position of each node, while "importance" is only a matter of how many child nodes any given node has. If a high-level node is removed, all child nodes go with it, but not siblings.

Mesh File Differences

Let's look at the result when a non-hierarchical mesh is loaded into a hierarchical mesh structure. Figure 13.5 shows an aircraft mesh with the frame names displayed on the screen. Since the left column is empty, that means there was no skeletal structure making up the aircraft's components, but there are individual frames.

In the following column, you can see the name of every item in this non-hierarchical model file. Under each named frame (the name being up to the 3D

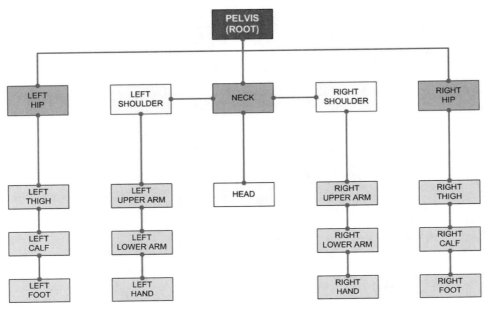

Figure 13.4
The hierarchical structure of a biped character in top-down view, prioritized by sibling and child nodes.

modeler who created it) is an unnamed frame and unnamed mesh. A modeler will usually only give names to important structures in the model file.

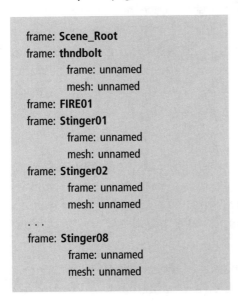

```
frame: Scene_Root
frame: thndbolt
        frame: unnamed
        mesh: unnamed
frame: FIRE01
frame: Stinger01
        frame: unnamed
        mesh: unnamed
frame: Stinger02
        frame: unnamed
        mesh: unnamed

. . .

frame: Stinger08
        frame: unnamed
        mesh: unnamed
```

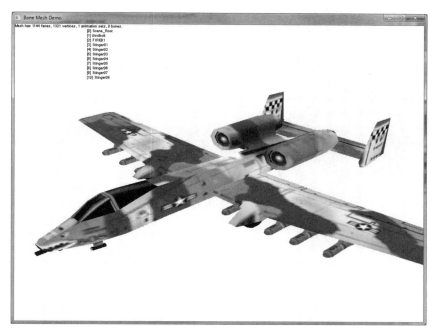

Figure 13.5
A non-hierarchical mesh may still have many frames containing sub-meshes, such as the detachable missiles on this "USAF A-10 Thunderbolt II" aircraft.

Let's look at another example. Figure 13.6 shows the rendering of an M-113 armored personnel carrier, which is a vehicle used by mechanized infantry units. The list shows that this model has only two parts—the "m113" mesh and the "Gun" mesh, with supporting frames. Since the small machine gun on top of the tank can be identified separately (as a frame called "Gun"), it is possible to affect transforms upon the mesh associated with that frame. We could search for the frame by name and apply an additional relative transform to cause the gun to swivel in place (via rotations), while continuing to remain "attached" to the vehicle. In that case, we would first identify the individual frames ("m113" and "Gun"), and render them individually using the same world matrix, with the additional changes to the gun as needed. (Note: the "FIRE01" frame is an unknown—it has no attached mesh so it is likely just a placeholder or an embedded code that a certain game is programmed to recognize.)

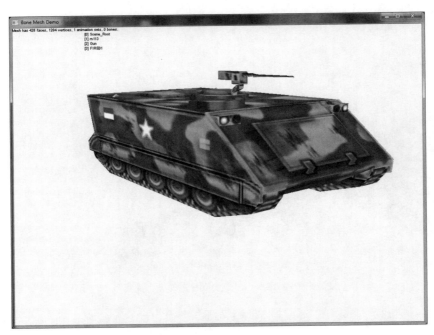

Figure 13.6
Another non-hierarchical mesh with even fewer parts than the previous model.

Added frame: **Scene_Root**
Added frame: **m113**
    Added frame: unnamed
    Added mesh: unnamed
Added frame: **Gun**
    Added frame: unnamed
    Added mesh: unnamed
Added frame: **FIRE01**

Advice

This chapter's resource files can be downloaded from www.jharbour.com/forum or www.courseptr. com/downloads. Not every line of code will be in print due to space considerations, only the most important sections of code.

Loading the Hierarchy

The function for loading animation data, skin info, and hierarchy is D3DXLoad-MeshHierarchyFromX(), which has this definition:

```
HRESULT D3DXLoadMeshHierarchyFromX(
    LPCTSTR Filename,
    DWORD MeshOptions,
    LPDIRECT3DDEVICE9 pDevice,
    LPD3DXALLOCATEHIERARCHY pAlloc,
    LPD3DXLOADUSERDATA pUserDataLoader,
    LPD3DXFRAME* ppFrameHeirarchy,
    LPD3DXANIMATIONCONTROLLER* ppAnimController
);
```

This is a very complicated function that requires us to create a C++ *class* to parse the hierarchical data inside the .X file. Fortunately, the DirectX SDK samples provide enough information to do this and we'll simply recycle the code without being too concerned about it needing to change. Here is a quick summary of the parameters:

Filename	File name of the .x file to be loaded.
MeshOptions	Mesh loading options.
pDevice	Pointer to the Direct3D device.
pAlloc	Required callback class used to allocate and deallocate memory and load the frames contained in the hierarchy.
pUserDataLoader	Used to load custom user data stored in a .X file.
ppFrameHeirarchy	Pointer to the root—the most important node.
ppAnimController	Pointer to the animation controller object.

We put this function to use in a general-purpose function called BoneMesh::Load.

```
bool BoneMesh::Load(std::string filename)
{
    MeshLoaderCallback *memoryAllocator=new MeshLoaderCallback;

    std::string currentDirectory = getTheCurrentDirectory();
    std::string xfilePath;
    splitPath( filename, &xfilePath, &filename);
    SetCurrentDirectory(xfilePath.c_str());
    HRESULT hr = D3DXLoadMeshHierarchyFromX(
```

```
                    filename.c_str(),
                    D3DXMESH_MANAGED,
                    g_engine->getDevice(),
                    memoryAllocator,
                    NULL,
                    &p_frameRoot,
                    &p_animController);

        delete memoryAllocator;
        memoryAllocator=0;

        SetCurrentDirectory(currentDirectory.c_str());
        if (hr != D3D_OK) {
            debug << "Error loading bone mesh" << endl;
            return false;
        }

        if(p_animController)
            p_numAnimationSets = p_animController->GetMaxNumAnimationSets();
        if (p_frameRoot) {
            createBoneMatrices((D3DXFRAME_NEW*)p_frameRoot, NULL);
            p_boneMatrices = new D3DXMATRIX[p_maxBones];
            ZeroMemory(p_boneMatrices, sizeof(D3DXMATRIX)*p_maxBones);
        }
        return true;
}
```

BoneMesh::Load() calls on a helper function called createBoneMatrices() to fill the skeletal structure from the incoming data from the .X file.

```
void BoneMesh::createBoneMatrices(D3DXFRAME_NEW *pFrame,
    LPD3DXMATRIX pParentMatrix)
{
    D3DXMESHCONTAINER_NEW* pMesh = (D3DXMESHCONTAINER_NEW*)
        pFrame->pMeshContainer;
    if (pMesh) {
        p_vertexCount += (int)pMesh->MeshData.pMesh->GetNumVertices();
        p_faceCount += (int)pMesh->MeshData.pMesh->GetNumFaces();
        if(!p_firstMesh) p_firstMesh = pMesh;
```

```
        //skinning info? then setup the bone matrices
        if(pMesh->pSkinInfo && pMesh->MeshData.pMesh) {
            D3DVERTEXELEMENT9 Declaration[MAX_FVF_DECL_SIZE];
            if (FAILED(pMesh->MeshData.pMesh->GetDeclaration(Declaration)))
                return;

            pMesh->MeshData.pMesh->CloneMesh(
                D3DXMESH_MANAGED,
                Declaration,
                g_engine->getDevice(),
                &pMesh->skinMesh);

            //total bones determines size of bone matrix array
            p_maxBones=max(p_maxBones,(int)pMesh->pSkinInfo->GetNumBones());

            //for each bone calculate its matrix
            for (unsigned int i=0; i<pMesh->pSkinInfo->GetNumBones(); i++)
            {
                D3DXFRAME_NEW* pTempFrame = (D3DXFRAME_NEW*)D3DXFrameFind(
                    p_frameRoot, pMesh->pSkinInfo->GetBoneName(i) );
                p_boneNames.push_back((std::string)
                    pMesh->pSkinInfo->GetBoneName(i));
                pMesh->frameCombinedMatrix[i] = &pTempFrame->combinedMatrix;
            }
        }
    }


    if(pFrame->pFrameSibling)
    {
        createBoneMatrices((D3DXFRAME_NEW*)pFrame->pFrameSibling,
            pParentMatrix);
    }


    if(pFrame->pFrameFirstChild)
    {
        createBoneMatrices((D3DXFRAME_NEW*)pFrame->pFrameFirstChild,
            &pFrame->combinedMatrix);
    }
}
```

Advice

The *complete* source code for the BoneMesh class and the MeshLoaderCallback class can be found in the project files for this chapter. Not every line of code is being put into print in the interest of conserving some space—the engine is too large to list it entirely in the pages of this book. We do cover the most important functions and structures, but not any of the minutia. Furthermore, some code listings will omit some comments and optional sections.

Allocating the Hierarchy

Before calling D3DXLoadMeshHierarchyFromX(), we need to derive a class based on ID3DXAllocateHierarchy (provided in the DirectX SDK). This new class will handle the mesh data, and it must implement the functions declared in the ID3DXAllocateHierarchy interface:

1. CreateFrame: requests memory allocation for one frame object

2. CreateMeshContainer: requests memory allocation for a mesh container object

3. DestroyFrame: de-allocates one frame object

4. DestroyMeshContainer: de-allocates one mesh container object

These four class methods are called during the internal processing of the .X file when you call the D3DXLoadMeshHierarchyFromX() function. The header for our loader class (derived from the ID3DXAllocateHierarchy interface) is shown below. We will look at the implementation of each of these four functions next.

```
class MeshLoaderCallback : public ID3DXAllocateHierarchy
{
public:
    STDMETHOD( CreateFrame )(LPCSTR Name, LPD3DXFRAME *retNewFrame);
    STDMETHOD( CreateMeshContainer )
        ( LPCSTR Name,
          const D3DXMESHDATA * meshData,
          const D3DXMATERIAL * materials,
          const D3DXEFFECTINSTANCE * effectInstances,
          DWORD numMaterials,
          const DWORD * adjacency,
          LPD3DXSKININFO skinInfo,
          LPD3DXMESHCONTAINER * retNewMeshContainer );
```

```
STDMETHOD( DestroyFrame )( LPD3DXFRAME frameToFree );
STDMETHOD( DestroyMeshContainer )(LPD3DXMESHCONTAINER meshContainerToFree);

bool findFile(std::string *filename);
bool doesFileExist(std::string &filename);
void splitPath(std::string& inputPath, std::string* pathOnly,
    std::string* filenameOnly);
};
```

Advice

The functions implemented in the `MeshLoaderCallback` function are *required*, and their parameters and return values cannot be changed because the functions are declared as pure virtual functions in `ID3DXAllocateHierarchy`. The source code listed in the text of this chapter is not meant to be typed in and compiled, but rather studied and discussed—some portions have been left out for the sake of brevity.

CreateFrame

The `CreateFrame()` method is called during processing of the mesh file when a new frame is encountered. A frame can contain pointers to additional frames (children or siblings) and/or the mesh data itself. By parsing the hierarchy, we can carry out animation and other functions on our mesh data. A *child* frame is one that is attached below, while a *sibling* frame is at the same level, attached above to the same parent. Processing all of the child and sibling nodes of the *root* will transform and render the whole model.

In Figure 13.7, note the "PELVIS (ROOT)" node. It has a mesh associated with it (namely, the body's torso), but some nodes (such as NECK) have no mesh data, even though such nodes may still have sibling and child nodes. As we have seen earlier, some modelers will insert tags into a model for future reference. Even though the NECK node is not rendered, it is *still transformed*, because both shoulders and all of their child nodes depend on the neck node to move with the pelvis. This flexibility in the model format makes it possible to create any kind of character, vehicle, or creature imaginable!

This function is called with a frame name and requires us to create a frame in memory. This memory is returned to the caller via the `retNewFrame` parameter. Therefore, we will need a new structure: `D3DXFRAME`. This is a structure provided

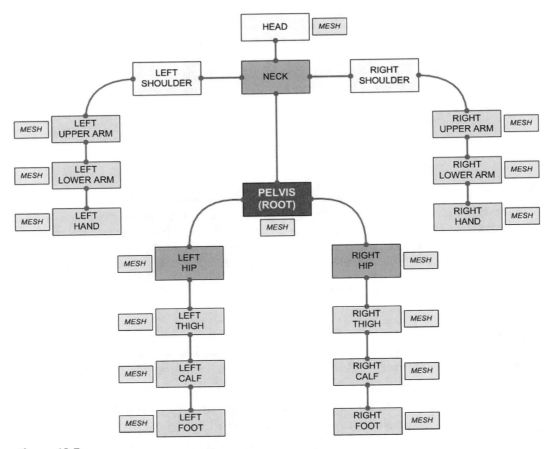

Figure 13.7
While bone data is purely mathematical (i.e., matrices), the embedded skinning data is tangible, as the mesh items in this diagram illustrate.

by Direct3D to hold information for a frame in a hierarchy. It contains properties representing the node's name (if it has one) and its matrix, a pointer to its mesh container, and pointers to any sibling or child nodes (which will be null if there are none). The code below is found in d3dx9anim.h within the DirectX SDK.

```
typedef struct _D3DXFRAME
{
    LPSTR                    Name;
    D3DXMATRIX               TransformationMatrix;
```

```
    LPD3DXMESHCONTAINER        pMeshContainer;
    struct _D3DXFRAME          *pFrameSibling;
    struct _D3DXFRAME          *pFrameFirstChild;
} D3DXFRAME, *LPD3DXFRAME;
```

To render a mesh hierarchy, traverse the frame tree applying each frame transformation matrix and rendering the mesh, then combine the transformation matrix as we go down the hierarchy. For this we need one more property in the struct—to keep track of the current combined matrix transform. If the transform for every node is not retained as we go through the hierarchy, then every node's matrix must be multiplied by every child and sibling's node matrix *over and over again* for each new child! The calculations would be a huge waste of time, and only slow down the performance of the game.

Instead, we want to keep track of the current combined matrix in order to perform just *one* multiplication—with the current combined matrix and the child's matrix. This will let us animate the character and have all child nodes follow along with the least amount of number crunching. The key to this working is by combining the matrices as we go along. Now, we aren't talking about skin data (which includes polygons, textures, etc.), but the bone data calculations can be quite a bottleneck, especially if you have a lot of objects in a scene.

A helpful optimization for these matrix calculations involves using a combined transformation matrix per frame (updated during the `BoneMesh::Animate` function coming up—stay tuned!). This combined matrix is not part of the frame structure, so we have to extend the structure a bit:

```
struct D3DXFRAME_NEW: public D3DXFRAME
{
    D3DXMATRIX combinedMatrix;
};
```

Advice

Direct3D provides a number of functions for working with frame hierarchies such as `D3DXFrameDestroy`, `D3DXFrameFind`, and `D3DXFrameCalculateBoundingSphere`. Since it takes quite a bit of work just to get a hierarchical mesh loaded, rendering, and animating, and because the gameplay coding requirements will vary from one project to the next, I will leave the higher-level functionality provided by functions such as these up to the reader.

Here's the code for `CreateFrame`. Remember, this is called once for every frame in the file.

```
HRESULT MeshLoaderCallback::CreateFrame(LPCSTR Name, LPD3DXFRAME *retNewFrame)
{
    *retNewFrame = 0;
    D3DXFRAME_NEW *newFrame = new D3DXFRAME_NEW;
    ZeroMemory(newFrame,sizeof(D3DXFRAME_NEW));
    D3DXMatrixIdentity(&newFrame->TransformationMatrix);
    D3DXMatrixIdentity(&newFrame->combinedMatrix);
    newFrame->pMeshContainer = 0;
    newFrame->pFrameSibling = 0;
    newFrame->pFrameFirstChild = 0;
    *retNewFrame = newFrame;
    if (Name && strlen(Name))
        newFrame->Name = duplicateCharString(Name);
    return S_OK;
}
```

CreateMeshContainer

The `CreateMeshContainer()` function is called during processing of the .X file by `D3DXLoadMeshHierarchyFromX()`, any time mesh data is encountered in the file. The function has this set of parameters:

```
HRESULT CreateMeshContainer(
    LPCSTR Name,
    const D3DXMESHDATA *pMeshData,
    const D3DXMATERIAL *pMaterials,
    const D3DXEFFECTINSTANCE *pEffectInstances,
    DWORD NumMaterials,
    const DWORD *pAdjacency,
    LPD3DXSKININFO pSkinInfo,
    LPD3DXMESHCONTAINER *ppNewMeshContainer

);
```

Here is a brief explanation for each of the parameters:

Name	The name of the mesh
pMeshData	A pointer to a mesh data structure
pMaterials	An array of materials
pEffectInstances	An array of effect instances
NumMaterials	The number of materials
pAdjacency	An array of adjacency information
pSkinInfo	Points to a struct containing skinning data
ppNewMeshContainer	A pointer to the new mesh container

All but the last parameter are input data defining the mesh. The function needs to use this data to create a new mesh container, provided by Direct3D. The D3DXMESHCONTAINER structure, which mimicks the parameters almost precisely, has these properties:

Name	The name of this mesh container
MeshData	A structure containing the mesh data as an ID3DXMesh, ID3DXPMesh, or ID3DXPatchMesh
pMaterials	An array of mesh materials
pEffects	An array of effect instances
NumMaterials	The number of materials
pAdjacency	The adjacency information
pSkinInfo	The skinning information
pNextMeshContainer	A pointer to a sibling mesh structure

As with the D3DXFRAME structure, we will extend the base D3DXMESHCONTAINER in order to add more properties, and call our new structure D3DXMESHCONTAINER_NEW. I was tempted to call this just "MeshContainer," but that may be confusing in the mesh loading code since our engine classes typically have that sort of code naming. We will normally load any textures specified in the mesh, so a texture array is needed, as well as skinning data. The structure used in the demo is shown below:

```
struct D3DXMESHCONTAINER_NEW: public D3DXMESHCONTAINER
{
    IDirect3DTexture9** textures;
    D3DMATERIAL9* materials;
    ID3DXMesh* skinMesh;
```

```
    D3DXMATRIX* boneOffsets;
    D3DXMATRIX** frameCombinedMatrix;


};
```

The base D3DXMESHCONTAINER has a pMaterials property, which is a D3DXMATERIAL structure that contains the texture filename and material data. It is easier to instead store the data in arrays of created textures and materials in our derived structure (IDirect3DTexture9** textures and D3DMATERIAL9* materials). Here's the code for CreateMeshContainer:

```
HRESULT MeshLoaderCallback::CreateMeshContainer(
    LPCSTR Name,
    CONST D3DXMESHDATA *meshData,
    CONST D3DXMATERIAL *materials,
    CONST D3DXEFFECTINSTANCE *effectInstances,
    DWORD numMaterials,
    CONST DWORD *adjacency,
    LPD3DXSKININFO pSkinInfo,
    LPD3DXMESHCONTAINER* retNewMeshContainer)
{
    D3DXMESHCONTAINER_NEW *newMeshContainer=new D3DXMESHCONTAINER_NEW;
    ZeroMemory(newMeshContainer, sizeof(D3DXMESHCONTAINER_NEW));
    *retNewMeshContainer = 0;
    if (Name && strlen(Name)) {
        newMeshContainer->Name = duplicateCharString(Name);
        debug << "Added mesh: " << Name << endl;
    } else {
        debug << "Added mesh: unnamed" << endl;
    }
    if (meshData->Type!=D3DXMESHTYPE_MESH) {
        DestroyMeshContainer(newMeshContainer);
        return E_FAIL;
    }
    newMeshContainer->MeshData.Type = D3DXMESHTYPE_MESH;

    //create adjacency data, required by ID3DMESH object
    DWORD dwFaces = meshData->pMesh->GetNumFaces();
    newMeshContainer->pAdjacency = new DWORD[dwFaces*3];
    memcpy(newMeshContainer->pAdjacency,
           adjacency, sizeof(DWORD) * dwFaces*3);
```

```
//get pointer to the Direct3D device
IDirect3DDevice9* device = g_engine->getDevice();
meshData->pMesh->GetDevice(&device);
newMeshContainer->MeshData.pMesh=meshData->pMesh;
newMeshContainer->MeshData.pMesh->AddRef();

//create material and texture arrays
newMeshContainer->NumMaterials = max(numMaterials,1);
newMeshContainer->materials = new
    D3DMATERIAL9[newMeshContainer->NumMaterials];
newMeshContainer->textures   = new
    LPDIRECT3DTEXTURE9[newMeshContainer->NumMaterials];
ZeroMemory(newMeshContainer->textures,
    sizeof(LPDIRECT3DTEXTURE9) * newMeshContainer->NumMaterials);
if (numMaterials>0) {
    // Load all the textures and copy the materials over
    for(DWORD i = 0; i < numMaterials; ++i)
    {
        newMeshContainer->textures[i] = 0;
        newMeshContainer->materials[i]=materials[i].MatD3D;
        if(materials[i].pTextureFilename)
        {
            string texturePath(materials[i].pTextureFilename);
            if (findFile(&texturePath))
            {
                if(FAILED(D3DXCreateTextureFromFile(
                    g_engine->getDevice(), texturePath.c_str(),
                    &newMeshContainer->textures[i])))
                {
                    debug << "Could not load texture: "
                        << texturePath << endl;
                }
            }
            else {
                debug << "Could not find texture: "
                    << materials[i].pTextureFilename << endl;
            }
        }
    }
}
```

```
        else {
        // make a default material in the case where the mesh did not provide one
            ZeroMemory(&newMeshContainer->materials[0], sizeof(D3DMATERIAL9) );
            newMeshContainer->materials[0].Diffuse.r = 0.5f;
            newMeshContainer->materials[0].Diffuse.g = 0.5f;
            newMeshContainer->materials[0].Diffuse.b = 0.5f;
            newMeshContainer->materials[0].Specular =
                newMeshContainer->materials[0].Diffuse;
            newMeshContainer->textures[0]=0;
        }

        //save skin data
        if (pSkinInfo) {
            newMeshContainer->pSkinInfo = pSkinInfo;
            pSkinInfo->AddRef();
            //save offset matrices
            UINT numBones = pSkinInfo->GetNumBones();
            newMeshContainer->boneOffsets = new D3DXMATRIX[numBones];
            //create the arrays for the bones and the frame matrices
            newMeshContainer->frameCombinedMatrix = new D3DXMATRIX*[numBones];
            //save each of the offset matrices
            for (UINT i = 0; i < numBones; i++)
                newMeshContainer->boneOffsets[i] =
                    *(newMeshContainer->pSkinInfo->GetBoneOffsetMatrix(i));

            debug << "Mesh has skin: bone count: " << numBones << endl;
        }
        else {
            newMeshContainer->pSkinInfo = 0;
            newMeshContainer->boneOffsets = 0;
            newMeshContainer->skinMesh = 0;
            newMeshContainer->frameCombinedMatrix = 0;
        }
        //reduce device reference count
        g_engine->getDevice()->Release();
        //does mesh reference an effect file?
        if (effectInstances) {
            if (effectInstances->pEffectFilename)
                debug << "Warning: mesh references an effect file" << endl;
        }
```

```
    // Set the output mesh container pointer to our newly created one
    *retNewMeshContainer = newMeshContainer;
    return S_OK;
}
```

DestroyFrame

The DestroyFrame() function frees memory used by each frame/node in the hierarchy as it is being de-allocated.

```
HRESULT MeshLoaderCallback::DestroyFrame(LPD3DXFRAME frameToFree)
{
    //create pointer to this frame
    D3DXFRAME_NEW *frame = (D3DXFRAME_NEW*)frameToFree;
    if (frame->Name) delete []frame->Name;
    delete frame;
    return S_OK;
}
```

DestroyMeshContainer

The DestroyMeshContainer() function removes a mesh contained within a hierarchy node from memory. This includes the name, material array and all materials, texture array and all textures, adjacency data, bone parts, the array of combined matrices (our optimization matrix for each frame), the skin mesh, the main mesh, and the container itself.

```
HRESULT MeshLoaderCallback::DestroyMeshContainer(
    LPD3DXMESHCONTAINER meshContainerBase)
{
    //create pointer to mesh container
    D3DXMESHCONTAINER_NEW* meshContainer =
    (D3DXMESHCONTAINER_NEW*)meshContainerBase;
    if (!meshContainer) return S_OK;
    //delete name
    if (meshContainer->Name) {
        delete []meshContainer->Name;
        meshContainer->Name=0;
    }
    //delete material array
    if (meshContainer->materials) {
        delete []meshContainer->materials;
        meshContainer->materials=0;
```

```
    }
    //release the textures before deleting the array
    if(meshContainer->textures) {
        for(UINT i = 0; i < meshContainer->NumMaterials; ++i)
        {
            if (meshContainer->textures[i])
                meshContainer->textures[i]->Release();
        }
    }
    //delete texture array
    if (meshContainer->textures)
        delete []meshContainer->textures;
    //delete adjacency data
    if (meshContainer->pAdjacency)
        delete []meshContainer->pAdjacency;
    //delete bone parts
    if (meshContainer->boneOffsets) {
        delete []meshContainer->boneOffsets;
        meshContainer->boneOffsets=0;
    }
    //delete frame matrices
    if (meshContainer->frameCombinedMatrix)
    {
        delete []meshContainer->frameCombinedMatrix;
        meshContainer->frameCombinedMatrix=0;
    }
    //release skin mesh
    if (meshContainer->skinMesh) {
        meshContainer->skinMesh->Release();
        meshContainer->skinMesh=0;
    }
    //release the main mesh
    if (meshContainer->MeshData.pMesh) {
        meshContainer->MeshData.pMesh->Release();
        meshContainer->MeshData.pMesh=0;
    }
    //release skin information
    if (meshContainer->pSkinInfo) {
        meshContainer->pSkinInfo->Release();
        meshContainer->pSkinInfo=0;
```

```
    }
    //delete the mesh container
    delete meshContainer;
    meshContainer=0;
    return S_OK;
}
```

RENDERING A SKELETAL MESH

We are going to learn how to render a skeletal mesh using a very rudimentary hardware skinning system. A professional hardware (that is, shader-based) skinned mesh renderer would pass the bone, skin, material, and texture data to the effect for rendering with the desired light sources all being managed inside the shader. We'll take a simpler approach by passing the texture and rendering each subset of the hierarchy within a skeletal mesh using a shader. This approach is not as elegant as a fully streamed skinning system, and there are a lot of GPU state changes, but it is still superior to the old software (i.e., fixed function) approach.

After having loaded a mesh from a .X file, we have the hierarchy loaded into a tree of frames and mesh data. We have a pointer to the root of the frame hierarchy (returned by D3DXLoadMeshHierarchyFromX() as ppFrameHeirarchy). In addition, if the .X file contained animation, there's a pointer to an animation controller (ppAnimController).

To render the hierarchical mesh, we have to traverse the tree and handle each node's transforms and rendering individually. There is no single function like "RenderHierarchy"—like the loading of a hierarchy, rendering is a very tedious, manual process! Why do you suppose Microsoft didn't just include a rudimentary rendering function? For one very good reason: a game engine programmer will optimize this process with a texture cache and other techniques. And that would not be possible unless Microsoft left these data structures and functions exposed. It's a lot more work up front, but once you have written the code to load, render, and animate a hierarchical mesh, you need not write that code again a second time.

At each limb or node of the tree, we have to calculate the new combined matrix for each frame in the tree. This could be done in the render function, but we will also want to handle animation so it's better to do this outside of rendering in an *update* function that's guaranteed to run as fast as possible. To render the tree, we call a recursive function, `drawFrame()`, passing it the root frame. This will render any mesh that it sees as a sibling or child via a call to `drawMeshContainer()`.

```
void BoneMesh::Render( Octane::Effect* effect )
{
    if (p_frameRoot) drawFrame(p_frameRoot, effect);
}
```

If the frame has any siblings it recursively calls `drawFrame` with them (these calls will only return once that branch has been completed), and then child frames are subsequently rendered recursively. Here is our `drawFrame()` function:

```
void BoneMesh::drawFrame(LPD3DXFRAME frame) const
{
    // draw all mesh containers in this frame
    LPD3DXMESHCONTAINER meshContainer = frame->pMeshContainer;
    while (meshContainer)
    {
        //draw this node/limb
        drawMeshContainer(meshContainer, frame, effect);
        //go to the next node/limb in the tree
        meshContainer = meshContainer->pNextMeshContainer;
    }
    // recursively draw siblings
    if (frame->pFrameSibling != NULL)
        drawFrame(frame->pFrameSibling, effect);
    // recursively draw children
    if (frame->pFrameFirstChild != NULL)
        drawFrame(frame->pFrameFirstChild, effect);
}
```

`DrawMeshContainer` is similar to our old static mesh rendering function, in that it goes through the materials, sets the texture, and calls `DrawSubset` for each one.

```
void BoneMesh::drawMeshContainer(LPD3DXMESHCONTAINER meshContainerBase,
    LPD3DXFRAME frameBase,   Octane::Effect* effect)
{
    D3DXFRAME_NEW *frame = (D3DXFRAME_NEW*)frameBase;
    D3DXMESHCONTAINER_NEW *meshContainer =
        (D3DXMESHCONTAINER_NEW*)meshContainerBase;
    //send the world transform to the shader
    effect->setWorldMatrix( frame->combinedMatrix );
```

```
//iterate through the materials, rendering each subset
for (unsigned int i = 0; i < meshContainer->NumMaterials; i++)
{
    //set shader's ambient color to the current material
    D3DXVECTOR4 material;
    material.x = meshContainer->materials[i].Diffuse.r;
    material.y = meshContainer->materials[i].Diffuse.g;
    material.z = meshContainer->materials[i].Diffuse.b;
    material.w = meshContainer->materials[i].Diffuse.a;
    effect->setParam("AmbientColor", material);
    //send the texture to the shader
    effect->setParam("Texture", meshContainer->textures[i]);
    //use either the skinned mesh or the normal one
    LPD3DXMESH mesh=NULL;
    if (meshContainer->pSkinInfo)
        mesh = meshContainer->skinMesh;
    else
        mesh = meshContainer->MeshData.pMesh;
    //draw the subset with passed shader
    effect->Begin();
    mesh->DrawSubset(i);
    effect->End();
}}
```

ANIMATING A SKELETAL MESH

Animating a hierarchical mesh is surprisingly easy thanks to the animation controller object, which will advance the vertices in the mesh according to a time value. Most of the code in this Animate() function is for updating the matrices after the animation frame changes the vertices—the actual animating is just a few lines of code!

```
void BoneMesh::Animate(float elapsedTime, D3DXMATRIX *matWorld)
{
    //adjust animation speed
    elapsedTime /= p_speedAdjust;
    //advance the time and set in the controller
    if (p_animController != NULL)
        p_animController->AdvanceTime(elapsedTime, NULL);
    p_currentTime += elapsedTime;
```

```
    //update the model matrices in the hierarchy
    updateFrameMatrices(p_frameRoot, matWorld);
    //if there's a skinned mesh, update the vertices
    D3DXMESHCONTAINER_NEW* pMesh = p_firstMesh;
    if(pMesh {
        unsigned int Bones = pMesh->pSkinInfo->GetNumBones();
        //transform each bone from bone space into character space
        for (unsigned int i = 0; i < Bones; ++i)
            D3DXMatrixMultiply( &p_boneMatrices[i],
                &pMesh->boneOffsets[i], pMesh->frameCombinedMatrix[i]);
        //lock the vertex buffers
        void *srcPtr=0, *destPtr=0;
        pMesh->MeshData.pMesh->LockVertexBuffer(D3DLOCK_READONLY,
            (void**)&srcPtr);
        pMesh->skinMesh->LockVertexBuffer(0, (void**)&destPtr);
        //update the skinned mesh via software skinning
        pMesh->pSkinInfo->UpdateSkinnedMesh(p_boneMatrices,
            NULL, srcPtr, destPtr);
        //unlock the vertex buffers
        pMesh->skinMesh->UnlockVertexBuffer();
        pMesh->MeshData.pMesh->UnlockVertexBuffer();
    }}
```

Updating the Frame Matrices

The updateFrameMatrices() function is called whenever the animation frame
changes. When animation occurs, the vertices in the mesh will change to reflect
the new animation frame. When this occurs (in the skeletal structure), we need
to recalculate the matrices with the transform changes as a result of the new
vertex positions. This function calls itself recursively as it goes through all of the
nodes of the hierarchy to update the combined matrix for each node.

```
void BoneMesh::updateFrameMatrices(D3DXFRAME *frameBase, D3DXMATRIX *parentMatrix)
{
    D3DXFRAME_NEW *currentFrame = (D3DXFRAME_NEW*)frameBase;
    //if parent matrix exists multiply with new frame matrix
    if (parentMatrix != NULL)
        D3DXMatrixMultiply(&currentFrame->combinedMatrix,
            &currentFrame->TransformationMatrix, parentMatrix);
    else
```

```
            currentFrame->combinedMatrix=currentFrame->TransformationMatrix;
        //recursively update siblings
        if (currentFrame->pFrameSibling != NULL)
            updateFrameMatrices(currentFrame->pFrameSibling, parentMatrix);
        //recursively update children
        if (currentFrame->pFrameFirstChild != NULL) {
            updateFrameMatrices( currentFrame->pFrameFirstChild,
                &currentFrame->combinedMatrix);
        }
    }
}
```

Changing the Animation Set

If there is more than one set of animation in the mesh, then we can change the animation from one set to another with interpolation. The setAnimationSet() function transitions animation from one set to another, performing a slight blending of the frames. If you want the transition to move quickly from one animation set to the next, then reduce the TransitionTime variable; likewise, increasing it will slow the transition, which looks cleaner but may not be responsive enough. It depends on the game, and this may be a value you will want to move into a script file so that it can be custom-set for each character in your game individually.

```
void BoneMesh::setAnimationSet(unsigned int index)
{
    //the timing with which to merge animations
    //(increasing slows down transition time)
    static float TransitionTime = 0.25f;
    if (index==p_currentAnimationSet) return;
    if (index>=p_numAnimationSets) index=0;
    //remember current animation
    p_currentAnimationSet=index;
    //get the animation set from the controller
    LPD3DXANIMATIONSET set;
    p_animController->GetAnimationSet(p_currentAnimationSet, &set);
    //alternate tracks for transitions
    DWORD newTrack = ( p_currentTrack == 0 ? 1 : 0 );
    //assign to the correct track
    p_animController->SetTrackAnimationSet( newTrack, set );
    set->Release();
```

```
    //clear any track events currently assigned
    p_animController->UnkeyAllTrackEvents( p_currentTrack );
    p_animController->UnkeyAllTrackEvents( newTrack );
    //disable the currently playing track
    p_animController->KeyTrackEnable( p_currentTrack, FALSE,
        p_currentTime + TransitionTime );
    //change the speed right away so the animation completes
    p_animController->KeyTrackSpeed( p_currentTrack, 0.0f, p_currentTime,
        TransitionTime, D3DXTRANSITION_LINEAR );
    //change the weighting (blending) of the current track
    p_animController->KeyTrackWeight( p_currentTrack, 0.0f, p_currentTime,
        TransitionTime, D3DXTRANSITION_LINEAR );
    //enable the new track
    p_animController->SetTrackEnable( newTrack, TRUE );
    //set the speed of the new track
    p_animController->KeyTrackSpeed( newTrack, 1.0f, p_currentTime,
        TransitionTime, D3DXTRANSITION_LINEAR );
    //change the weighting of the current track (0.0 to 1.0)
    p_animController->KeyTrackWeight( newTrack, 1.0f, p_currentTime,
        TransitionTime, D3DXTRANSITION_LINEAR );
    //save current track
    p_currentTrack = newTrack;
}
```

THE BONE MESH DEMO

There are several mesh files included with this chapter's sample project, called Bone Mesh Demo. One is the Viking spearman mesh shown in Figure 13.8.

Advice

This Viking character is one of the many characters included in the FPS Creator Model Pack 25, and is provided courtesy of The Game Creators (www.thegamecreators.com). There are buildings, animals, and other scenery objects included in this model pack, plus there are many more model packs available (43 at the time of this writing!) for a great price. This is a great resource for any aspiring or even experienced indie game developer—avail yourself of it!

Following is the core source code for the Bone Mesh Demo program (with some redundant portions omitted—open the project for the complete source code). This is a fairly useful program as far as using it to view various mesh files, because it has automatic camera control. When a mesh is loaded, a bounding

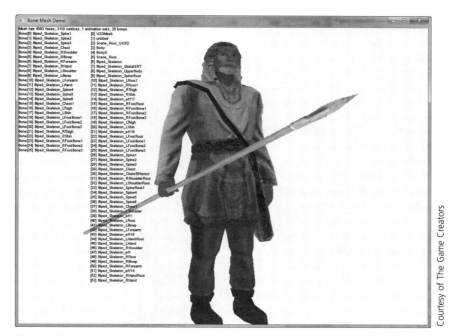

Courtesy of The Game Creators

Figure 13.8
This Viking spearman mesh has 26 bones and 1 animation set.

sphere is calculated with `D3DXFrameCalculateBoundingSphere()` to get the radius of the mesh. Then, the camera is moved away from the mesh based on that radius distance, and its "look at" angle is set to the center of the mesh so it appears, roughly, in the center of the screen regardless of its size.

```
const int BLACK = D3DCOLOR_XRGB(0,0,0);
Font* font;
BoneMesh* mesh;
Camera* camera;
Effect* effect;
vector<string> names;

bool game_init(HWND hwnd)
{
    g_engine->setBackdropColor(D3DCOLOR_XRGB(250,250,250));
    font = new Font("Arial",12);

    mesh = new BoneMesh();
    mesh->Load("viking3.x");
```

```
        mesh->Rotate(0, 0, 0);
        mesh->setScale(1.0);
        names = mesh->getAllBoneNames();
        //get a bounding sphere for this model
        D3DXVECTOR3 center;
        float radius;
        D3DXFrameCalculateBoundingSphere(mesh->getRootFrame(),&center,&radius);

        camera = new Camera();
        camera->setPosition(0.0f, radius*0.6f, -radius*1.5f);
        camera->setTarget(0.0f, radius*0.6f, 0.0f);
        camera->Update();

        effect = new Effect();
        effect->Load("ambient.fx");

        return true;
    }

    void game_update(float deltaTime)
    {
        mesh->Transform();
        mesh->Animate( deltaTime, &mesh->getMatrix() );
    }

    void game_render3d()
    {
        effect->setTechnique("Ambient");
        effect->setProjectionMatrix( camera->getProjMatrix() );
        effect->setViewMatrix( camera->getViewMatrix() );
        effect->setWorldMatrix( mesh->getMatrix() );
        mesh->Render( effect );
    }

    void game_render2d()
    {
        //print out mesh properties
        std::ostringstream ostr;
        ostr << "Mesh has " << mesh->getFaceCount() << " faces, ";
        ostr << mesh->getVertexCount() << " vertices, ";
        ostr << mesh->getAnimationSetIndex() << " animation sets, ";
        ostr << mesh->getBoneCount() << " bones." << endl;
```

```
    //print out bone names
    for(int i = 0; i < mesh->getBoneCount(); i++)
        ostr << "Bone[" << i << "] " << mesh->getBoneName(i) << endl;
    font->Print(0, 0, ostr.str(),BLACK);
    int x=180,y=12;
    for (int n=0; n< names.size(); n++) {
        ostr.str("");
        ostr << "[" << n << "] " << names[n] << endl;
        font->Print(x,y,ostr.str(),BLACK);
        y += 12;
        //add another column if we reach the bottom
        if (y > 750) {
            x += 180; y = 12;
        }
    }
}


void game_event(Octane::IEvent* e)
{
    float speed = 1.0f;
    switch(e->getID()) {
        case EVENT_KEYRELEASE: {
            KeyReleaseEvent *evt = (KeyReleaseEvent*) e;
            switch(evt->keycode) {
            case DIK_ESCAPE:
                g_engine->Shutdown();
                break;
            }
        }
        break;
        case EVENT_KEYPRESS: {
            KeyPressEvent *evt = (KeyPressEvent*) e;
            switch(evt->keycode) {
                case DIK_LEFT:   {
                    Vector3 pos = camera->getPosition();
                    pos.x -= speed;
                    camera->setPosition(pos);
                    camera->Update();
                }
```

```
                break;
                case DIK_RIGHT: {
                    Vector3 pos = camera->getPosition();
                    pos.x += speed;
                    camera->setPosition(pos);
                    camera->Update();
                }
                break;
                case DIK_UP: {
                    Vector3 pos = camera->getPosition();
                    pos.z -= speed;
                    camera->setPosition(pos);
                    camera->Update();
                }
                break;
                case DIK_DOWN: {
                    Vector3 pos = camera->getPosition();
                    pos.z += speed;
                    camera->setPosition(pos);
                    camera->Update();
                }
                break;
                case DIK_HOME: {
                    Vector3 pos = camera->getPosition();
                    pos.y -= speed;
                    camera->setPosition(pos);
                    camera->Update();
                }
                break;
                case DIK_END:   {
                    Vector3 pos = camera->getPosition();
                    pos.y += speed;
                    camera->setPosition(pos);
                    camera->Update();
                }
                break;
            }
        }
    break;
}}
```

Summary

We now have added to the engine support for one of the most crucial features of any 3D game—animated, hierarchical models. Combined with the other classes, our new `BoneMesh` class affords us with almost enough features to build a very decent 3D game, perhaps even a first-person shooter (although a scene optimization manager and texture cache would be needed for that).

References

Ditchburn, Keith; http://www.toymaker.info.

Granberg, Carl; http://www.cjgraphic.com.

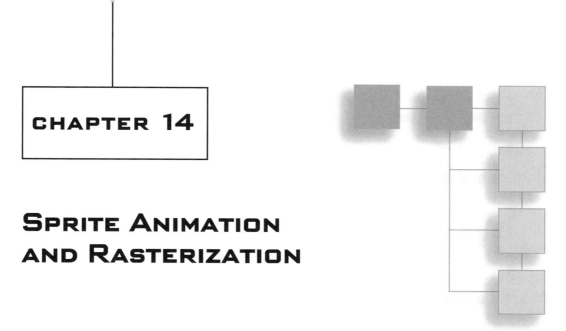

CHAPTER 14

SPRITE ANIMATION AND RASTERIZATION

This chapter covers the subject of sprite animation. We will learn how to render sprites with 2D transformation matrices with full support for translation, rotation, and scaling. That process is called *rasterization*, which describes the rendering of an object onto a 2D screen. Technically, the video card *rasterizes* all rendered output based on our projection matrix settings. But in the context of this chapter, sprite rasterization is an appropriate term because `ID3DXSprite` renders rectangular shapes using orthogonal projection. This new functionality, combined with our existing vector code, will produce a truly robust, highly usable sprite engine. Not merely for 2D games, a sprite engine is used quite often to render particles and bitmapped fonts—two supplemental topics covered later in the chapter.

There are two ways to render 2D objects in Direct3D. First, you can create a quad (or rectangle) comprised of two triangles with a texture representing the 2D image you wish to draw. This technique works and even supports transparency, responds to lighting, and can be moved in the Z direction. The second method available in Direct3D for rendering 2D objects is with sprites—and this is the method we will focus on in this chapter. A *sprite* is a 2D representation of a game entity that usually must interact with the player in some way. A tree or rock might be rendered in 2D and interact with the player by simply getting in the way, stopping the player by way of collision physics. We must also deal with game characters that interact with the player's character, whether it's an arrow fired from a bow or a missile fired from a spaceship.

This chapter will cover the following:

- Sprite rasterization
- Rectangles
- Drawing with transparency
- Sprite transformations
- Sprite animation
- Sprite-based particles
- Sprite-based fonts
- Zip file asset loading

SPRITE RASTERIZATION

It's one thing to know how to render a sprite—even a complex sprite with transparency and animation—but it's quite another matter to do something *useful* with it. Some software engineers cannot see beyond the specifications, are unable to design creative gameplay, and, as a result, focus their time on the mechanics of the game. What we're doing now is managing the *logistics* of 2D games by building this game engine and providing support facilities within the engine to simplify the *engineering* side of 2D game development. There are literally hundreds of game engines at repositories such as SourceForge, but they are mostly the result of failed game projects. When you design an engine from the outset with reuse and multi-genre support in mind, then you will more likely finish the game you have planned, as well as end up with a useful engine out of the deal.

We need to build a sprite engine that is powerful enough to support myriad game genres—from fixed-screen arcade-style games, to scrolling shooters, to board games, and so on. In other words, our 2D rendering system must be robust, fully featured, and versatile. That calls for some iterative programming!

Advice

Iterative game programming is a development methodology in which a game is built in small stages and is more like the growth of a life-form than the construction of a building (a common analogy in software engineering theory). The term "iterative" comes from the edit-compile-test process that is repeated over and over until the code functions as desired. Speeding up the iterative process results in more robust code and less propensity for bugs.

ID3DXSprite

We use the ID3DXSprite object to perform transformed 2D rendering (in which 2D bitmapped graphics are drawn in a process called *rasterization*). The core engine already initializes this object at startup, and we can access it via g_engine->getSpriteObj(). So, we're good to go there already, and just need to learn what to do with this object. There really is just one important function: Draw(), and two logistical functions: Begin() and End(). ID3DXSprite will batch all of the rendered output at once when the End() function is called. The Octane engine core calls game_render2D() inside these two function calls, so our game entities can then draw themselves from within this function.

The Draw() function has these parameters:

LPDIRECT3DTEXTURE9 pTexture	The source texture to be rendered
RECT *pSrcRect	The source rectangle on the texture
D3DXVECTOR3 *pCenter	The pivot point on the image for rotation purposes
D3DXVECTOR3 *pPosition	The target location for output
D3DCOLOR Color	The color used to draw the sprite (usually white) with support for alpha

It is possible to draw a sprite from a source texture using just this Draw() function alone, and we can even get animation by manipulating the source rectangle corresponding with timing. But, what's even more powerful is the ability for ID3DXSprite to render our sprites with *full 2D matrix-based transformations*: translation, rotation, and scaling—via the SetTransform() function. We'll see how that works later in the chapter.

Advice

This chapter's resource files can be downloaded from www.jharbour.com/forum or www.courseptr.com/downloads. Not every line of code will be in print due to space considerations, only the most important sections of code.

At its most basic usage, we can just load up a texture and draw it with ID3DXSprite. But to what end? We need the ability to manipulate *game entities* that will move on the screen in interesting ways and interact with each other, not to mention animate themselves. A complete entity manager would be nice (a topic addressed in more detail in Chapter 16). Here is an example usage of `Render()` for a non-animated image and the rotation pivot set to the upper left:

```
D3DXVECTOR3 pivot(0.0f, 0.0f, 0.0f);
D3DXVECTOR3 position(sprite_x, sprite_y, 0.0f);
g_engine->getSpriteObj()->Draw( image->getTexture(),
    NULL, &pivot, &position, color );
```

This is the simplest way to call `Draw()`. Assuming there are no animation frames, the `NULL` second parameter will cause the entire source image to be rasterized. We will look at transformed rendering and animation later in the chapter.

Vectors

Transforms will require position, rotation, and scaling data, which is facilitated most effectively with vectors (covered previously in Chapter 7). A *vector* is a mathematical construct that can represent two things—a point or a direction. A vector is not merely a point, nor is it merely a direction; otherwise, we would use one term or the other to describe it. However, we *can* use a vector to represent simple points or positions for game entities such as sprites and models. Since we already studied vectors, a detailed review is not needed now—we'll just put them to good use.

Our `Vector2` and `Vector3` classes will help provide some solid functionality to a new sprite class with very little new code required. We will be able to give a sprite some properties such as position, direction, and velocity, calculate the trajectory to a target, calculate normals, length, distance, and other helpful functions. The `Vector2` class will assist with the heavy lifting for advanced sprite rendering.

Rectangles

The Windows SDK provides a `RECT` structure with rudimentary properties but no functionality on its own, we we'll build our own `Rect` class with all of the modern comforts. This class will also facilitate 2D collision detection.

Following is the `Rectangle` class interface. Note that the class has only public properties and functions—and as such, it is similar to just a simple struct. I did not want to hide the four properties (left, top, right, and bottom) because they may be needed elsewhere in the engine and sometimes accessor/mutator functions, while enforcing good OOP structure, just get in the way.

```
class Rect {
public:
    double left;
    double top;
    double right;
    double bottom;
    Rect();
    Rect( const Rect& rect );
    Rect( const RECT& rect );
    Rect(int l,int t,int r,int b);
    Rect(double l,double t,double r,double b);
    virtual ~Rect(){}
    Rect& operator=( const Rect& R );
    Rect& operator=( const RECT& R );
    void Set(const Rect& R);
    void Set(const RECT& R);
    void Set(int l,int t,int r,int b);
    void Set(double l,double t,double r,double b);
    double getLeft() { return left; }
    double getTop() { return top; }
    double getRight() { return right; }
    double getBottom() { return bottom; }
    double getWidth() { return right-left; }
    double getHeight() { return bottom-top; }
    bool Contains(Vector3 point);
    bool Contains(int x,int y);
    bool Contains(double x,double y);
    bool Intersects(Rect rect);
    bool operator==( const Rect& R ) const;
    bool operator!=( const Rect& R ) const;
};
```

Here is the `Rectangle` class implementation:

```
Rect::Rect() {
    left = top = right = bottom = 0;
}
Rect::Rect( const Rect& R ) {
    Set(R);
```

```
}
Rect::Rect( const RECT& R ) {
    Set(R);
}
Rect::Rect(int l,int t,int r,int b) {
    Set(l,t,r,b);
}
Rect::Rect(double l,double t,double r,double b) {
    Set(l,t,r,b);
}
//assignment operator
Rect& Rect::operator=(const Rect& R) {
    Set(R); return *this;
}
Rect& Rect::operator=(const RECT& R) {
    Set(R); return *this;
}
void Rect::Set(const Rect& R) {
    left = R.left; top = R.top;
    right = R.right; bottom = R.bottom;
}
void Rect::Set(const RECT& R) {
    left=R.left; top=R.top;
    right=R.right; bottom=R.bottom;
}
void Rect::Set(int l,int t,int r,int b) {
    left = (double)l;
    top = (double)t;
    right = (double)r;
    bottom = (double)b;
}
void Rect::Set(double l,double t,double r,double b) {
    left = l;
    top = t;
    right = r;
    bottom = b;
}
bool Rect::Contains(Vector3 point) {
    return Contains(point.getX(), point.getY());
}
```

```
bool Rect::Contains(int x,int y) {
    return Contains((double)x, (double)y);
}
bool Rect::Contains(double x,double y) {
    return (x > left && x < right && y > top && y < bottom);
}
bool Rect::Intersects(Rect rect) {
    //check four corners of incoming Rect
    if (Contains(rect.getLeft(),rect.getTop()) ||
        Contains(rect.getLeft(),rect.getBottom()) ||
        Contains(rect.getRight(),rect.getTop()) ||
        Contains(rect.getRight(),rect.getBottom()))
        return true;
    //check four corners of self
    if (rect.Contains(getLeft(),getTop()) ||
        rect.Contains(getLeft(),getBottom()) ||
        rect.Contains(getRight(),getTop()) ||
        rect.Contains(getRight(),getBottom()))
        return true;
    return false;
}


//equality operator comparison includes double rounding
bool Rect::operator==( const Rect& R ) const {
    return ( left == R.left && top == R.top &&
            right == R.right && bottom == R.bottom );
}
//inequality operator
bool Rect::operator!=( const Rect& V ) const {
    return (!(*this == V));
}
```

The Sprite Class

We're going to create a C++ class to encapsulate all of the properties and methods needed to effectively use sprites in a game, as well as to support more advanced features like bitmapped fonts and particles (coming up later in the chapter). The Vector2 class will greatly simplify the code in the Sprite class, which otherwise would have to calculate things such as velocity on its own. In some cases, we'll use Vector2 just for a simple X-Y position.

Advice

As far as this `Sprite` class is concerned, and regarding object-oriented programming in C++ in general, there is such a thing as too much of a good thing. An overzealous OOP programmer tends to hide every property and make an accessor (for retrieving the property) and a mutator (for changing the property) for every single property in the class. This is generally a good thing, as it isolates potentially volatile data from manipulation. But a strong OOP design can also get in the way of getting things done.

For instance, updating a sprite's position will require several lines of code using a strong OOP implementation, while just exposing the *position* property would greatly simplify the code, not to mention result in higher productivity for anyone using the class.

I have a tendency toward simplicity when it comes to game programming, as long as the potential for harm is minimal. For instance, a simple position variable should be exposed as public, while a volatile *texture pointer* should be hidden and protected. I usually follow this rule: if the class *allocates* memory for something, then the class should also *de-allocate* it as well as hide the variable or pointer from outside manipulation, and instead provide it via an accessor (i.e., "get") function.

In a large studio environment, there will usually be coding standards that every programmer has to follow, so that everyone is not rewriting each other's code due to one or another preference for variable or function naming, or accessor/mutator usage. Let us keep it simple for the sake of learning.

What do we want to do with sprites? When it comes right down to it, the answer is *almost everything* involving 2D graphics. Sprites are at the very core of 2D games. We need to load and draw simple sprites (with no animation, just a single image), as well as the more complex animated sprites (with frames of animation). There is a need for both static and animated sprites in every game. In fact, most game objects are animated, which begs the questions how do we *create* an animation, and how do we *draw* the animation? We'll get to the first question later with several example programs, and we'll get to the second question in just a moment.

To answer the second question requires a bit of work. Let's take a look at the `Sprite` class header first. This class is feature rich, meaning that it is loaded with features we haven't even gone over yet, and will not go over until we use some of these features in future chapters (for instance, collision detection, which is not covered until Chapter 17).

```
class Sprite {
protected:
    Texture *image;
    bool imageLoaded;
    D3DXMATRIX matTransforms;
public:
    Sprite();
```

```
virtual ~Sprite();
bool Load(std::string filename, Color transcolor=Color(255,0,255,0));
void setImage(Texture *);
//managed functions
void Update(float deltaTime);
void Render();
void RenderFast(); //fast draw with no animation
void Render(bool autoPivot); //draw with animation
//center-pivot property
Vector2 pivotPoint;
Vector2 getPivot() { return pivotPoint; }
void setPivot(Vector2 pivot) { pivotPoint = pivot; }
//position on screen
Vector2 position;
Vector2 getPosition() { return position; }
void setPosition(Vector2 value) { position = value; }
void setPosition(double x, double y) { position.Set(x,y); }
double getX() { return position.x; }
double getY() { return position.y; }
void setX(double x) { position.x=x; }
void setY(double y) { position.y=y; }
//movement velocity
Vector2 velocity;
Vector2 getVelocity() { return velocity; }
void setVelocity(Vector2 value) { velocity = value; }
void setVelocity(double x, double y) {
    velocity.x=x; velocity.y=y;
}
//image dimensions
Vector2 size;
void setSize(Vector2 dim) { size = dim; }
void setSize(int width, int height) {
    size.x=width; size.y=height;
}
int getWidth() { return (int)size.x; }
int getHeight() { return (int)size.y; }
//multi-use sprite state
int state;
int getState() { return state; }
void setState(int value) { state = value; }
//animation columns
int animationColumns;
```

```
int getColumns() { return animationColumns; }
void setColumns(int value) { animationColumns = value; }
//current animation frame
float currentFrame;
int getCurrentFrame() { return (int)currentFrame; }
void setCurrentFrame(int value) { currentFrame = (float)value; }
//animation range
int firstFrame;
int lastFrame;
int getFirstFrame() { return firstFrame; }
int getLastFrame() { return lastFrame; }
void setAnimationRange(int first,int last) {
    firstFrame=first; lastFrame=last;
}
//animation direction property
int animationDirection;
int getAnimationDirection() { return animationDirection; }
void setAnimationDirection(int value) {
    animationDirection = value;
}
//rotation transform
double rotation;
double getRotation() { return rotation; }
void setRotation(double value) { rotation = value; }
//scale transform
Vector2 scale;
double getScaleHoriz() { return scale.x; }
double getScaleVert() { return scale.y; }
void setScale(double horiz,double vert) {
    scale.x = horiz; scale.y = vert;
}
void setScale(double scale) { setScale(scale,scale); }
//rendering color
Color color;
Color getColor() { return color; }
void setColor(Color col) { color = col; }
//returns boundary of sprite
Rect getBounds();
//use to adjust location of source rectangle
Vector2 sourcePosition;
```

```
    //facing and moving angles are helpful for targeting
    double facingAngle;
    double getFacingAngle() { return facingAngle; }
    void setFacingAngle(double angle) { facingAngle = angle; }
    double movingAngle;
    double getMovingAngle() { return movingAngle; }
    void setMovingAngle(double angle) { movingAngle = angle; }
};
```

That was a large header file, I'll admit, but it was jam-packed with features that we'll need later, and—as I mentioned back at the Vector3 listing—I prefer to give you the complete listing for a reusable class rather than modifying it when possible. There are some features built in to the Sprite class now that we will need in the next three chapters. Here is the Sprite class implementation (note that some comments and error handling code is left out for space considerations):

```
Sprite::Sprite() {
    image = NULL;
    imageLoaded = false;
    velocity = Vector2(0,0);
    state = 0;
    facingAngle = 0;
    movingAngle = 0;
    color = Color(255,255,255,255);
    pivotPoint = Vector2(0,0);
    //animation properties
    sourcePosition = Vector2(0,0);
    currentFrame = 0;
    firstFrame = 0;
    lastFrame = 0;
    animationDirection = 1;
    animationColumns = 1;
    //transformation properties
    position = Vector2(0,0);
    rotation = 0;
    scale = Vector2(1,1);
    size = Vector2(1,1);
}
Sprite::~Sprite() {
    if (imageLoaded) delete image;
}
```

```cpp
bool Sprite::Load(std::string filename, Color transcolor) {
    //de-allocated existing texture
    if (!image) {
        delete image;
        image = NULL;
    }
    //create new texture
    image = new Texture();
    if (image->Load(filename,transcolor)) {
        size.x = image->getWidth();
        size.y = image->getHeight();
        imageLoaded = true;
        return true;
    } else
        return false;
}
void Sprite::setImage(Texture *img) {
    if (!img) {
        debug << "Sprite::setImage: texture is null\n";
        return;
    } else {
        if (imageLoaded) {
            delete image;
            image = NULL;
        }
    }
    //set new image
    image = img;
    size.x = image->getWidth();
    size.y = image->getHeight();
    imageLoaded = false;
}
//optimized rendering without animation
void Sprite::RenderFast() {
    D3DXVECTOR3 pivot(0.0f, 0.0f, 0.0f);
    g_engine->getSpriteObj()->Draw( image->getTexture(),
        NULL, &pivot, &position.ToD3DXVECTOR3(), color.ToD3DCOLOR() );
}
//Entity::Render implementation
void Sprite::Render() {
```

```
        Render(false);
    }
    //full animation frame rendering
    void Sprite::Render(bool autoPivot) {
        if (autoPivot) {
            pivotPoint.x = (float)((size.x*scale.x)/2);
            pivotPoint.y = (float)((size.y*scale.y)/2);
        }
        D3DXVECTOR2 center((float)pivotPoint.x, (float)pivotPoint.y);
        D3DXVECTOR2 trans((float)position.x, (float)position.y);
        D3DXVECTOR2 scale((float)scale.x,(float)scale.y);
        D3DXMatrixTransformation2D(&matTransforms,NULL,0,&scale,&center,
            (float)rotation,&trans);
        g_engine->getSpriteObj()->SetTransform(&matTransforms);
        //draw animation frame
        int fx = (int)(((int)currentFrame % animationColumns) * size.x);
        int fy = (int)(((int)currentFrame / animationColumns) * size.y);
        RECT srcRect = {fx,fy, (int)(fx+size.x), (int)(fy+size.y)};
        g_engine->getSpriteObj()->Draw(image->getTexture(),
            &srcRect,NULL,NULL,color.ToD3DCOLOR());
        //set identity
        g_engine->setSpriteIdentity();
    }
    void Sprite::Update(float deltaTime) {
        //move sprite by velocity amount
        position.x += velocity.x * deltaTime;
        position.y += velocity.y * deltaTime;
        //increment animation frame
        currentFrame += (float)((float)animationDirection * deltaTime);
        //keep current frame within bounds
        if ((int)currentFrame < firstFrame) currentFrame = (float)lastFrame;
        if ((int)currentFrame > lastFrame) currentFrame = (float)firstFrame;
    }
    Rect Sprite::getBounds() {
        Rect rect;
        rect.left = position.x; rect.top = position.y;
        rect.right = position.x + size.x * scale.x;
        rect.bottom = position.y + size.y * scale.y;
        return rect;
    }
```

This is a very effective implementation of a sprite class. We have here the ability to render a sprite to any desired scale, at any angle of rotation, with timed animation, using alpha channel transparency, and timed animation and movement. The Sprite class has some functionality that we're not using yet, but which will be needed in the next three chapters.

Drawing with Transparency

ID3DXSprite doesn't care whether your sprite's source image uses a color key or an alpha channel for transparency—it just renders the image as requested. If you have an image with an alpha channel—for instance, a 32-bit targa—then it will be rendered with alpha, including translucent blending with the background. But if your image has no alpha because you are using a background color key for transparency—for instance, a 24-bit bitmap—then it will be drawn by simply not drawing the color-keyed pixels. Looking at the sprite functionality at a lower level, you can tell the sprite renderer (ID3DXSprite) what color you want to use for the color key; our Sprite class defines magenta (with an RGB of 255, 0, 255) as the default transparent color key. Figure 14.1 shows just such an image.

A better approach is to use alpha channel transparency. The image file itself can have an alpha channel—and most artists will prefer to define their own translucent pixels for best results (rather than leaving it to chance in the hands of a programmer). The main reason to use alpha rather than color-key transparency is the limitation on quality when using the latter technique. An alpha channel can define pixels with shades of translucency, while a color key is an all-or-nothing, on/off setting with solid edges and pixelization—because such an image will have discrete pixels. We can do alpha blending at runtime to produce some awesome special effects (such as the particle emitters discussed later in the chapter), but for best quality it's best to prepare artwork in advance.

The preferred method for rendering with transparency (especially among artists) is using an alpha channel. One great advantage to alpha-blended images is support for partial transparency—that is, translucent blending. Rather than using a black border around a color-keyed sprite (the old-school way of highlighting a sprite), an artist will blend a border around a sprite's edges using an alpha level for partial translucency (which looks fantastic in

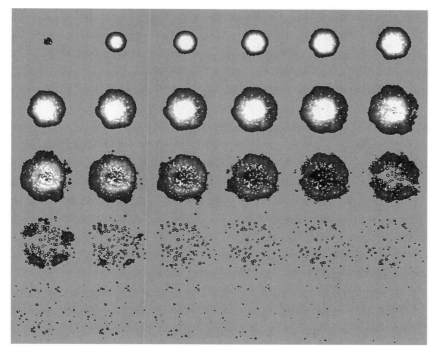

Figure 14.1
A sprite animation sheet with color key transparency.

comparison!). To do that, you must use a file format that supports 32-bit RGBA images. Truevision Targa (TGA) is a good choice, and Portable Network Graphics (PNG) files work well, too. Let's take a look at the spaceship sprite again—this time with an alpha channel rather than a color-keyed background. Note the checkerboard pattern in the background; this is a common way of showing the alpha channel in graphic editors. Figure 14.2 shows an example image with an alpha channel.

SPRITE TRANSFORMATIONS

Rendering a sprite at any desired location is fairly easy, as you have seen. But we have the ability to use a full matrix transformation to apply the translation, rotation, and scaling to a sprite, which obviously will be far more useful. We can rotate and scale a sprite with relative ease due to D3DX library functions. If we

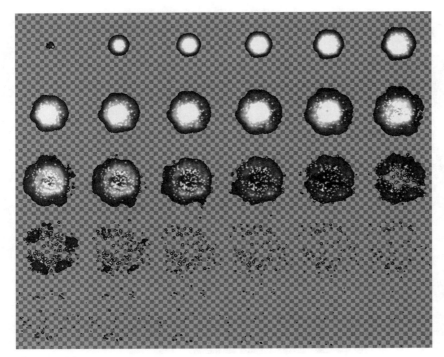

Figure 14.2
A sprite animation sheet with an alpha channel (shown as a checkerboard pattern in GIMP).

want to draw a single-frame sprite or draw a single frame from an animation sheet, we can use the same multi-purpose drawing function from our new Sprite class.

We can apply this functionality to animation as well. Since ID3DXSprite is used to draw single- or multi-frame sprites, you can use the same transformation to rotate and scale a sprite regardless of whether it's animated.

Calculating Transforms

The transformed matrix is created with a function called D3DXMatrixTransformation2D(). Here is how it looks:

```
D3DXVECTOR2 pivot((float)pivotPoint.x, (float)pivotPoint.y);
D3DXVECTOR2 trans((float)position.x, (float)position.y);
D3DXVECTOR2 scale((float)scale.x,(float)scale.y);
D3DXMATRIX matrix;
```

```
D3DXMatrixTransformation2D (
    &matrix,            //output matrix
    NULL,               //scaling center
    0,                  //scaling rotation
    &scale,             //scaling factor
    &pivot,             //rotation center
    (float)rotation,    //rotation angle
    &trans              //translation
);

g_engine->getSpriteObj()->SetTransform(&matrix);
```

The Render() function performs the transformations internally based on the sprite's properties—position, rotation, and scale—and it is therefore a self-contained function. This function creates a matrix with scaling, rotation, and translation all combined. We use the same D3DXMATRIX to transform a sprite as we do for a mesh. Let me show you what you can do with sprite transformations. Note that only the important code is listed, while redundant code (such as game_preload) has been omitted for space.

Sprite Transform Demo

Let's see how transforms work within the engine with a little test program. The Sprite Transform Demo is shown in Figure 14.3.

```
Sprite *backgrnd;
Font* font;
float delta;
Texture* phat;
const int NUMSPRITES = 1000;
std::vector<Sprite*> sprites;

bool game_init(HWND hwnd) {
    g_engine->setBackdropColor(D3DCOLOR_XRGB(0,50,50));
    font = new Font("Arial Bold",18);

    backgrnd = new Sprite();
    backgrnd->Load("pinkgeometry.bmp");
    backgrnd->scale.x = ((float)g_engine->getScreenWidth() /
        (float)backgrnd->getWidth());
```

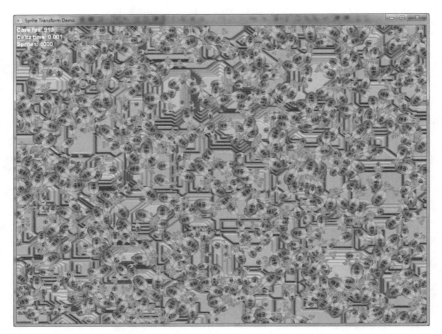

Figure 14.3
The Sprite Transform Demo program draws many sprites with full matrix transforms.

```
backgrnd->scale.y = ((float)g_engine->getScreenHeight() /
    (float)backgrnd->getHeight());

phat = new Texture();
phat->Load("fatship256.tga");

Vector2 res = Vector2(g_engine->getScreenWidth(),
    g_engine->getScreenHeight());

//create a group of sprites using std::vector
for (int n=0; n<NUMSPRITES; n++) {
    Sprite* S = new Sprite();
    S->setImage( phat );
    S->setScale( 0.1f + (rand() % 10) / 50.0f );
    int sx = (int)(S->size.x*S->scale.x/2);
    int sy = (int)(S->size.y*S->scale.y/2);
    int cx = rand() % (int)res.x - sx;
```

```
            int cy = rand() % (int)res.y - sy;
            S->setPosition(cx,cy);
            S->setRotation( (double)(rand()%360));
            sprites.push_back( S );
        }
        return true;
}

void game_end() {
    delete font;
    delete backgrnd;
    delete phat;
    BOOST_FOREACH(Sprite* S, sprites)
        delete S;
    sprites.clear();
}

void game_update(float deltaTime) {
    delta = deltaTime;
    BOOST_FOREACH(Sprite* S, sprites) {
        double r = S->getRotation();
        r += deltaTime;
        S->setRotation(r);
    }
}

void game_render2d() {
    backgrnd->Render();
    BOOST_FOREACH(Sprite* S, sprites)
        S->Render();
    std::ostringstream ostr;
    ostr << "Core fps: " << g_engine->getCoreFrameRate() << endl;
    ostr << "Delta time: " << delta << endl;
    ostr << "Sprites: " << sprites.size() << endl;
    font->Print(0, 0, ostr.str());
}

void game_event(Octane::IEvent* e) {
    switch(e->getID()) {
        case EVENT_KEYRELEASE:
```

```
        g_engine->Shutdown();
        break;
  }}
```

We will only see *very* basic sprite example programs in this chapter with no real intelligence or behavior behind any of the objects being rendered. We have just added some quite advanced vector and sprite support to the game engine and verified that 2D rendering is working (with both color-keyed and alpha transparency). So let's move into animation next.

SPRITE ANIMATION

Let's talk about sprite animation. A *sprite animation sheet* is an image containing many frames for an animation sequence laid out in tiles that are arranged into rows and columns, as shown in Figure 14.4. In this sprite sheet there are 6 columns across and 30 total frames of animation.

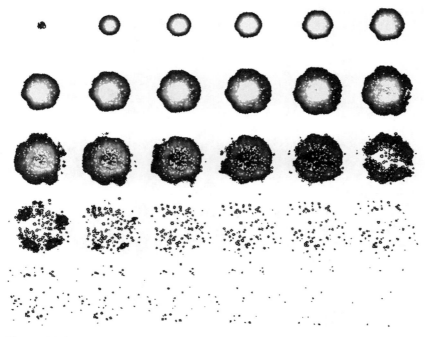

Figure 14.4
Animated explosion sprite stored on a sheet of rows and columns.

Animation with a Touch of Class

Using the Sprite class we could create an explosion sprite with code like this:

```
Sprite *explosion = new Sprite();
explosion->loadImage( "explosion.tga" );
```

Each sprite can have its own individual properties for animation, such as the total frames, number of columns (in the sprite sheet), and animation timing. Let's see how those might be set for the sample explosion sprite. First, we have to tell the Sprite class how large each frame is, because it sets the width and height to the full size of the image by default. The image size is the size of the whole sprite sheet, while the frame size is the size of each cell of animation.

```
explosion->setSize( 128, 128 );
```

The number of frames of animation (called the animation range) must be set as well. When we're doing animation, the range of valid frame numbers (which are zero based) will be 0 to the total frames minus one. The following line of code will cause the animation system to animate the sprite based on frames 0 to 29, and then auto-wrap around to 0.

```
explosion->setAnimationRange( 0, 29 );
```

Once a sprite is configured with the desired properties, you can animate and draw a sprite using the Sprite::Update() and Sprite::Render() functions. The Update() function will do two basic tasks automatically: move the sprite (if velocity is set), and animate the sprite (if appropriate). Animation is based on the delta time passed from the engine core to the game_update() function (usually found in main.cpp of a project). The deltaTime will usually be about 4 microseconds, but of course it's totally dependent on processor speed.

```
void Sprite::Update(float deltaTime)
{
    //move sprite by velocity amount
    position.x += velocity.x * deltaTime;
    position.y += velocity.y * deltaTime;
    //increment animation frame
    currentFrame += (float)((float)animationDirection * deltaTime);
    //keep current frame within bounds
    if ((int)currentFrame < firstFrame) currentFrame = (float)lastFrame;
    if ((int)currentFrame > lastFrame) currentFrame = (float)firstFrame;
}
```

Animation speed should be based on the delta time multiplied by any modifier you wish to use to slow down the animation rate. The Sprite class uses a float for the frame counter so it will accurately keep track of partial frames and perform the animation at sub-framerates as a result. (Without this capability, animation would be forced into a discrete minimum framerate.) Since the time is specified in floating-point milliseconds, the value you use will be based on the desired framerate for the sprite. The average rate for animation is usually 30 frames per second (at 33 milliseconds per frame).

Animation Demo

Now we will create an example program to demonstrate a single animated sprite. By keeping the demos short and simple, it's my belief that the code is easier to understand and learn. This short program will animate a single explosion, rendering an alpha-transparent targa image at random locations around the screen, as shown in Figure 14.5.

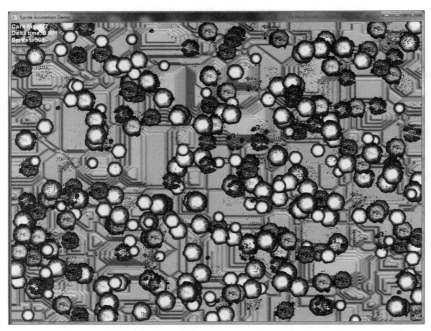

Figure 14.5
The Sprite Animation Demo program draws a large number of animated explosion sprites.

The explosion is composed of thirty 128×128 sprite frames in a sheet with six columns. Note the effective use of alpha to produce transparent regions as the explosion dissipates. This shows just how much better alpha is versus the older color-key technology. You can also very easily cause sprites to fade in or out to produce effects like cloaking or shielding (in the case of a spaceship, for instance). Another popular trick with alpha is to cause a sprite to flicker on and off repeatedly after a collision. One of my favorite tricks is to cycle a sprite's alpha through the red color component when the object "dies."

This sort of demo is interesting because it affords an opportunity to resume exploring multi-threaded programming—which has admittedly been put on hold for a while as the engine has been developed. Let's observe the same program running with 10,000 animated sprites. Figure 14.6 shows a screenshot with a reported 45 core fps and delta time of 0.021 ms (or 21 microseconds). This delta time should be producing hundreds of frames per second at such a low value, so that's good—we know that the timing system is functioning as expected. This is a good candidate for a thread test, so we'll revisit this program

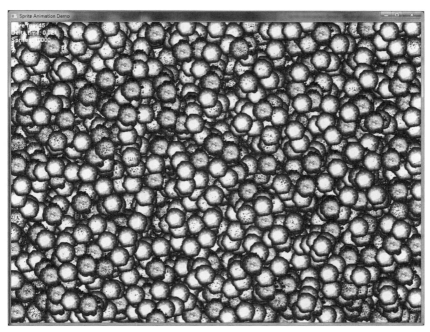

Figure 14.6
Animating 10,000 sprites (single core version) slows the engine core to 45 fps.

again in a later chapter to see how well it runs with more cores available. (For the complete source code to this project, see the complete project included in this chapter's resource files.)

Advice

The explosion animation was provided courtesy of Reiner Prokein and is available at www .reinerstileset.de.

```
Sprite *backgrnd;
Font* font;
float delta;
Texture* explosion;
const int NUMSPRITES = 1000;
std::vector<Sprite*> sprites;

bool game_init(HWND hwnd) {
    g_engine->setBackdropColor(D3DCOLOR_XRGB(0,50,50));
    font = new Font("Arial Bold",18);

    backgrnd = new Sprite();
    backgrnd->Load("pinkgeometry.bmp");
    backgrnd->scale.x = ((float)g_engine->getScreenWidth() /
        (float)backgrnd->getWidth());
    backgrnd->scale.y = ((float)g_engine->getScreenHeight() /
        (float)backgrnd->getHeight());

    explosion = new Texture();
    explosion->Load("explosion_30_128.tga");

    //create a group of sprites using std::vector
    for (int n=0; n<NUMSPRITES; n++) {
        Sprite* spr = new Sprite();
        spr->setImage( explosion );
        spr->setPosition( rand()%g_engine->getScreenWidth(),
            rand()%g_engine->getScreenHeight() );
        spr->setAnimationRange( 0,29 );
        spr->setCurrentFrame( rand()%30 );
        spr->setColumns( 6 );
        spr->setSize( 128,128 );
```

```
            sprites.push_back( spr );
        }
        return true;
}

void game_update(float deltaTime) {
        static float factor = 0;
        delta = deltaTime;
        factor += deltaTime * 0.5f;
        //adjust sprite scale with delta time
        if(factor > 3.0f) factor = 0.01f;
        //update sprites
        BOOST_FOREACH(Sprite* S, sprites) {
            S->Update(deltaTime*30.0f);
            if (S->getCurrentFrame() == S->getLastFrame()-1) {
                //adjust scaling
                S->scale.x = factor;
                S->scale.y = factor;
                //set random location
                int sx = (int)(S->size.x*S->scale.x/2);
                int sy = (int)(S->size.y*S->scale.y/2);
                int cx = rand() % g_engine->getScreenWidth() - sx;
                int cy = rand() % g_engine->getScreenHeight() - sy;
                S->setPosition(cx,cy);
            }
        }
}

void game_render2d() {
        backgrnd->Render();
        BOOST_FOREACH(Sprite* S, sprites)
            S->Render();
        std::ostringstream ostr;
        ostr << "Core fps: " << g_engine->getCoreFrameRate() << endl;
        ostr << "Delta time: " << delta << endl;
        ostr << "Sprites: " << sprites.size() << endl;
        font->Print(0, 0, ostr.str());
}

void game_event(Octane::IEvent* e) {
```

```
switch(e->getID()) {
    case EVENT_KEYRELEASE:
        g_engine->Shutdown();
        break;
}
}
```

SPRITE-BASED PARTICLES

Particles are tiny sprites that are rendered with about 50 percent alpha transparency so that they seem to glow. The key to creating a particle system—that is, an emitter or other special effect—is to start with a good source particle image. Figure 14.7 shows an enlarged view of a 16 × 16 particle sprite. Note the amount of alpha transparency in the image—only the central white portion is fully opaque, while the rest will blend with whatever background the particle is rendered over.

Sprite-based particles differ significantly from shader-based particles rendered by the 3D hardware (known as *point sprites* and used to optimize the rendering of objects in the far distance). Three-dimensional particles can emit light (emissive)

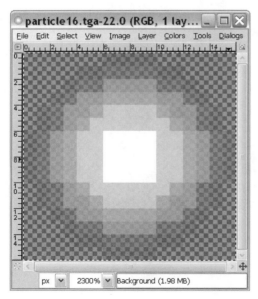

Figure 14.7
The source particle image is 16 × 16 pixels with alpha channel.

or reflect light (reflective) and can be used to simulate *real* smoke and fog. Sprite-based particles can be used to generate smoke trails behind missiles and spaceships, among other things.

A so-called *particle system* is a managed list of particles that are rendered in creative ways. That list is based on either a std::vector or std::list. A std::vector will work *slightly* faster than a std::list when your list does not need to change very often. Our particle emitter will create particles but not remove any (until the object is destroyed, that is). A std::list would be preferred if you needed to add and remove items regularly, but it's not quite as fast as a std::vector when it comes to sequential iteration[1].

To make working with particles as reasonable and practical as possible, we'll code up the most obvious functionality into a class. Following is the definition for a ParticleEmitter class. This class uses a std::vector filled with Sprite objects to represent the entities in the emitter. The class is otherwise completely self-contained and can handle most types of particle systems that I have seen over the years. Basically, a great particle system works in such a way that the player shouldn't notice that it's a particle at all. When a spaceship is cruising through space, it can emit a flame and smoke with the use of two particle emitters, for example. Here is the interface:

```
class ParticleEmitter {
private:
    typedef std::vector<Octane::Sprite*>::iterator p_iter;
    std::vector<Octane::Sprite*> p_particles;
    Texture *p_image;
    Vector2 p_position;
    double p_direction;
    double p_length;
    int p_max;
    int p_alphaMin,p_alphaMax;
    int p_minR,p_minG,p_minB,p_maxR,p_maxG,p_maxB;
    int p_spread;
    double p_velocity;
    double p_scale;
public:
    ParticleEmitter();
    virtual ~ParticleEmitter();
```

```cpp
    bool Load(std::string imageFile);
    void Render();
    void Update(float deltaTime);
    void Add();
    void setPosition(double x, double y) { p_position.Set(x,y); }
    void setPosition(Vector2 vec) { p_position = vec; }
    Vector2 getPosition() { return p_position; }
    void setDirection(double angle) { p_direction = angle; }
    double getDirection() { return p_direction; }
    int getCount() { return (int)p_particles.size(); }
    void setMax(int num) { p_max = num; }
    void setAlphaRange(int min,int max);
    void setColorRange(int r1,int g1,int b1,int r2,int g2,int b2);
    void setSpread(int value) { p_spread = value; }
    void setLength(double value) { p_length = value; }
    void setVelocity(double value) { p_velocity = value; }
    void setScale(double value) { p_scale = value; }
};
```

Following is the implementation file for the ParticleEmitter class. We'll go over an example to fully illustrate how it works shortly.

```cpp
ParticleEmitter::ParticleEmitter() {
    p_image = NULL;
    p_max = 100;
    p_length = 200;
    p_direction = 0;
    p_alphaMin = 254; p_alphaMax = 255;
    p_minR = 0; p_maxR = 255;
    p_minG = 0; p_maxG = 255;
    p_minB = 0; p_maxB = 255;
    p_spread = 10;
    p_velocity = 1.0f;
    p_scale = 1.0f;
}
bool ParticleEmitter::Load(std::string imageFile) {
    if (p_image) {
        delete p_image;
        p_image = NULL;
    }
    p_image = new Texture();
```

```
        if (!p_image->Load(imageFile)) {
            debug << "Error loading particle image\n";
            return false;
        }
        return true;
    }
ParticleEmitter::~ParticleEmitter() {
        delete p_image;
        BOOST_FOREACH(Sprite* sprite, p_particles) {
            delete sprite;
            sprite = NULL;
        }
        p_particles.clear();
    }
void ParticleEmitter::Add() {
        double vx,vy;
        Sprite *p = new Sprite();
        p->setImage(p_image);
        p->setPosition(p_position.getX(), p_position.getY());
        //add some randomness to the spread
        double variation = (rand() % p_spread - p_spread/2) / 100.0f;
        //set linear velocity
        double dir = Math::wrapAngleDegs( p_direction-90.0f );
        dir = Math::toRadians( dir );
        vx = cos( dir ) + variation;
        vy = sin( dir ) + variation;
        p->setVelocity(vx * p_velocity,vy * p_velocity);
        //set random color based on ranges
        int r = rand()%(p_maxR-p_minR)+p_minR;
        int g = rand()%(p_maxG-p_minG)+p_minG;
        int b = rand()%(p_maxB-p_minB)+p_minB;
        int a = rand()%(p_alphaMax-p_alphaMin)+p_alphaMin;
        Color col(r,g,b,a);
        p->setColor(col);
        //set the scale
        p->setScale( p_scale,p_scale );
        //add particle to the emitter
        p_particles.push_back(p);
    }
void ParticleEmitter::Render() {
```

```
    BOOST_FOREACH( Sprite* sprite, p_particles )
        sprite->Render();
}
void ParticleEmitter::Update(float deltaTime) {
    static Timer timer;
    //do we need to add a new particle?
    if ((int)p_particles.size() < p_max) {
        //trivial but necessary slowdown
        if (timer.Stopwatch(100)) Add();
    }

    BOOST_FOREACH( Sprite* sprite, p_particles ) {
        //update particle's position
        sprite->Update(deltaTime * 50.0f);
        //is particle beyond the emitter's range?
        double dist = Math::Distance( sprite->getPosition(), p_position );
        if ( dist > p_length) {
            //reset particle to the origin
            sprite->setX(p_position.getX());
            sprite->setY(p_position.getY());
        }
    }
}
void ParticleEmitter::setAlphaRange(int min,int max) {
    p_alphaMin=min; p_alphaMax=max;
}
void ParticleEmitter::setColorRange(int r1,int g1,int b1,int r2,int g2,int b2)
{
    p_minR = r1; p_maxR = r2;
    p_minG = g1; p_maxG = g2;
    p_minB = b1; p_maxB = b2;
}
```

Using the ParticleEmitter class is very easy if you don't need to change any of the default properties—just supply the source image and destination position. That image can be any reasonably nice-looking circle on a bitmap, or perhaps a simple square image if you want to produce a blocky effect. I have created a circle on a 16×16 bitmap with several shades of alpha built into the image. Combined with the color and alpha effects we'll apply when drawing the image, this will produce the particles in our emitter. However, you can produce quite different particles using a different source image—something to keep in mind!

Here is how you can create a simple emitter. This example code creates a new particle emitter using the `particle16.tga` image; sets it at screen location 400,300; sets the angle to 45 degrees; sets a maximum of 200 particles; sets an alpha range of 0 to 100 (which is faint); sets the random spread from the given angle to 30 pixels; and sets the length to 250 pixels.

```
ParticleEmitter *p new ParticleEmitter();
p->loadImage("particle16.tga");
p->setPosition(400,300);
p->setDirection(45);
p->setMax(200);
p->setAlphaRange(0,100);
p->setSpread(30);
p->setLength(250);
```

After creating the emitter, you need to give it a chance to update its particles and draw itself. The `ParticleEmitter::Update()` function should be called from `game_update()` since it will need the `deltaTime` parameter. `ParticleEmitter::Render()` should be called from the `game_render2d()` function.

Following is an example program called Sprite Particle Demo that demonstrates one of the most common uses for particles—chimney smoke! This example draws a house with a chimney and uses a particle emitter to simulate smoke. Figure 14.8 shows the output. (Note: the complete project includes error handling and comment code omitted from this listing.)

```
Sprite* backgrnd;
Font* font;
float delta;
Sprite* house;
ParticleEmitter *part;

bool game_init(HWND hwnd) {
    g_engine->setBackdropColor(D3DCOLOR_XRGB(0,50,50));
    font = new Font("Arial Bold",18);
    backgrnd = new Sprite();
    backgrnd->Load("selection_highlight.png");
```

Figure 14.8
Particle demonstration simulating smoke coming out of a chimney.

```
backgrnd->scale.x = ((float)g_engine->getScreenWidth() /
    (float)backgrnd->getWidth());
backgrnd->scale.y = ((float)g_engine->getScreenHeight() /
        (float)backgrnd->getHeight());
//load the house
house = new Sprite();
house->Load("house.tga");
house->setPosition(400,300);
//create particle emitter
part = new ParticleEmitter();
part->Load("particle16.tga");
part->setPosition(440,310);
part->setDirection(0);
part->setMax(200);
part->setAlphaRange(30,40);
part->setColorRange(240,240,240, 255,255,255);
part->setScale( 4.0 );
```

```
        part->setSpread( 50 );
        part->setVelocity( 0.5 );
        part->setLength( 400 );
        return true;
}

void game_update(float deltaTime) {
        delta = deltaTime;
        part->Update(deltaTime);
}

void game_render2d() {
        backgrnd->Render();
        house->RenderFast();
        part->Render();
        std::ostringstream ostr;
        ostr << "Core fps: " << g_engine->getCoreFrameRate() << endl;
        ostr << "Delta time: " << delta << endl;
        ostr << "Particles: " << part->getCount() << endl;
        font->Print(0, 0, ostr.str());
}

void game_event(Octane::IEvent* e) {
        switch(e->getID()) {
                case EVENT_KEYRELEASE:
                        g_engine->Shutdown();
                        break;
        }
}
```

SPRITE-BASED FONTS

One of the most crucial features of a game engine is the ability to display text on the screen using *font output*. This is a challenging problem because font output has the potential to bring a game engine to its knees if it is not implemented properly. The font system included with DirectX (ID3DXFont) does a fair job of rendering text, and this is the technique we have used up to this point to do so. But it can become slow, especially if the font size is changed often (which is one reason why we have used only one type of font in the examples). Why is it slow? ID3DXFont renders text with Windows GDI functions rather than Direct3D. In

Figure 14.9
System 12 font represented as a bitmap reminiscent of an animated sprite sheet.

contrast, professional game engines use *bitmapped fonts*. A bitmapped font is an image containing characters stored in rows and columns—like a sprite animation sheet. Figure 14.9 shows a bitmapped font. Note that some characters are illegible or just not available in this low-resolution bitmapped font. Rendering a bitmapped font is extremely fast because we use the Sprite class and render text with ID3DXSprite—which, as you'll recall, batches sprites into a group for efficiency.

Creating a Font

I've included several bitmapped fonts in the project folder for your use. These fonts were created with a very useful tool called Bitmap Font Builder by Thom Wetzel, Jr. (www.lmnopc.com), which is also included in this chapter's files. You can use Bitmap Font Builder (shown in Figure 14.10) to create a bitmapped font from any TrueType font installed on your Windows system. The font shown in the figure is 10-point Verdana.

The settings are important. I recommend setting the Texture Size field to Auto with 0-pixel spacing for best results. If the Character Set is configured to render

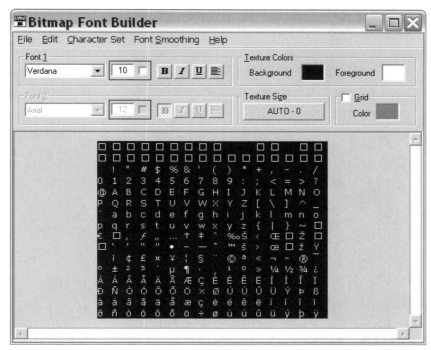

Figure 14.10
Bitmap Font Builder is used to render a TrueType font onto a bitmap.

two fonts, change it using the menu to a single ASCII font, as shown in the figure. Although you will never use most of those unusual ASCII characters, the source code for rendering the font is simpler when using a font with characters numbered 0–255 (which are simply treated as sequential animation frames).

After configuring the font to produce, open the File menu, choose Save 32-bit TGA (RGBA), and enter a filename. This will save a new Targa file—and most importantly, it will have an *alpha channel*. Saving the 10-point Verdana font produces a Targa file shown in Figure 14.11. You can experiment with different fonts to come up with one you like for your games. When you are setting up a font, note that it will look sharper in your game than it looks in the BFB preview; although you may be tempted to output a font in bold, that usually is not needed.

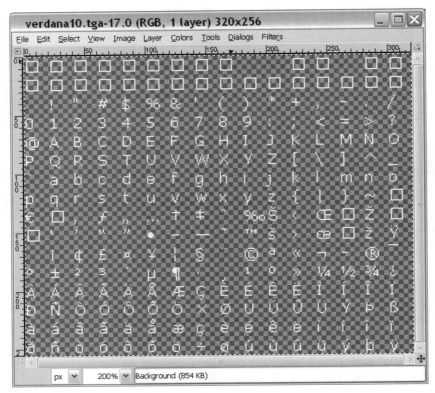

Figure 14.11
Bitmap Font Builder automatically generates an alpha channel for transparency.

The bitmapped font could be used as is for text output in a game, but we're actually only half done. The next step is to output the *width data* for the font, in order to render the text *proportionally*. This is extremely important for producing attractive-looking text. After saving the font to a Targa image, you will need to export the font width data in order to render the font proportionally. BFB makes this very easy by exporting the width data into a simple binary data file that can be read and used when rendering characters as an animated sprite.

Open the File menu in BFB and choose "Save Font Widths (Byte Format)" and enter a filename at the prompt. I find it makes sense to use the same filename that I used for the font, but append a .dat extension. This data file will be composed of 256 font width values stored in binary format for a total of 512 bytes (two bytes per ASCII character width).

Advice

If you aren't crazy about the idea of distributing two files with your game just for each font, there is a way to combine the two files into one—or all of your game's assets into one, for that matter. A zip library is available that makes it possible to read your game's assets from a single zip data file—it's called *zlib*. See the final section of this chapter for an example.

We can read the proportional width data from this 512-byte file with an `ifstream` reader.

```
unsigned char buffer[512];
std::ifstream infile;
infile.open(filename.c_str(), std::ios::binary);
infile.read( (char *)(&buffer), 512 );
infile.close();
for (int n=0; n<256; n++)
        widths[n] = (int)buffer[n*2];
```

Loading and Rendering a Font

We *could* load a bitmapped font into a `Sprite` object and render it by treating each character as a frame in the font "animation" sheet. In fact, this is exactly what we will do. But there is too much configuration and custom code to be duplicated that way. Instead, a new subclass of `Sprite` will do nicely. The new class will be called `Font` and will inherit its basic functionality from `Sprite` and add some of its own new features.

BitmapFont Header

Let's take a look at the new `BitmapFont` class, which is now available in the Engine project. Here's the header file:

```
class BitmapFont : public Sprite {
private:
    int p_widths[256];
public:
    BitmapFont();
    virtual ~BitmapFont(void) { }
    void Print(int x, int y, std::string text,
        Color color = Color(255,255,255,255) );
    int getCharWidth() { return (int)size.x; }
    int getCharHeight() { return (int)size.y; }
```

```
    void setCharWidth(int width) { size.x = width; }
    void setCharSize(int width, int height) {
        setCharWidth( width );
        size.y = height;
    }
    bool loadWidthData(std::string filename);
};
```

BitmapFont Implementation

Now let's take a look at the implementation file BitmapFont.cpp. There are just two methods in the implementation file, with the most important method being Print, which actually displays text on the screen. The Print method accepts four parameters that are self-explanatory: x, y, text, and color. The code in Print goes through each character of the string and prints out a character from the font image based on the ASCII code of the character (from 0 to 255). This is *done very easily* by just setting the sprite's current frame to the ASCII code! When that's done, presto—the character corresponding to that "animation frame" will be rendered. Furthermore, because BFB saved the Targa with an alpha channel, we have automatic transparency support built in.

The second method, aside from the constructor, loads the proportional font width data. A std::ifstream reads 512 bytes at once and then copies out the width data from every other byte in the buffer. The end result is an array called widths that contains custom proportional values for each character in the bitmapped font.

```
BitmapFont::BitmapFont() : Sprite() {
    //set character widths to default
    memset(&p_widths, 0, sizeof(p_widths));
}
void BitmapFont::Print(int x,int y,std::string text,Color color) {
    float fx = (float)x;
    float fy = (float)y;
    setColor( color );
    //draw each character of the string
    for (unsigned int n=0; n<text.length(); n++) {
        int frame = (int)text[n];
        setCurrentFrame( frame );
        setX( fx );
        setY( fy );
```

```
            Render();
            //use proportional width if available
            if (p_widths[frame] == 0) p_widths[frame] = (int)size.x;
            fx += (float)(p_widths[frame] * scale.x);
        }
    }
}
bool BitmapFont::loadWidthData(std::string filename) {
    unsigned char buffer[512];
    //open font width data file
    std::ifstream infile;
    infile.open(filename.c_str(), std::ios::binary);
    if (!infile) return false;
    //read 512 bytes (2 bytes per character)
    infile.read( (char *)(&buffer), 512 );
    if (infile.bad()) return false;
    infile.close();
    //convert raw data to proportional width data
    for (int n=0; n<256; n++)
        p_widths[n] = (int)buffer[n*2];
    return true;
}
```

Using the BitmapFont Class

We now have a multipurpose bitmapped font class that can load and render proportional fonts, so let's put it to the test. Figure 14.12 shows the Bitmapped Font Demo program. Without the font width data, we would have to condense the font by hard-coding the width data inside the program because non-proportioned text just looks too unprofessional. As you can see from the figure, we can display any TrueType font once it has been converted using a tool such as BFB. As a bonus, we have all of the features of the sprite renderer available, too. That means you can print text in any color with rotation and scaling support. See the complete project for detailed code with comments and error handling.

```
BitmapFont *bmpfont;
std::string text;
Color white(255,255,255,255);
Color black(0,0,0,255);

bool game_init(HWND hwnd) {
    g_engine->setBackdropColor(white);
```

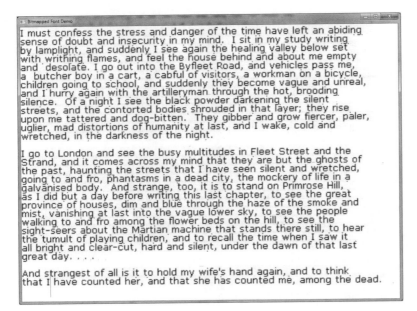

Figure 14.12
The Bitmapped Font Demo program demonstrates proportional bitmapped font rendering.

```
//load sample text
string line;
ifstream file("hgwells2.txt");
if (!file.is_open()) {
    debug << "Error loading text file\n";
    return false;
}
while (!file.eof()) {
    getline(file,line);
    text += line + '\n';
}
file.close();
//load the bitmapped font
bmpfont = new BitmapFont();
bmpfont->Load("system12.tga");
bmpfont->setColumns(16);
bmpfont->setCharSize(14,16);
bmpfont->loadWidthData("system12.dat");
return true;
}
```

```
void game_render2d() {
    int y=0;
    string line;
    istringstream iss(text);
    while ( getline(iss, line, '\n') ) {
        bmpfont->setScale(1.0f);
        bmpfont->Print(0,y,line,black);
        y+=20;
    }
}


void game_event(Octane::IEvent* e) {
    switch(e->getID()) {
        case EVENT_KEYRELEASE:
            g_engine->Shutdown();
            break;
    }
}
```

LOADING ASSETS FROM A ZIP FILE

As was mentioned earlier in the chapter, it can be annoying to distribute assets and data files with a game with their individual files exposed to snooping by fans or just creative programmers wanting to borrow your game's assets. The easiest solution is to rename all data files to a generic extension—this alone will throw off the casual asset hacker, but not a more determined (i.e., experienced) person who knows better. The best solution is to embed all of your game's data and assets inside a *password encrypted* zip file. That's extremely easy with all of the free zip archive programs available (such as 7Zip, a multi-format archiver available from www.7-zip.org). The hard part is this: how do we get assets out of the zip file?

There is a zip archive library available that can do this for us with a minimum of fuss—*zlib*, available from www.zlib.net and is included in the book's support files.

A good asset manager will initialize the zip data file, repeatedly read from it while open, and then close the data file when done. The drawback to encapsulating an asset manager into a class is that every game has different needs, and every engine programmer will want to do this in a different way—implementing a texture cache, mesh cache, audio cache, etc. So, we will instead just look at an example using global zlib variables and leave it up to the reader to implement an asset or content manager.

At a minimum, these files need to be added to the project:

- `ioapi.c`
- `iowin32.c`
- `unzip.c`

These files must be available in the project folder:

- `zdll.lib`
- `iowin32.h`
- `unzip.h`
- `zconf.h`
- `zlib.h`
- `crypt.h`

And this file must be added to the output folder:

- `zlib1.dll`

Reading from a Zip File

We need to create variables from `unzFile` (the main object) and `unz_file_info` (the zip info struct):

```
unzFile zip=NULL;
unz_file_info info;
```

The zlib library will return a data file out of the zip archive as a `void*`, so we need only typecast it to our desired structure or buffer, or use the `void*` buffer directly when reading binary data (as is the case when converting the buffer into a Direct3D texture) or copying the buffer into a new data structure such as an array. The helper functions to follow will assume the use of these two global variables, on the assumption that this code will soon find itself in a C++ class.

To open the zip file, first use the `unzOpen()` function like so:

```
zip = unzOpen( "assets.zip" );
```

If the zip object is `NULL`, then you may assume the file was not found or was corrupted. Otherwise, it's now ready to be used. When finished with the zip file, it should be closed with `unzClose()`:

```
unzClose( zip );
```

Reading Raw Data

We'll write a function to read the raw data of a file stored inside the zip file and then use that `void*` buffer as a data source for the various file types needed for a game. The first step is to try to locate the filename inside the zip archive using a function called `unzLocateFile()`; if found, then this function will return `UNZ_OK`.

```
HRESULT rez = unzLocateFile( zip, "cursor.tga", 1 );
```

Next, we can use the `unzOpenCurrentFile()` function to open the file that was located.

```
rez = unzOpenCurrentFile( zip );
```

Again, if the function returns `UNZ_OK`, then we can proceed; otherwise, a problem should be reported—the most common being that the filename supplied was not found in the zip archive.

```
rez = unzGetCurrentFileInfo( zip, &zipinfo, NULL, 0, NULL, 0, NULL, 0 );
```

If we reach this step, then the file has been loaded and opened, and is ready to be pulled out of the zip archive and into memory. We do that with `unzReadCurrentFile()`, but the memory must first be created:

```
void *buffer = malloc( zipinfo.uncompressed_size + 1 );
rez = unzReadCurrentFile( zip, buffer, zipinfo.uncompressed_size );
```

At this point, if the function returns `UNZ_OK`, then we have our data in memory and the file may be closed (the current data file, not the zip archive—which should stay open for repeated file reading).

```
unzCloseCurrentFile( zip );
```

So, what do we do with the `void*` buffer now that it contains the file read into memory? This pointer to the data buffer can contain absolutely *anything*—a mesh, a texture, an audio sample, an XML file, a LUA script, *anything*! If you know that the file was a simple binary, then it can be typecast into an array or struct of your own design. Following is a reusable function that encapsulates the loading process:

```
void* LoadAsset(std::string filename) {
    // locate the file (1 = case sensitive)
    HRESULT rez = unzLocateFile(zip, filename.c_str(), 1);
    if( rez != UNZ_OK ) return NULL;
    //try to open the file
    rez = unzOpenCurrentFile( zip );
    if( rez != UNZ_OK ) return NULL;
    // find current file info (uncompressed file size)
    rez = unzGetCurrentFileInfo( zip, &zipinfo, NULL, 0, NULL, 0, NULL, 0 );
    if( rez != UNZ_OK ) return NULL;
    //create a buffer big enough to hold uncompressed file in memory
    void *buffer = malloc( zipinfo.uncompressed_size + 1 );
    if (!buffer) return NULL;
    memset(buffer, 0, zipinfo.uncompressed_size + 1);
    // load into memory
    rez = unzReadCurrentFile( zip, buffer, zipinfo.uncompressed_size );
    if( rez < 0 ) {
        free(buffer); return NULL;
    }
    //close the read file
    unzCloseCurrentFile( zip );
    return buffer;
}
```

Reading a Texture

Reading an image out of the zip file in memory and converting it to a Direct3D texture is not as easy as just typecasting the void* buffer into an LPDIRECT3D-TEXTURE9. That would be nice, but it won't work. Instead, we'll use a function called D3DXCreateTextureFromFileInMemoryEx() to convert the void* buffer into a texture. After that, the texture can be used normally for any purpose—to skin a mesh or fill in the frames of an animated sprite. For some strange reason this process feels like cloning to me. We'll use the LoadAsset() function above to read in the raw data for a texture, and then convert the data into a fully mature Direct3D texture.

```
Texture* LoadTextureFromZip(std::string filename) {
    //load the raw data file
    void* buffer = NULL;
    buffer = LoadAsset(filename);
    if (!buffer) return NULL;
    //create new texture
    Texture *texture = new Texture();
    //get image info from memory buffer
    D3DXGetImageInfoFromFileInMemory(
        buffer, zipinfo.uncompressed_size, &texture->info);
    //load texture from memory buffer
    D3DXCreateTextureFromFileInMemoryEx( g_engine->getDevice(),
        buffer, zipinfo.uncompressed_size, texture->info.Width,
        texture->info.Height, 1, D3DUSAGE_DYNAMIC, texture->info.Format,
        D3DPOOL_DEFAULT, D3DX_FILTER_NONE, D3DX_FILTER_NONE,
        0xFF000000, NULL, NULL, &texture->texture );
    //free the buffer memory
    free( buffer );
    return texture;
}
```

Reading a Text File

Imagine storing all of your game's effect (.FX) files in a password-encrypted zip archive, and then pulling them out of the data file when the game starts up, rather than storing them as raw text in the game's runtime folder? Yes, that is entirely possible and extremely easy to do now that we have working code around zlib. What other uses are there for a text data file reader? Besides an effect file, how about XML data and LUA scripts?

```
std::string LoadTextFromZip(std::string filename) {
    //load the raw data file
    void* buffer=NULL;
    buffer = LoadAsset(filename);
    if (!buffer) return NULL;
    //convert raw buffer into text
    char* data = (char*) buffer;
    std::string text = data;
    return text;
}
```

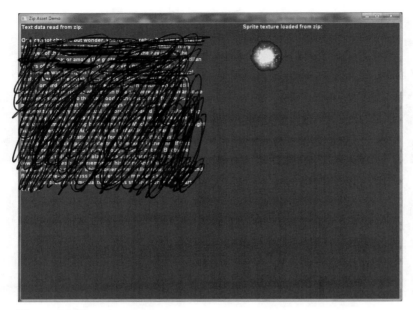

Figure 14.13
The sprite's animated image and text data displayed here were read from a zip file.

Zip Asset Demo

The Zip Asset Demo program shows how to use zlib in a very practical way by loading the image for an animated sprite and drawing it, and loading a text file and printing out its contents on the screen. The program is shown in Figure 14.13.

This project (included with the chapter files) has the zlib files integrated only within the gameplay project, not the game engine project—to avoid messing up the earlier projects in this chapter. In the very next chapter, the zlib code will be embedded inside the engine. There is an added benefit to keeping zlib on the front lines at this point, since you can learn from it and use the zlib code for other purposes beyond this engine if you have the need. Due to the zlib requirements, this is the complete source code listing, not just a subset.

Advice

The zlib-specific source code has been added to the gameplay source code file (main.cpp), not to the engine. Since this code will need to be wrapped into specific classes or (better yet) an asset manager, it makes no sense to add the zip code to the engine at this time—although it could be just added to the Engine class.

```cpp
#include "Engine.h"
using namespace std;
using namespace Octane;
#include "zlib/unzip.h"
#pragma comment(lib,"../zlib/zdll.lib")
Font* font=NULL;
Texture* imgExpl=NULL;
Sprite* explosion=NULL;
std::string textData="";
//zlib variables
unzFile zip=NULL;
unz_file_info zipinfo;

void* LoadAsset(std::string filename);
Texture* LoadTextureFromZip(std::string filename);
std::string LoadTextFromZip(std::string filename);

bool game_preload() {
    g_engine->setScreen(1024,768,32,false);
    g_engine->setAppTitle("Zip Asset Demo");
    return true;
}

bool game_init(HWND hwnd) {
    g_engine->setBackdropColor(D3DCOLOR_XRGB(0,50,50));
    font = new Font("Arial Bold",18);

    //open zip file
    zip = unzOpen( "assets.zip" );
    if( !zip ) {
        debug << "Zip file not found\n";
        return false;
    }

    //load explosion image from zip data file
    imgExpl = LoadTextureFromZip("explosion_30_128.tga");
    //create sprite using zip asset image
    explosion = new Sprite();
    explosion->setImage( imgExpl );
    explosion->setPosition( 600, 30 );
```

```
        explosion->setAnimationRange( 0,29 );
        explosion->setColumns( 6 );
        explosion->setSize( 128,128 );

        //load text data file from zip archive
        textData = LoadTextFromZip("data.txt");

        unzClose( zip );
        zip = NULL;
        return true;
    }

void game_end() {
    delete font;
    delete imgExpl;
    delete explosion;
}

void game_update(float deltaTime) {
    explosion->Update(deltaTime*20);
}

void game_render2d() {
    std::ostringstream ostr;
    ostr << "Text data read from zip:\n\n";
    ostr << textData << endl;
    font->Print(0, 0, ostr.str());
    font->Print(600, 0, "Sprite texture loaded from zip:");
    explosion->Render();
}

void game_render3d(){}
void game_event(Octane::IEvent* e) {
    switch(e->getID()) {
        case EVENT_KEYRELEASE:
            g_engine->Shutdown();
            break;
    }
}
```

Advice

Be sure to add the three zip asset functions (`LoadAsset`, `LoadTextureFromZip`, and `LoadTextFromZip`) covered previously to complete the Zip Asset Demo program. For the sake of brevity, and since they were already provided in their entirety above, the source code for these functions will be omitted from the program listing.

SUMMARY

This has been one of the most productive chapters as far as adding new features to the engine—extremely vital, core features at that! The `Sprite` class and associated features that were made available as a result of the sprite code greatly enhances the engine with very strong 2D rendering support. All of these topics are based on the `Sprite` class, and it was quite a bit to cover all at once, but there are several examples that go with this chapter and each topic has its own example.

REFERENCES

1. Reese, Greg; *C++ Standard Library Practical Tips*; Charles River Media.

CHAPTER 15

RENDERING TO A TEXTURE

In this chapter we will explore some of the unusual things we can do with vector (line-based) shapes after gaining the capability to render to an off-screen texture. The texture that receives the rendered output from Direct3D is a normal texture, capable of being used for a sprite or the skin of a mesh. This technique is often used to create an environment map for the special effect called *cube mapping*, where the environment around a mesh is mapped onto the mesh in a mirror-like manner. By adding this functionality to the engine, we gain some impressive new capabilities such as drawing shapes out of vector lines and points, and scrolling background layers (i.e., platformer games).

The following topics will be covered:

- Rendering to a Texture
- Drawing vector shapes
- Comparing ID3DXLine and VectorShape
- Drawing scrolling bitmap layers
- Drawing tiled layers

RENDERING TO A TEXTURE

Off-screen rendering is a powerful technique that we will use in this chapter to create vector lines, scrolling layered backgrounds, and graphical user interface elements. There are further uses for this capability, such as camera viewports, environmental cube mapping, mirroring, and texture animation (i.e., security camera monitors). We'll start by reviewing the existing rendering capability built into our old Texture class. It's been a while since we wrote the code for Texture, but it has harbored this capability from the beginning. Our Texture class has three functions that can be used to render onto the texture's surface (rather than to the screen like usual):

- createRenderTarget()
- renderStart()
- renderStop()

Advice

This chapter's resource files can be downloaded from www.jharbour.com/forum or www.courseptr.com/downloads. Not every line of code will be in print due to space considerations, only the most important sections of code.

Creating a Render Target

To create an off-screen render target, first create a normal Texture. But, instead of using Load to load an image file, or Create to create the new texture in memory, use the createRenderTarget() function instead, passing the desired resolution when calling the function. These features were included in the Texture class first presented back in Chapter 11. Here is the createRenderTarget() function again for reference:

```
bool Texture::createRenderTarget(int width,int height) {
    if (texture) {
        texture->Release();
        texture = NULL;
    }
    g_engine->getDevice()->CreateTexture( width, height,
        1, D3DUSAGE_RENDERTARGET, D3DFMT_A8R8G8B8,
        D3DPOOL_DEFAULT, &texture, NULL );
    g_engine->getDevice()->CreateDepthStencilSurface( width, height,
        D3DFMT_D16, D3DMULTISAMPLE_NONE, 0, false,
        &renderDepthStencilSurface, NULL );
    texture->GetSurfaceLevel( 0, &renderSurface );
```

```
//save texture info
info.Width = width;
info.Height = height;
info.Format = D3DFMT_A8R8G8B8;
return true;
}
```

Rendering to the Alternate Target

As we have seen, a texture created as a render target requires a special-purpose texture surface created with the D3DUSAGE_RENDERTARGET parameter, as well as a special-purpose depth stencil buffer surface. These are *heavy* objects, so you would not want to haphazardly create a large number of render targets for normal textures that *might* be used as such—a normal Texture object is a lightweight in comparison. Think of a render target as another frame buffer, capable of representing the entire screen for rendering purposes.

The key to rendering onto this special-purpose texture is to have our Direct3D device set it as the new render target (and likewise, set the new depth stencil surface). When that is done, then rendering proceeds like normal with all the usual function calls: Clear(), BeginScene(), EndScene(), as well as sprite drawing. Our renderStart() function sets up the render target so that any rendering will be sent to the texture. After rendering is complete, then render-Stop().

```
bool Texture::renderStart(bool clear, bool sprite, Color clearColor) {
    g_engine->getDevice()->SetRenderTarget( 0, renderSurface );
    g_engine->getDevice()->SetDepthStencilSurface( renderDepthStencilSurface );
    if (clear) {
            g_engine->getDevice()->Clear( 0, NULL, D3DCLEAR_TARGET,
                clearColor.ToD3DCOLOR(), 1.0f, 0 );
    }
    g_engine->getDevice()->BeginScene();
    if (sprite) g_engine->getSpriteObj()->Begin(D3DXSPRITE_ALPHABLEND);
    D3DXMATRIX identity;
    D3DXMatrixIdentity(&identity);
    g_engine->getSpriteObj()->SetTransform(&identity);
    return true;
}
```

```
bool Texture::renderStop(bool sprite) {
    if (sprite) g_engine->getSpriteObj()->End();
    g_engine->getDevice()->EndScene();
    return true;
}
```

One thing we must be very careful to do when changing the render target is to *restore* the primary render surface and depth stencil surface when finished. In the core engine class is a pair of functions to facilitate this: SavePrimaryRenderTarget() and RestorePrimaryRenderTarget(). These functions were included in the core engine code in Chapter 1 but not used until now.

```
void Engine::savePrimaryRenderTarget()
{
    //save primary rendering & depth stencil surfaces
    p_device->GetRenderTarget( 0, &p_MainSurface );
    p_device->GetDepthStencilSurface( &p_MainDepthStencilSurface );
}

void Engine::restorePrimaryRenderTarget()
{
    //restore normal render target
    p_device->SetRenderTarget( 0, p_MainSurface );
    p_device->SetDepthStencilSurface( p_MainDepthStencilSurface );
}
```

DRAWING VECTOR SHAPES

Direct3D has the ability to render 2D lines using 3D hardware with a class called ID3DXLine. This is an efficient way to draw lines because they are rendered as a line list with shared vertices, but if you only need to draw one line at a time then no performance improvement will be found with the two points of a single line. We will also create our own line-drawing mechanism as an alternative to ID3DXLine, and it will be called VectorShape. This class will be the basis for potentially many vector shapes that could be rendered from the basic point- and line-drawing functions we'll develop. For example, you could use the Bresenham circle-drawing algorithm to draw circles from the basic line code in the VectorShape class.

VectorShape Class

The VectorShape class basically just draws lines, but it has the ability to draw points as well, and these two building blocks could be used to draw other shapes such as circles, boxes, triangles, and so on. Consider it a multi-purpose class for vector graphics.

```
class VectorShape {
private:
    Texture *texture;
    Sprite *sprite;
    int size;
    ID3DXLine* d3dxline;
public:
    VectorShape(void);
    ~VectorShape(void);
    void MakeTexture();
    void drawPoint(Vector2 point, int linesize, Color color = Color(255,
        255,255,255));
    void drawPoint(double x, double y, int linesize,
        Color color = Color(255,255,255,255));
    void drawLine(Vector2 point1, Vector2 point2, int linesize,
        Color color = Color(255,255,255,255));
    void drawLine(double x1, double y1, double x2, double y2, int linesize,
        Color color = Color(255,255,255,255));
    void drawBox(Vector2 point1, Vector2 point2, int linesize,
        Color color = Color(255,255,255,255));
    void drawBox(double x1, double y1, double x2, double y2, int linesize,
        Color color = Color(255,255,255,255));
    void drawBox(Rect rect, int linesize, Color color = Color(255,255,
        255,255));
    void drawFilledBox( Rect rect, Color color = Color(255,255,255,255));
    void drawD3DXLine(Vector2 start, Vector2 end, float size, Color color);
};
```

The implementation for VectorShape includes support for ID3DXLine as well as the Sprite-based points, lines, and rectangles. The Vector Shape Demo project coming up compares the performance of the two.

```
VectorShape::VectorShape(void) {
    texture = NULL;
    sprite = NULL;
```

```
        size = -1;
        d3dxline = NULL;
        D3DXCreateLine(g_engine->getDevice(), &d3dxline);
}
void VectorShape::MakeTexture() {
    //validate VectorShape size
    if (size < 1) return;
    //create the texture
    if (texture) delete texture;
    texture = new Texture();
    if (!texture->Create(128,size,true))
        debug << "VectorShape: Error creating texture\n";
    //create the sprite
    if (sprite) delete sprite;
    sprite = new Sprite();
    sprite->setImage( texture );
}
VectorShape::~VectorShape(void) {
    if (texture) delete texture;
    if (sprite) delete sprite;
    d3dxline->Release();
    d3dxline = NULL;
}
void VectorShape::drawLine(Vector2 point1, Vector2 point2,
    int linesize, Color color) {
    //if VectorShape size changed, texture must be recreated
    if (size != linesize) {
        size = linesize;
        MakeTexture();
    }
    //position start of line at startpos
    sprite->setPosition( point1 );
    //set scale so line reaches point2
    double dist = Math::Distance( point1, point2 );
    double w = (double)sprite->getWidth();
    double scale = dist / w;
    sprite->setScale( scale, 1.0 );
    //rotate VectorShape to aim it at endpos
    double angle = Math::angleToTarget( point1, point2 );
    sprite->setRotation( angle );
```

```cpp
    //line will be drawn from upper-left corner at
    //point1 with pivot at 0,0 and rotated toward point2
    sprite->setColor( color );
    Vector2 pivot(0,0);
    sprite->setPivot(pivot);
    sprite->Render(false);
}
void VectorShape::drawLine(double x1, double y1, double x2, double y2,
    int linesize, Color color) {
    Vector2 p1(x1,y1);
    Vector2 p2(x2,y2);
    drawLine( p1, p2, linesize, color );
}
void VectorShape::drawPoint(Vector2 point, int linesize, Color color) {
    Vector2 stretch(point.x+linesize, point.y);
    drawLine(point, stretch, linesize, color);
}
void VectorShape::drawPoint(double x, double y, int linesize, Color color) {
    Vector2 point(x,y);
    drawPoint(point, linesize, color);
}
void VectorShape::drawBox(Vector2 point1, Vector2 point2,
    int linesize, Color color) {
    //top line
    Vector2 upperRight(point2.x, point1.y);
    drawLine(point1, upperRight, linesize, color);
    //left line
    Vector2 lowerLeft(point1.x, point2.y);
    drawLine(lowerLeft, point1, linesize, color);
    //right line
    drawLine(upperRight, point2, linesize, color);
    //bottom line
    drawLine(point2, lowerLeft, linesize, color);
}
void VectorShape::drawBox(double x1, double y1, double x2, double y2,
    int linesize, Color color) {
    Vector2 p1(x1,y1);
    Vector2 p2(x2,y2);
    drawBox( p1, p2, linesize, color );
}
```

```
void VectorShape::drawBox(Rect rect, int linesize, Color color) {
    Vector2 p1(rect.left, rect.top);
    Vector2 p2(rect.right, rect.bottom);
    drawBox( p1, p2, linesize, color );
}
void VectorShape::drawFilledBox( Rect rect, Color color) {
    Vector2 p1( rect.left, rect.top );
    Vector2 p2( rect.right, rect.top );
    drawLine( p1, p2, rect.bottom-rect.top, color );
}
void VectorShape::drawD3DXLine(Vector2 start, Vector2 end,
    float size, Color color) {
    D3DXVECTOR2 lineList[] = { start.ToD3DXVECTOR2(),
                               end.ToD3DXVECTOR2() };
    d3dxline->SetWidth(size);
    d3dxline->Begin();
    d3dxline->Draw(lineList, 2, color.ToD3DCOLOR());
    d3dxline->End();
}
```

Vector Shape Demo

The Vector Shape Demo program is shown in Figure 15.1. The results are intriguing if not unsurprising: ID3DXLine outperforms VectorShape by 600%, with 42,000 shapes per second and 7,000 shapes per second, respectively. D3DXLine is rendering lines in the GPU while VectorShape is rendering lines using ID3DXSprite. Performance *might* have been closer if VectorShape did not have to call two very slow math functions—Distance() and AngleToTarget(). I don't need a profiler to prove that these two function calls are the bottleneck, knowing that ID3DXLine is using Direct3D's basic line list rendering capability in the GPU which requires no trigonometric calculations. The important thing is that we get similar results with both line-drawing tools, meaning they are interchangeable. Where VectorShape may come in handy is when we need to render lines in the midst of a sprite batch update, while ID3DXSprite is in the middle of rendering a bunch of game objects, where it would be inconvenient to switch out of 2D mode, back into 3D mode, just to render the line(s). Knowing about the performance bottleneck with VectorShape should not affect a gameplay decision, since it does fine at rendering a few hundred lines without any

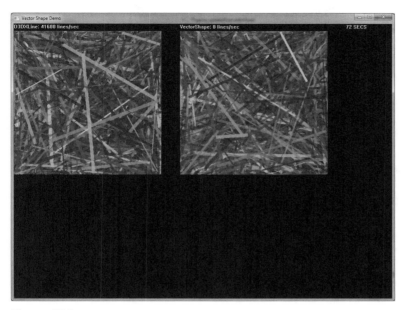

Figure 15.1
The Vector Shape Demo is a performance comparison between our VectorShape class and
D3DXLine.

noticeable performance degradation—it's only up in the thousands of lines that the frequent trig function calls started slowing things down.

However, there is one very easy optimization that could be made here—the calls to Distance() and AngleToTarget() could be moved into the update function, separating these calculations from the actual rendering. That would go a long way toward closing the performance gap between ID3DXSprite and VectorShape, and worth trying out if the need arises for extra performance. Note that this is a subset of the source code—see the project in this chapter's resource files for full commenting and error handling code.

Advice

> Note: The line-drawing performance in this program does not represent absolute performance, just performance of a comparative nature in which 10 lines at a time are drawn by each method (ID3DXLine and VectorShape) repeatedly for one full second at a time. The hardware is capable of much higher line counts, of course.

Following is the source code.

```
Texture* renderTarget1=NULL;
Texture* renderTarget2=NULL;
Font* font=NULL;
VectorShape* shape=NULL;
Timer timer;
bool flip=false;
int seconds=0;
int counter1=0,counter2=0;
int rate1=0,rate2=0;

bool game_init(HWND window) {
    font = new Font("System",12);
    renderTarget1 = new Texture();
    renderTarget1->createRenderTarget(400,400);
    renderTarget2 = new Texture();
    renderTarget2->createRenderTarget(400,400);
    shape = new VectorShape();
    return true;
}

void game_update(float deltaTime) {
    if (flip) {
        g_engine->savePrimaryRenderTarget();
        renderTarget1->renderStart(false, true);
        for (int n=0; n<100; n++) {
                Vector2 start( rand()%400, rand()%400 );
                Vector2 end( rand()%400, rand()%400 );
                float size = (float)(rand()%10);
                Color color(rand()%255,rand()%255,rand()%255,rand()%255);
                shape->drawD3DXLine(start,end,size,color);
                counter1++;
            }
            renderTarget1->renderStop();
            g_engine->restorePrimaryRenderTarget();
    } else {
            g_engine->savePrimaryRenderTarget();
            renderTarget2->renderStart(false, true);
            for (int n=0; n<100; n++) {
```

```
                    Color color(rand()%255,rand()%255,rand()%255,rand()%255);
                    Vector2 start( rand()%400, rand()%400 );
                    Vector2 end( rand()%400, rand()%400 );
                    int size = rand()%10;
                    shape->drawLine(start, end, size, color);
                    counter2++;
                }
                renderTarget2->renderStop();
                g_engine->restorePrimaryRenderTarget();
        }
}

void game_render2d() {
    static ostringstream ostr;
    ostr.str("");
    ostr << "D3DXLine: " << rate1 << " lines/sec";
    font->Print(0,0,ostr.str());
    //draw render target 1
    {
        Sprite* target = new Sprite();
        target->setPosition(0,20);
        target->setImage( renderTarget1 );
        target->RenderFast();
        delete target;
    }
    ostr.str("");
    ostr << "VectorShape: " << rate2 << " lines/sec";
    font->Print(450,0,ostr.str());
    //draw render target 2
    {
        Sprite* target = new Sprite();
        target->setPosition(450,20);
        target->setImage( renderTarget2 );
        target->RenderFast();
        delete target;
    }
    font->Print(900,0, Octane::ToString(seconds) + " SECS");
    if (timer.Stopwatch(1000)) {
        flip = !flip;
```

```
            rate1=counter1;
            counter1=0;
            rate2=counter2;
            counter2=0;
            seconds++;
        }
    }
}

void game_event(Octane::IEvent* e) {
    switch (e->getID()) {
    case EVENT_KEYRELEASE:
        KeyReleaseEvent* evt = (KeyReleaseEvent*) e;
        switch (evt->keycode) {
                case DIK_ESCAPE:
                    g_engine->Shutdown();
                    break;
        }
        break;
    }
}
```

SCROLLING BACKGROUND LAYERS

There are quite a few game genres that are based on scrolling backgrounds. There are the *vertical scrollers*, usually shoot-em-up games, and the *sideways scrollers*. Of the latter, there are two main categories of games—side-scrolling *platformer games*, and side-scrolling *shoot-em-ups*. But there's also a third type of game that can be made when a background scroller is available—a top-down view game such as the traditional RPG (role-playing game) popularized by games such as *Zelda* and *Ultima*.

Bitmap Layers

We'll start by learning how to create a scroll buffer in memory using our Texture class, and then render something onto that memory texture—and presto, we'll have a scrolling layer. Beyond that, the ability to render the layer at any location, to any target rectangle size, and with any alpha level, provides for some very advanced gameplay capabilities for the aforementioned genres. Our Layer class will function at a high level, taking care of most of the lower-level details like creating the scroll buffer, filling in the scroll buffer with a bitmap, and making it possible to render anything onto the scroll buffer (such as tiles from a tile sheet). We'll see how to use the Layer class shortly.

Layer Class Header

Here is the interface definition for the Layer class. Of particular note is the createBounded() and createWrapping() functions. These two functions will create a scrollable layer buffer (as a Texture) that is suited for rendering a scrolling level with distinct boundaries, as well as being suited for rendering a seamless texture repeatedly so that the appearance of endless scrolling is achieved. An endless scrolling layer is helpful in a game when you want the background to appear to go on for a long time without actually consuming huge amounts of memory in the process—so we fake it with a repeating or *seamless* texture and just wrap it around the edges. For this to work, we have to create a scroll buffer that is four times larger than the source image, and then paste the source image into the four corners of the buffer. This makes it possible to wrap the texture endlessly, as long as the scroll buffer is twice the resolution of the viewport (which might be the entire screen or just a small window).

```
class Layer {
private:
    int bufferw,bufferh;
    int windoww,windowh;
public:
    Texture *texture;
    double scrollx,scrolly;
    Layer();
    virtual ~Layer();
    int createBounded(int bufferw, int bufferh, int windoww, int windowh);
    int createWrapping(Texture *seamlessTex);
    //these are just passed on to Texture
    bool renderStart(bool clear = true, Color color = Color(0,0,0,0));
    bool renderStop();
    //updating the scroller
    void updateBounded(double scrollx,double scrolly);
    void updateBounded(Vector3 scroll);
    void updateWrapping(double scrollx,double scrolly);
    void updateWrapping(Vector3 scroll);
    //drawing
```

```
    void drawBounded(int x,int y, Color color = Color(255,255,255,255));
    void drawWrapping(int x,int y, Color color = Color(255,255,255,255));
};
```

Layer Class Implementation

The Layer class does a lot of work for us, making it actually quite easy to build a scrolling game out of it. Note the two update functions, updateBounded() and updateWrapping()—these functions must be called from the game's update() function, as they will refresh the scroll buffer based on the current scroll position. Note secondly the two rendering functions—drawBounded() and drawWrapping(). You can't draw a bounded scroll buffer with the drawWrapping() function, and vice versa, because they are not interchangeable. It might be interesting to abstract the two forms of scrolling with a property and have the Layer class decide how to update and render its buffer based on the programmer's preference. But the class does a good job as is, and that might be suitable for a subclass suited for a specific game genre.

```
Layer::Layer() {
    bufferw = bufferh = 0;
    windoww = windowh = 0;
    texture = NULL;
    scrollx = scrolly = 0.0;
}
Layer::~Layer() {
    if (texture) {
        delete texture;
        texture = NULL;
    }
}


/** Creates a layer; dimensions must be within 256 to 4096 for
    the primary window output used for all rendering **/
int Layer::createBounded(int bufferw, int bufferh, int windoww, int windowh) {
    this->bufferw = bufferw;
    this->bufferh = bufferh;
    this->windoww = windoww;
    this->windowh = windowh;
    //these are arbitrary, just chosen to prevent huge memory
    if (bufferw < 256) return 1;
```

```
    else if (bufferw > 4096) return 2;
    if (bufferh < 256) return 3;
    else if (bufferh > 4096) return 4;
    texture = new Texture();
    texture->createRenderTarget(bufferw,bufferh);
    return 0;
}

// A seamless image can be wrapped top/bottom or left/right
int Layer::createWrapping(Texture *seamlessTex) {
    windoww = seamlessTex->getWidth();
    windowh = seamlessTex->getHeight();
    bufferw = windoww*2;
    bufferh = windowh*2;
    texture = new Texture();
    texture->createRenderTarget(bufferw,bufferh);
    texture->renderStart(true, true, Color(0,0,0,0));
    RECT source = seamlessTex->getBounds();
    D3DXVECTOR3 center(0.0f, 0.0f, 0.0f);
    //upper left quadrant of scroll buffer
    D3DXVECTOR3 position(0.0f, 0.0f, 0.0f);
    g_engine->getSpriteObj()->Draw(seamlessTex->texture,
        &source, &center, &position, 0xffffffff);
    //upper right quadrant of scroll buffer
    position.x = (float) source.right;
    g_engine->getSpriteObj()->Draw(seamlessTex->texture,
        &source, &center, &position, 0xffffffff);
    //lower left quadrant of scroll buffer
    position.x = 0;
    position.y = (float)source.bottom;
    g_engine->getSpriteObj()->Draw(seamlessTex->texture,
        &source, &center, &position, 0xffffffff);
    //lower right quadrant of scroll buffer
    position.x = (float)source.right;
    g_engine->getSpriteObj()->Draw(seamlessTex->texture,
        &source, &center, &position, 0xffffffff);
    texture->renderStop(true);
    return 0;
}
// Pass thru to Texture: begin rendering to texture
```

```cpp
bool Layer::renderStart(bool clear, Color color) {
    return (texture->renderStart(clear, true, color));
}
// Pass thru to Texture: done rendering to texture
bool Layer::renderStop() {
    return (texture->renderStop(true));
}
void Layer::updateBounded(double vx,double vy) {
    scrollx += vx;
    scrolly += vy;
    if (scrollx < 0) scrollx = 0;
    if (scrollx > bufferw - windoww - 1)
        scrollx = bufferw - windoww - 1;
    if (scrolly < 0) scrolly = 0;
    if (scrolly > bufferh - windowh - 1)
        scrolly = bufferh - windowh - 1;
}
void Layer::updateBounded(Vector3 vel) {
    updateBounded(vel.x,vel.y);
}
void Layer::updateWrapping(double vx,double vy) {
    scrollx += vx;
    scrolly += vy;
    if (scrolly < 0)
        scrolly = bufferh - windowh - 1;
    if (scrolly > bufferh - windowh - 1)
        scrolly = 0;
    if (scrollx < 0)
        scrollx = bufferw - windoww - 1;
    if (scrollx > bufferw - windoww - 1)
        scrollx = 0;
}
void Layer::updateWrapping(Vector3 vel) {
    updateWrapping(vel.x,vel.y);
}
void Layer::drawBounded(int x,int y, Color color) {
    RECT srect = { (long)scrollx, (long)scrolly,
        (long)scrollx+windoww, (long)scrolly+windowh };
    D3DXVECTOR3 pos( (float)x, (float)y, 0.0f );
    g_engine->getSpriteObj()->Draw( texture->texture,
        &srect, NULL, &pos, color.ToD3DCOLOR() );
```

```
}
void Layer::drawWrapping(int x,int y, Color color) {
    RECT srect = { (long)scrollx, (long)scrolly,
        (long)scrollx+windoww, (long)scrolly+windowh };
    D3DXVECTOR3 pos( (float)x, (float)y, 0.0f);
    g_engine->getSpriteObj()->Draw( texture->texture,
            srect, NULL, &pos, color.ToD3DCOLOR() );
}
```

Scrolling Layer Demo

To demonstrate the Layer class, I present you with a program called the Scrolling Layer Demo. This demo creates *four* layers, each with random shapes rendered onto them so you can clearly discern each one. Figure 15.2 shows the deepest layer that is behind the other three. This layer scrolls at the slowest speed to simulate parallax distance. These layer images are quite large—1800×1800—because that is the size of the scroll buffer.

Figure 15.2
The fourth background layer does not scroll so it is only the size of the viewport (900×600).

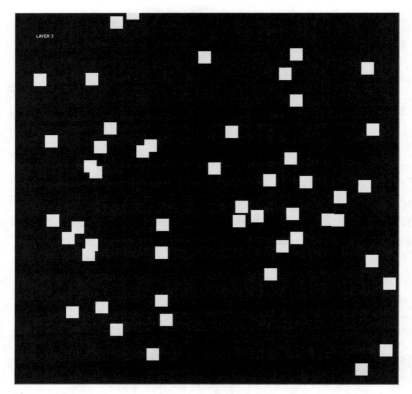

Figure 15.3
The third background layer is the size of the bounded scroll buffer (1800 × 1800) and filled with random yellow boxes.

The next figure shown in Figure 15.3 shows the third layer, drawn over the top of the fourth layer, and containing similar box shapes in a different color. This layer will also scroll more slowly than the two in front of it, but slightly faster than the fourth one behind it.

The second layer is shown in Figure 15.4. This layer moves slightly faster than the previous one, and is filled with random boxes.

Finally, the first and final layer, shown in Figure 15.5, is drawn over all of the others with alpha transparency making it possible to see each successive layer below, all the way to the fourth layer at the bottom (or back, depending on how you visualize it).

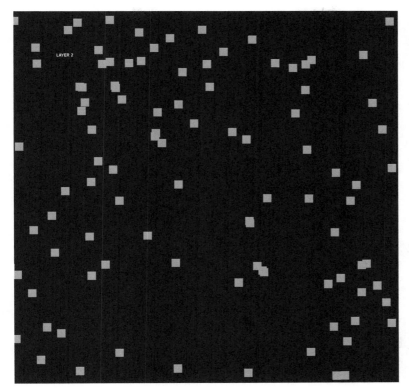

Figure 15.4
The second background layer is the size of the bounded scroll buffer (1800 × 1800) and filled with random green boxes.

The Scrolling Layer Demo is shown with all four layers moving together at different speeds to produce a parallax effect. See Figure 15.6. In the code listing for this program, note that redundant code (including most of the comment and error handling lines) has been omitted for space. Please see the complete project for these details.

```
Font* font = NULL;
Font* font2 = NULL;
Layer *layer1 = NULL;
Layer *layer2 = NULL;
Layer *layer3 = NULL;
Layer *layer4 = NULL;
VectorShape *shape = NULL;
```

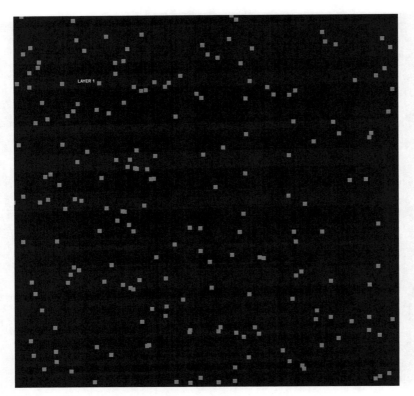

Figure 15.5
The first background layer is the size of the bounded scroll buffer (1800 × 1800) and filled with random red boxes.

```
const int WINDOWW = 900;
const int WINDOWH = 600;
const int BUFFERW = WINDOWW * 2;
const int BUFFERH = WINDOWH * 3;
double scrollx=0, scrolly=0;
double basevel = 4.0;
double velx=basevel, vely=0.0;
int direction = 1;

void createlayer4() {
    //create non-moving layer that is rendered first
    layer4 = new Layer();
    layer4->createBounded( WINDOWW, WINDOWH, WINDOWW, WINDOWH );
```

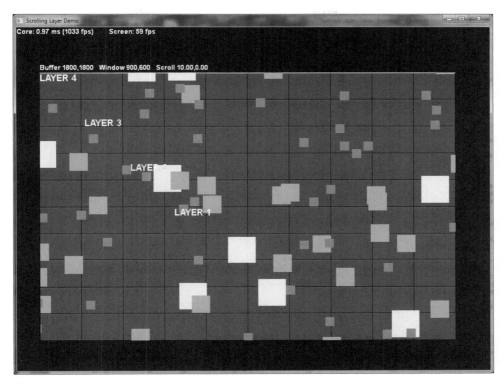

Figure 15.6
The Scrolling Layer Demo program.

```
    layer4->renderStart();
    int sizew = WINDOWW/10;
    int sizeh = WINDOWH/10;
    for (int y=0; y<sizeh; y++) {
        for (int x=0; x<sizew; x++) {
            Vector2 p1(x*sizew, y*sizeh);
            Vector2 p2(p1.x+sizew-1, p1.y);
            shape->drawLine(p1, p2, sizeh-1, Color(60,60,200,255));
        }
    }
    font2->Print(0,0,"LAYER 4");
    layer4->renderStop();
}

void createlayer3() {
```

```
        //create slow scrolling layer filled with random dark red boxes
        layer3 = new Layer();
        layer3->createBounded( BUFFERW, BUFFERH, WINDOWW, WINDOWH );
        layer3->renderStart();
        Vector2 p1(0.0, 0.0);
        Vector2 p2(BUFFERW-1, BUFFERH-1);
        shape->drawBox( p1, p2, 2, Color(100,255,0,255) );
        for (int n=0; n<50; n++) {
            int x = rand() % BUFFERW-60;
            int y = rand() % BUFFERH-60;
            shape->drawPoint( (double) x, (double) y, 60, Color(255,255,0,255) );
        }
        font2->Print(100,100,"LAYER 3");
        layer3->renderStop();
}

void createlayer2() {
    //create medium scrolling layer filled with random green boxes
    layer2 = new Layer();
    layer2->createBounded( BUFFERW, BUFFERH, WINDOWW, WINDOWH );
    layer2->renderStart(true, Color(0,0,0,0));
    for (int n=0; n<100; n++) {
        int x = rand() % BUFFERW-40;
        int y = rand() % BUFFERH-40;
        shape->drawPoint( (double) x, (double) y, 40, Color(0,200,0,255) );
    }
    font2->Print(200,200,"LAYER 2");
    layer2->renderStop();
}

void createlayer1() {
    //create medium scrolling layer filled with random green boxes
    layer1 = new Layer();
    layer1->createBounded( BUFFERW, BUFFERH, WINDOWW, WINDOWH );
    layer1->renderStart();
    for (int n=0; n<200; n++) {
        double x = (double)(rand() % BUFFERW-20);
        double y = (double)(rand() % BUFFERH-20);
        shape->drawPoint( x, y, 20, Color(250,0,0,255) );
```

```
    }
    font2->Print(300,300,"LAYER 1");
    layer1->renderStop();
}

bool game_init(HWND window) {
    font = new Font("Arial Bold",18);
    font2 = new Font("Arial Bold",24);
    shape = new VectorShape();
    g_engine->savePrimaryRenderTarget();
    createlayer4();
    createlayer3();
    createlayer2();
    createlayer1();
    g_engine->restorePrimaryRenderTarget();
    g_engine->setSpriteIdentity();
    return true;
}

void game_update(float deltaTime) {
    switch (direction) {
    case 1: //right
        velx = basevel; vely = 0.0; break;
    case 2: //down
        velx = 0.0; vely = basevel; break;
    case 3: //left
        velx = -basevel; vely = 0.0; break;
    case 4: //up
        velx = 0.0; vely = -basevel; break;
    }
    //update scroll position
    scrollx += deltaTime*velx*50.0;
    scrolly += deltaTime*vely*50.0;
    if (scrollx <0) {
        scrollx = 0; direction = 4;
    }
    if (scrollx > BUFFERW - WINDOWW - 1) {
        scrollx = BUFFERW - WINDOWW - 1;
        direction = 2;
    }
```

```
        if (scrolly < 0) {
            scrolly = 0; direction = 1;
        }
        if (scrolly > BUFFERH - WINDOWH - 1) {
            scrolly = BUFFERH - WINDOWH - 1;
            direction = 3;
        }
    }

void game_render2d() {
    ostringstream os;
    //draw layers
    layer4->scrollx = 0;
    layer4->scrolly = 0;
    layer4->drawBounded(50,100);
    layer3->scrollx = scrollx/3;
    layer3->scrolly = scrolly/3;
    layer3->drawBounded(50,100);
    layer2->scrollx = scrollx/2;
    layer2->scrolly = scrolly/2;
    layer2->drawBounded(50,100);
    layer1->scrollx = scrollx;
    layer1->scrolly = scrolly;
    layer1->drawBounded(50,100);

    //print debugging info
    font->Print(50,80,
        "Buffer " + ToString(BUFFERW) + "," + ToString(BUFFERH) +
        " Window " + ToString(WINDOWW) + "," + ToString(WINDOWH) +
        " Scroll " + ToString(scrollx) + "," + ToString(scrolly) );
    long core = g_engine->getCoreFrameRate();
    font->Print(0,0, "Core: " + ToString((double)(1000.0f/core)) +
        " ms (" + ToString(core) + " fps)" );
    long fps = g_engine->getScreenFrameRate();
    font->Print(200,0, "Screen: " + ToString(fps) + " fps" );
}

void game_event(Octane::IEvent* e) {
    switch (e->getID()) {
    case EVENT_KEYRELEASE:
```

```
        KeyReleaseEvent* evt = (KeyReleaseEvent*) e;
        switch (evt->keycode) {
                case DIK_ESCAPE:
                        g_engine->Shutdown();
                        break;
        }
        break;
    }
}
```

Tiled Layers

The Layer class already has the capability to render a layer suitable for a side-scrolling platformer game (*Mario, Sonic, Mega Man, Contra,* etc.). Rendering the tile blocks onto an empty layer texture is the key to making this type of game. When the tiled layer has been created, then the process is to open it up for rendering with Layer::renderStart(), then draw the tiles onto the layer's internal texture just as if we're drawing them onto the screen (with Sprite animation code used to process the tilemap numbers as animation frames). Once rendered onto the layer, we do not need the tile sheet any longer so it can be disposed. In the drawTilemap() function below you can see that it is self-contained, loading its tile block assets, rendering them onto a render target layer, and then cleaning up afterward. The LEVELW and LEVELH constants are global, so a more reusable function would use parameters.

```
void drawTilemap() {
    Sprite* blocks = new Sprite();
    blocks->Load("blocks.bmp", Color(0,0,0,0));
    blocks->setColumns(4);
    blocks->setSize(32,32);
    blocks->setAnimationRange(0,3);
    for (int y=0; y<LEVELH; y++) {
        for (int x=0; x<LEVELW; x++) {
            double xp = x * 32;
            double yp = y * 32;
            blocks->setPosition(xp, yp);
            int frame = level[y][x];
            if (frame>0) {
                blocks->setCurrentFrame( frame );
                blocks->Render();
```

```
            }
        }
    }
    delete blocks;
}
```

The gameplay code for a tile scroller would involve calculating the position of the player, loot, and enemy sprites and rendering them with collision among the tiles. Calculating the position of each tile is similar to the process used to render them onto the layer, by going through each tile and noting its value (0 to 3 in this example). Tile number 0 is empty, while anything else would be a collision. There are four layers in the example.

Layer 1 is shown in Figure 15.7, and is the layer rendered first so it appears in the back behind the other three.

Figure 15.7
The first layer of the tiled layer demo is in the far background.

Figure 15.8
The second layer of the tiled layer demo is drawn over the first one.

The second layer (Figure 15.8) is similar to the first one, but it is rendered with a bit of alpha so that the layer beneath it is discernible.

The third layer (Figure 15.9) is our gameplay layer, which the player's sprite and other game objects would use to determine how to behave—using the tile blocks as walking platforms. This layer is rendered with 100% opacity (zero alpha) so it stands out when rendered on the screen.

The fourth and final layer (Figure 15.10) is rendered over the top of the gameplay layer with a high amount of alpha, so it is only barely visible, but it is enough to obstruct some of the third layer and those below. Depending on a game's design goals, this may be desired to increase the difficulty of the game. In a real game, this fourth layer would represent a foreground wall in a building or it may reveal the gameplay through windows as if the camera is outside a building looking in (reminiscent of the *Castlevania* series).

Figure 15.9
The third layer of the tiled layer demo is filled with platformer gameplay tiles.

It will be almost impossible to discern any detail in the screenshot of this project, shown in Figure 15.11, but you can make out the platformer tiles showing through more clearly in the fully transparent regions of the fourth layer. The alpha blending of the four layers looks remarkable on the screen, but it is impossible to appreciate it in print. Granted, the fourth layer is vanity, but I wanted to show how a fully opaque tile layer looks behind one of the translucent bitmap layers. Note that include lines, comments, and error handling code has been omitted for space.

```
Font *font = NULL;
int mouse_x, mouse_y, mouse_b;
VectorShape *shape = NULL;
Texture* texBackgrnd=NULL;
Layer* layer1 = NULL;
Layer* layer2 = NULL;
```

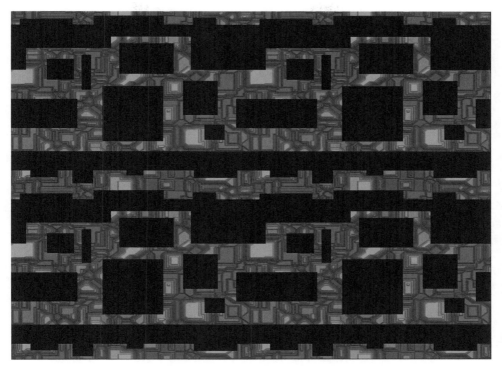

Figure 15.10
The fourth layer of the tiled layer demo is drawn over the tiled layer.

```
Layer* layer3 = NULL;
Layer* layer4 = NULL;
const int WINDOWW = 800;
const int WINDOWH = 600;
const int BUFFERW = WINDOWW * 3;
const int BUFFERH = WINDOWH * 1;
double basevel = 4.0;
double velx=basevel, vely=0.0;
int direction = 1;


const int LEVELW = 60;
const int LEVELH = 36;
const int level[LEVELH][LEVELW] = {
{1,1,1,1,1,1,1,0,0,0,0,0,0,0,0,0,0,3,3,3,3,3,3,3,3,0,0,0,0,0,0,0,0,0,1,1,1,1,1,1,1,0,0,0,0,0,0,1,1,1,1,1,1},
{1,1,1,1,1,0,0,0,0,0,0,0,0,0,0,0,0,3,3,3,3,3,3,3,3,0,0,0,0,0,0,0,0,0,0,0,1,1,1,0,0,0,0,0,0,0,0,0,0,0,1,1},
```

Figure 15.11
The Tiled Layer Demo program shows the output of all four layers being rendered together.

```
{1,1,1,0,0,0,0,0,0,0,0,0,0,0,0,0,0,0,0,0,0,0,0,0,0,0,0,0,0,0,0,0,0,0,0,0,0,0,0,0,0,0,0,0,0,0,0,0,1},
. . . //portion omitted to save space-see complete project for details
{0,0,1,1,1,1,0,0,0,1,1,1,1,0,1,0,0,1,0,0,0,1,1,1,0,0,0,1,1,1,1,0,0,1,1,1,1,0,0,1,1,1,1,0,1,0,0,1,0,0},
{0,0,0,0,0,0,0,0,0,0,0,0,0,0,0,0,0,0,0,0,0,0,0,0,0,0,0,0,0,0,0,0,0,0,0,0,0,0,0,0,0,0,0,0,0,0,0,0,0,0},
{0,0,0,0,0,0,0,0,0,0,0,0,0,0,0,0,0,0,0,0,0,0,0,0,0,0,0,0,0,0,0,0,0,0,0,0,0,0,0,0,0,0,0,0,0,0,0,0,0,0},
};

void drawTilemap() {
    Sprite* blocks = new Sprite();
    blocks->Load("blocks.bmp", Color(0,0,0,0));
    blocks->setColumns(4);
    blocks->setSize(32,32);
    blocks->setAnimationRange(0,3);
    for (int y=0; y<LEVELH; y++) {
```

```
        for (int x=0; x<LEVELW; x++) {
            double xp = x * 32;
            double yp = y * 32;
            blocks->setPosition(xp, yp);
            int frame = level[y][x];
            if (frame>0) {
                blocks->setCurrentFrame( frame );
                blocks->Render();
            }
        }
    }
    delete blocks;
}

void createlayer4() {
    Texture* image = new Texture();
    image->Load("steel.tga");
    layer4 = new Layer();
    layer4->createWrapping( image );
    delete image;
}

void createlayer3() {
    Texture* image = new Texture();
    image->Create(800,600);
    layer3 = new Layer();
    layer3->createWrapping( image );
    layer3->renderStart();
    drawTilemap();
    layer3->renderStop();
    delete image;
}

void createlayer2() {
    Texture* image = new Texture();
    image->Load("plastic.bmp");
    layer2 = new Layer();
    layer2->createWrapping( image );
    delete image;
}
```

```cpp
void createlayer1() {
    Texture* image = new Texture();
    image->Load("alloy.bmp");
    layer1 = new Layer();
    layer1->createWrapping( image );
    delete image;
    layer1->renderStart(false);
    font->Print(0,0,"LAYER 1");
    layer1->renderStop();
}

bool game_init(HWND window) {
    font = new Font("Arial Bold",18);
    shape = new VectorShape();
    g_engine->savePrimaryRenderTarget();
    createlayer1();
    createlayer2();
    createlayer3();
    createlayer4();
    g_engine->restorePrimaryRenderTarget();
    g_engine->setSpriteIdentity();
    return true;
}

void game_update(float deltaTime) {
    float vx = deltaTime*velx*20.0;
    float vy = deltaTime*vely*20.0;
    layer1->updateWrapping( vx/4, vy/4 );
    layer2->updateWrapping( vx/3, vy/3 );
    layer3->updateWrapping( vx/2, vy/2 );
    layer4->updateWrapping( vx, vy );
}

void game_render2d() {
    ostringstream os;
    //draw layers
    layer1->drawWrapping(50,100, Color(255,255,255,255));
    layer2->drawWrapping(50,100, Color(255,255,255,120));
    layer3->drawWrapping(50,100, Color(255,255,255,255));
    layer4->drawWrapping(50,100, Color(255,255,255,150));
```

```
    //print debugging info
    long core = g_engine->getCoreFrameRate();
    long fps = g_engine->getScreenFrameRate();
    os << "Core: " << (double)(1000.0f/core) << " ms (" << core << " fps)";
    os << " Screen: " << fps << " fps";
    font->Print(0,0,os.str());
    os.str("");
    os << "Buffer " << BUFFERW << "," << BUFFERH;
    os << " Window " << WINDOWW << "," << WINDOWH;
    os << " Scroll " << layer1->scrollx << "," << layer1->scrolly;
    font->Print(50,80,os.str());
}

void game_event(Octane::IEvent* e) {
    switch (e->getID()) {
    case EVENT_KEYRELEASE:
        KeyReleaseEvent* evt = (KeyReleaseEvent*) e;
        switch (evt->keycode) {
            case DIK_ESCAPE:
                    g_engine->Shutdown();
                    break;
        }
        break;
    }
}
```

Summary

This was a challenging chapter because we did some rather unusual things in 2D with a technique often used solely for environmental cube mapping—rendering to a different target texture. There are more uses for this advanced technique than those presented here. For instance, it's possible to use the VectorShape class to draw GUI components such as a label and a button, using our existing Font class, and the Event system, and without any extra GUI management code, build a very decent graphical user interface.

CHAPTER 16

ENTITY MANAGEMENT

An entity is usually an instance of an encapsulated object that fulfills some aspect of gameplay. For instance, you might think of a sound effect as an entity, and that might be a valid description, but it doesn't quite fit. I think of a sound effect as a result of some action performed by an entity, not as an entity itself. What types of objects in a game are likely to perform actions or interact in some way? Most likely, only a mesh or a sprite is likely to interact in a game. So, let's imagine that mesh and sprite objects share at least one behavior—they are both *entities* in a game. By sharing basic properties, such as position and velocity, we can manipulate both sprites and meshes using a single call to shared function names. This takes the form of virtual functions in the class definition. Pure virtuals are functions declared with $= 0$ in the definition, which is equivalent to setting the function pointer to null. On the technical side of C++, class function names are actually pointers to the shared function code in memory, and a pure virtual means that the subclasses override the base class' function pointer. (I'm using the word "function" to describe the work performed by an entity, which is interchangeable with the word "method.") From these entities we should drive the *gameplay objects* required by a game's design.

Topics covered in this chapter include:

- Building an entity manager
- Updating entities
- Rendering 3D entities

- Rendering 2D entities
- Adding and removing entities
- Managed timer
- Managed sprites
- Managed meshes

BUILDING AN ENTITY MANAGER

The entity management system in a game engine shouldn't care what type of object you add to it, as long as that object is derived from a base entity. You should be able to subclass an entity into as many different entity types as you want to use in your game! For our game engine, we'll support the Sprite, Mesh, and BoneMesh classes (created in previous chapters) so they can be used as entities and add one or more new entity types as needed. You could even treat things such as lights and cameras as entities. It is also essential to support objects in the entity manager that you want to control with script code down the road.

Up to this point, we have been adding new features to the game engine via new C++ classes for such things as meshes, sprites, terrain, and so forth. Those classes do not make a game engine; they are merely tools. A true engine must do something other than just offer up classes! Imagine it this way: You have a block, crankshaft, heads, camshafts, pistons, spark plugs, a fuel injection intake, and a throttle body; do these parts individually produce power? An engine performs work. Every component is crucial to the correct running of the engine, but the engine is far more than just the sum of its parts. Let's follow the same analogy when thinking about our game engine, and then work on putting the components together, from individual pieces to a whole machine that can produce work. An entity manager is one such means to producing work within the engine. Rather than just consuming the classes provided *by the engine*, we will have the engine itself actually perform some gameplay processing internally. Up to this point, we have been manually cranking our engine, but now it's time to start it up!

An entity class should provide base properties and functions that will be shared by all entities (regardless of gameplay functionality). We want to be able to add an entity by name or identifier number, among other things, and the entity class should provide these facilities.

An entity manager will automatically process the entities and then report the results to the game (or rather, to *you*, the programmer). This will only work if the entities are properly initialized before they are added. The properties will affect how each entity is drawn, moved, animated, and so forth. If we set an entity's properties a certain way, it should automatically move and animate. In the future, we may want to add behavior to game entities so they interact with their environment in an even higher level of automation (which is the subject of A.I.). Before that will be possible, however, the entity manager must be programmed with the basic logistics of managing entities.

The entity manager should make it easy to manipulate entities once they're in the system. We need functionality that makes it possible to add, find, and delete entities from the game code. In the engine itself, we need to automatically move, animate, and draw entities based on their properties. This is the part where game programming really starts to get fun, because at this point we're working at a higher level, more in the realm of designing gameplay than doing low-level stuff like rendering. This automated functionality is possible through the use of the Standard Template Library; specifically, a `std::list` or a `std::vector`. While a `std::list` is better at adding and deleting items, a `std::vector` is better at processing data in sequences. To simplify iteration, we'll use `BOOST_FOREACH` from the boost/foreach.hpp library and avoid using iterators.

Advice

If your standard library knowledge is a bit rusty, I recommend *C++ Standard Library Practical Tips* (Course PTR, 2005) by Greg Reese—it was a good reference while I was working on the code in this book.

The entity list will be defined as a `std::vector` of type `Entity*`, and it will manage all entities in the engine. We will revisit the entity manager again to add multi-threaded optimizations in Chapter 18.

```
std::vector<Entity*> p_entities;
```

Advice

This chapter's resource files can be downloaded from www.jharbour.com/forum or www.courseptr.com/downloads. Not every line of code will be in print due to space considerations, only the most important sections of code.

The Entity Class

Let's start with a new class called `Entity`. This simple class is more of a placeholder with a few minor properties used to identify the type of entity being subclassed. Some of the functions in `Entity` are declared as pure virtual, meaning you *must* subclass `Entity` into a new class; you cannot use an `Entity` alone. The properties are all important and are used by the entity manager to process the entities. Actually, the manager doesn't really care whether your entity is a sprite, a mesh, or a timer; it will just process the virtual methods and use the properties you provide it. Properties will determine whether an entity is used for processing (such as a timer), for 3D rendering (such as a mesh), or for 2D rendering (such as a GUI control).

Although a strongly typed engine might define specific entity types with an enumeration or some constant values (such as `EntityType`), I did not want to regulate the engine too much—it's up to *you* to set the properties when you create your entity objects and add them to the manager, and then write the code to respond to the events based on object type. One very interesting property is `lifetime` (composed of two variables—`lifetimeStart` and `lifetimeLength`). Using this property, you can set an entity to auto-expire after a fixed amount of time (measured in milliseconds). If you want an entity to participate in the game for only 10 seconds, you can set its `lifetime` to `10000`, and it will be automatically removed when the time expires. This can be extremely handy for many types of games in which you would otherwise have to add logic to terminate things such as bullets and explosions manually. After adding a bullet to the game with a specified lifetime, you will not need to keep track of it as it will be removed from the game automatically when its *time is up*!

There is one property that we *must* set in order to perform the correct type of rendering: NONE (for a process), 2D, or 3D—so this property will be a constructor parameter to make sure it is set. You cannot render 2D and 3D objects together because 2D sprites must be rendered by `ID3DXSprite` within the 3D rendering pipeline. The `Entity` class, defined in a moment, includes an enumeration called `RenderType` that also falls inside the overall Octane namespace (so it's visible to the `Entity` class). We need to use this simple enumeration to determine whether an entity should be rendered, and whether it falls into the 2D or 3D category. It's automatic once the various classes are revised.

First, our managed entities must be identifiable, and by more means than one. Internally, the manager should be able to (if we desire) sort the entity list by identifier (ID), by entity type (sprite, mesh, etc.), or by rendering type (2D, 3D, etc.). The entity type will grow in time as new classes are added to the manager.

```
enum EntityType {
    ENTITY_UNKNOWN=-1,ENTITY_TIMER=0,ENTITY_MESH,ENTITY_SPRITE };
```

Next we have the rendering type. While `EntityType` will grow to add new types of entities in time, the `RenderType` enumeration will most likely not change since it is of a simpler type of state.

```
enum RenderType { RENDER_NONE = 0, RENDER_2D, RENDER_3D };
```

Below is the `Entity` class implementation. All we need here is the constructor to initialize the property variables; otherwise, the `Entity` class is mostly made up of accessors and mutators in the header. Note that `Entity` does not have a default constructor, only one with the `RenderType` parameter. You *must* tell an entity whether it should be rendered in 2D or 3D or NONE, and this takes care of that requirement.

```
class Entity {
protected:
    int id;
    std::string name;
    bool alive;
    bool visible;
    enum RenderType renderType;
    enum EntityType entityType;
    float lifetimeStart;
    float lifetimeCounter;
    float lifetimeLength;
public:
    Entity(enum RenderType renderType);
    virtual ~Entity() { };

    //pure virtuals required in sub-classes
    virtual void Update(float deltaTime) = 0;
    virtual void Render() = 0;

    void setID(int value) { id = value; }
    int getID() { return id; }
```

```
void setRenderType(enum RenderType type) {renderType=type;}
enum RenderType getRenderType() { return renderType; }
std::string getName() { return name; }
void setName(std::string value) { name = value; }
bool getVisible() { return visible; }
void setVisible(bool value) { visible = value; }
bool getAlive() { return alive; }
void setAlive(bool value) { alive = value; }
float getLifetime() { return lifetimeLength; }
void setLifetime(float value) { lifetimeLength = value; }
bool lifetimeExpired() {
    return (lifetimeStart + lifetimeCounter > lifetimeLength);
}
EntityType getEntityType() { return entityType; }
void setEntityType(enum EntityType value) { entityType = value; }
};
```

Implementation of the `Entity` class will be short and simple because most of the class is interface and the real functionality will be found in subclasses like `Sprite`.

```
Entity::Entity(enum RenderType type) {
    renderType = type;
    id = -1;
    name = "";
    visible = true;
    alive = true;
    entityType = ENTITY_UNKNOWN;
    lifetimeStart = 0;
    lifetimeCounter = 0;
    lifetimeLength = 0;
}
```

The two pure virtual functions defined in the `Entity` class are `Entity::Update()` and `Entity::Render()`, which means these two functions *must* be implemented in a subclass. We'll get to that in a bit, with modifications to some of the classes. First, we need to make some changes to the core engine.

Advice

There are too many modifications and additions taking place in the engine project to point them all out and list every line of code. This chapter will present the most important changes but gloss over the many smaller details that would become too tedious to cover line by line. Please refer to the Engine project in this chapter's resource files.

Modifying the Engine

The engine will need to be modified to support entity management. This is the part where we begin to take the components (Entity, Sprite, Mesh, and so on) and assemble them into a functional engine. We'll begin with some changes to the Engine class. When a managed entity is being updated or rendered, there are times when we will want to make changes to it. For instance, if we want to render a force field around a spaceship without incurring a large amount of memory for new artwork, then it may be more desirable to add the force field over the ship as it is being rendered. When the spaceship is being updated—moved based on velocity, tested for collisions, etc.—we may want to apply behaviors to the object to influence it according to the requirements of the gameplay. These two events are fired off through the engine's event system and received by the gameplay code's game_event() function.

Event Changes

We have need for two new events in the engine to accommodate entity update and render notifications.

```
enum eventtype {
    EVENT_TIMER = 10,
    EVENT_KEYPRESS = 20,
    EVENT_KEYRELEASE = 30,
    EVENT_MOUSECLICK = 40,
    EVENT_MOUSEMOTION = 50,
    EVENT_MOUSEWHEEL = 60,
    EVENT_MOUSEMOVE = 70,
    EVENT_ENTITYUPDATE = 80,
    EVENT_ENTITYRENDER = 90,
};
```

Advice

Does it seem wasteful to send a notice (like a "delivery confirmation") every time an entity is updated and rendered? Imagine how many function calls and Event objects that will generate in a game with a couple thousand entities! The performance impact will be less important than something like scene management (eliminating objects in the scene that are not visible, i.e., those behind the camera), but it is still noticeable. This most certainly *would* benefit from an additional property that would specify whether an entity needs to generate the update and render events—perhaps an EventToggle property?

The new event classes (which subclass from IEvent) are EntityRenderEvent and EntityUpdateEvent. These two events are generated in the engine core (i.e., Engine::Update()) as the entity manager is iterating through the list to update and render each entity—if its properties allow.

```
class EntityRenderEvent : public IEvent {
public:
    Octane::Entity* entity;
    EntityRenderEvent(Entity* e);
};
class EntityUpdateEvent : public IEvent {
public:
    Octane::Entity* entity;
    EntityUpdateEvent(Entity* e);
};
```

We already added timing support to the event system back in Chapter 6, but here it is again for reference. We will be using the TimerEvent event with the AutoTimer class shortly as an example of non-rendering event handling.

```
class TimerEvent : public IEvent {
public:
    int timerid;
    TimerEvent(int tid);
};
```

The implementation of these class interfaces is also fairly simple—remember, these classes will be generated and destroyed quickly and repeatedly while the engine is running, so they should be lightweight.

```
EntityRenderEvent::EntityRenderEvent(Entity* e) {
    id = EVENT_ENTITYRENDER;
    entity = e;
}
EntityUpdateEvent::EntityUpdateEvent(Entity* e) {
    id = EVENT_ENTITYUPDATE;
    entity = e;
}
TimerEvent::TimerEvent(int tid) {
    id = EVENT_TIMER;
    timerid = tid;
}
```

We've been exploring a new "entity manager" quite a bit in the chapter so far, but have not yet really explained what it is. The manager is not a class (although it uses the Entity class); rather, it is new functionality in the engine, in the form of new code that automatically updates and renders the managed entities. Again, we define the entity list in the Engine.h private section:

```
std::vector<Entity*> p_entities;
```

This is template-based code. When the std::vector class is used to create the instance called p_entities, we must tell the container what type of object it will contain. The std::vector is a container for other objects. When this code is compiled, the C++ compiler creates a new class based on a container of Entity objects. When a class like Sprite is defined as a subclass of Entity, it can be added to the list as well (the C++ compiler handles the differences in memory size needed by each object, even when they are different).

Also in the private section of the Engine class are several new management functions used internally by the engine to update, draw, and delete entities. These functions are internal and not accessible outside of the engine core.

```
void updateEntities(float deltaTime);
void entitiesRender3D();
void entitiesRender2D();
void drawEntities();
void buryEntities();
```

There is also one new public function needed to add entities to the manager:

```
void addEntity( Entity* entity );
```

That odd-sounding buryEntities() function is actually quite descriptive, because its job is to remove all "expired" entities from the list. But how does an entity expire? Very simply: by setting its "alive" property to false.

Advice

The magnificent thing about the entity manager (from a gameplay perspective) is that we can dynamically add new entities to a game, and they are *automatically* updated and rendered. And, if the lifetime property is used, the entity manager will even terminate an entity when its lifetime is reached and remove it from memory. This functionality makes it possible to build a fully scripted game engine using a script language such as LUA or Python.

Engine::Update

Located in the Engine.cpp file, the Engine::Update() function is the engine core, called directly from the WinMain while loop, and residing at the lowest level of the engine. Here is the complete source code for the function with the new entity manager code highlighted in bold:

```
void Engine::Update( float deltaTime ) {
    static float accumTime=0;
    //calculate core framerate
    p_coreFrameCount++;
    if (p_coreTimer.Stopwatch(1000))  {
        p_coreFrameRate = p_coreFrameCount;
        p_coreFrameCount = 0;
    }

    //fast update
    game_update( deltaTime );

    //update entities
    if (!p_pauseMode) updateEntities(deltaTime);

    //60fps = ~16 ms per frame
    if (!timedUpdate.Stopwatch(16)) {
        timedUpdate.Rest(1);
    } else  {
        //calculate screen framerate
        p_screenFrameCount++;
        if (p_screenTimer.Stopwatch(1000)) {
            p_screenFrameRate = p_screenFrameCount;
            p_screenFrameCount = 0;
        }

        //update input devices
        p_input->Update();
        updateKeyboard();
        updateMouse();

        //begin rendering
        if (p_device->BeginScene() == D3D_OK)  {
            g_engine->clearScene(p_backdropColor);
```

```
            entitiesRender3D();
            game_render3d();
            p_spriteObj->Begin(D3DXSPRITE_ALPHABLEND);
            entitiesRender2D();
            game_render2d();
            p_spriteObj->End();
            p_device->EndScene();
            p_device->Present(0,0,0,0);
        }
    }
    //clean up expired entities
    buryEntities();}
```

Updating Entities

The updateEntities() function is called from Engine::Update to process everything in the entity list. "Process" here means to move, animate, and check the lifetime of each entity, and call the game event functions for each entity that is updated (but rendering is done elsewhere). If you want to add additional functionality to the entity manager, this is where you will want to do that because this code runs at the core clock speed—not the slow framerate speed. This is where we will add some physics code in the near future.

```
void Engine::updateEntities(float deltaTime) {
    BOOST_FOREACH( Entity* entity, p_entities ) {
        if ( entity->getAlive() ) {
            //move/animate entity
            entity->Update(deltaTime);

            //tell game that this entity has been updated
            raiseEvent( new EntityUpdateEvent( entity ) );

            //see if this entity will auto-expire
            if ( entity->getLifetime() > 0 ) {
                if ( entity->lifetimeExpired() )
                    entity->setAlive(false);
            }
        }
    }
}
```

Rendering 3D Entities

The `Engine::entitiesRender3D()` function is called from `Engine::Update()` to process all 3D entities (if any). The entire entity list is iterated through; any entities with a `RenderType` of `RENDER_3D` have their `Render()` method called. Any other entities are ignored. If the gameplay design of a game requires that something is rendered over the top of an entity (such as clothing, or a force field, or a glowing effect), then that should be handled with a state variable when the `EntityUpdateEvent` event is received—always be careful to preserve the render stage framerate and use the untimed updated stage for logic.

```
void Engine::entitiesRender3D()
{
    BOOST_FOREACH( Entity* entity, p_entities ) {
        if (entity->getRenderType() == RENDER_3D) {
            if (entity->getAlive() && entity->getVisible()) {
                entity->Render();
                raiseEvent( new EntityRenderEvent(entity) );
            }
        }
    }
}
```

Advice

Do your instincts tell you that it's wasteful to iterate through the entire entity list *twice* to process the 3D and 2D entities separately? That means you are anticipating how the entity manager can be optimized, which is a good thing. However, processors are extremely good at doing loops today, with their multiple pipeline architectures and cache memory, so don't worry about duplicating loops for different processes. In the end, the only code that takes clock cycles is the code in called functions, while the code in the loop is pipelined and probably would not even show up in profiling. As it turns out, we cannot combine these loops anyway because the 2D and 3D rendering must be done at different times. One possible enhancement is a `std::map`—worth looking into!

Rendering 2D Entities

Like the `entitiesRender2D()` function, `entitiesRender2D()` also iterates through the entity list and picks out objects with a `RenderType` of `RENDER_2D` and calls the `Render()` method for each one. If it turns out during the development of a game that you need to respond to an entity's render event *before* rather than *after* it takes place, you might consider adding another event or, better yet, handle such things in the update event instead.

```
void Engine::entitiesRender2D()
{
    BOOST_FOREACH( Entity* entity, p_entities ) {
        if (entity->getRenderType() == RENDER_2D) {
            if (entity->getAlive() && entity->getVisible()) {
                entity->Render();
                raiseEvent( new EntityRenderEvent(entity) );
            }
        }
    }
}
```

Advice

> Don't worry about slowing down your game by drawing too many sprites, because Direct3D *batches* sprite rendering and does it extremely quickly in the 3D hardware. What you *should* be concerned with is code that performs *updates* such as collision detection (covered in the next chapter).

Removing "Dead" Entities

The last of the private entity manager support methods is BuryEntities. This method iterates through the entity list (p_entities), looking for any objects that are "dead" (where the alive property is false). Thus, to delete an object from the entity manger, just call setAlive(false), and it will be removed at the end of the frame update loop. Although you will create a new entity on the heap (with new) and then add it to the entity manager, you will not need to remove entities because the list::erase method automatically calls delete for each object as it is destroyed. As a result, we can use a "fire and forget" policy with our entities and trust that the container is cleaning up afterward.

```
void Engine::buryEntities()
{
    std::vector<Entity*>::iterator iter = p_entities.begin();
    while (iter != p_entities.end()) {
        if ( (*iter)->getAlive() == false ) {
            iter = p_entities.erase( iter );
        }
        else iter++;
    }
}
```

498 Chapter 16 ■ Entity Management

Adding Entities

Now that the entity manager has been added to the engine for internal processing, we need to add a public access method to give the gameplay code access to the entity manager. The `Engine::addEntity()` function is used by the game to add an entity to the manager (that is, any object derived from `Entity`—which includes `Sprite`, `Mesh`, and any of their subclasses. First, you must create a new object from a class derived from `Entity`, instantiate the class, set its properties, and then add it to the list.

```
void Engine::addEntity(Entity *entity)
{
    static int id = 0;
    entity->setID(id);
    p_entities.push_back( entity );
    id++;
}
```

Managed AutoTimer—Non-Rendering

To test whether the engine's new entity manager is working, we'll write a test program that uses a new class that does not require any rendering—`AutoTimer`. This class has a couple of properties that determine how often it will fire (as a timer) and how long it will last. The `AutoTimer` can be added to the entity manager to generate regular timing events at any specified interval (in seconds with fractional second support—such as 2.5 or 0.005).

AutoTimer.h

```
class AutoTimer : public Entity {
private:
    float elapsedTime;
    float repeatTime;
    float repeatStart;
    int id;
public:
    AutoTimer(int timerid, float cycletime, float lifetime=0);
    ~AutoTimer(void);
    int getID() { return id; }
    //entity functions
```

```
    void Update(float deltaTime);
    void Render();
};
```

AutoTimer.cpp

```
AutoTimer::AutoTimer(int timerid, float cycletime, float lifetime)
: Entity(RENDER_NONE) {
    setEntityType(ENTITY_TIMER);
    id = timerid;
    elapsedTime = 0;
    repeatStart = 0;
    repeatTime = cycletime;
    setLifetime(lifetime);
    setVisible(false);
}
AutoTimer::~AutoTimer() {}
void AutoTimer::Update(float deltaTime) {
    if (repeatTime > 0) {
        elapsedTime += deltaTime;
        if (elapsedTime > repeatStart + repeatTime) {
            repeatStart = elapsedTime;
            g_engine->raiseEvent(new TimerEvent(id));
        }
    }
}

void AutoTimer::Render() { /* not used */ }
```

Testing AutoTimer

Here is an example of how to create an AutoTimer object and add it to the entity manager, then watch for AutoTimer events coming in:

```
AutoTimer* timer = new AutoTimer( 1, 1.0 );
timer->setName("TIMER");
g_engine->addEntity( timer );
```

Now for the timer events. The game_event function receives all events, and the one we want to watch for in this case is called EVENT_TIMER. Note that TimerEvent does not maintain an elapsed running time or a delta time between events; because those properties were used to *create* the timer it's assumed that the firing time occurs at the desired interval and we need only respond to it as needed.

```
void game_event(Octane::IEvent* e) {
    switch (e->getID()) {
    case EVENT_TIMER: {
            TimerEvent* t = (TimerEvent*) e;
            debug << "Timer: " << t->getID() << endl;
            timerFired = true;
        }
        break;
    }
}
```

ENTITY-FYING THE ENGINE CLASSES

Any type of object in a game can be added to the entity manager if you want it to be managed (and as a result, made available to scripting). Our first example added a new class called AutoTimer with a RenderState setting of RENDER_NONE, which means this object should be updated (via it's Update() function) but not rendered. While we could have modified Timer to work in this manner, it is used by the engine core and is best left alone at this point. Some of our existing classes that might be given support for managed rendering include:

- Sprite (RENDER_2D)
- Mesh (RENDER_3D)
- BoneMesh (RENDER_3D)
- VectorShape (RENDER_2D)
- Camera (RENDER_NONE)
- Particles (RENDER_2D)
- Layer (RENDER_2D)
- Skybox (RENDER_3D)
- Terrain (RENDER_3D)

Some of these examples are more intuitive than others. For instance, how would a Camera object work from within the managed environment? Well, for one thing, we probably *will* want to manipulate one or more cameras from script code so this is a good idea in general. But what about rendering the scene with a Camera's view and projection matrices? These are all maintained in the Camera class, so perhaps every Camera object found in the managed list will be used for rendering. Furthermore, perhaps a `Texture` render target can be associated with a `Camera` so that views of the scene from various angles can be rendered onto a texture automatically?

Do not hesitate to create a new class to suit your needs, as you can't have *too many* (although it may be confusing for a new programmer to make sense of your engine's architecture). It is perfectly normal to create a new class that encapsulates both a `Camera` and a `Texture`. Or, imagine combining a `Sprite` and a `ParticleEmitter` together in a new subclass of `Entity` (with a `RenderType` of `RENDER_2D`), so that when this new entity is rendered, the particles will automatically move with the spaceship sprite and appear to come out of the engine as fire or smoke. Such a class might find use in many a game, and could be configured with script code (i.e., setting the position and angle of the particle emitter relative to the sprite).

For the sake of clarity, we will only convert `Sprite` and `Mesh` to a subclass of `Entity`, but I encourage you to use this example on some or all of the classes listed, as well as your own new classes. The whole purpose of a class like `Sprite` and `Mesh` is to be the foundation for new gameplay classes such as `Ship`, `Person`, `Dragon`, `Bullet`, `Cloud`, `Boulder`, `Tree`, `House`, and so forth.

Managing Sprites

Let's see what must be changed in the `Sprite` class to support the entity manager. As it turns out, we only need to change the class name definition by adding `Entity` as the parent class, and no other changes are needed to either the definition or the implementation file.

```
class Sprite : public Entity
{
    ...
};
```

Now that `Sprite` is a subclass of `Entity`, we need to make sure it implements any pure virtual functions required by the base class. As you'll recall, `Entity::Update()` and `Entity::Render()` are the two pure virtuals that we must implement. This works out fine for the existing `Sprite::Update` function, which was declared with the same definition so it needn't change.

```
void Update(float deltaTime);
```

The Render() function is a bit of a problem though. It was defined back in Chapter 14 with a parameter (bool autoPivot=true):

```
void Render(bool autoPivot=true);
```

Our Entity class requires a Render() function with no parameters, but the default value in the existing Render() will confuse the compiler. So we will have to remove the default value (=true) and add the void parameter version of Render():

```
void Render();
void Render(bool autoPivot);
```

We can handle the autoPivot parameter in Render() manually. Since we have no way of knowing whether the sprite should have an automatically centered pivot point or not, we can't make the assumption and will have to call Render(false) in this new function. When creating a new managed sprite, we must be careful to set the properties correctly.

The Sprite constructor needs some modification as well.

```
Sprite::Sprite() : Entity(RENDER_2D){
    setEntityType(ENTITY_SPRITE);
    image = NULL;
    imageLoaded = false;
    velocity = Vector2(0,0);
    state = 0;
    facingAngle = 0;
    movingAngle = 0;
    color = Color(255,255,255,255);
    collidable = false;
    pivotPoint = Vector2(0,0);
    //animation properties
    sourcePosition = Vector2(0,0);
    currentFrame = 0;
    firstFrame = 0;
    lastFrame = 0;
    animationDirection = 1;
    animationColumns = 1;
    //transformation properties
    position = Vector2(0,0);
    rotation = 0;
```

```
    scale = Vector2(1,1);
    size = Vector2(1,1);
}
```

Managing Meshes

The Mesh class was first introduced way back in Chapter 9 and provided basic 3D rendering support to the engine (a feature that will get little use in actual practice, since we're focusing our attention on 2D games). Here is the only change that is needed to bring the Mesh class into the Entity family.

```
class Mesh : public Entity{
    ...
};
```

One immediate problem we have with Mesh is the Render() function which has parameters, while our Entity::Render() function definition has none. A Mesh object is rendered with an Effect object, so this is a problem. Instead of passing the Effect as a parameter, we need to make it a property in the class. Also, the Texture effect parameter will need to be assumed. While the existing two-parameter Render() function will be retained, it is not possible to use it from within the entity manager without a lot of custom code that would slow down the engine—it's better to use properties with a single Render() function instead. Here is the new Mesh class constructor:

```
Mesh::Mesh() : Entity(RENDER_3D) {
    entityType = ENTITY_MESH;
    mesh = 0;
    materials = 0;
    material_count = 0;
    textures = 0;
    position = Vector3(0.0f,0.0f,0.0f);
    rotation = Vector3(0.0f,0.0f,0.0f);
    scale = Vector3(1.0f,1.0f,1.0f);
}
```

We'll add this property to the Mesh class interface and a mutator function for it:

```
Effect *p_effect;
void setEffect(Effect* effect) { p_effect = effect; }
```

The Mesh::Update() function will need to call Mesh::Transform() to set up the matrices for rendering.

```
void Mesh::Update(float deltaTime) {
    Transform();
}
```

The `Mesh::Render()` function (which now has one overload) will be modified a bit to work with the entity managed function variation.

```
void Mesh::Render() {
    Render( p_effect, "Texture" );
}

void Mesh::Render(Effect *effect,std::string fxTextureParam) {
    //save the effect object
    p_effect = effect;
    p_effect->setWorldMatrix( matWorld );
    p_effect->Begin();
    if (material_count == 0) {
        mesh->DrawSubset(0);
    } else {
        //draw each mesh subset
        for( DWORD i=0; i < material_count; i++ ) {
            // set the texture used by this face
            if (textures[i])  {
                p_effect->setParam(fxTextureParam,(textures[i]));
            }
            // Draw the mesh subset
            mesh->DrawSubset( i );
        }
    }
    p_effect->End();
}
```

Advice

If you see a linker warning that refers to "uuid.lib," you may ignore it. This is an unavoidable warning caused by a "#pragma comment" statement in one of the DirectX header files.

Freeing Memory

Only one thing remains—freeing memory used by the entity manager when the engine is shutting down.

```
Engine::~Engine() {
    delete p_input;
```

```
    if (p_device) p_device->Release();
    if (p_d3d) p_d3d->Release();
    //destroy entities
    BOOST_FOREACH( Entity* entity, p_entities ) {
        delete entity;
        entity = NULL;
    }
    p_entities.clear();
}
```

ENTITY DEMO

The Entity Demo program (shown in Figure 16.1) shows how the entity manager can handle sprites, timers, and meshes already (and more entity types can be added in time). Most of the functionality in this program occurs in the event handler—note, in particular, that both the game_render3d() and

Figure 16.1
The Entity Demo program demonstrates the entity manager.

game_update() functions are *empty*! All of the updating and rendering is taking place in the engine core's new entity manager. This is a simple example with just one sprite, one mesh, and one timer, but it's fascinating to think that our familiar old gameplay functions are now empty and most of the code is in the event handler. *Now* we have a real engine running. (As is usually the case, only the most relevant code is included in the listing—see the complete project for more details.)

```
Font *font = NULL;
Camera* camera = NULL;
Effect* effect = NULL;
bool timerFired = false;

bool game_init(HWND window)   {
    font = new Font("Arial Bold",36);

    camera = new Camera();
    camera->setPosition(0,0,50);
    camera->Update();

    //add a managed timer
    AutoTimer* timer = new AutoTimer( 1, 1.0 );
    timer->setName("TIMER");

    //add a managed mesh
    Mesh* mesh = new Mesh();
    //mesh = new Mesh();
    mesh->setName("OILDRUM");
    mesh->Load("oil-drum.x");
    mesh->setScale(0.25);
    mesh->setPosition(-12,15,0);
    mesh->setRotation(0,45,0);
    mesh->Transform();

    //create an effect
    effect = new Effect();
    effect->Load("directional.fx");
    effect->setTechnique("TexturedDirectionalLight");
    effect->setViewMatrix( camera->getViewMatrix() );
```

```
    effect->setProjectionMatrix( camera->getProjMatrix() );
    effect->setWorldMatrix( (D3DXMATRIX) mesh->getMatrix() );

    //calculate inverse transpose matrix
    D3DXMATRIX inverse, wit;
    D3DXMatrixInverse( &inverse, 0, &(mesh->getMatrix()) );
    D3DXMatrixTranspose( &wit, &inverse );
    effect->setParam( "WorldInverseTranspose", wit );

    //use this effect to render the mesh
    mesh->setEffect( effect );

    //add a managed sprite
    Sprite* sprite = new Sprite();
    sprite->Load("fatship256.tga");
    sprite->setName("FATSHIP");

    //add objects to entity manager
    g_engine->addEntity( timer );
    g_engine->addEntity( sprite );
    g_engine->addEntity( mesh );

    return true;
}

void game_render2d() {
    if (timerFired) {
        Color color(rand()%256,rand()%256,rand()%256,255);
        font->Print(450,350,"TIMER FIRED!",color);
        timerFired = false;
    }
}

void game_event(Octane::IEvent* e) {
    switch (e->getID()) {
    case EVENT_TIMER: {
        TimerEvent* t = (TimerEvent*) e;
        //WARNING: this slows down the game!
        debug << "Timer: " << t->getID() << endl;
        timerFired = true;
    }
```

```
            break;
            case EVENT_ENTITYUPDATE: {
                EntityUpdateEvent* evt = (EntityUpdateEvent*) e;
                //WARNING: this slows down the game!
                debug << "EntityUpdateEvent: "
                    << evt->entity->getName() << endl;
                if (evt->entity->getEntityType() == ENTITY_SPRITE) {
                    Sprite* sprite = (Sprite*) evt->entity;
                    if (sprite->getName() == "FATSHIP") {
                        //set the pivot
                        sprite->setPivot( Vector2(127,127) );
                        //rotate the sprite
                        float angle = sprite->getRotation();
                        sprite->setRotation( angle + 0.01 );
                    }
                }
            }
            break;
            case EVENT_ENTITYRENDER: {
                EntityRenderEvent* evt = (EntityRenderEvent*) e;
                //WARNING: this slows down the game!
                debug << "EntityRenderEvent: "<<evt->entity->getName()<<endl;
            }
            break;
            case EVENT_KEYRELEASE:
                KeyReleaseEvent* evt = (KeyReleaseEvent*) e;
                switch (evt->keycode) {
                    case DIK_ESCAPE:
                    g_engine->Shutdown();
                    break;
                }
                break;
    }}
```

Summary

That wraps up entity management, at least for the time being. We'll be using this new capability of the engine for the remaining chapters and will be making modifications soon to thread the entity manager!

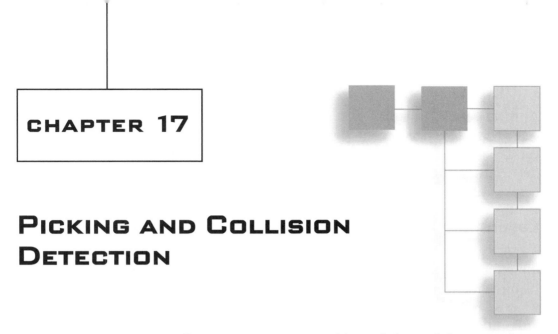

CHAPTER 17

PICKING AND COLLISION DETECTION

This chapter covers one of the most common and basic "physics" features of any game engine—collision detection. We will explore two different ways to detect collisions between entities with support for both sprite and mesh collision. Most games have entities that interact, such as bullets and missiles that hit enemy ships and cause them to explode; characters that must navigate a maze without going through walls; or avatars that can run and jump over crates and land on top of enemy characters (such as how Mario jumps onto turtles in *Super Mario World* to knock them out). All of these situations require the ability to detect when two objects have collided, or intersected each other. The ability to detect a collision between two gameplay objects brings a real-world capability to a game engine that is otherwise just a graphics renderer. The key to collision testing is to identify where two objects are located and then compare their radii or bounding rectangles to see if an intersection occurs. In this chapter we will study how to detect collisions between sprites and meshes (a crossover of 2D and 3D collision) and how to perform *picking*.

This chapter covers the following topics:

- Casting rays
- Ray-mesh intersection
- Converting object space to screen space
- Point-rectangle intersection
- Automated collision detection

PICKING

Any 3D object in the viewport (the projected camera view) can be "picked" by converting its transformed position in the scene (i.e., its matrix) to screen coordinates. We can use this technique to select 3D objects with a mouse click (by transforming the mouse coordinates into a *ray*) or to test for collisions between 2D and 3D objects (such as a sprite and mesh).

Casting Rays

To pick an object in the viewport with the mouse, we have to create a ray from the mouse cursor's position into the Z-axis (into the depth of the screen). This requires the camera's current projection and view matrices, obviously, because what we're looking at in the scene represents the view projected by the camera's position and orientation. It's actually rather challenging to "grab" an object in the scene based solely on the mouse's position. This *might* work if your camera is oriented so that the origin (0,0,0) is at the upper-left corner of the viewport, which will probably never happen (and even if it does, the camera is rarely fixed!).

Advice

This chapter's resource files can be downloaded from www.jharbour.com/forum or www.courseptr.com/downloads. Not every line of code will be in print due to space considerations, only the most important sections of code.

Let's learn how to cast a ray from the mouse cursor into the scene to select an object. First, we'll need a vector to represent the ray:

```
Vector3 ray;
```

Next, we need the screen dimensions:

```
int w = g_engine->getScreenWidth();
int h = g_engine->getScreenHeight();
```

Next, the camera's projection matrix is used to calculate the projected mouse coordinates using the matrices diagonal positions for X and Y, and a fixed length of 1.0 for Z.

```
Matrix matProj = camera->getProjMatrix();
ray.x =  (((2.0f * vec.x) / w ) - 1) / matProj._11;
ray.y = -(((2.0f * vec.y) / h) - 1) / matProj._22;
ray.z =  1.0f;
```

Next, we have to transform the screen space (representing the mouse cursor's position) into 3D space using an inverse matrix of the camera's view matrix (with the `D3DXMatrixInverse()` function). We'll need both the origin and direction for the ray, with the origin set to the camera's position. So, if your camera is at coordinates $(10,20,-50)$ then that is precisely what the ray's origin will be as well. This vector represents the ray with a normalized direction (and length of 1.0). You could use this code almost without change to fire the weapon in a first-person shooter game (using the center of the viewport as the coordinate with "mouse look" for aiming the weapon).

```
D3DXMATRIX m;
D3DXMatrixInverse( &m, NULL, &camera->getViewMatrix() );
D3DXVECTOR3 rayOrigin,rayDir;
rayDir.x  = ray.x*m._11 + ray.y*m._21 + ray.z*m._31;
rayDir.y  = ray.x*m._12 + ray.y*m._22 + ray.z*m._32;
rayDir.z  = ray.x*m._13 + ray.y*m._23 + ray.z*m._33;
rayOrigin.x = m._41;
rayOrigin.y = m._42;
rayOrigin.z = m._43;
```

We now have a ray that can be used to test for collisions with transformed geometry in the scene, which will usually be the mesh objects transformed and rendered in a game. This ray extends into the scene from the mouse cursor's position, or from the position of a *sprite*!

Ray-Mesh Intersection

Using the calculated ray (from the mouse or a game sprite or any other *screen space* entity), we can determine whether the ray extending from that screen position intersects with any geometry in the scene, determined by the camera's projection and view matrices. In other words, the ray will extend in the same direction that the camera is looking (recall the "look at" property). We can use a Direct3D helper function called `D3DXIntersect()` to find out if a ray is intersecting with any mesh in the scene (using its matrix transform). In other words, we perform the ray-mesh collision test using *model space* rather than *global space* (the camera's matrices).

One incredibly helpful calculation that `D3DXIntersect()` gives us, in addition to a collision flag, is the distance to the collision—that is, the distance from the mouse cursor to the *face* of the mesh that was intersected. I like to think of this as a laser targeting system, and visualize a laser's red dot hitting the object.

Next, to create a normalized direction vector for the ray, we use the `D3DXMatrixInverse()` function to get an inverse matrix of the current world transform.

```
D3DXMATRIX matInverse;
D3DXMatrixInverse(&matInverse, NULL, &mesh->getMatrix());
D3DXVECTOR3 rayObjOrigin,rayObjDir;
D3DXVec3TransformCoord(&rayObjOrigin, &rayOrigin, &matInverse);
D3DXVec3TransformNormal(&rayObjDir, &rayDir, &matInverse);
D3DXVec3Normalize(&rayObjDir, &rayObjDir);
```

There are two additional ways to detect ray-mesh intersection. The former method just covered checks the mesh faces for an intersection, which can be time consuming. An optimization is to use a bounding cube or sphere as a container for the collision test, and then use that simpler shape for the ray intersection test. Direct3D provides two helper functions to facilitate this: `D3DXBoxBoundProbe()` and `D3DXSphereBoundProbe()`. This culminates in a reusable function:

```
float intersectsCoordsToMesh(Mesh* mesh, Vector2 vec) {
    //convert coords to projection space
    Vector3 ray;
    int w = g_engine->getScreenWidth();
    int h = g_engine->getScreenHeight();
    Matrix matProj = camera->getProjMatrix();
    ray.x =  (((2.0f * vec.x) / w ) - 1) / matProj._11;
    ray.y = -(((2.0f * vec.y) / h) - 1) / matProj._22;
    ray.z =  1.0f;
    //transform screen space pick ray into 3D space
    D3DXMATRIX m;
    D3DXMatrixInverse( &m, NULL, &camera->getViewMatrix() );
    D3DXVECTOR3 rayOrigin,rayDir;
    rayDir.x  = ray.x*m._11 + ray.y*m._21 + ray.z*m._31;
    rayDir.y  = ray.x*m._12 + ray.y*m._22 + ray.z*m._32;
    rayDir.z  = ray.x*m._13 + ray.y*m._23 + ray.z*m._33;
    rayOrigin.x = m._41;
    rayOrigin.y = m._42;
    rayOrigin.z = m._43;
    //create normalized ray
```

```
    D3DXMATRIX matInverse;
    D3DXMatrixInverse(&matInverse,NULL,&mesh->getMatrix());
    D3DXVECTOR3 rayObjOrigin,rayObjDir;
    D3DXVec3TransformCoord(&rayObjOrigin,&rayOrigin,&matInverse);
    D3DXVec3TransformNormal(&rayObjDir,&rayDir,&matInverse);
    D3DXVec3Normalize(&rayObjDir,&rayObjDir);
    //ray-mesh intersection test
    int hasHit;
    float distanceToCollision;
    D3DXIntersect( mesh->getMesh(), &rayObjOrigin, &rayObjDir, &hasHit,
        NULL, NULL, NULL, &distanceToCollision, NULL, &hits );
    if (hasHit) return distanceToCollision;
    else return -1.0f;
}
```

Converting Object Space to Screen Space

We can get the screen position of any 3D object (such as a mesh) by using a Direct3D helper function called D3DXVec3Project(). This function projects the vector from 3D object space to screen space as a 2D position.

```
Vector2 getScreenPos(Vector3 pos) {
    D3DXVECTOR3 screenPos;
    D3DVIEWPORT9 viewport;
    g_engine->getDevice()->GetViewport(&viewport);
    D3DXMATRIX world;
    D3DXMatrixIdentity(&world);
    D3DXVec3Project( &screenPos, &pos.ToD3DXVECTOR3(), &viewport,
        &camera->getProjMatrix(), &camera->getViewMatrix(), &world );
    return Vector2((int)screenPos.x, (int)screenPos.y);
}
```

Point-Rectangle Intersection

One fairly easy way to test for collisions in the 2D realm is with point-rectangle intersection, where we test to see if a point falls within the boundary of a rectangle. Our Rect class already has a Contains() function that reports true if a passed vector falls within its boundary. We can use this function to make a simple collision function suitable for a sprite-based game. The version of intersectsCoordsToRect() can be overloaded to work directly with a Sprite object or the result of Sprite::getBounds() can be passed to this function. In the case of a sprite-to-sprite collision, either the center of the sprite or each corner of the sprite's bounding Rect can be used for the intersection test. The Picking Demo program shows how it works.

```
bool intersectsCoordsToRect(Rect rect, Vector2 vec) {
    return rect.Contains(vec.x, vec.y);
}
```

The Picking Demo

The Picking Demo program demonstrates how to perform ray-mesh intersection as a form of 2D-to-3D collision detection. Since this example uses the mouse cursor position to test for a ray-mesh collision, this process could be used to simulate collisions between sprites and meshes as well. Figure 17.1 shows a positive collision between the ray projected by the mouse cursor over a mesh.

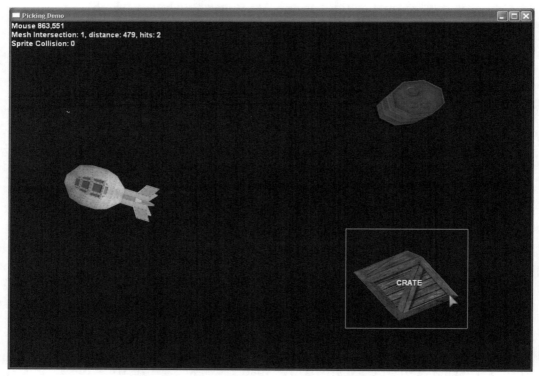

Figure 17.1
A ray is fired from the mouse cursor position to test for mesh collisions.

Figure 17.2
No collision occurs this time because the crate mesh has rotated away from the ray.

To demonstrate how precise the ray-mesh collision technique is, take a look at Figure 17.2. In this case, the mouse cursor is clearly within the same range of the crate mesh as it was before, but due to the rotation of the crate there are no faces intersecting the mouse cursor's ray so no collision is reported.

This program also tests point-rectangle intersection testing, which is a form of *sprite collision detection* (see Figure 17.3).

Custom Mouse Cursor

Since we'll be using a custom mouse cursor in this program, we need the ability to selectively hide and show the default mouse cursor over our program window. These new functions are added to the Engine.h file to handle it. Or, if you prefer, just use the ShowCursor function directly, but I prefer to abstract both the Windows SDK and DirectX SDK as much as possible.

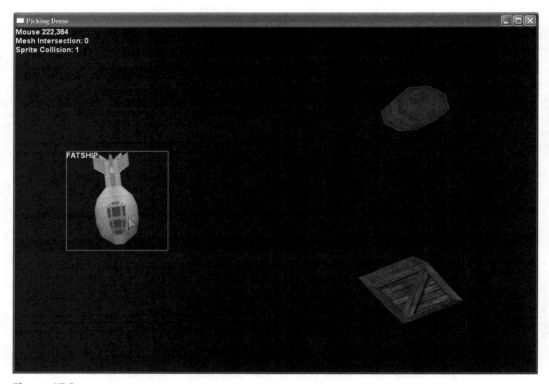

Figure 17.3
"Picking" with the mouse cursor and a sprite is a much simpler affair because no ray is needed, just a simple point-rectangle intersection test will suffice.

```
//mouse cursor
void showCursor() { ShowCursor(true); }
void hideCursor() { ShowCursor(false); }
```

Picking Demo Source

Here is the source code for the Picking Demo. Note that some #include statements, comments, and error handling lines have been omitted to conserve space.

```
Font *font = NULL;
Camera* camera = NULL;
Effect* effect1 = NULL;
Effect* effect2 = NULL;
VectorShape* shape = NULL;
```

```cpp
Sprite* cursor = NULL;
ID3DXLine* line = NULL;
Vector2 mouse;
D3DXVECTOR3 mouseVec;
int hasHit=0;
int hitDistance=0;
std::string objectName="";
DWORD hits;
ostringstream os;
Vector3 objectPos(0.0,0.0,0.0);
Vector2 p1(0.0,0.0);
Vector2 p2(0.0,0.0);
int spriteCollision=0;

//picking function prototypes
Vector2 getScreenPos(Vector3 pos);
bool intersectsCoordsToRect(Rect rect, Vector2 vec);
float intersectsCoordsToMesh(Mesh* mesh, Vector2 vec);

bool game_init(HWND window) {
    font = new Font("Arial Bold",18);
    shape = new VectorShape();
    shape->MakeTexture();
    D3DXCreateLine(g_engine->getDevice(), &line);
    line->SetAntialias(true);
    line->SetWidth(2.0f);

    camera = new Camera();
    camera->setPosition(0,0,50);
    camera->Update();

    cursor = new Sprite();
    cursor->Load("cursor.tga");
    g_engine->hideCursor();

    effect1 = new Effect();
    effect1->Load("ambient.fx");
    effect1->setTechnique("Ambient");
    effect1->setViewMatrix( camera->getViewMatrix() );
    effect1->setProjectionMatrix( camera->getProjMatrix() );
```

```
    effect2 = new Effect();
    effect2->Load("ambient.fx");
    effect2->setTechnique("Ambient");
    effect2->setViewMatrix( camera->getViewMatrix() );
    effect2->setProjectionMatrix( camera->getProjMatrix() );

    //add a managed oildrum mesh
    {
        Mesh* mesh = new Mesh();
        mesh->setName("OILDRUM");
        mesh->Load("oil-drum.x");
        mesh->setScale(0.15);
        mesh->setPosition(-10,10,0);
        mesh->setEffect( effect1 );
        g_engine->addEntity( mesh );
    }

    //add a managed crate mesh
    {
        Mesh* mesh = new Mesh();
        mesh->setName("CRATE");
        mesh->Load("crate.x");
        mesh->setScale(0.1);
        mesh->setPosition(-10,-10,0);
        mesh->setEffect( effect2 );
        g_engine->addEntity( mesh );
    }

    //add a managed sprite
    Sprite* sprite = new Sprite();
    sprite->Load("fatship256.tga");
    sprite->setName("FATSHIP");
    sprite->setPosition(100,250);
    sprite->setScale(0.75);
    sprite->setPivot( Vector2(128*0.75,128*0.75) );
    g_engine->addEntity( sprite );

    return true;
}

void draw3DBox(Vector2 p1, Vector2 p2, Color color)
    D3DXVECTOR2 lines[] = {
```

```
            D3DXVECTOR2((float)p1.x, (float)p1.y),
            D3DXVECTOR2((float)p2.x, (float)p1.y),
            D3DXVECTOR2((float)p2.x, (float)p2.y),
            D3DXVECTOR2((float)p1.x, (float)p2.y),
            D3DXVECTOR2((float)p1.x, (float)p1.y) };
    line->Begin();
    line->Draw(lines, 5, color.ToD3DCOLOR());
    line->End();
}


void game_render3d() {
    Color color = Color(255,0,0,255);
    //mesh translation is at center
    if (hasHit) {
        p1 = getScreenPos(objectPos);
        p1.x -= 100; p1.y -= 100;
        p2 = p1;
        p2.x += 240; p2.y += 200;
        draw3DBox(p1, p2, color);
    }


    //sprite translation is at upper-left
    if (spriteCollision) {
        p1 = objectPos.ToD3DXVECTOR2();
        p2 = p1;
        p2.x += 200; p2.y += 200;
        draw3DBox(p1, p2, color);
    }
}

void game_render2d() {
    font->Print(0,0, os.str() );
    //ray-mesh collision
    if (hasHit) {
        Vector2 pos = getScreenPos(objectPos);
        font->Print( (int)pos.x, (int)pos.y, objectName);
    }
    hasHit = 0;
    hitDistance = 0;
```

```
        //coord-sprite collision
        if (spriteCollision) {
            Vector2 pos = objectPos.ToD3DXVECTOR2();
            font->Print( (int)pos.x, (int)pos.y, objectName);
        }

        //draw cursor
        cursor->setPosition(mouse);
        cursor->RenderFast();
}

//helper function for game_event
void sprite_update(Sprite* sprite) {
    if (sprite->getName() == "FATSHIP") {
        //rotate the sprite
        float angle = (float) sprite->getRotation();
        sprite->setRotation( angle + 0.005 );
    }
    spriteCollision = 0;
    Rect b = sprite->getBounds();
    if (intersectsCoordsToRect(b,mouse)) {
        spriteCollision = 1;
        objectName = sprite->getName();
        objectPos = sprite->getPosition().ToD3DXVECTOR3();
    }
    os << "Sprite Collision: " << spriteCollision << endl;
}

//helper function for game_event
void mesh_update(Mesh* mesh) {
    string name = mesh->getName();
    if (name == "OILDRUM" || name == "CRATE") {
        //rotate the mesh
        Vector3 rot = mesh->getRotation();
        rot.z += 0.1;
        mesh->setRotation(rot);
    }
    os.str("");
    os << "Mouse " << mouse.x << "," << mouse.y << endl;
    //create a ray based on mouse coords, test for collision
    if (!hasHit) {
        hitDistance = (int) intersectsCoordsToMesh(mesh, mouse);
```

```
            hasHit = (hitDistance != -1.0f);
            objectName = mesh->getName();
            objectPos = mesh->getPosition();
        }
        os << "Mesh Intersection: " << hasHit;
        if (hasHit) {
            os << ", distance: " << hitDistance;
            os << ", hits: " << hits;
        }
        os << endl;
}

void game_event(Octane::IEvent* e) {
    switch (e->getID()) {
        case EVENT_ENTITYUPDATE: {
            EntityUpdateEvent* evt = (EntityUpdateEvent*) e;
            switch(evt->entity->getEntityType()) {
                case ENTITY_SPRITE: {
                    Sprite* sprite = (Sprite*) evt->entity;
                    sprite_update(sprite);
                }
                break;
                case ENTITY_MESH: {
                    Mesh* mesh = (Mesh*) evt->entity;
                    mesh_update(mesh);
                }
                break;
            }
        }
        break;
        case EVENT_ENTITYRENDER:
            EntityRenderEvent* evt = (EntityRenderEvent*) e;
            break;
        case EVENT_KEYRELEASE: {
            KeyReleaseEvent* evt = (KeyReleaseEvent*) e;
            switch (evt->keycode) {
                case DIK_ESCAPE:
                g_engine->Shutdown();
                break;
            }
        }
```

```
            break;
        case EVENT_TIMER:
            TimerEvent* t = (TimerEvent*) e;
            break;
        case EVENT_MOUSEMOVE: {
            MouseMoveEvent* evt = (MouseMoveEvent*) e;
            mouse.x = evt->posx;
            mouse.y = evt->posy;
        }
        break;
    }
}
```

COLLISION DETECTION

The two types of collision testing we will utilize are *bounding rectangle* and *distance* (or bounding circle). If you know the location of two sprites and you know the width and height of each, then it is possible to determine whether the two sprites are intersecting. Likewise, if you know the position and size of two meshes, you can determine whether they are intersecting as well. Bounding rectangle collision detection describes the use of a sprite's image or animation frame boundary for collision testing. You can get the upper-left corner of a sprite by merely looking at its X and Y values. To get the lower-right corner, add the width and height to the position. Collectively, these values may be represented as *left*, *top*, *right*, and *bottom* of a rectangle.

Automated Collision Detection

The game engine should be capable of calculating and reporting collision events automatically using its entity list. What we want the engine to do is automatically perform collision detection, but then *notify* the game when a collision occurs in a *pull* or *polled* manner. We could fire off an event when a collision occurs, but collisions are highly dependent on the gameplay—we simply do not need to test for collisions among all entities, since that does not reflect realistic gameplay. For instance, it's a waste of processing to test for collisions between the player's ship and its own missiles, while we *do* want to test for collisions between those same missiles and *enemy ships*. So, instead of firing off an event, we'll set a flag within each entity (*collided*) and reset the flags every frame. The flag approach also has the added performance benefit of allowing us to skip any entities that already have the flag set.

First, we need a new global collision property in the engine so that it is possible to globally enable or disable collisions (for game states or conditions where we do not want collision to take place, possibly for performance reasons).

```
bool p_globalCollision;
void enableGlobalCollisions(){ p_globalCollision = true; }
void disableGlobalCollisions(){ p_globalCollision = false; }
void setGlobalCollisions(bool value) { p_globalCollision = value; }
bool getGlobalCollisions() { return p_globalCollision; }
```

We want support for collision testing for sprite-to-sprite and sprite-to-mesh via these new engine functions. The `Entity-to-Entity` function is called from the main `Engine::testForCollisions()` function and selectively calls one of the other two based on the `EntityType` property of each entity.

```
bool Collision(Entity* entity1, Entity* entity2);
bool Collision(Sprite* sprite1, Sprite* sprite2);
bool Collision(Sprite* sprite, Mesh* mesh);
```

Advice

The `collidable` property for entities is set to false by default. When creating a new managed entity, be sure to manually enable its collision property.

These three overload functions should be expanded if new entity types are added to the entity manager. The first `Collision()` function (with `Entity` parameters) will call on the other three to perform specific collision tests between the entity types. Testing for a collision or intersection between a sprite and a mesh calls for a special technique called *ray casting*. What we need to do is calculate the sprite's position in 3D space (based on our camera's projection and view matrices) and cast a ray in the direction of that position on the screen parallel to the camera's orientation, and then see if the ray intersects with any geometry in the scene at that location.

In order to perform sprite-to-mesh collision testing, we have to make use of the "picking" function developed earlier, called `intersectsCoordsToMesh()`. But that leads to a problem: this function requires the projection and view matrices, and those are found in the `Camera` class, which has nothing at all to do with collision testing, and is a gameplay object not managed in the engine. We have to come up with a rather ugly workaround, unfortunately, but one that will be easy to use. In the Mesh class, which is therefore available to BoneMesh as well, is a pair of new properties to handle the projection and view matrices: p_collision_proj and p_collision_view. There are helper functions to assist:

*   void setCollisionMatrices(**Matrix** proj, **Matrix** view)
*   **Matrix** getCollisionProjMatrix()
*   **Matrix** getCollisionViewMatrix()

If the camera does not move, then it's easy enough to call Mesh::setCollision-Matrices() when creating the new Mesh object. But if the camera changes its position or target then this function will need to be called again while the game is running. With these new properties available, then sprite-to-mesh collision testing can be done with a newly modified version of intersectsCoordsToMesh(), which is now integrated into the Engine class.

```
float Engine::intersectsCoordsToMesh(Mesh* mesh, Vector2 vec) {
    D3DXMATRIX projection = mesh->getCollisionProjMatrix();
    D3DXMATRIX view = mesh->getCollisionViewMatrix();
    //convert coords to projection space
    Vector3 ray;
    int w = g_engine->getScreenWidth();
    int h = g_engine->getScreenHeight();
    ray.x =  (((2.0f * vec.x) / w ) - 1) / projection._11;
    ray.y = -(((2.0f * vec.y) / h) - 1) / projection._22;
    ray.z =  1.0f;
    //transform screen space pick ray into 3D space
    D3DXMATRIX m;
    D3DXMatrixInverse( &m, NULL, &view );
    D3DXVECTOR3 rayOrigin,rayDir;
    rayDir.x   = (float) (ray.x*m._11 + ray.y*m._21 + ray.z*m._31);
    rayDir.y   = (float) (ray.x*m._12 + ray.y*m._22 + ray.z*m._32);
    rayDir.z   = (float) (ray.x*m._13 + ray.y*m._23 + ray.z*m._33);
    rayOrigin.x = m._41;
    rayOrigin.y = m._42;
    rayOrigin.z = m._43;
    //create normalized ray
    D3DXMATRIX matInverse;
    D3DXMatrixInverse(&matInverse,NULL,&mesh->getMatrix());
    D3DXVECTOR3 rayObjOrigin,rayObjDir;

D3DXVec3TransformCoord(&rayObjOrigin,&rayOrigin,&matInverse);
```

```
D3DXVec3TransformNormal(&rayObjDir,&rayDir,&matInverse);

    D3DXVec3Normalize(&rayObjDir,&rayObjDir);
    //ray-mesh intersection test
    int hasHit;
    float distanceToCollision;
    D3DXIntersect( mesh->getMesh(), &rayObjOrigin, &rayObjDir, &hasHit,
        NULL, NULL, NULL, &distanceToCollision, NULL, NULL );
    if (hasHit) return distanceToCollision;
    else return -1.0f;
}
```

Advice

Although we have an opportunity to support collision with other types of objects, the code here is written specifically for `Sprite` and `Mesh` classes (and through inheritance, `BoneMesh` as well). If you want to support collision detection with other types of objects (for instance, `VectorShape`), you can duplicate this code and adapt them to subclass `Entity` in a similar manner.

The `testForCollisions()` function goes through the entities and performs several conditional tests before actually calling on the collision support function to perform a collision test. First, the `RenderType` of the entity is tested because we are currently only concerned with collisions between like objects. When the entity has been verified to be collidable—its `alive` and `collidable` properties are true—then it becomes the focus of attention for collision testing. For every *other* like object in the list, the same set of comparisons is made.

```
void Engine::testForCollisions() {
    //reset all collided properties
    BOOST_FOREACH( Entity* entity, p_entities )
    entity->setCollided(false);
    //escape if global collisions are disabled
    if (!p_globalCollision) return;
    BOOST_FOREACH( Entity* first, p_entities )
    {
        if (first->getAlive() && first->isCollidable() && !first->isCollided())
        {
            //test all other entities for collision
            BOOST_FOREACH(Entity* second, p_entities) {
                //do not test object with itself
                if (second->getID() != first->getID()) {
```

```
                    if (second->getAlive() && second->isCollidable() &&
                        !second->isCollided()) {
                        //test for collision
                        if (Collision( first, second )) {
                            //set collision flags
                            first->setCollided(true);
                            second->setCollided(true);
                        }
                    }//if
                }//if
            }//foreach
        }//if
    }//foreach
}
```

Now let's check out the collision methods that do all the real work of performing a collision test.

```
bool Engine::Collision(Entity* entity1, Entity* entity2) {
    switch (entity1->getEntityType()) {
    case ENTITY_SPRITE:
        switch (entity2->getEntityType()) {
            case ENTITY_SPRITE:
                //sprite-to-sprite
                return Collision((Sprite*)entity1, (Sprite*)entity2);
                break;
            case ENTITY_MESH:
                //sprite-to-mesh
                return Collision((Sprite*)entity1, (Mesh*)entity2);
                break;
        }
        break;
    case ENTITY_MESH:
        switch (entity2->getEntityType()) {
            case ENTITY_SPRITE:
                //sprite-to-mesh
                return Collision((Sprite*)entity2, (Mesh*)entity1);
                break;
        }
        break;
    }
```

```
        return false;
    }
bool Engine::Collision(Sprite* sprite1, Sprite* sprite2) {
    Rect r1 = sprite1->getBounds();
    Rect r2 = sprite2->getBounds();
    if (r1.Intersects(r2)) return true;
    else return false;
    }
bool Engine::Collision(Sprite* sprite, Mesh* mesh) {
    //get sprite position
    Vector2 pos = sprite->getPosition();
    //adjust for sprite center
    pos.x += sprite->getWidth()/2;
    pos.y += sprite->getHeight()/2;
    //test for ray-to-mesh intersection
    float dist = intersectsCoordsToMesh(mesh, pos);
    if (dist > -1.0) return true;
    else return false;
    }
```

Bounding rectangle collision testing makes use of the Rect class (introduced in Chapter 14). While we could have expanded the existing RECT struct, the problem with RECT is that it uses integers while we need floating-point precision. Refer back to Chapter 14 for the sources for the Rect class.

The Collision Demo

We will put the new automated collision detection features to the test with a program called Collision Demo, included with this chapter's resource files. In Figure 17.4, you can see the result of a sprite-to-sprite collision reported (see message at upper left). The mouse is actually in control of the large "lightning ball" sprite, which you can use to move on the screen to test for collisions with an example sprite and example mesh. The next screenshot shown in Figure 17.5 shows the collision report when the mouse cursor sprite is moved over the mesh. Only the most relevant portions of this program are included in the code listing—refer to the complete project for the complete source listing with comments and error handling intact.

```
Font *font = NULL;
Camera* camera = NULL;
Effect* effect = NULL;
```

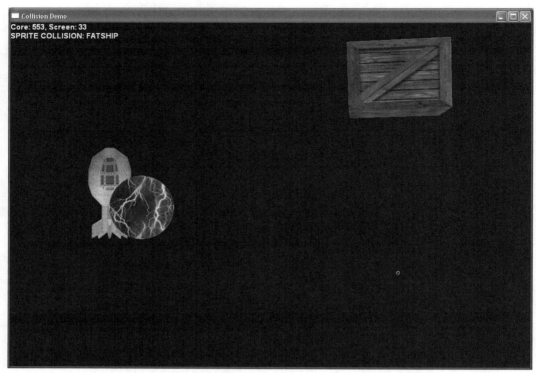

Figure 17.4
The engine now supports automatic sprite-to-sprite collision detection.

```
Vector2 mouse;
ostringstream os;
string collisionMessage="";

bool game_init(HWND window) {
    g_engine->hideCursor();
    font = new Font("Arial Bold",18);
    camera = new Camera();
    camera->setPosition(0,0,50);
    camera->Update();

    effect = new Effect();
    effect->Load("ambient.fx");
    effect->setTechnique("Ambient");
```

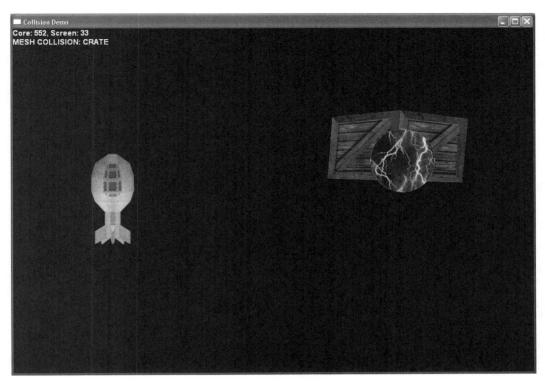

Figure 17.5
The engine also supports automatic sprite-to-mesh collision detection.

```cpp
effect->setViewMatrix( camera->getViewMatrix() );
effect->setProjectionMatrix( camera->getProjMatrix() );

//add a managed mesh
{
    Mesh* mesh = new Mesh();
    mesh->setName("CRATE");
    mesh->Load("crate.x");
    mesh->setScale(0.15);
    mesh->setPosition(-10,10,0);
    mesh->setRotation( rand()%360, rand()%360, rand()%360 );
    mesh->setEffect( effect );
    mesh->setCollidable(true);
```

```
            mesh->setCollisionMatrices( camera->getProjMatrix(),
                camera->getViewMatrix() );
            g_engine->addEntity( mesh );
        }
        //add a managed sprite
        {
            Sprite* sprite = new Sprite();
            sprite->Load("fatship256.tga");
            sprite->setName("FATSHIP");
            sprite->setPosition(100,250);
            sprite->setScale(0.75);
            sprite->setPivot( Vector2(128*0.75,128*0.75) );
            sprite->setCollidable(true);
            g_engine->addEntity( sprite );
        }
        //add a managed cursor
        {
            Sprite* cursor = new Sprite();
            cursor->Load("lightningball.tga");
            cursor->setPivot( Vector2(32,32) );
            cursor->setName("CURSOR");
            cursor->setCollidable(true);
            g_engine->addEntity( cursor );
        }
        return true;
    }


void game_render2d() {
    os.str("");
    os << "Core: " << g_engine->getCoreFrameRate();
    os << ", Screen: "<<g_engine->getScreenFrameRate()<<endl;
    os << collisionMessage << endl;
    font->Print(0,0, os.str() );
    collisionMessage = "";
}


//helper function for game_event
void sprite_update(Sprite* sprite) {
    string name = sprite->getName();
```

```
    if (name == "CURSOR") {
        sprite->setPosition(mouse);
        return;
    }
    if (sprite->isCollided())
        collisionMessage = "SPRITE COLLISION: " + name;
}

Vector2 getScreenPos(Vector3 pos) {
    D3DXVECTOR3 screenPos;
    D3DVIEWPORT9 viewport;
    g_engine->getDevice()->GetViewport(&viewport);
    D3DXMATRIX world;
    D3DXMatrixIdentity(&world);
    D3DXVec3Project(&screenPos, &pos.ToD3DXVECTOR3(),
        &viewport, &camera->getProjMatrix(),
        &camera->getViewMatrix(), &world);
    return Vector2((int)screenPos.x, (int)screenPos.y);
}

//helper function for game_event
void mesh_update(Mesh* mesh) {
    string name = mesh->getName();
    Vector2 pos = getScreenPos(mesh->getPosition());
    if (mesh->isCollided())
        collisionMessage = "MESH COLLISION: " + name;
}

void game_event(Octane::IEvent* e) {
    switch (e->getID()) {
        case EVENT_ENTITYUPDATE: {
            EntityUpdateEvent* evt = (EntityUpdateEvent*) e;
            switch(evt->entity->getEntityType()) {
                case ENTITY_SPRITE: {
                    Sprite* sprite = (Sprite*) evt->entity;
                    sprite_update(sprite);
                }
                break;
                case ENTITY_MESH: {
```

```
                    Mesh* mesh = (Mesh*) evt->entity;
                    mesh_update(mesh);
                }
                break;
            }
        }
        break;
        case EVENT_ENTITYRENDER:
            EntityRenderEvent* evt = (EntityRenderEvent*) e;
            break;
        case EVENT_KEYRELEASE: {
            KeyReleaseEvent* evt = (KeyReleaseEvent*) e;
            switch (evt->keycode) {
                case DIK_ESCAPE:
                    g_engine->Shutdown(); break;
            }
        }
        break;
        case EVENT_MOUSEMOVE: {
            MouseMoveEvent* evt = (MouseMoveEvent*) e;
            mouse.x = evt->posx;
            mouse.y = evt->posy;
        }
        break;
    }
}
```

Mesh Collision

Mesh-to-mesh collision detection can be done with bounding boxes (cubes) or bounding spheres. To calculate a bounding cube around a mesh, we can use the Direct3D function D3DXComputeBoundingBox, and for a bounding sphere, the function D3DXComputeBoundingSphere. Using a bounding cube, we can use simple conditional code to determine whether any corner of one cube-bound mesh is within the bounds of any other cube-bound mesh. The following code will help generate the bounding cube. Once you have the BBOX.min and BBOX.max properties filled in, then the BBOX struct can be used in a conditional statement to test for mesh collisions (without a ray-casting scheme).

```
struct BBOX {
    Vector3 min;
    Vector3 max;
};
BBOX Mesh::getBoundingBox() {
    BYTE* pVertices=NULL;
    mesh->LockVertexBuffer(D3DLOCK_READONLY, (LPVOID*)&pVertices);
    D3DXVECTOR3 minBounds,maxBounds;
    D3DXComputeBoundingBox( (D3DXVECTOR3*)pVertices, mesh->GetNumVertices(),
        D3DXGetFVFVertexSize(mesh->GetFVF()), &minBounds, &maxBounds );
    mesh->UnlockVertexBuffer();
    BBOX box;
    box.min = Vector3(minBounds);
    box.max = Vector3(maxBounds);
    return box;
}
```

Calculating a bounding sphere is a similar process, and we'll make use of a custom struct called BSPHERE. When the bounding sphere is calculated from the vertices of a mesh, it can then be used in a *much* simpler manner to perform distance-based collision detection between two bounding spheres. Basically, you have the center of each mesh to use for the distance calculation. If the distance between two centers is less than the sum of their radii, then they are intersecting.

```
struct BSPHERE {
    Vector3 center;
    float radius;
};
BSPHERE Mesh::getBoundingSphere() {
    BYTE* pVertices=NULL;
    mesh->LockVertexBuffer(D3DLOCK_READONLY, (LPVOID*)&pVertices);
    D3DXVECTOR3 center;
    float radius;
    D3DXComputeBoundingSphere( (D3DXVECTOR3*)pVertices, mesh->GetNumVertices(),
        D3DXGetFVFVertexSize(mesh->GetFVF()), &center, &radius );
    mesh->UnlockVertexBuffer();
    BSPHERE sphere;
    sphere.center = Vector3(center);
    sphere.radius = radius;
    return sphere;
}
```

Summary

That wraps up collision detection for our game engine. As with any solution to a programming problem, there are alternatives, and even better ways of doing things. As we discussed in this chapter, there are ways to optimize collision algorithms. You should consider optimizing the collision system to work best with the type of game you're building at any particular time, as the code presented here is meant to be a foundation for a gameplay collision handler.

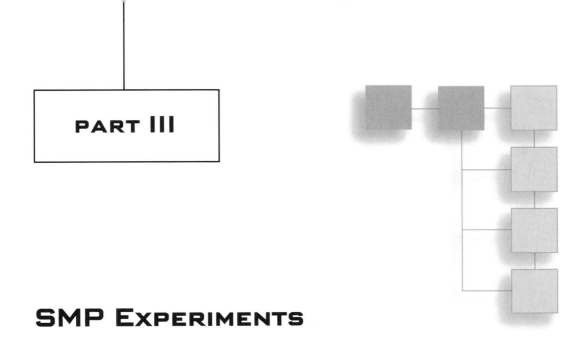

PART III

SMP Experiments

In this final part of the book we have one heavy-hitting chapter to address a most important issue—adding threading technology studied back in Part I to the game engine developed in the chapters of Part II. The rudimentary threading techniques will be tested first before we explore more complex threading code, such as running engine modules in separate threads. The goal is to explore optimization techniques, including threading.

- Chapter 18: Threading the Engine

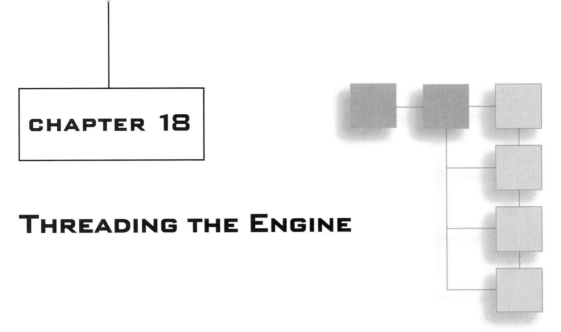

CHAPTER 18

THREADING THE ENGINE

We now have a competent game engine with which to use as a test environment for symmetric multi-processing experiments. Without digging into too much detail, this final chapter explores some possibilities with threaded code and encourages the reader to take it to the next level. We will be studying optimization techniques to improve framerates by hitting the CPU with a large population count and the GPU with high-quality shaders to push the hardware in a way that reflects actual gameplay (without an environment).

This chapter covers the following topics:

- OpenMP external experiment
- OpenMP engine improvements
- OpenMP internal experiment
- Gravity experiment
- Sprite collision experiment

OpenMP Experimentation

There's one important fact that I want to convey again before we get started: Direct3D is *not* thread safe! It would be great if we could do something like this in our engine's core while loop:

```
#pragma omp parallel
while (msg.message != WM_QUIT) {
    if (PeekMessage(&msg, NULL, 0, 0, PM_REMOVE))  {
        TranslateMessage(&msg);
        DispatchMessage(&msg);
    } else {
        long t = timer.getElapsed();
        float deltaTime = (t - startTime) / 1000.0f;
        g_engine->Update( deltaTime );
        startTime = t;
    }
}
```

No, of course this will not work, because we need to run updating code separately from rendering code, which run at different speeds, and such an over-arching approach to threading the engine would prevent us from synchronizing objects that need to interact in a game.

However, we *can* thread the `Engine::Update()` function and others in the `Engine` class!

The performance of the two or three experiments we'll be conducting is not as important as the *comparisons* that will be observed using the different threading techniques. There are *painfully obvious* optimizations that we could make to this code to improve the framerates, but that's a given—the threaded code will scale with any optimizations made to the code (such as a scene manager). In other words, the experiments should not be judged in comparison to other engines or demos, which will be using totally different techniques.

Advice

> If you are sensitive to the performance of this code and want to see how much you can improve it, be sure to set your DirectX runtime to Retail mode rather than Debug mode using the DirectX Control Panel.

The first thing we need to do is experiment within the *gameplay* side of the engine—that is, in our engine consumer project, and our `main.cpp` to be specific. The first experiment with OpenMP will use the existing engine as a renderer and event manager while all entities will be managed outside the engine in our gameplay code. The second experiment will use the engine's entity manager and OpenMP internally.

Advice

Visual C++ Express Edition (which is free) does not support OpenMP, a feature of the Professional and more expensive versions of Visual Studio. If an error comes up when you try to run a program using OpenMP referring to a missing file called VCOMP90D.DLL, that's a sign that your version of Visual C++ does not support OpenMP. Or, it could mean that OpenMP support is just not turned on!

OpenMP External Experiment

This project (including a copy of the engine) is found in the "OpenMP External" folder in the book's resource files. "External" refers to the fact that this project does not have any threading code embedded in the engine—it's all in the gameplay project (main.cpp). The "OpenMP Internal" project in the chapter's resource files is the version with OpenMP integrated into the engine. Figure 18.1 shows the first test run of the first thread experiment using the new engine. Figure 18.2 shows a similar test but with more objects—note the difference in performance.

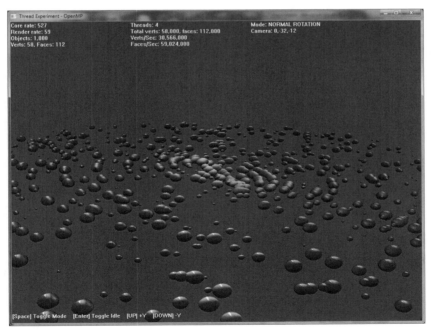

Figure 18.1
The first thread demo with 1000 low-resolution spheres.

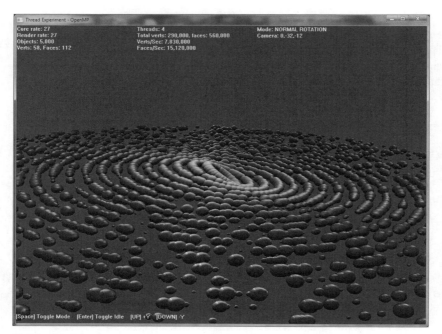

Figure 18.2
The second thread demo with 5000 low-resolution spheres.

A d v i c e

This chapter's resource files can be downloaded from www.jharbour.com/forum or www.courseptr.com/downloads. Not every line of code will be in print due to space considerations, only the most important sections of code.

Object Class

This project makes use of a helper class called Object. The purpose of the Object class is to represent one mesh entity but with additional "actor" properties and functions that make it a bit higher-level in functionality than a traditional entity such as a Sprite or Mesh.

```
//these two are bound--keep zeros balanced
const double STARTMASS = 0.00000001;
const double SCALE_MULTIPLIER = 10000000.0;
class Object {
public:
    double mass;
```

```
        double ax, ay, az;
        double vx, vy, vz;
        Octane::Matrix matrix,wit;
        Octane::Matrix matPosition,matRotation,matScale;
        Octane::Vector3 position, rotation, scale;
        float radius,angle,angVel;
        Object();
        virtual ~Object(){};
        void Reset();
        void Update();
};
```

Next up is the source code for the Object class. Included in this code is a function called Attract(), which simulates attraction between two objects of mass (i.e., *gravity*).

```
Object::Object() {
    Reset();
}
void Object::Reset() {
    mass = STARTMASS * (double) (rand() % 6);
    ax = ay = az = 0;
    position.x = cos( (double)(rand()%6) );
    position.y = sin( (double)(rand()%6) );
    position.z = 0;
    vx = (double)((rand() % 10) / 100);
    vy = (double)((rand() % 10) / 100);
    vz = (double)((rand() % 10) / 100);
    radius = (float)(rand()%20)+1;
    angle = (float)(rand()%360);
    angVel = (float)(rand()%5) / radius + 0.1f;
    scale = Vector3(1.0f, 1.0f, 1.0f);
    rotation = Vector3(0.0f, 0.0f, 0.0f);
}
void Object::Update() {
    //see if object has gone too far out of bounds
    if (position.x < -100000 || position.x > 100000) position.x *= -1;
    if (position.y < -100000 || position.y > 100000) position.y *= -1;
    if (position.z < -100000 || position.z > 100000) position.z *= -1;
    //copy mass values into mesh scaling
    scale.x = mass * SCALE_MULTIPLIER;
    if (scale.x > 2.0) scale.x = 2.0;
```

```
    scale.z = scale.y = scale.x;
    //slight rotation
    rotation.x += 0.001f;
    //transforms
    matPosition.Translate( position );
    matRotation.rotateYawPitchRoll( rotation );
    matScale.Scale( scale );
    matrix = matRotation * matScale * matPosition;
}
```

OpenMP Experiment Source Code

Here is the source code for the OpenMP experiment using threaded code in the gameplay (main.cpp) file—outside of the actual engine. This is to differentiate it from the other project in this chapter which incorporates the threading code *inside* the engine. Only the most relevant code is included here—see the complete project for additional details such as comment lines and error handling code.

```
const double SPHERE_RADIUS = 0.75;
const int SPHERE_QUALITY = 16;
const int NUM_OBJECTS = 1000;
std::vector<Object*> objects;
Mesh *sphere=NULL;
float cameraAngle = 0.0f;
Camera* camera = NULL;
Font *font = NULL;
Effect* effect = NULL;
string modes[]={"NORMAL ROTATION","TANGENT ROTATION","ARCTANGENT ROTATION"};
int mode = 0;
bool idle=false;
int numThreads = 0;

void addObject() {
    Object* object = new Object();
    object->position.x = (float) (rand() % 30 - 15);
    object->position.y = (float) (rand() % 30 - 15);
    object->position.z = (float) (rand() % 30 - 15);
    object->scale.x = object->mass * SCALE_MULTIPLIER;
    object->scale.z = object->scale.y = object->scale.x;
    objects.push_back(object);
}
```

```
bool game_init(HWND) {
    camera = new Camera();
    camera->setPosition(0.0f, -32.0f, -12.0f);
    camera->setTarget(0.0f, 0.0f, 0.0f);
    camera->Update();
    font = new Font("System", 12);
    effect = new Effect();
    effect->Load("specular.fx");
    effect->setTechnique("Specular");
    //light the meshes from the camera's direction
    Vector3 lightDir = Vector3(0.0, 0.0, -1.0);
    effect->setParam("DiffuseLightDirection", lightDir);
    //set diffuse color
    Color diffuse(150,255,255,255);
    effect->setParam("DiffuseColor", diffuse.ToD3DXVECTOR4());
    //create sphere mesh
    sphere = new Mesh();
    sphere->createSphere( SPHERE_RADIUS, SPHERE_QUALITY, SPHERE_QUALITY );
    //create list of objects
    for (int n=0; n<NUM_OBJECTS; n++) addObject();
    return true;
}

void game_update(float deltaTime) {
    if (idle) return;
    #pragma omp parallel for
    for (int n=0; n < (int)objects.size(); n++) {
            numThreads = omp_get_num_threads();
        //calculate world/inverse/transpose for lighting
        D3DXMatrixInverse( &objects[n]->wit, 0, &objects[n]->matrix );
        D3DXMatrixTranspose( &objects[n]->wit, &objects[n]->wit );
        //update object angle
        objects[n]->angle += objects[n]->angVel;
        float rad = (float)Math::toRadians((double)objects[n]->angle);
        //calculate new position based on radius
        objects[n]->position.x = cosf(rad) * objects[n]->radius;
        objects[n]->position.y = sinf(rad) * objects[n]->radius;
        //tweak z based on mode
        if (mode == 0)
            objects[n]->position.z = objects[n]->position.x / objects[n]->
radius;
```

```
            else if (mode == 1)
                objects[n]->position.z = tanf(rad) * objects[n]->radius;
            else if (mode == 2)
                objects[n]->position.z = atanf(rad) * objects[n]->radius;
            objects[n]->Update();
        }
}

void game_render3d() {
    effect->setProjectionMatrix(camera->getProjMatrix());
    effect->setViewMatrix(camera->getViewMatrix());
    for (int n=0; n < (int)objects.size(); n++) {
        effect->setParam( "WorldInverseTranspose", objects[n]->wit );
        sphere->setMatrix( objects[n]->matrix );
        sphere->Render( effect );
    }
}

void game_render2d() {
    ostringstream os;
    os.imbue(std::locale("english-us"));
    os << "Core rate: " << g_engine->getCoreFrameRate() << endl;
    os << "Render rate: " << g_engine->getScreenFrameRate() << endl;
    os << "Objects: " << (int)objects.size() << endl;
    os << "Verts: " << sphere->getVertexCount() << ", Faces: "
        << sphere->getFaceCount() << endl;
    font->Print(0,0, os.str());
    os.str("");
    os << "Threads: " << numThreads << endl;
    long vertices = sphere->getVertexCount() * (int)objects.size();
    long faces = sphere->getFaceCount() * (int)objects.size();
    os << "Total verts: " << vertices << ", faces: " << faces << endl;
    unsigned long vps = (unsigned long)(vertices *
        g_engine->getCoreFrameRate());
    unsigned long fps = (unsigned long)(faces *
        g_engine->getCoreFrameRate());
    os << "Verts/Sec: " << vps << endl;
    os << "Faces/Sec: " << fps << endl;
    font->Print(300,0, os.str());
    os.str("");
    os << "Mode: " << modes[mode] << endl;
    Vector3 pos = camera->getPosition();
```

```
    os ≪ "Camera: " ≪ pos.x ≪ "," ≪ pos.y ≪ "," ≪ pos.z ≪ endl;
    font->Print(600,0,os.str());
    int y = g_engine->getScreenHeight()-25;
    os.str("");
    os ≪ "[Space] Toggle Mode     ";
    os ≪ "[Enter] Toggle Idle     ";
    os ≪ "[UP] +Y       ";
    os ≪ "[DOWN] -Y";
    font->Print(0,y,os.str());
}

void game_event(Octane::IEvent* e) {
    switch (e->getID()) {
        case EVENT_KEYRELEASE: {
            KeyReleaseEvent* evt = (KeyReleaseEvent*) e;
            switch (evt->keycode) {
                case DIK_ESCAPE: g_engine->Shutdown(); break;
                case DIK_SPACE:  if (++mode > 2) mode = 0; break;
                case DIK_RETURN: idle = !idle; break;
            }
        }        break;
        case EVENT_KEYPRESS: {
            KeyPressEvent* evt = (KeyPressEvent*) e;
            switch(evt->keycode) {
                case DIK_UP: {
                    Vector3 cameraPos = camera->getPosition();
                    cameraPos.y += 1.0f;
                    camera->setPosition( cameraPos );
                    camera->Update();
                }
                break;
                case DIK_DOWN: {
                    Vector3 cameraPos = camera->getPosition();
                    cameraPos.y -= 1.0f;
                    camera->setPosition( cameraPos );
                    camera->Update();
                }
                break;
            }
        }
        break;
```

```
case EVENT_MOUSEWHEEL: {
    MouseWheelEvent* evt = (MouseWheelEvent*) e;
    float zoom = 2.0f;
    Vector3 cameraPos = camera->getPosition();
    if (evt->wheel > 0) {
        cameraPos.z += zoom;
        if (evt->wheel > 200)
            cameraPos.z += zoom*10.0f;
    }
    else if (evt->wheel < 0) {
        cameraPos.z -= zoom;
        if (evt->wheel < -200)
            cameraPos.z -= zoom*10.0f;
    }
    if (cameraPos.z > 0.0) cameraPos.z = 0.0;
    camera->setPosition( cameraPos );
    camera->Update();
}
break;
    }
}
```

Reviewing the Results

Table 18.1 shows the results of the experimental program with 1000 objects with various face counts (which determines the quality of the sphere used in the demo). Table 18.2 shows similar data for 5000 objects with various sphere quality values. Note that results will vary widely from one system to the next.

Table 18.1 OpenMP Experiment Results: 1000 Objects

Objects	Faces	Threads	Update	Render
1000	24	4	*3,400 M*	90 M
1000	112	4	1,600 M	430 M
1000	480	4	3,000 M	1,700 M
1000	1984	4	2,400 M	2,100 M
1000	4512	4	3,200 M	2,300 M
1000	8064	4	3,600 M	*2,500 M*

Table 18.2 OpenMP Experiment Results: 5000 Objects

Objects	Faces	Threads	Update	Render
5000	24	4	***2,800 M***	25 M
5000	112	4	1,700 M	156 M
5000	480	4	1,900 M	208 M
5000	1984	4	228 M	228 M
5000	4512	4	338 M	338 M
5000	8064	4	403 M	***403 M***

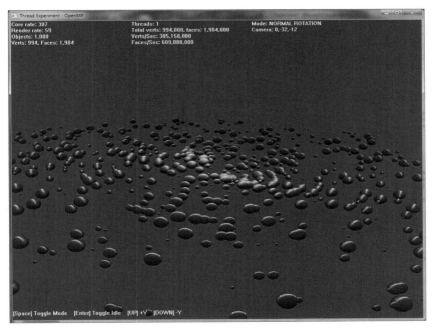

Figure 18.3
The OpenMP external experiment project rendering 1000 high-quality spheres.

Let's see where some of these numbers came from by viewing the screenshots of the project running. Figure 18.3 shows a new run of the program with 1000 higher-quality spheres, while Figure 18.4 shows the same version but without the calculations (just transform and rendering)—note the difference in the faces-per-second value!

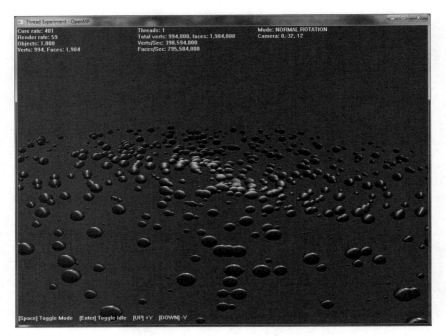

Figure 18.4
The same project running in render-only mode.

The next pair of figures show an alternate version of the program logic that produces quite interesting results with just a single line change (affecting the Z-axis position of each object). Figure 18.5 shows the result of object positioning when Z is set to the arc-tangent of the object's angle around the center of the scene, while Figure 18.6 shows the tangent.

Advice

The resource folder for this chapter has separated versions of the Engine folder since changes are being made to the engine in different ways that cannot be merged together (without making a mess of the code).

Removing the Rev Limiter

In automotive terms, the rev limiter is a device or computer setting that limits the engine to a maximum crankshaft RPM (revolutions per minute). This is used in NASCAR to balance the playing field so that racing is more of a driver-versus-driver sport rather than a competition among car builders. NASCAR also

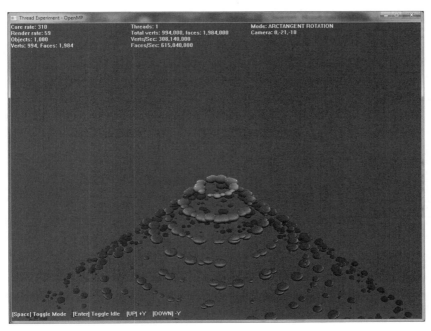

Figure 18.5
Dramatic difference in the scene when the Z-axis is calculated using arc-tangent (using the `atanf()` function).

applies other limits such as intake restrictions and fuel octane to keep racing more predictable. Older cars, especially muscle cars, equipped with a carburetor intake (rather than a modern fuel injection intake) will "open up" the carburetor when the throttle is mashed.

In hot rod terms, we call this "opening the butterflies" or "opening the secondaries." This refers to the fact that most older muscle cars were equipped with four-barrel carburetors, which would run two barrels while cruising to achieve better gas mileage, reserving the other two for when more power is needed. Flooring the gas pedal had the effect of not just down-shifting the transmission (if it is an automatic) but also opening up the second pair of barrels, which is what gives classic muscle cars such a "growl."

In terms of *our* engine, we have been playing up to this point with a framerate-hobbling limitation in order to run the CPU at a reasonable rate, without pushing it. Time to take the rev limiter off our engine to let it run fast and

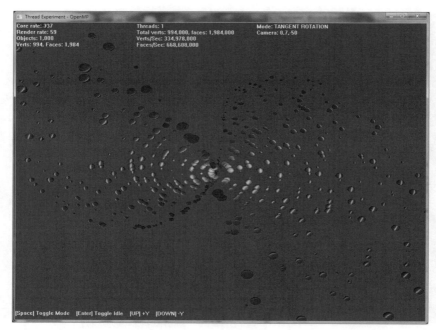

Figure 18.6
The Z-axis is calculated with tangent (using the `tanf()` function).

furious without concern for longevity! The best game engine developers in the business run their benchmarks with the limiters turned off, so we will do the same now that we're in the experimentation chapter. Let's take a look at the OpenMP External project again—and this time, we'll run it at maximum processor usage. To do this, we'll need to open up `Engine.cpp` and comment out the limiter line. Here is the code, found in `Engine::Update`. Commenting out that line turns off processor throttling.

```
//60fps = ~16 ms per frame
if (!timedUpdate.Stopwatch(16)) {
    //free the CPU for 1 ms
    //timedUpdate.Rest(1);
}
```

Figure 18.7 shows the result. Just to show that this is not a flip of a switch just to make threading look good (here at the end), I'll run the program with and without threading so we can note the difference. With threading *disabled*, the

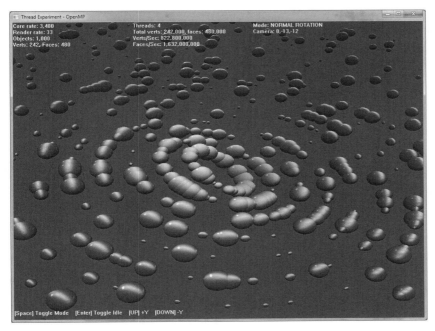

Figure 18.7
Removing the "rev limiter" in the engine results in 300% framerate improvement.

unlimited engine build cranks out about 570 million faces per second—single threaded. That's about the performance we saw with the limited engine running in multiple threads. Running it again with the full power of the CPU enabled and OpenMP turned back on, we get *1.6 billion* faces per second (1000 objects)! Suffice it to say, we will leave the rev limiter off for the remainder of the chapter.

DirectX Runtime—Retail Version

The next optimization we can make is kind of a no-brainer, but it is worth mentioning here because it has such an impact on performance. Open up the DirectX Control Panel application, shown in Figure 18.8. We really do want to run our Direct3D projects using the debug setting for Direct3D, as this will cause detailed output to appear in Visual Studio when a program is running. But when performance is important, we should turn this off. Having done so, the new run of the program has an additional 13% better performance at 1.855 billion faces per second!

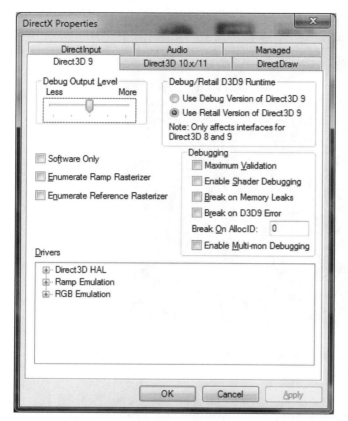

Figure 18.8
Setting DirectX runtime to retail (rather than debug) to improve performance.

OpenMP Engine Improvements

We can take advantage of OpenMP within the engine to a certain degree, but must be cautious that no shared data is exposed to more than one thread at a time. I'm not going to list the entire source code listing here, because the complete project is available in the chapter resources. I will go over the key code improvements. You may recall the Engine::Update() function, which was first created back in Chapter 6, "Engine Startup." Here is the function again for review since we haven't looked at it in quite some time:

```
void Engine::Update( float deltaTime ) {
    p_coreFrameCount++;
    if (p_coreTimer.stopwatch(1000)) {
```

```
        p_coreFrameRate = p_coreFrameCount;
        p_coreFrameCount = 0;
    }
    game_update( deltaTime );
    if (!p_pauseMode) {
        updateEntities(deltaTime);
        testForCollisions();
    }
    if (!timedUpdate.stopwatch(16)) {
        //timedUpdate.Rest(1);
    } else {
        p_screenFrameCount++;
        if (p_screenTimer.stopwatch(1000)) {
            p_screenFrameRate = p_screenFrameCount;
            p_screenFrameCount = 0;
        }
        //update input devices
        p_input->Update();
        updateKeyboard();
        updateMouse();
        //begin rendering
        if (p_device->BeginScene() == D3D_OK) {
            g_engine->clearScene(p_backdropColor);
            entitiesRender3D();
            game_render3d();
            p_spriteObj->Begin(D3DXSPRITE_ALPHABLEND);
            entitiesRender2D();
            game_render2d();
            p_spriteObj->End();
            p_device->EndScene();
            p_device->Present(0,0,0,0);
        }
    }
    buryEntities();
}
```

Since we can't interrupt Direct3D's rendering with threads without crashing the program, there is not a lot we can do inside the rendering section of code inside `Engine::Update()`, but we can address the helper functions such as `updateEntities()` and `testForCollisions()`. The original version of `updateEntities()` is shown below (with comments removed for clarity). Note the efficient use of BOOST_FOREACH to iterate the container of entities.

```
void Engine::updateEntities(float deltaTime) {
    BOOST_FOREACH( Entity* entity, p_entities ) {
        if ( entity->getAlive() )  {
            entity->Update(deltaTime);
            raiseEvent( new EntityUpdateEvent( entity ) );
            if (entity->getLifetime() > 0) {
                if (entity->lifetimeExpired())
                        entity->setAlive(false);
            }
        }
    }
}
```

I will suggest a possible change to updateEntities() here for your perusal. First, we must do away with the Boost iterator and revert to a for loop since OpenMP does not like iterators (at least not in version 2.0, although 3.0 is supposed to support them). Not only will we switch to a for loop, but we will also break up the update code into three distinct blocks of threaded code so that OpenMP can attack it more efficiently. This threaded function will only really show its strength if there are a *large number* of entities in the managed list.

```
void Engine::updateEntities(float deltaTime) {
    #pragma omp parallel {
        //get thread count
        p_numThreads = omp_get_num_threads();
        int size = p_entities.size();
        #pragma omp for
        for (int n=0; n < size; n++) {
            if ( p_entities[n]->getAlive() ) {
                if (p_entities[n]->getLifetime() > 0) {
                    if (p_entities[n]->lifetimeExpired())
                        p_entities[n]->setAlive(false);
                }else {
                    //move/animate entity
                    p_entities[n]->Update(deltaTime);
                    //tell game that this entity has been updated
                    raiseEvent( new EntityUpdateEvent( p_entities[n]) );
```

```
                        }
                    }
                }
            }
        }
```

Since there are nested for loops in the `testForCollisions()` function, each coded with a `BOOST_FOREACH`, we would write similar code to convert this function to an OpenMP implementation. Another possibility is using a `Boost.Thread` for the `Collision` function call (refer to the collision code covered in the previous chapter and the `Boost.Thread` code covered in Chapter 2).

```cpp
void Engine::testForCollisions() {
    if (!p_globalCollision) return;
    //reset all collided properties
    int size = p_entities.size();
    #pragma omp parallel for
    for (int n=0; n < size; n++)
        p_entities[n]->setCollided(false);
    #pragma omp parallel for
    for (int n=0; n < size; n++) {
        if (p_entities[n]->getAlive() &&
            p_entities[n]->isCollidable() &&
            !p_entities[n]->isCollided() ) {
            //test all other entities for collision
            #pragma omp parallel for
            for (int m=0; m < size; m++)
            {
                //do not test object with itself
                if (n != m &&
                    p_entities[n]->getID() != p_entities[m]->getID())
                {
                    if (p_entities[m]->getAlive() &&
                        p_entities[m]->isCollidable() &&
                        !p_entities[m]->isCollided())
                    {
                        //test for collision
                        if (Collision(p_entities[n], p_entities[m])) {
                            p_entities[n]->setCollided(true);
                            p_entities[m]->setCollided(true);
                        }
```

```
                      }//if
                  }//if
              }//for
          }//if
      }//for
}
```

OpenMP Internal Experiment

Using a threaded `updateEntities()` function and a slightly modified version of the `Object` class to support the entity manager, we can simplify the code of our project quite a bit (which is the goal of our engine code). The `Object` class now looks like this:

```
class Object : public Octane::Entity {
public:
    double mass;
    double ax, ay, az;
    double vx, vy, vz;
    Octane::Matrix matrix,wit;
    Octane::Matrix matPosition,matRotation,matScale;
    Octane::Vector3 position, rotation, scale;
    float radius,angle,angVel;
    Octane::Mesh *mesh;
    Octane::Effect* effect;
    Object();
    virtual ~Object( ){ }
    void Reset();
    void Update(float deltaTime);
    void Render();
    static void Attract(Object* A, Object* B);
};
```

Moving along to the implementation, here is the new `Object.cpp` code. First, there is a new entity type used by this program, requiring an addition to the `Entity.h` file:

```
    enum EntityType {ENTITY_UNKNOWN=-1,ENTITY_TIMER=0,ENTITY_MESH,
ENTITY_SPRITE, ENTITY_OBJECT, };
```

Note the changes made to the constructor in particular, which now calls on the base `Entity` constructor as well. We'll come to use the as-yet-unknown `Object::Attract()` function shortly. Only the relevant code is provided, while functions that have not changed or are not important at this point are left out to conserve space—see the full project for the complete code.

```
Object::Object() : Entity(RENDER_3D) {
    effect=NULL;
    mesh = NULL;
    entityType = ENTITY_OBJECT;
    Reset();
}
void Object::Reset() {
    mass = STARTMASS * (double) (rand() % 6);
    ax = ay = az = 0;
    position.x = cos( (double)(rand()%6) );
    position.y = sin( (double)(rand()%6) );
    position.z = 0;
    vx = (double)((rand() % 10) / 100);
    vy = (double)((rand() % 10) / 100);
    vz = (double)((rand() % 10) / 100);
    radius = (float)(rand()%20)+1;
    angle = (float)(rand()%360);
    angVel = (float)(rand()%5) / radius + 0.1f;
    scale = Vector3(1.0f, 1.0f, 1.0f);
    rotation = Vector3(0.0f, 0.0f, 0.0f);
}
void Object::Render() {
    effect->setParam( "WorldInverseTranspose", wit );
    mesh->setMatrix( matrix );
    mesh->setEffect( effect );
    mesh->Render(effect);
}
void Object::Update(float deltaTime) {
    //update object angle
    angle += angVel;
    float rad = (float)Math::toRadians((double)angle);
    //calculate new position based on radius
    position.x = cosf(rad) * radius;
    position.y = sinf(rad) * radius;
    position.z = position.x / radius;
    //see if object has gone too far out of bounds
    if (position.x < -100000 || position.x > 100000) position.x *= -1;
    if (position.y < -100000 || position.y > 100000) position.y *= -1;
```

```
        if (position.z < -100000 || position.z > 100000) position.z *= -1;
        //copy mass values into mesh scaling
        scale.x = mass * SCALE_MULTIPLIER;
        if (scale.x > 2.0) scale.x = 2.0;
        scale.z = scale.y = scale.x;
        //slight rotation
        rotation.x += 0.001f;
        //transforms
        matPosition.Translate( position );
        matRotation.RotateYawPitchRoll( rotation );
        matScale.Scale( scale );
        matrix = matRotation * matScale * matPosition;
        mesh->setMatrix( matrix );
        //calculate world/inverse/transpose for lighting
        D3DXMatrixInverse( &wit, 0, &matrix );
        D3DXMatrixTranspose( &wit, &wit );
    }
    void Object::Attract(Object* A, Object* B) {
        double distance=0;
        //calculate distance between particles
        double distX = A->position.x - B->position.x;
        double distY = A->position.y - B->position.y;
        double distZ = A->position.z - B->position.z;
        double dist = distX*distX + distY*distY + distZ*distZ;
        if (dist != 0) distance = 1 / dist;
        //adjust position by velocity value
        A->position.x += A->vx;
        A->position.y += A->vy;
        A->position.z += A->vz;
        //translation
        double transX = distX * distance;
        double transY = distY * distance;
        double transZ = distZ * distance;
        //acceleration = mass * distance
        A->ax = -1 * B->mass * transX;
        A->ay = -1 * B->mass * transY;
        A->az = -1 * B->mass * transZ;
        //increase velocity by acceleration value
        A->vx += A->ax;
        A->vy += A->ay;
```

```
    A->vz += A->az;
}
```

Now for the OpenMP Internal project source code. Note the more complex `game_init()`, but empty `game_update()` and `game_render3d()` functions as a result of switching to managed entities! Portions of duplicated code have been removed due to redundancy so refer to the chapter's resource files for the complete project. Again, only relevant code is provided here—see the complete project for the full source code.

```
const double SPHERE_RADIUS = 0.75;
const int SPHERE_QUALITY = 32;
const int NUM_OBJECTS = 1000;
float cameraAngle = 0.0f;
Camera* camera = NULL;
Font *font = NULL;
Effect* effect=NULL;
Mesh *sphere=NULL;
int numVerts=0;
int numFaces=0;

bool game_init(HWND) {
    g_engine->disableGlobalCollisions();
    camera = new Camera();
    camera->setPosition(0.0f, -32.0f, -12.0f);
    camera->setTarget(0.0f, 0.0f, 0.0f);
    camera->Update();
    font = new Font("System", 12);

    effect = new Effect();
    effect->Load("specular.fx");
    effect->setTechnique("Specular");

    //light the meshes from the camera's direction
    Vector3 lightDir = Vector3(0.0, 0.0, -1.0);
    effect->setParam("DiffuseLightDirection", lightDir);
    //set diffuse color
    Color diffuse(150,255,255,255);
    effect->setParam("DiffuseColor", diffuse.ToD3DXVECTOR4());
    //create the object's mesh
    sphere = new Mesh();
```

```
    sphere->createSphere( SPHERE_RADIUS, SPHERE_QUALITY, SPHERE_QUALITY );
    numVerts = sphere->getVertexCount();
    numFaces = sphere->getFaceCount();
    //create objects
    #pragma omp parallel for
    for (int n=0; n<NUM_OBJECTS; n++) {
        Object* object = new Object();
        object->mesh = sphere;
        object->effect = effect;
        object->setCollidable(false);
        object->position.x = (float) (rand() % 30 - 15);
        object->position.y = (float) (rand() % 30 - 15);
        object->position.z = (float) (rand() % 30 - 15);
        object->scale.x = object->mass * SCALE_MULTIPLIER;
        object->scale.z = object->scale.y = object->scale.x;
        g_engine->addEntity( object );
    }
    return true;
}

void game_update(float deltaTime) {
    effect->setProjectionMatrix(camera->getProjMatrix());
    effect->setViewMatrix(camera->getViewMatrix());
}
```

Advice

The OpenMP Internal project, with several sections of the core engine now supporting multiple threads, sphere quality of 32, and 1000 objects, we easily see over 4.0 billion faces per second running at 1,900 FPS. In terms of faces per *frame*, to give us a basic idea of our rendering capability, that's well over 65 million faces *per frame*. That is a very high quality scene, and that's with just an old 8800GT video card and Intel Q6600 running at 2.6GHz—which is quite obsolete hardware by 2010 standards. We also have not even addressed scene management optimizations such as removing objects not in the view frustum. These are very encouraging stats to say the least.

The result of these changes to internalize the sphere entities is a faces per second rate of over 4.0 billion, up from the high mark of 1.8 billion when all of the updating and rendering was taking place in the gameplay code rather than in the engine. This gain in performance is seen even with the engine's overhead— events are generated for every entity as it is updated and rendered. By commenting out the calls to `Engine::raiseEvent()`, performance would be improved even more.

Another factor to consider is the size of each entity and the quality settings used to render it. I have kept to a standard sphere quality (band size) of 16 and radius of 0.75 for all of these experiments, but by making small changes to these variables, huge changes can be seen in the output. A sphere quality of 16 to 24 seems to produce the best results in this project, but a typical production-quality mesh will have 10,000 or more faces.

GRAVITY EXPERIMENT

This so-called "Gravity Experiment" is a simulation I've enjoyed tweaking and experimenting with for many years. It started life in 1997 in Visual Basic 5.0. It was then revived and upgraded to the C language and the Allegro SDK in 2004, still functioning entirely in 2D. Now, at last, the old particle/gravity/star system demo is running in full 3D with the advantage of having true 3D motion and rendering with DirectX, thanks to the Octane engine! Figure 18.9 shows the

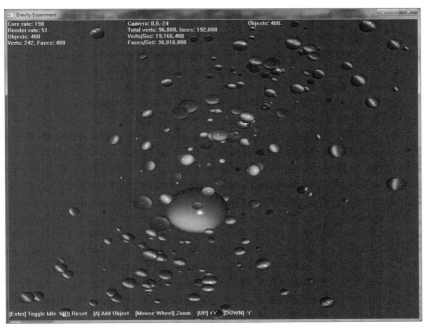

Figure 18.9
The Gravity Demo is an intriguing test bed.

program running. This is probably the least functional version of the simulation compared to the earlier ones, which featured sliders and buttons to configure the simulation and re-run it without making changes to the code. By simply tweaking some of the values you will get quite different results. Now all we can really do here is add new entities (A key) and reset the simulation (R key), as well as move the camera around. Go ahead, carry on the torch and see what you can come up with—I would love to hear from you if you do anything interesting with it! Of course, the screenshot (Figure 18.9) does not do this or any other project in this chapter justice, so be sure to open up the sources and watch it run.

THREADED SPRITE COLLISION EXPERIMENT

One of the last things we'll try out is threaded sprite collision testing. The results will not be as impressive as our earlier mesh examples because screen space limits the number of sprites that can be moved independently in order to track collision rates—a too-crowded screen renders the demo useless because of non-stop collisions taking place. Since the original collision code dealt only with bounding rectangles, I've decided to add distance-based (i.e., "circular" or "spherical") collision testing to improve the accuracy of the sprites being used in this example. For reference, here is one of the previously undocumented functions in the Engine class that is used for this example:

```
Entity* Engine::getEntity(int index) {
    if (index >= 0 && index < p_entities.size())
        return p_entities[index];
    else
        return NULL;
}
```

We will need this function to retrieve information about sprites that have collided. As you may recall, the Engine::testForCollisions() function performs collision testing among all managed entities that have the collision enable property set—which includes both sprites and meshes. We'll fill the entity manager with sprites and enable collision among them all, then observe performance with collision testing being done in multiple threads. When running this program, observe the CPU in Task Manager and you should see all cores running at maximum potential. See Figure 18.10. See the complete project for the entire code listing.

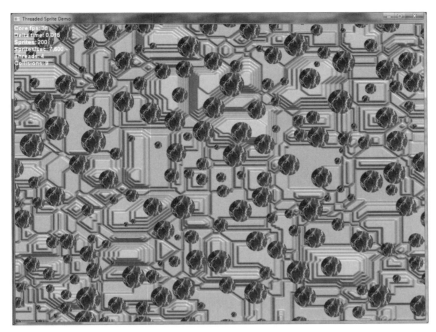

Figure 18.10
Testing for sprite collisions using multiple threads.

DISTRIBUTING YOUR GAME

The runtime file requirements for a Visual C++ binary file can be quite a challenge to sort out, so here are some suggestions to help when you wish to distribute or share your game with others. To see an example for yourself, just open up the folder for any installed game and note which runtime files the studio has included with the game! You may be surprised to find older runtimes, which means some games are still being built with Visual Studio 2003 or 2005! A lot of this depends on the engine a studio uses for their game (if not an in-house engine).

For instance, Firaxis has used the Gamebryo engine for many of their products, including *Civilization IV*, and it was built with Visual C++ 2003 (including more recent expansions that used the same engine).

Another good example is Blizzard's *World of Warcraft*. Perusing the install folder reveals many files including, notably, `Microsoft.VC80.CRT.manifest` and `msvcr80.dll`. What these files tell us is that *World of Warcraft* was built with

Visual C++ 2005. Since even the latest expansion (at the time of this writing, that would be *Lich King*) still requires the same runtime file means that Blizzard has not upgraded to Visual C++ 2008. That, I have found, is a fairly common practice in the industry—as long as a compiler works, there's no compelling reason to upgrade in the middle of a product's life cycle and potentially introduce new bugs (a project manager's worst nightmare).

For a Debug build of a project, these files are required (located in \Program Files \Microsoft Visual Studio 9.0\VC\redist) and should be copied into the bin or output folder where the .exe file is located.

- Microsoft.VC90.DebugCRT.manifest
- msvcr90d.dll

For a Release build, include these files:

- Microsoft.VC90.CRT.manifest
- msvcr90.dll

When using OpenMP (as we are) we also need to include the OpenMP runtime files:

- Microsoft.VC90.DebugOpenMP.manifest
- vcomp90d.dll

and the release build version:

- Microsoft.VC90.OpenMP.manifest
- vcomp90.dll

REFERENCES

Isensee, Pete; "Utilizing Multicore Processors with OpenMP"; *Game Programming Gems 6*. 2006. pp: 17–23.

Jones, Toby; "Lock-Free Algorithms"; *Game Programming Gems 6*. Charles River Media. 2006. pp: 5–15.

INDEX